The Poetry of Class

Historical Materialism Book Series

VOLUME 305

The titles published in this series are listed at *brill.com/hm*

Female Figure (blowing bubbles) as allegory of Christian Peter Wilhelm Beuth, riding Pegasus over an industrial city

BY KARL FRIEDRICH SCHINKEL, DATED 1837, FROM THE KUPFERSTICH KABINETT OF THE STAATLICHEN MUSEEN ZU BERLIN. VIA WIKIMEDIA COMMONS, PUBLIC DOMAIN

The Poetry of Class

Romantic Anti-Capitalism and the Invention of the Proletariat

By

Patrick Eiden-Offe

Translated by

Jacob Blumenfeld

BRILL

LEIDEN | BOSTON

The Library of Congress Cataloging-in-Publication Data is available online at https://catalog.loc.gov
LC record available at https://lccn.loc.gov/2023035815

First published in 2017 as *Die Poesie der Klasse. Romantischer Antikapitalismus und die Erfindung des Proletariats*, Copyright © MSB Matthes & Seitz Berlin Verlagsgesellschaft mbH, Berlin 2017. All rights reserved.

This book was originally funded by the Cluster of Excellence at the University of Konstanz 'Cultural Foundations of Integration', established as part of the Excellence Initiative of the Federal Government and the Länder.

The translation of this work was funded by Geisteswissenschaften International – Translation Funding for Work in the Humanities and Social Sciences from Germany, a joint initiative of the Fritz Thyssen Foundation, the German Federal Foreign Office, the collecting society VG WORT and the Börsenverein des Deutschen Buchhandels (German Publishers & Booksellers Association).

Typeface for the Latin, Greek, and Cyrillic scripts: "Brill". See and download: brill.com/brill-typeface.

ISSN 1570-1522
ISBN 978-90-04-68545-1 (hardback)
ISBN 978-90-04-68553-6 (e-book)

This book is printed on acid-free paper and produced in a sustainable manner.

For Valentin and Martha and for Johanna

Contents

Translator's Note XIII

Introduction 1
1 Class and Classification, Proletariat and Proletarianisation 5
2 The Proletariat: a Non-identical Subject 10
3 Romantic Anti-capitalism 14
4 Historiography of Rescue 17
5 Proletarian Identity: Openness and (Self-)Enclosure 19
6 Inverse Relevance of the Vormärz 21
7 Literary History as Social History: Class as Figure 22

1 **Small Masters and Journeymen: from Guild to Movement** 25
1 Romantic Anti-capitalism: Ludwig Tieck's *The Young Master Carpenter* 25
1.1 *The Death of the House and the Life of the Factory* 27
1.2 *The Bourgeoisie as Whole and Part* 29
1.3 *Becoming Rabble: from Servants to Scum* 31
1.4 *The Decline of the Guilds* 32
1.5 *Guild Representation* 35
1.6 *Affect Politics from Above* 38
1.7 *Passions and Interests: Leonhard, Adam Smith and Albert O. Hirschman* 40
1.8 *Political Passions, Aesthetic Taste* 42
1.9 *Enclosing Class Struggle: Tieck's Guilds as Invention of Tradition* 45
1.10 *The End of the Guilds and the Beginnings of the Labour Movement. 'Traditions' of Social History* 47
2 Journeymen Culture and the Workers' Movement: Wilhelm Weitling 51
2.1 *Journeymen Language* 55
2.2 *Journeymen Song* 58
2.3 *Journeymen Association* 61
3 Georg Weerth and the Break with Guild Traditions 65

2 **'We? Tricky Question!' on the Search for Class Identity in Proletarian Journals** 75
1 Negations: 'Bourgeois' and 'Intellectual Prolatarians' 78
2 Ascension: 'We' Want to Be *Bürger* 82
3 Activation: What 'We' Should Be 85
4 Affirmation: 'We' Who Raise Our Voices 92

3 **Counting the People: Class Statistics** 100
1 Statistics and Social Agitation: *The Hessian Messenger* 101
2 Statistics in the Service of Revolution: *Gesellschaftsspiegel* 110
2.1 *Rhetoric of Facts: Statistics and Description* 110
2.2 *Exaggeration and Distance: the Style of Criticism* 112
2.3 *Fiction and Correction: Statistics of Prostitution* 117

4 **Miserabilism and Critique: from the Poverty of Literature to the Poverty of Theory** 122
1 Ludwig Tieck and the Wolves of London 122
2 German Misery, German Verse: Engels as Narrative Theorist 124
3 Striking Stereotypes: Ernst Dronke's 'Rich and Poor' 128
4 The Family Romance of the Proletarian 131
5 Relentlessness 137
6 Mystères – Misère 142
7 Misery in Relations: Production, World Market, Needs 148
8 Poverty and Quality of Life: Disposable Time 151

5 **Wage Labour and Slavery: Unfulfilled Promises of Freedom** 157
1 Allegories of Class: 'Steam King' and 'White Slaves' 158
2 Point of Comparison: Weitling's 'Politics of Slavery' 160
3 The 'Semblance of Liberty' and Real Slavery: Engels 163
4 Class Slavery 167
5 Why '*White* Slaves'? 169
6 Theory as Mystification: the Cult of the Industrial Worker and Global Critique 171
7 The Universality of Proletarianisation 174

6 **Representing the 'Labouring Poor'** 179
1 The Possibilities of Literature: Ernst Willkomm's *White Slaves or the Sufferings of the People* 179
2 Engels and the Invention of Social Reportage 185
3 The Reporter in the Field: 'The Great Towns' 192

7 **Class in Struggle** 197
1 Witches' Sabbath as Early Modern Class Struggle: Tieck 199
2 The Witches' Sabbath of the Class Struggles in France: Börne 203
3 Social War on Lake Zurich: Weitling 205
4 *Primitive Rebels* in Lower Lusatia: Willkomm 207
5 Rescuing the Rebels 214
6 Revenge and Class 216
7 The Machine Breakers 221
8 Is It O.K. to Be a Luddite? 224
9 Towards a Pure Strike: Georg Weerth's Fragment of a Novel 230
10 The Struggle for the Family Wage, the Feminisation of Factory Work and the Masculinisation of the Workers' Movement 240

Conclusion: the Return of Romantic Anti-capitalism 252

Epilogue: Romantic 'Anti-capitalism' from Above 266

Bibliography 281
Name Index 301

Translator's Note

The original German title of this book is *Die Poesie der Klasse*. The word *Poesie* has a double meaning. On the one hand, it simply means poetry; on the other hand, with reference to its roots in the Ancient Greek word *poiesis*, it can also mean *composition*, or *making*. Thus, while *The Poetry of Class* is an apt translation of the title, another equally suitable one would be *The Composition* or *Making of Class*. It helps to keep both in mind while reading this book.

There are two words in the text for which it is particularly difficult to find a single, consistent word in English: *Bürger* and *Bildung*. Depending on the time period to which it refers, the word *Bürger* can have slightly different meanings in German: citizen, bourgeois, middle-class, burgher, townsperson. I have chosen to mostly use the terms bourgeois and burgher, depending on the context, or leave it untranslated altogether. The word *Bildung* is an expansive term in German meaning culture, education, development, or cultivation. I have translated it mostly as culture in the broad sense or, when appropriate, education.

References to Marx and Engels' Collected Works are written as MECW followed by the volume and page numbers.

Thanks to Loren Balhorn for setting this up, my family for giving me the time to finish it, and Patrick Eiden-Offe for feedback on the translation.

Hunter Bolin and Eric-John Russell helped with key parts of the translation, and I would like to emphatically thank them here. They are, undoubtedly, my co-translators.

Introduction

In August 1830, Eduard Gans, full professor of law at Berlin University, friend of Heinrich Heine and head of the Hegelian school, travelled to Paris. Only a few weeks earlier, the pent-up social tensions there had erupted in a brief revolutionary outbreak with barricade fights, in the course of which the last Bourbon king, Charles X, was driven out and the 'citizen king' Louis-Philippe placed on the throne.[1] The Saint-Simonians, followers of an early socialist group – often confused in their religious views but profound in their social criticism – were particularly active during the July Revolution.[2] As an emissary of the Berlin Hegelians, Gans met with representatives of this revolutionary group in Paris to discuss the state of the social movement. Despite many common points of criticism of the emerging capitalist social order, Gans quickly became aware of a crucial difference between the two doctrines: while the Saint-Simonians lamented the 'evil of competition … in bourgeois society' and wanted to see it 'transformed into order and hierarchy', Gans saw in the Saint-Simonian utopia of order a horror that far surpassed the social chaos of the present. The 'evil' of the Saint-Simonians, however, is a promise to him:

> But whoever wants to exclude competition from it [bourgeois civil society] creates another slavery of supervision, which, even if it offered happier conditions, would be unbearable. Antiquity worked with its slaves; we with our own persons. For this, however, the person also belongs to himself, and to take away his happiness or unhappiness, success or misfortune, would mean depriving him today of the only poetry of which he is capable. For the negative sides of life also belong to it: just as good presupposes evil, so must a full unhappiness be possible, so that happiness may receive a concrete and appropriate shape.[3]

The following sections of his memoirs show that Gans, in keeping with the language of the time and especially that of the Saint-Simonians, had the problem of class formation in mind with 'competition', where 'proletarians' and 'factory owners' confront each other, with an impending 'struggle of the proletarians

1 Ludwig Börne and Heinrich Heine brought the class character of the July Revolution home to the German public in their Paris correspondent articles. Cf. Börne 1986; Heine 1976, pp. 89–279.

2 For a classification of the Saint-Simonists in their time, see Harvey 2006, especially pp. 59–89.

3 Gans 1995, pp. 98–9.

 | DOI:10.1163/9789004685536_002

against the middle classes of society'.[4] But why does Gans think that a root of the 'poetic' capacity of modern man (the 'person') can be seen precisely in 'competition', which should under no circumstances be removed? For Gans, the 'poetry' of modern life is based on its economic precariousness; 'poetry' is guaranteed by the 'concrete', the ever-present possibility of economic ruin. The autonomy of the person, one's belonging (only) to oneself, at the same time exposes oneself to a new form of heteronomy: an external determination by the economy. It is only in this heteronomy that autonomy finds its reality, with which it must prove itself. Only by openly facing the contingency and unpredictability of social and economic conditions can modern human beings give their lives the full 'appropriate shape' and form.

The ever-possible socio-economic ruin, the ever-present threat of being pushed down into the 'rabble' – this, according to Gans, is what constitutes the 'poetry' of modern life.[5] This point gains its explosiveness from the fact that it unsettles and readjusts a common pattern of self-understanding of the time, which Hegel of all people had put into a universally quotable formula. In modernity, as he postulated in his *Lectures on Aesthetics*, man is confronted with a 'reality already ordered into *prose*', with the modern novel as the appropriate artistic medium for articulating and resolving the necessarily resulting 'conflict between the poetry of the heart and the opposing prose of circumstances'.[6]

Hegel gave his lectures on aesthetics a total of four times between the winter semester of 1820–1 and the winter semester of 1828–9. The 'prose of circumstances' became so popular as a phrase in the following years because it captured precisely the new socio-economic reality. The two decades after 1830 are referred to in German as the Vormärz (pre-March) since in them all signs of the times point ahead to the revolution that will break out first again in Paris in February 1848 and then set the whole continent aflame in March. During this period, industrialisation makes a breakthrough in Europe, and society is penetrated by the market. All the essential elements of what we call 'modernity' today were established in the Vormärz. It was the beginning of *our* modern history – with all its upheavals, standardisations and divisions.

The aesthetic conceptions of the time reflect these developments. In his theory of the novel, the 'left' Hegelian disciple, Friedrich Theodor Vischer, contrasts the poetic as irruption of 'striking, surprising occurrences', as openness, with the 'prose of conditions', which he sees as determined by predictability and routine. Vischer outlines the 'prosaic arrangement of things of the world'

4 Gans 1995, pp. 100–1.

5 Cf. Gans, 1995, p. 100. On the subject of the rabble in Hegel, cf. Hegel 1991, § 244, pp. 266–67.

6 Hegel 1975, pp. 1092–93. Translation revised.

in historically concrete terms. It is the 'division of labour' that, together with a 'general trend towards the mechanisation of technical products, jewellery, etc'., characterises modernity.[7]

Jacob Grimm already wrote in the registry of the epoch that the historical-philosophical signature of the present could be read from the defining relationship between poetry and prose: 'Poetry is passing away and prose (not the common, but the spiritual) is becoming more appropriate for us', he says in the introduction to the *German Grammar* of 1819.[8] This is quoted again and again throughout the Vormärz, by Theodor Mundt in his *Art of German Prose* from 1837, for example, or in Berthold Auerbach's political-poetological manifesto *Writing and People* from 1846.[9] In contrast to Grimm and also to Hegel, who define the trend towards prose as an inescapable historical-philosophical trait of the epoch, poets, scientists and philosophers in the Vormärz, and later also political activists and propagandists, try to find a way out of the 'prose of modernity' (Peter Bürger) and achieve a re-poetisation of life. Initially, in Vischer's formulation, 'green spots' of the poetic are sought in the grey of 'well-worn prose': islands of the extraordinary, as it were, reserves of the 'wild' in the midst of civilisation.[10] Ultimately, however, what are sought are possibilities for making modernity itself, modern life precisely in all its modernness, the resource of a new poetry. This is where Gans's proposal comes into play: anyone who – with Hegel, but also beyond Hegel – is serious about justifying the real as rational cannot bemoan the course of history, but must penetrate it. Whoever still does not want to resign themselves to the 'prose of circumstances' must then look for the poetic where the doxa would least expect it. To put it bluntly, they must also accept the social 'division of labour' and, along with it, the class divide as sources of the poetic. Whoever seeks a poetry of modern life, therefore, will hardly be able to avoid a *poetry of class*.

It is not without reason that in the two decades after Hegel's death – and, in terms of literary history, after Goethe's death, in the 'final phase of the "Goethean art period"' (Heine) – the concept of social class becomes common in German and, in parallel, a momentous redefinition of the concept of poetry takes place. Both, as will be shown in the following, still belong together in the Vormärz, and not only – as we can see with Gans – as poetry with a black ribbon.

7 Vischer 1986, pp. 240–1 (original: Vischer 1857, pp. 1317–21).
8 Grimm 1819, p. XXVII.
9 Mundt 1837, pp. 20, 131, 359; Auerbach 2014, p. 67.
10 Vischer 1986, pp. 240–1.

Berthold Auerbach also refers to the increasing class divide in his 1846 manifesto, where he uncovers another dimension of the poetic – an 'epistemic-poetic' dimension.[11] Based on Grimm's definition of the powerful 'old language' of the 'savages', Auerbach postulates that precisely the new – '[e]ven the newest technical environment' – can only be grasped linguistically and conceptually at all if one assumes an irreducibly poetic element, an element that can lead us from prose 'back to poetry'. Poetic power and 'strength', however, had been preserved according to Auerbach especially in the language of the simple, the common or 'lower folk'.[12] 'Folk language' possesses the special ability of a 'child-like groping around, where one does not yet have ready-made templates and set phrases for everything, but first looks for the features oneself, creates new words and re-forms old ones' – where the speaker, to sum up, becomes poetically active.

Through the elective affinity of poetry and the 'lower folk', the latter in turn could first appear in society in general: 'It is undeniable that at no time have the conditions of the so-called lower folk been pushed so much into the considerations of the higher-ups as in our days. Poetry has contributed significantly to this'.[13] When Auerbach then cites 'Boz', an early pseudonym of Charles Dickens, and the 'Corn Law Poet' – the *Corn Law Rhymer*, an activist of Chartism, the first major organised force of the English labour movement – as examples from the English-speaking world, then there can be no doubt that by the 'so-called lower folk', Auerbach has in mind not only his beloved Black Forest peasants, but also 'pauperism and the proletariat', to whom he devotes the last paragraph of his pamphlet.[14] As a poetically produced and pronounced fact, 'class' quickly becomes a central component of the political imaginary of the epoch.

The *poetry of class* can thus also be read as subjective genitive. The class itself appears as subject, as author and recipient of its own poetry. The *Corn Law Rhymer* mentioned by Auerbach is not a bad candidate in this respect. In the German-speaking world, for example, one might think of Wilhelm Weitling, who, besides and because of his 'communist' agitational activities, was given enough time by the authorities to write *Dungeon Poetry*.[15] Or, one may consider the *Album of Original Poetry*, published in 1847 by the early socialist project-maker Hermann Püttmann, with poems by Georg Weerth, Friedrich Sass, Percy

11 Cf. Rancière 1994.
12 Auerbach 2014, p. 67.
13 Auerbach 2014, p. 76.
14 On Boz/Dickens, see the section 'Engels and the Invention of Social Reportage' in the sixth chapter of this study. Cf. Auerbach 2014, pp. 164–72.
15 Weitling 1844.

Shelley, Ferdinand Freiligrath, Anastasius Grün and Heinrich Heine in addition to Weitling, and which, according to Püttmann's preface, shows once again that 'the poets, the *true ones of* course, always walk with the *people* and never with the *kings*'.[16]

'The term poetry', writes Georges Bataille, 'can be considered synonymous with expenditure'.[17] In the following, the talk of a *poetry of class* aims to release the class question – as it first arose in the Vormärz and as it *still* or *again* arises today in one form or another – from the paradigm of lack. The point is not to express ignorance or snobbery in the face of hardship and exploitation, but rather to marvel at the lavish wealth of social, cultural and literary forms in which people have historically struggled with these problems and fought against them. But the poetry of class, which we can still observe everywhere in the Vormärz, will soon be suppressed and made invisible – by the powers of the old and new world, but also and not least by the very workers' movement born from the spirit of poetry in the Vormärz. The stronger, more united and more successful the movement will become in the following decades, the more *prosaic* it will appear. The poetic founding figures, however, must then increasingly look like wandering cranks to the movement itself. The aim of the following study is to unearth the poetry of class from the burial sites of history and to put it up for debate in the present.

1 Class and Classification, Proletariat and Proletarianisation

Whether in poetry or prose, social reality manifests in language and condenses into concepts. Linguistic forms of expression, in turn, shape social reality, giving direction to historical development or confusing it; concepts must thus always also be seen as themselves powerful historical actors. To do justice to this reciprocal determination is to engage in 'social theory as conceptual history' –

16 Püttmann 1847, p. 1. The *Album* also includes 'Edward P. Mead in Birmingham', whose poem 'King Steam' appears in the collection in Friedrich Engels' translation On Mead and 'King Steam', see the section 'Allegories of Class: "Steam King" and "White slaves"' in the fifth chapter of the present study.

17 Bataille 1997, p. 171. Bataille's general economy, which starts from the 'insufficiency of the principle of classical utility' and progresses to an 'insubordination of material facts', forms the background in many respects to the following remarks. The basis of this reference lies in Bataille's adoption of a specific form of 'romantic anti-capitalism', which may be closer to the authors examined below (like Ludwig Tieck) than is usually assumed. One should not forget that William Blake's 'Exuberance is Beauty' serves as the epigraph for Bataille's main economic work, *The Accursed Share* (cf. Bataille 1988).

as the somewhat forced but quite appropriate German translation of Raymond Williams's work from 1958, *Culture and Society*, puts it. Furthermore, as we shall see, it also means engaging in the history of transnational translation at the same time.[18] The question of when certain terms are used (or rejected) by whom for which circumstances is clearly a political one: conceptual history is also always conceptual politics. The first half of the nineteenth century is characterised by an extremely lively, at times almost overheated poetic and political activity of conceptual formation. The Vormärz is the great semantic marshalling yard where the political and social language of modernity works itself out – especially terms like 'class' and 'proletariat'.

At the same time, however, the conceptual creativity of the Vormärz has a long prehistory that goes back to antiquity. The concept of class, for example, comes from Roman tax law, and the original meaning of class is the tax class; the term thus originally refers to a classification, a hierarchical subdivision of the social. From here on, the term subsequently undergoes a far-reaching social neutralisation, it becomes the concept of classification par excellence, with which taxonomies and tables are produced and made representable. In this way, however, it loses its reference to the social in general; it becomes a term of natural history and grammar and is applied almost exclusively to fauna, flora and language. From the middle of the seventeenth century, the concept returns to its original scope. The fact that people or human collectives are now to be classified again – and not, for example, flowers or words – still had to be linguistically marked off in German at the end of the eighteenth century. Hence, there is often talk of 'classes of people' or 'human classes'.[19]

Since around 1800 and increasingly after 1820, in response to a series of socio-historical changes, the term 'class' becomes used in German to describe and interpret contemporary society. The concept of class first enters, or rather, creeps in wherever the old ordering scheme of the estates is slowly dismantled socio-economically and finally abolished by political decision. While this is spectacularly carried out in the French Revolution, essential parts of the so-called Prussian reforms can also be understood as a socio-economic and political gutting of the estate system, even and especially when the old order officially continues to exist. This is how the abolition of serfdom and the introduction of 'freedom of trade' as well as the abolition of compulsory guild membership and the granting of the right to choose one's profession should be seen. If 'status' or 'estate' meant the legal codification of social hierarchies, then 'class'

18 Williams 1960; Williams 1972.

19 On the intellectual history of the concept of class, see Poovey 1994.

was often chosen as a descriptive term where the legal marking of difference was omitted, but social differences still had to be outlined. It was precisely its supposed scientific neutrality that qualified the use of the concept of class as a makeshift solution.

The 'proletariat' also has a long history. The term arises parallel to the concept of 'class' in the military constitution of Servius Tullius in the fifth century BC. There, 'proletarii' refers to the 'members of the 6th class, i.e. the propertyless and thus unarmed', who 'were unable to make a (military) contribution to the community due to their poverty'.[20] According to a widespread etymology, the name 'proletarius' comes from 'proles', or descendants, the only thing the proletarius has to contribute to the preservation of the *patria* (and its army).[21] The intrinsic link between the proletarian and his offspring has survived and will accompany us again and again in the following investigation – whether as the reproach that proletarians multiply like animals, or as praise that they at least supply the 'industrial reserve army' with ever new recruits.

Unlike the concept of class, which finds refuge in the classifications of natural history and classical grammar post-antiquity, the concept of the *proletarii* already becomes uncommon in late antiquity and then falls into oblivion altogether. It was not until the Renaissance that proletarians experience a rebirth, in England. In the seventeenth century, the century of civil war and accompanying class struggles, the term *proletarii* becomes popular again and finally anglicised as 'proletary'.[22] The question of when 'proletarians' first appears in German to describe the present is difficult to answer. Early evidence can be found in a letter by Baron vom Stein from 21 September 1829, in which the long-retired reform minister warns a friend of England's unreliability in foreign policy: 'In England, proletarians and the national debt predominate'.[23] The use of the term had been earlier prepared by German classical studies. Niebuhr's *Roman History* from 1811 discusses in detail the status of proletarians – already Germanised here – and, in the following years, an academic debate arises over how to distinguish between *proletarii* and *capite censi* in light of unclear sources. After all, the *capite censi* are also propertyless and thus only count 'by their heads'. The debate about the difference between the two

20 Conze 1984, p. 27.

21 Cf. the entry on 'Proletarii' in the *New Pauly*: 'The Latin word *proletarii*, derived from *proles* ('descendant'), describes people without property, who mattered only for their progeny (Cic. Rep. 2, 40), i.e. were liable neither to military service nor to taxation' (Ungern-Sternberg 2003).

22 For instance, in the most important global utopia of the time, James Harrington's 1656 *The Commonwealth of Oceana*. See Harrington 1992, p. 207.

23 Stein 1833, p. 269.

groups raises the question of whether one can still make distinctions in the social *underground*. That proletarians pose a problem for scientific classification (among other things) was thus clear from the beginning.[24]

In the mid-1830s, a broad debate about proletarians and the proletariat broke out in Germany, although the linguistic form of the group was not yet standardised. The Munich Catholic-Romantic social philosopher Franz von Baader baroquely entitled his famous memorandum *On the Present Disproportion of the Propertyless or Proletairs to the Propertied Classes of Society with regard to their Livelihood, both Materially and from the Standpoint of Law*.[25] The 'proletair' comes from far away, and belongs to a 'homeless class', linguistically as well.[26] After the July Revolution of 1830, many restless and homeless exiles, revolutionary tourists, poets and journalists such as Ludwig Börne and Heinrich Heine ensure that, in addition to revolutionary ideas, the highly developed and differentiated political-social language of the French is imported into Germany as an intellectual 'contrebande'. The history of linguistic import can be seen, like with 'proletairs', particularly well in non- or half-translations, especially in Heine's work. For example, in his correspondent articles, which he regularly sends from Paris to the Augsburg *Allgemeine Zeitung* from 1831 onwards, he speaks of 'Ouvrier-Emeuten' when referring to the silk weavers' revolts in Lyon of 1831, or the 'Crapüle' when referring to the street urchins of Paris.[27] The 'peuple', the simple, lowly folk, appears assonantly in Heine as 'pöbel', or rabble, his attempt to neutralise the pejorative connotation of the German word by remembering the glorious role of the *peuple* in the Revolution. He does not succeed, and so Heine quickly distinguishes again between the rejected 'pöbel' and the honourable 'ouvriers' – an early prelude to the later constitutive division of the class into workers and lumpenproletariat.[28]

The effusive character of the linguistic attempts at clarification reflects the fluid basis to which the language refers. In the linguistic usage of the Vormärz, the 'proletariat' was still an extremely heterogeneous conglomerate, a 'motley crowd', as Marx would later write.[29] Its genesis can be traced back to the fifteenth century, as Peter Linebaugh and Marcus Rediker have shown in their ground-breaking work *The Many-Headed Hydra*.[30] Whether this hetero-

---

24 Niebuhr 1811.
25 Baader 1957, pp. 235–50.
26 Freiherr vom Stein, quoted in Wehler 1987, p. 282.
27 Cf. Heine 1976, pp. 27–87, especially the Delacroix discussion pp. 39–42.
28 Cf. Heine, 1976, p. 220.
29 Marx 1976, p. 364.
30 Linebaugh and Rediker 2000.

geneous historical collective can be identified with a uniform signature was already questionable in the Vormärz. Heinrich Wilhelm Bensen, in his 'historical memorandum' of 1847, *The Proletarian*, additively subsumes and explicitly enumerates:

> 1) the actual factory workers; 2) the assistants and workers in all businesses and trades operated in a factory-like manner; 3) the farm workers, that is, both the actual day labourers, who, without property, support themselves merely by the work of their hands, and the innumerable subtenants ranked last, who, after the termination of the lease, do not have enough capital left to exist independently with their families for a while; 4) the poor, who revert to public support; 5) the common soldiers; 6) the crooks, prostitutes, bandits, etc; 7) the small civil and religious servants.[31]

The concept of *proletarianisation* makes it possible to grasp the identity of all those who have been called 'proletarians'. The term appears in the late nineteenth century – with the old Engels – and later becomes an important social-scientific tool.[32] 'Proletarianisation' turns the 'proletariat' into a processual category; the focus of attention is no longer the result, but the process of producing a social collective. The term thus belongs to a whole series of (nominalised) verbalisations that all follow the same pattern. Just as Simmel inferred processes of 'socialisation' from 'society', so Freud inferred processes of 'identification' from 'identity'.[33] To go back from the proletariat to the process of proletarianisation undertakes the old Hegelian step, according to which substance must always also be understood as subject, and goes one post-Hegelian step further from *subject* to *subjectivation*: the 'proletariat' is thus, in a nutshell, the result of a socio-historical process of proletarianisation *and* the result of a political act of *subjectivation*, the political identification with its own proletarianisation.

The proletarianisation of society initially means nothing other than the fact that the proportion of wage labourers in the population rises, that peasants, for example, are turning into wage labourers. The preconditions of this process, however, are most adequately defined in the negative: that someone performs

31 Bensen 1847, p. 344.

32 See, for example, Engels' late 1891 introduction to Marx's Vormärz text, *Wage-Labour and Capital*, where Engels writes that 'the great mass of society [is] proletarianised, transformed into wage-workers, and thereby made incapable of appropriating this abundance of products' (MECW 27, p. 201, translation revised).

33 Cf. Simmel 1910; Freud, 1990, pp. 46–53.

wage labour indicates the absence of other, traditional possibilities of material reproduction. Historically, proletarianisation takes place as the 'destruction of the previously dominant forms of labour and subsistence'.[34] Yet this destruction does not automatically mean that the proletarianised are placed into regular employment. To mark this difference, Gero Lenhardt and Claus Offe have proposed the distinction between 'passive proletarianisation' and 'active proletarianisation'. The former does not necessarily entail the latter; the proletarianised can also seek 'alternatives to "active" proletarianisation in wage labour existence', and this is exactly what they have historically done in huge numbers. The 'deviant' forms of proletarian existence that Bensen enumerates, the growth of the 'classes dangereuses' fervently discussed at the time, the flight into 'emigration' – all this shows that for the newly proletarianised, anything was better than going directly into the labour market.

In the Vormärz, these two *analytically* distinct phases of proletarianisation also diverge *historically*. The separation appears before our eyes in quasi-real analytical clarity. It is precisely because of this that the transitional society of the Vormärz is so well suited to confound us with forms of perception and thinking that have become 'second nature' (Hegel). The truism that *whoever does not work* – whoever does not pursue regular and gainful employment – *shall not eat* still appears to people in the Vormärz as a cruel imposition.[35]

2 The Proletariat: a Non-identical Subject

Since the 1830s, proletarianised individuals made their living conditions and experiences the reference point for a collective identification, from which the 'proletariat' (or the 'working class') finally emerges as a political subject. From this perspective, one could say that the emergence of the working class is inseparable from the rise of the labour movement; without a labour movement – no matter how rudimentary it may be at the beginning – there is no working class. Proletarians interpret their *condition proletariénne* for themselves and others and recognise the self-interpretation of their experiences as the constitution of a *we* that transcends all individual differences. Without class consciousness – to

34 Offe 1984, p. 92.

35 The most radical critique of society was thus not only (and perhaps not even primarily) sparked by the unjust distribution of the product of labour, but by the always presupposed compulsion to work in general, which historically follows from passive proletarianisation. This tradition spans from Marx's son-in-law Paul Lafargue and his manifesto *The Right to be Lazy* of 1880 to the *Glücklichen Arbeitslosen* [Happy Unemployed] of 1996.

push the point further – there is no class. The category of class consciousness, however, should not be understood in a narrow psychologistic way: 'Class consciousness is the way', according to E.P. Thompson, 'in which these experiences are handled in cultural terms: embodied in traditions, value-systems, ideas, and institutional forms'.[36] In other words, class consciousness is inextricably linked to that dimension of social interpretation identified by the concept of the *imaginary*. Class consciousness is imaginary because it is articulated in images, stories and myths, in ways of speaking, patterns of thinking and pictorial languages, what Thompson calls 'imagery'. Class consciousness is neither tangibly real nor simply fictitious; it moves in the realm of cultural invention – from poem to institution – and, thus, proletarian class identity is also *imaginary*, just as the class-conscious proletariat is *an invention*. Invention: this is, as Mary Shelley noted in her great machine-wrecking novel *Frankenstein* of the same time, not a 'creating out of void' but the new and unexpected combination of found materials.[37] And so, proletarian class consciousness is constituted in the Vormärz by the combination of found historical-cultural artefacts, not least by the invention of its own tradition: the tradition of rebellious journeymen and the justice-loving social rebels. This tradition is imaginary: it is invented and imagined, yet incredibly influential.[38]

The texts that will be discussed in-depth below are read in this sense as embodiments of an imaginary proletarian class consciousness, as manifestations and configurations of collectively shared experiences. Such texts bear witness to these experiences, making comprehensible how the manifestations and embodiments not only follow their own conditions (like a programme), but also change them (rewriting the programme). One must be careful not to distinguish too hastily between primary and secondary aspects of class formation – like base and superstructure – and thus already predetermine their priority. This study is based on an 'objective' concept of class, which is determ-

36 Thompson 1966, p. 10. 'Class consciousness' should not be placed in opposition with the unconscious: it is precisely in the cultural embodiments of class consciousness that the political-economic unconscious expresses itself quite forcefully. On the methodological self-understanding of a 'Social History of Art' under the sign of the unconscious see Clark 1982, especially pp. 9–20.

37 Cf. Shelley 2009, p. 440: 'Invention, it must be humbly admitted, does not consist in creating out of void, but out of chaos; the materials must, in the first place, be afforded: it can give form to dark, shapeless substances, but cannot bring into being the substance itself'. On Mary Shelley and the Luddites, see the conclusion of this book, 'The Return of Romantic Anti-Capitalism'.

38 Cf. Hobsbawm and Ranger 2012, and the section 'Enclosing Class Struggle: Tieck's Guilds as *Invention of Tradition*', in the first chapter of this book.

ined by economic processes and their political and juridical moderation. But the 'subjective' dimension of this process, the way in which the 'objective' conditions are imaginatively processed and thus culturally lived, how they are made intelligible and imaginable in the first place, is not determined by the objective conditions. Proletarianisation is first of all a process of 'destruction', 'dispossession', 'undermining', 'disorganisation', in short, comprehensive disintegration.[39] The subjective (and collective) handling of this disintegration need not necessarily lead to the system of productive wage labour, which will only later become widely established and then presented as inevitable. The Vormärz is precisely the historical epoch of enormous teething problems for these attempts at integration. Nor do subversive subjectivations automatically come about here. In his study on the genesis of the early workers' movement in France, *Proletarian Nights*, Jacques Rancière meticulously traces the coils of the serpent: the struggle between 'subversive' departures and 'conformist' recuperations, above all the drift that threatens to turn every departure into the motor of a new integration in the system of wage labour from which one had just sought to escape. These processes, too, outline a poetry of class, and – as Rancière forcefully shows – it is often even poetry in the narrow sense: poems and the poetic imagination make both the departures and their failure possible. The break with given identities comes from reading and writing poems at night, from discussions about metaphysics, from walks in nature, from sunrises experienced together. It is only against this background that the intolerability of the workshop and the factory reveals itself to the workers. The education acquired in this development, the new knowledge and broader horizons of the literate workers, however, in turn predestine them to become the new bosses in the next industrial cycle of innovation.[40]

What Rancière writes about the individual identity politics of his heroes can be said in a more general sense about proletarian identity, the identity of the proletariat as such: the process of subjective proletarianisation, the constitution of a culturally diverse, embodied class consciousness does not lead to a seamless identity, an identity of the proletariat with itself, which would then merely have to be affirmed and stabilised. Proletarian identity is as precarious as the mode of existence that expresses itself in it, as precarious as its political-economic preconditions. From the outset, proletarian class identity has a transitory character, a tendency towards self-abolition. All versions of proletarian identity in the Vormärz ultimately aimed at making

39 Offe 1984, pp. 92–3.
40 Cf. Rancière, 2012, p. xi.

this identity disappear: whether 'socio-politically' through bourgeoisification and 'domestication' of the proletariat, or 'communistically' in a classless society.

This precarious aspect of proletarian identity finds unsurpassed expression in the first ever mention by Karl Marx of the proletariat. At the end of his 'Introduction' to the *Critique of Hegel's Philosophy of Right*, Marx answers his own question about the 'possibility of German emancipation' with a long cascade of sentences that culminates in a battle cry:

> *Answer*: In the formation of a class with *radical chains*, a class of civil society which is not a class of civil society, an estate which is the dissolution of all estates, a sphere which has a universal character by its universal suffering and claims no *particular right* because no *particular wrong* but *wrong generally* is perpetrated against it; which can no longer invoke a *historical* but only a *human* title … a sphere, finally, which cannot emancipate itself without emancipating itself from all other spheres of society and thereby emancipating all other spheres of society, which, in a word, is the *complete loss* of man and hence can win itself only through the *complete rewinning of man*. This dissolution of society as a particular estate is the *proletariat*.[41]

For Marx, the proletariat embodies the fact that the present world order brings with it a permanent dissolution of every possible world order: fundamental, radical disintegration, 'creative destruction', as the economist Schumpeter will aphoristically put it almost one hundred years later. Society in the present is thus always already synonymous with the 'dissolution of society', and to identify with this paradox – to embody this paradox – is the task of the proletariat.

Marx's negative definition of the proletariat may seem philosophically exaggerated, but it should be noted that there is no affirmation, no celebration of a positive proletarian identity in the Vormärz. At best, proletarian identity is accepted as a passing phase; the proletariat remains a transitional figure. But since a proletarian identity is not meant to be permanent, the contours of this identity do not have to be sharply drawn, no hard inclusions and exclusions made, no defining list of characteristics laid down. This conceptual vagueness on which historians grit their teeth – *what exactly did the term 'proletariat' mean in the Vormärz, who called themselves 'workers'?* – was made, for instance, by

---

41 Marx 1844, MECW 3, p. 186. The text first appeared in the *Deutsch-Französische Jahrbücher*.

Wilhelm Weitling and his comrades in the 'League of the Just' into the positive basis for their own political and organisational work. The indeterminacy of proletarian identity was interpreted as the boundlessness of their own political mission: the 'communist', the class-conscious proletarian, ultimately always addresses 'everyone': 'We have addressed all working classes, indeed all classes of society; proving that our voice has been heard by all and its value recognised', programmatically proclaims the first issue of Weitling's 1841 journal, *Hülferuf der deutschen Jugend* [*Cry for Help of German Youth*].[42] The *poetry of class* thus also refers to the 'enthusiasm' of the class towards its own abolition.

3 Romantic Anti-capitalism

The transcendence of class society, inscribed in the concept of class from the beginning, is announced in the Vormärz for the future, yet consistently articulated in relation to the past, in which, accordingly, there was no class division. This viewpoint will be defined in the following as 'romantic anti-capitalism'.

The expression comes from Georg Lukács. In his essay on Eichendorff from 1940, Lukács uses the formula 'romantic anti-capitalism' to salvage the social and critical dimension in Eichendorff's work.[43] Lukács wants to reinforce an impulse in Eichendorff's writing that turns against the 'pointless and inhuman bustle of modem life, against the "efficiency" and "diligence" of the old and new philistine', an impulse that sharply rejects the 'capitalist prose' of life; instead, Lukács sees in Eichendorff a 'struggle for a meaningful life of human dignity under capitalism'.[44] The rebellion against the 'capitalist "religion of labour"', as Lukács puts it with Paul Lafargue, is at the same time a 'struggle for leisure'; this last point, according to Lukács, should be regarded as an essential element of any romantic anti-capitalism.[45]

At this point, however, as Lukács mobilises the critical force of the phrase, romantic anti-capitalism falls short. Although it 'exposes with great accuracy

42 *Hülferuf* 1841, No. 1, p. 6.

43 Lukács 1940, p. 52. An alternative formulation on p. 62 speaks of a 'Romantic opposition to the nascence of capitalism'.

44 Lukács 1940, pp. 52, 61–2.

45 Lukács 1940, 62, 64. Lukács quotes the formulation of the 'religion of labour' from Paul Lafargue's 'witty essay', *The Right to Be Lazy* (1880): 'And to think that the sons of the heroes of the Terror have allowed themselves to be degraded by the religion of work, to the point of accepting, since 1848, as a revolutionary conquest, the law limiting factory labor to twelve hours. They proclaim as a revolutionary principle the Right to Work' (Lafargue 1907, pp. 15–16).

the contradictions of capitalist society and combats them with genuine bitterness and hard-hitting scorn', it nevertheless maintains an 'inability to grasp the essence of these contradictions'.[46] Romantic anti-capitalism simply lacks the analytical tools and categories to conceptualise its opposition; thus, the opposition remains vague, the identification of the enemy blurred. At the centre of Lukács' critique of romantic anti-capitalism, however, is its relationship to history. Here, its conceptual inadequacy is revealed: 'Thus, the exposure of the contradictions of the capitalist division of labour turns into an uncritical glorification of the social conditions which existed at a time when this division of labour was still unknown; here is the source of the infatuation with the Middle Ages'.[47] It is only a short step from 'uncritical glorification' to the desire to politically restore the past conditions as well. This would certainly make romantic anti-capitalism plainly reactionary.

Romantic anti-capitalism remains virulent well after Romanticism; indeed, it is only when the capitalist mode of production fully develops that the concept really begins to take hold. To understand this, however, we need to readjust Lukács' critical understanding of Romanticism and romantic anti-capitalism. In the French context, Michael Löwy and Jacques Rancière have in recent years reappraised Romanticism as the historical code of the critique of capitalism; the social historians of the British New Left – E.P. Thompson, Raymond Williams, Eric Hobsbawm, to name only the most well-known representatives – have also consistently referred positively to Romanticism as a point of departure for anti-capitalist critique, and drawn methodological inspiration from it.[48]

Michael Löwy and Robert Sayre define Romanticism as a 'critique of modernity, that is, of modern capitalist civilization, in the name of values and ideals drawn from the past'.[49] The past as a resource of critique leads Löwy and Sayre to call Romanticism 'nostalgic' or 'melancholic' critique.[50] The striking thing about this approach is that the 'nostalgic' programme of Romantic criticism does not lead Löwy and Sayre to reject it as 'backward-looking'. Rather, it is precisely the nostalgic element that allows Romantic criticism to register the consequences and costs of modernity. For Löwy and Sayre, the fact that the

46 Lukács 1940, pp. 62–63. Translation revised.

47 Lukács 1940, pp. 63. Translation revised.

48 Cf. Löwy and Sayre 2001; cf. also Löwy 2005; Thompson 1997; Thompson 2011. The subtitle of Thompson's monograph on Morris ('Romantic to Revolutionary') is almost identical to the English title of Michael Löwy's major study of the young Lukács: *Georg Lukács. From Romanticism to Bolshevism* (Löwy 1979).

49 Löwy and Sayre 2001, p. 17. Cf. Sayre and Löwy, 2016, p. 145.

50 Löwy and Sayre 2001, p. 24, on the Romantic vision as one of 'melancholic nostalgia'.

foil of a lost past can lead to its idealisation is only a *possible* (and even then, not necessarily reprehensible) consequence of critique, but it is not a logically necessary one (as is usually assumed in the German critical tradition after Lukács).[51]

Following Lucien Goldmann, Löwy and Sayre understand romantic anti-capitalism as a 'signifying structure' which allows a critique to be articulated that would not be intelligible without this structure; a necessary part of this structure is the assumption of a 'better' past that has been lost in capitalist modernity.[52] The historical interpreter does not have to then ask whether this belief is substantially justified or not. The belief produces its own form of critique, the validity of which needs to be examined and historically located on its own terms. The proof that the past was not 'actually' the way it is supposed to have been completely misses the point: even invented pasts express a real desire for change and can be deciphered accordingly.

If one regards anti-capitalism in the Vormärz as romantic, then new, previously unseen connections come into view. In England, it has always been taken for granted that the Romantics were contemporaries and vehement critics of the industrial revolution and new capitalist social relations. Shelley's poem 'Queen Mab', for example, was, as Peter Linebaugh writes, the 'bible of the working class' for two generations, and the German protagonists of the early socialist movement were also avid Shelley readers.[53] Shelley himself took a firm stand in the struggles of the early movement before his untimely death.[54] The same cannot be said of any German author of the 'Romantic school'. Despite this, the formula of 'romantic anti-capitalism' reveals similarities between the critique of modernity in late Romantic texts by Ludwig Tieck and the social cri-

51 On the possible but not necessary turn into 'reactionary modernism', cf. Löwy and Sayre 2001, p. 29.

52 Löwy and Sayre 2001, p. 18.

53 Linebaugh 2104, p. 96. On the German reception, see, for example, Moses Hess, 'Über das Geldwesen' [On the Essence of Money] in Püttmann 1845, Vol. 1, pp. 1–34. Hess prefaced his treatise-with a one-and-a-half-page excerpt from Shelley's *Queen Mab*. Karl Marx's lifelong enthusiasm for Shelley has been pointed out by none other than his daughter and son-in-law, see Aveling and Aveling-Marx 1888.

54 Shelley's commitment is evident, for example, in his poem 'The Mask of Anarchy', his direct response to the Peterloo Massacre, where fifteen workers were killed and several hundred injured when cavalry attacked a huge proletarian mass demonstration with an estimated 60,000 to 80,000 demonstrators. The final stanza reads, 'Rise like lions after slumber / In unvanquishable number – / Shake your chains to earth like dew / Which in sleep had fallen on you – / Ye are many – they are few' (Percy Bysshe Shelley, 'The Mask of Anarchy. Written on the Occasion of the Massacre at Manchester', in Shelley 1987, p. 401). For a modern perspective on Peterloo, see Krantz 2011.

tique of early socialist authors such as Georg Weerth and Ernst Dronke. Even early socialist theorising, from Wilhelm Weitling and Moses Hess to Marx and Engels, can be examined for its Romantic motifs, without this being taken as a theoretical denunciation. Especially in German literary history, where eras are always divided according to political differences of opinion, such connections were often not seen or even actively obscured. Perhaps it has been a missed opportunity in German literary and social history that there were no places or mediums of encounter for the radical critique of the system of 'freedom of trade', as presented by Tieck, for example, and the early socialist movement.[55]

4 Historiography of Rescue

Romantic critique is 'bound up with an experience of loss', its vision 'characterized by the painful and melancholic conviction that in modern reality something precious has been lost'.[56] Romantic anti-capitalism is therefore inextricably bound to a programme of rescue or restitution. One of the most important ways of implementing this programme has been historiography from the very beginning. E.P. Thompson, as Löwy also points out, can be regarded as one of the most pronounced representatives of a romantic anti-capitalist historiography, a historiography that chooses its subject precisely where the industrial revolution not only destroys all 'previous' forms of work and life, but also mercilessly and violently breaks all forms of resistance to it, giving 'no alternative'. These famous sentences from the introduction to Thompson's classic *The Making of the English Working Class* sum up his programme of a romantic anti-capitalist historiography of rescue:

> I am seeking to rescue the poor stockinger, the Luddite cropper, the 'obsolete' hand-loom weaver, the 'Utopian' artisan, and even the deluded follower of Joanna Southcott, from the enormous condescension of posterity. Their crafts and traditions may have been dying. Their hostility to the new industrialism may have been backward-looking. Their communitarian ideals may have been fantasies. Their insurrectionary conspiracies may have been foolhardy. But they lived through these times of acute

55 The tragic nature and intellectual homelessness of the late Tieck is elaborated in Wergin 1979.

56 Löwy and Sayre 2001, p. 21.

> social disturbance, and we did not. Their aspirations were valid in terms of their own experience; and, if they were casualties of history, they remain, condemned in their own lives, as casualties.[57]

The aforementioned textile artisan, the stocking maker, the cloth shearer and the hand weaver may have expressed 'romantic anti-capitalism' in Lukács's pejorative sense. They may have long since been overrun by developments, they may have argued and acted in a deluded and backward-looking manner, pursued illusory and foolish goals. Thompson *nevertheless* wants to rescue them because they not only had to live through times we can hardly imagine, as he writes, but also because they actively and defiantly sought to shape these times. The three highly skilled trades that Thompson lists were not only displaced by the system of manufacture and a thoroughgoing mechanisation of labour in the course of the Industrial Revolution, their representatives were declassed and pauperised. The stocking makers, cloth shearers and hand weavers also militantly resisted this, forming the core troops of the 'Luddites', the organised machine breakers. The struggles of the Luddites – named after General Ludd, their mythical leader – reached their climax in 1811–12 in northern England; the rebellion could only be put down with massive military force. The Luddites were defeated long ago, and yet they still need saving. For now, the 'enormous condescension of posterity' has not ceased to triumph; it renews itself with the 'progress' with which it believes to be in league, and sustains itself not least in the 'left', 'Marxist', and 'progressive' condemnation of romantic anti-capitalism. Should there not be historical solidarity with the defeated instead?

Thompson's melancholic (or Hobsbawm's picaresque) social history revolves around 'blind alleys', 'lost causes' and 'losers'.[58] It is concerned with disclosing 'opportunities not taken', missed encounters in historiography and in history itself.[59]

With this orientation, however, social history becomes a history of latencies. It is no longer only about 'how it actually was', but about what could have happened, what did not happen either by chance or necessity, but thereby might have had an impact on the possibilities of thinking, on assumptions and imaginations. If romantic anti-capitalism always operates with imagined

57 Thompson 1966, pp. 12–13.

58 Thompson 1966, p. 12. Here, at the latest, a kinship becomes apparent between Thompson's concept of history and that of Walter Benjamin. See Benjamin 2006.

59 Cf. Joyce 2010, pp. 213–14.

pasts, then a history of romantic anti-capitalism must at the same time be a history of (mostly) counterfactual, but politically effective imaginaries. What is missing – and what will be attempted in the following – is a *social history with a sense of possibility*. One must try, following Rancière, to 'find a poetics' of 'social and workers' history' which can hear 'the multiplicity of languages and modes of subjectivation' at work. Indeed, this is something that the Vormärz in particular can offer, but which has subsequently been largely forgotten and suppressed – not least by a social historiography enthralled by modernisation.[60]

5 Proletarian Identity: Openness and (Self-)Enclosure

The Vormärz proletariat has an open, assembling, 'multiversal' character. The still disordered proletarian class movement finds its adequate expression in the texts that will be examined below, which themselves appear disordered in many respects. The Vormärz presents us with a discursive melange in which the now familiar boundaries of social spheres and subsystems, disciplines and genres are first drawn – or previously established boundaries are deliberately and experimentally called into question. Anyone in the Vormärz who wanted to write about social issues could do so philosophically or literarily, they could join the nascent and not yet academically institutionalised fields of sociology or ethnology, they could even as scholars or militant activists write a novella or a 'social poem' to articulate their findings and intentions. And when they finally seek a place to publish what they created, they can choose from a variety of scientific and literary periodicals, or they can start one of the numerous and usually extremely short-lived journals themselves in order to avoid any trouble with the censors from the outset, almost certainly leading to economic bankruptcy. Writers in the Vormärz, especially those who were socially committed, were always also project-makers. The ubiquitous political repression and censorship of the Restoration era not only produced a very unique, disguised, ironic 'art of writing', but also a highly independent explosion of journalistic project-making.[61]

To this wild writing scene, I bring a wild, even undisciplined reading attitude, reading literature like theory and theory like literature, neither of which should enjoy epistemic priority. Both types of texts are first and foremost mediums in

60 Rancière 1994, pp. 99–100. Translation revised.

61 Cf. Strauss 1988, pp. 22–37.

which the imaginary formation of class identities and forms of consciousness occurs and can be reconstructed. The perhaps aesthetically mediocre 'social poem' by a poet largely forgotten today promises the same insight as the social-theoretical treatise by a later world-famous philosopher; and that treatise in turn only reveals its full content when its artistic form is also considered. That both Georg Herwegh's poem 'Treason!' and Karl Marx's *Critique of Hegel's Philosophy of Right* are printed next to each other in the same journal (here, the one-time published *Deutsch-Französische Jahrbücher*) must not be viewed as a coincidence, but on the contrary, must be taken as the starting point of interpretation.

Every Vormärz eventually comes to an end. A short summer, then comes autumn and winter; the time of opening and openness is over, survival must be ensured. With regard to class configurations – and the proletariat in particular – one can also observe such a process of closure and (self-)enclosure in the post-March period, the time after the revolutionary outbreaks of 1848–9. Out of the 'motley crowd' of the Vormärz proletariat emerges the increasingly solidified collective of a nationally contained, adult white male working class, and this process too can be traced in literature, or is even developed by it – as in Georg Weerth's posthumous novel fragment.

At the level of literary and theoretical texts, the clarification of class configurations is accompanied by a clarification and straightening of genre boundaries; the social disciplining corresponds to a disciplinary classification and codification of the (literary and non-literary) texts in which class and class consciousness are expressed. The literary experiments that characterise the Vormärz end at the latest by the mid-1850s. Sometime around 1855, the *realist* literary programme is established, which will then remain decisive for at least two decades. The theoretical expressions of the Vormärz do not end until 1859, the year in which Marx publishes *A Contribution to the Critique of Political Economy*. This, in turn, establishes the method and programme of what will later be called 'Marxism'.[62] In the *Grundrisse*, which originated as an unpublished 'rough draft' of *Capital* in 1857–8, Marx once again tries out various concepts and forms of representation that he had worked out in the Vormärz.[63] After that, the phase of experimentation is over. Genre boundaries and disciplines are no longer at issue.

62 Marx 1859, *Contribution to the Critique of Political Economy. Part One*, MECW 29, pp. 257–417.

63 Marx 1993.

6 Inverse Relevance of the Vormärz

> The present forms of capitalism, the collapse of the labor market, the destruction of systems of social solidarity, and the precarious nature of employment are creating experiences of work and forms of life that may well be closer to those of the artisans of the past than that world of non-material work and frenetic consumption whose complacent picture we are offered.
>
> JACQUES RANCIÈRE[64]

∴

The homogenisation and uniformisation of the proletariat has proven to be an extraordinarily profound and long-lasting affair. Even today, the word 'proletariat' still spontaneously evokes in most readers the (frightful) image of a closed mass of grey men whose strong arm creates the world, keeps it running or even plunges it into chaos. Of course, this image has always been a bourgeois-ideological one, expressing fear and loathing of the lower classes. However, the image does reveal – albeit in an ideologically distorted form – the historical process of the formation and containment of the working class, a formation in which the labour movement itself played a crucial role. In the following, the (ideological) image of a massive, unbroken working-class identity will serve as historical foil against which the protean Vormärz proletariat takes shape. That 'class' and 'proletariat' have not always signified the massive, visible identities that we have associated them with since the end of the nineteenth century will be made clear in the study of the Vormärz. That 'class' and 'proletariat' do not lose all reality, however, when the massive historical identities that we initially and mostly still associate with these names dissolve, lends our historical investigation a perhaps surprising relevance. If there is talk everywhere in our present of a 'return of class society', then the historical model for the present would surely be sought in the Vormärz rather than in the time that separates us from it.

For what recurs today under terms like 'precariat' or 'new proletariat' has little in common with the formed working class that disappeared in the 1970s, at the latest, except the most general names and some very global regula-

64 Rancière 2012, p. xi.

tions. The 'old' working class (of the metropolises) was politically nurtured and equipped with social guarantees that largely cushioned 'proletarian risk'. What comes after the end of this formed working class is the proletariat in a once again raw, wild, heterogeneous motley form. The steady erosion of the 'normal employment relationship' is driving class configurations that increasingly resemble those of the Vormärz. They are unregulated, 'unguaranteed', always only temporary labour relations, combining a structural overqualification of the workforce – as in the Vormärz with the hand weavers and cloth shearers – with systematic over-exploitation. When Marx wrote in the *Grundrisse* that the worker always remains a 'virtual pauper', then today, at least tendentially, the actualisation of this virtuality is at hand in the metropolises.

The relevance of the Vormärz, however, is an *inverse* one: inverse because in the Vormärz we can historically observe the congealing process of that modern constellation whose long decomposition we have witnessed since the crises of the 1970s. In the process of dissolution, however, images of the social emerge which – in their own right and as historical *snapshots* – look confusingly similar to those from the formative phase of the proletariat, but which stem from an opposing sequence. An investigation of the Vormärz must capture both moments: the similarities as well as the differences. The modernity that takes shape in the Vormärz is still ours, but it disintegrates in the present and becomes irrevocably alien to us.

7 Literary History as Social History: Class as Figure

The inverse relevance of the Vormärz also allows historical insights into class constitution that might not have been possible in the heyday of class society, that is, in the century between 1860 and 1960. If today, as in the Vormärz, proletarianisation occurs without a clearly defined, unambiguous and 'visible' working-class identity, then, in retrospect, it will have to be stated that the reality of class relations is by no means necessarily bound to clear and definite class identities at all. The firm and fixed, *welded* unity of political-imaginary class identity and political-economic proletarianisation, as it existed in the century of class society, then appears in retrospect as a historical exception that could only seem normal due to its particularly rigid form. The proverbial *farewell to the working class* applies to this special case.[65]

65 Gorz 1982.

Conversely, one will have to understand as the historical rule what must be considered a deviation from the point of view of a 'strong', normatively loaded class theory: namely, that there can be contradictions and incompatibilities between socio-cultural class consciousness, political class standpoint and economically determined class interest. The historical study carried out here shows that the category of class has been inherently contradictory from the very beginning. Class *figures* are thus mentioned here in order to mark the fact that class is subject to multiple cultural, political and theoretical claims of validity, which in extreme cases can even be mutually exclusive; yet class *as a figure* remains able to keep the various claims in play and to settle them narratively. This is why class can be narrated even before there are clear definitions, and why class must continue to be narrated precisely when fixed and firm definitions are enforced. Narrative keeps flexible and adaptable what definitions threaten to harden. This applies in an overarching sense to the relationship between literature and social theory, but it also applies to the narrative element within theories. That which theory cannot cope with must be narratively 'managed', but this does not leave theory untouched either. Class as a figure operates, so to speak, as a partisan in the conceptual framework of class theories; ironically, however, the theories only remain functional through this 'subversive' figurative dimension of their concepts. Entire generations of *Capital* reading groups can tell you a thing or two about the fact that Marx's metaphorical mode of presentation cannot be simply 'defined away'.

The cultural and literary study of class figures can help us take class more seriously. The notion that class has been dissolved and replaced by individualisation, as claimed by German sociology since the 1980s, can be historically questioned by pointing out that individualisation was seen from the beginning only as the other side of class formation, and not as its opposite. One need only read Thomas Carlyle or Moses Hess. With only a little exaggeration, one can say from this perspective that the gesture of parting with class society is an essential part of the history of class society itself. The diagnosis of having finally left the class divide behind constantly repeats itself. Patrick Joyce has shown, for example, that in the middle of the nineteenth century – that is, precisely at the moment when class society was completely and undisputedly installed – the English working class turned away from the concept of class in its self-understanding and imagined itself (again) as a 'people'.[66] If we take class as a figure and as a category of historical process (and not simply as a designation of given identities), then class is always just emerging or having passed. In

66 Joyce 1991.

the words of David Cannadine, we are always both 'Beyond Class – Forward To Class'.[67] If, however, the reference to class is never simply tangible, but always one of *memory or expectation*, if therefore every presentist access to class is always already blocked to us, then the romantic path becomes the only realistic one.[68] Romantic anti-capitalism would then not be proof of an attitude turned away from the world, but a medium of historical insight, an insight that cannot be had any other way.

From this realisation, in turn, conclusions can also be drawn about our own political situation. For what the present lacks – *lacks*, however, only measured against the claims of the 'old' class society before its departure – is that imaginary formation that once gave classes their 'visible', powerful identity. In this situation – 'everywhere proletarianised individuals, nowhere the proletariat, not as a recognisable group of people and certainly not as a collective actor' – it seems natural, in the desire for contemporary political agency, to fall back on those imaginary armaments that once made up the old working-class identity.[69] But here too, when it comes to the question of an imaginary configuration of class identity, we are well advised to resist the discreet charm of reinforced concrete modernity. Even with the newly forming class configuration of the present, we should try to learn to appreciate the 'merits of a political entity' that wants, can or must 'do without a strong self-narrative'.[70] Here, historical work on the Vormärz can perhaps offer alternatives to that 'strong' self-narrative of class that shaped modernity in the heroic yet catastrophic century between 1860 and 1960, alternatives that were historically crushed by the very 'strong' self-narrative that they themselves helped set in motion.

---

67 Cannadine 1993, pp. 1–24.

68 Zygmunt Bauman structures his book on class by means of the operations of memory and expectation; it is always about 'Class: before and after' (Bauman 1982).

69 Cf. Freundinnen und Freunde der klassenlosen Gesellschaft 2007, p. 11.

70 Koschorke 2015, p. 31, on Europe.

CHAPTER 1

Small Masters and Journeymen: from Guild to Movement

1 Romantic Anti-capitalism: Ludwig Tieck's *The Young Master Carpenter*

Romanticism may be backward-looking, defensive and nostalgic, as has been argued time and again over the last two hundred years, but it is definitely not *modest*. Thus, in the preface to his late major novella *Der junge Tischlermeister* [*The Young Master Carpenter*] of 1836, Ludwig Tieck, the long grown old 'king of Romanticism', blasts his contemporary opponents – progressive, modern, and critical – and insists that he is much more current (more modern and more critical) than they have been for a long time. Although unnamed, Tieck undoubtedly meant the writers of the *Junges Deutschland* [*Young Germany*] movement, with whom he had waged a fierce polemic in the previous years. For them, as for Heinrich Heine, Tieck was the prototypical representative of an old, outdated conception of literature, a dinosaur of a classical-romantic aesthetic of autonomy, who can no longer understand the new age and therefore must almost inevitably become a lackey of the old powers.[1] After a long and heated exchange, Tieck finally counters these accusations and defamations with 'indulgent irony':[2]

> When the younger, impetuous world now so often calls me and scolds me to learn, to experience, to go along, to understand and to grasp, and I once take a look at these products of my newest and freshest contemporaries, I cannot help smiling, because so many of these new great discoveries and truths have long been in my writings, some of them the earliest.[3]

The Young Master Carpenter is more than four hundred pages long – probably one of the longest novellas in German literary history – and has a complicated origin, which Tieck reveals in his preface. This lengthy genesis, however, sup-

1 cf. Bunzel 2011.

2 Bunzel 2011, p. 128.

3 Tieck 1988, p. 12. *Der junge Tischlermeister* is cited according to this edition in the body of the text in brackets with the initials JTM and the page number.

 | DOI:10.1163/9789004685536_003

posedly justifies the novella's particular relevance. For Tieck, much of what erupted in crisis everywhere in the mid-1830s – and was now perceived by Tieck's 'newest and freshest contemporaries' as new and fresh – had just as long a run-up as his now finally published work. The first drafts were composed 'as early as spring 1795', and already here he sought 'to truly depict clear and specific details of our real German life, its circumstances and prospects' (JTM, p. 11). Most of the work seems to date from 1811. The subject matter gains shape over time, since now 'thoughts about guilds, bourgeois life and the like are on the agenda'; of what Tieck has to contribute, however, 'much remains, in a sense, new and as yet unspoken' (JTM, p. 11).

The guilds were on the agenda in 1811 because they had just been deprived of power and economically gutted in Prussia by the 'Trade Tax Edict' of 2 November 1810, which introduced the freedom of trade that had long been discussed in scholarly circles, thus implementing a central issue of the Stein-Hardenberg reforms.[4] In order to – as it says in the preamble – 'liberate the trades from their most oppressive shackles', compulsory guild membership was abolished and the right to free choice of profession introduced. A uniform trade law replaced the colourful patchwork of old and regionally differentiated privileges and concessions, through which the guilds had previously regulated prices, wages and market access; anyone wishing to pursue a trade now needed a state trade licence (and *only* a state trade licence) and to pay a trade tax to the state (and *only* to the state). The nationalisation of commercial life, in its move against the old feudal guilds, still lies on this side of the later decisive opposition between market and state. It creates for the very first time, according to Reinhart Koselleck, a 'nationwide market' to which 'everyone' has access who is willing and able to pay 'the corresponding tax … as an entrance ticket to the free economy'.[5]

The introduction of freedom of trade, implemented in Prussia in the remarkably prosaic way of tax law, can hardly be overestimated in its significance. With this act, the whole composition of what Tieck calls 'bourgeois life and the like' changes; society is structurally transformed. What was discussed as *freedom of trade* in 1810 would be conceptualised as *capitalism* a short time later. The effects of this great transformation, in turn, only become fully visible in the 1830s, and this is where the relevance that Tieck ascribes to his *Master Carpenter* becomes apparent.

Tieck presents his titular character, the young master carpenter Leonhard, as a clear-sighted observer of his present. By moving the plot of his novella back

4 Vogel 1983. On the trade tax edict of November 1810, see pp. 179–183.

5 Koselleck 1987, pp. 587–8.

to 1802, Tieck allows Leonhard to describe and predict social changes early on, which were only politically and legally sanctioned with the freedom of trade in 1811, the year the novella was written, and which do not begin to fully develop socially until the 1830s, the time of publication.

Leonhard's (and Tieck's) observation of the present is situated on three levels. First, Leonhard notes a fundamental social division in the new system of freedom of trade, which, for a large part of the people, goes together with a previously unseen impoverishment; the term pauperism is coined for this in the 1830s. Leonhard then shows that the poverty of the great 'masses' is material, but not *only* material. It is not the insecurity of bare survival that is so scandalous for Leonhard, but the fact that the lives of most people today are already exhausted in bare survival *and should be*; any further demands, needs and passions are considered unacceptable. This is followed by the observations on the third level: the lives of most 'ordinary' people have lost any collective sense of meaning in the new system of freedom of trade. For Leonhard, the guilds also had the function of providing a social order of representation in which everyone could feel at home in their own place. With this gone, only isolation, despair and emptiness remain.

1.1 *The Death of the House and the Life of the Factory*

Leonhard's romantic anti-capitalism reveals its full diagnostic power and foresight in long conversations he has with an old friend, Baron Elsheim. The two conversation partners approach their subject, the ongoing transformation of society, from its institutional side: from the 'impression that the guilds and all their related establishments will perish' (JTM, p. 74).[6] The starting point of Leonhard's observations is always his own position as a craftsman; his reflections unfold from the small to the large, from the near to the far.

The guild 'establishment' nearest to Leonhard in his immediate vicinity is 'his house' (JTM, p. 16). This consists of a small carpentry shop that Leonhard owns and which, in addition to himself, employs a senior journeyman, three other journeymen and three apprentices. With the carpentry shop growing and 'trade increasing every week' (JTM, p. 16), Leonhard is constantly adding new journeymen to his business. The 'whole house' that Leonhard and his wife Friederike preside over together also includes the young foster son Franz – 'the legacy of a neighbour who died poor' (JTM, p. 29) – and several servants.[7] They gather daily for lunch and dinner at a 'round table' where all

6 For an introduction, see Kluge 2007.

7 On the 'whole house', cf. Ghanbari, Haag and Twellmann 2011.

the members of the household sit to the left and right of the father of the house 'in the order in which they had earlier or later come to his house' (JTM, p. 16).[8]

Baron Elsheim now enters life in Leonhard's house, triggering the narration in the first place. He is a 'schoolmate' (JTM, p. 24) of Leonhard's, they travelled together a lot in their youth. After a long period of separation, the Baron suddenly reappears in the city and makes Leonhard an offer: to 'establish' a theatre with Elsheim in one of his castles and 'act' with the Baron there in an amateur troupe (JTM, p. 35). After Leonhard initially refuses the offer so as not to endanger the peace in his house, business and marriage, he finally agrees enthusiastically after he learns that Elsheim wants to perform the common 'favourite work' from their youth: '"Götz von Berlichingen!" exclaimed Leonhard, hastily embracing his friend, "yes, I'll travel with you, everything can stay put, it works quite well without me, and the wife must find her way around"' (JTM, p. 35).

The conversations below take place on their journey to the castle. Leonhard has already stepped out of his everyday life in the house, but he and Elsheim are not yet immersed in the castle society that will then occupy the central three of the seven sections of the novella. In the transitory situation of the journey, Leonhard can now confess that he is no longer entirely satisfied with his personal and professional life. Leonhard's reflections are triggered by a teasing remark by Elsheim, who pretends not to understand why Leonhard does not modernise his business:

> And how long will it last, then, until I see you setting up a large warehouse of furniture, masters working under you, to whom you only give drawings and orders, and commission councillors, or whatever else it is called; according to your wealth, and since it is the tone of the day, you could do it right away (JTM, p. 74).

Leonhard reacts 'vividly': 'That will never happen'. For it is precisely the 'tone of the day', as Elsheim put it, that spoils Leonhard's profession; in what Elsheim recommends to him, Leonhard can only see a 'dead and deathly factory life' that threatens the craft everywhere (JTM, p. 74).

What would first 'die out' through 'factory life' would be life in the 'whole house', and that would affect both the social form and the material labour process. If the head of the house no longer 'looks after [his] employees as a father

8 On the common lunch and dinner in the 'whole house', see Riehl, 1873, pp. 153–54 and p. 263.

and teacher and helps them along', Leonhard says, then he must inevitably become their exploiter. He could then no longer do anything else but 'oppress other masters and feast off their skill and their sweat'. Merely by using capital – 'by spending money' – he would 'acquire the right ... to despotise and torment others' and thereby to 'destroy their lives, serenity and prosperity' (JTM, p. 74).

The death of the house, however, is linked to the demise of the guilds as institutions of social order. If 'the venerable guild has to make way for new fashionable establishments', the heads of the house – each formerly 'father and teacher' of his household members – now appear 'as condescending gentlemen or businessmen', while the 'younger craftsmen', now degraded, try to gain a reputation outside the house 'by drifting about coffee houses and making frivolous tavern chatter in semi-fashionable tailcoats' (JTM, p. 76). Life in the house, however, was still 'linked to a completely different civic honour', an honour of the whole that now counts for nothing (JTM, p. 76). 'Factory life' is 'dead and deathly' also because it renders one honourless. One might say, with the decline of the guilds, social death attends the masters, journeymen and apprentices alike.

1.2 *The Bourgeoisie as Whole and Part*

The house and the guilds institutionally embodied a unified social order, encompassing both masters and assistants. When the house and guilds perish, all the social bonds that previously held society together are ripped apart. In a brilliant tirade, Leonhard describes this process as an extreme form of social polarisation. *Is this really worth it?* – reads the question that finally pushes Leonhard over the edge:

> I only ask whether one can really find in those trades where the industrial establishment has long taken place, or in those countries where factory towns exist, a happiness which could tempt us to overthrow everything in order to have the same with us. Instead of many well-to-do people, a few rich people and a mass of poor, stunted and lazy riff-raff, always in the most tormenting dependence on their employer and his torturous and meagre advances, with no lust for life, no capacity, virtue or love to raise sickly children, becoming stultified in a completely mechanical and soulless business, and thereby driven to seek pleasure, which man cannot and will not do without, in bad, intoxicating drinks, dying early without having lived, despairing and self-loathing, inclined to all base tricks, and unable to experience or endure happiness and unhappiness. Thus, I have seen many hundreds, worse than slaves, languish in famous factories, and

> shrugged my shoulders at the rising culture like rising barbarism, that we consider it profitable by our spreadsheets to sacrifice men, the highest powers of the state, in order to deliver goods more cheaply (JTM, p. 75).

With the passing of the guilds, the group of 'many well-to-do people' breaks up into 'a few rich people' on the one hand and 'a mass of poor, stunted and lazy riff-raff' on the other. The social pact that was still valid for Leonhard in the house and the guilds has been replaced by mere 'dependence', which must be addressed as a new form of slavery, as a form of reproduction in which people themselves have become commodities whose use and application is calculated on the basis of utility and profit.

Leonhard condemns modern 'factory life' because it bursts open the social continuum guaranteed by tradition. But this social *whole*, Leonhard maintains, was 'the true bourgeoise, the core and the marrow of all states', which must now 'disappear' (JTM, p. 74 f.).[9]

This claim has a remarkable implication: Leonhard disidentifies the 'true bourgeoisie', which is in the process of 'disappearing', and the emerging bourgeoisie of his present; he denies this bourgeoisie, which will stabilise as a semantic and social entity in the course of the nineteenth century, the right to represent the 'true bourgeoisie'. The latter, as a representation of the whole, is from the outset not dependent on that operation which will remain constitutive for the bourgeoisie of the nineteenth century: the social demarcation 'from the "lower classes", the people, the fourth estate and the proletariat'.[10]

For Leonhard, a bourgeoisie that has to demarcate itself from below can only be *one* of the decaying products of that bemoaned social class; the proletariat, the 'riff-raff' dependent on the 'employer', is the other. Both parts are only precipitates of a whole, and if one of these parts, the bourgeoisie, in the further course of the nineteenth century, poses as the whole or as the 'middle' or centre of this whole, as the 'middle class', in order to marginalise the other parts and deny them social visibility and recognition, then this will also have to be characterised from Leonhard's position as an ideological operation.[11] Of course, Leonhard cannot yet have a view of the full extent of this process, but it can be stated that the nineteenth century, which has only just begun, will

9 On the connection between master title, guild master and civil law, cf. Haupt 2002, pp. 26–7.

10 Kocka 1995, p. 16.

11 On the semantic and political-linguistic shift from 'bourgeoisie' to 'middle class' in English, see Moretti 2013, pp. 6–12.

certainly not become the much-vaunted 'century of the bourgeoisie' for Tieck's hero. At best, it will be the century of a bourgeoisie that is precisely no longer the 'true bourgeoisie' which it culturally pretends to be.

Tieck shows us a society that no longer consists of integral parts and that therefore can no longer develop integrity, wholeness, in its totality; Tieck gives us the outline of a *decaying society*, a society that is already composed of decaying products. Any assertion of integrity, be it of the whole or of the parts, has thus become ideology, aesthetically kitsch.

1.3 *Becoming Rabble: from Servants to Scum*

Mirroring the new bourgeoisie, the proletariat emerges in the process of disintegration. When Leonhard describes the downward movement that takes hold of the 'mass', he uses all the topoi of the contemporary discussion of pauperism. Yes, the 'mass of poor, stunted and lazy riff-raff' is easily deciphered as a transcription of the 'rabble', which was recognised as a mass phenomenon in the first third of the nineteenth century and whose 'production' was analysed not least by Hegel in his *Philosophy of Right*. The rabbleisation of dependent workers affects their entire 'movement of life': wage labour keeps them in the 'most tormenting dependence', the 'mechanical and soulless operations' affect the workers themselves, with 'stultifying' effects. They become that 'mechanick part of mankind', as the father of Robinson Crusoe says.[12] With the 'tortuous and meagre advances' they can only give birth to 'sickly children' whom they bring up with 'no lust for life, no capacity, virtue or love'.[13] The residual humanity, which this 'mass' has not yet completely lost, only shows itself in the fact that it, too, seeks that 'pleasure' which 'man cannot and will not do without'. Now, however, the pleasure that alone is still open to the rabble fatally exacerbates the tendency towards rabbleisation: the 'bad, intoxicating drinks' – the rampant 'brandy plague', as it was called at the time – rob people of their last self-respect, driving them, 'despairing and self-loathing', into criminality, which Leonhard trivialises as 'base tricks'.[14] However, the fact that people are 'dying early without having lived' cannot be played down; they have lost the elementary ability to 'experience happiness and unhappiness' at all.

In a certain sense, however, the 'rising barbarism' has gripped Leonhard himself, as he only 'shrugs his shoulders' about it and the 'rising culture'. 'There is no document of culture which is not at the same time a document of barbarism',

12 Defoe 2007, p. 6.

13 On the theme of the paupers' lack of love for children, see Rancière 1978, p. 151.

14 On the 'plague of brandy' and all the other aspects of pauperism mentioned, see Engels 1839, 'Letters from Wuppertal', MECW 2, pp. 7–25.

Walter Benjamin will write a hundred years later.[15] The social polarisation that Leonhard attacks has already seized himself when he repeats that gesture of notorious indifference with which citizens also morally confront mass poverty. Nothing has remained of the caring attitude of the father of the house, who 'lived in a truly patriarchal way with his own people and the local and foreign assistants' (JTM, p. 76).

1.4 *The Decline of the Guilds*

Elsheim's remark that the guilds 'will perish' (JTM, p. 74) is not only socially and historically precise in substance, but also in its formulation. The 'old craft' and with it the guild system had already had a long 'autumn', or less elegiac, a long history of erosion and transformation, which was only officially sealed by the introduction of freedom of trade.[16] Tieck, the son of craftsmen, was familiar with this up close. Tieck's father, the renowned master ropemaker Johann Ludwig Tieck, is said to have been part of a delegation of Berlin craftsmen who presented Frederick the Great with a petition at the Sanssouci Palace window to protect the guild order and asked him to intervene.[17]

Leonhard knows that 'factories and the much-lauded division of labour are already an old invention'; in the case of simple trades, '[the] craft and art were converted into a factory institution early on' (JTM, p. 76). This process of transformation, however, not only makes the work in the institutions 'entirely mechanical', as was said before, it also has far-reaching consequences for the structure of society. The former craftsmen, now as manufacturing labourers, fall out of the order of house and guild, while more and more members of the lower classes, who never belonged to this order anyway, enter the manufactories as unskilled workers. The enormous population growth that can be seen throughout Europe at the end of the eighteenth century makes itself felt in the production of free workers who are pumped into the manufactories of the late mercantilist era. Mass production, which makes it possible 'to offer goods ever more cheaply', also leads to a massification of labour, which itself becomes ever 'cheaper', because 'the supply of unskilled labour' was, as Jürgen Kocka succinctly notes, 'abundant'.[18]

In the medium of a lament that submits to what is historically imposed, but still dares asking about the costs, Leonhard sums up the characteristics of the old guild system for the last time: the guilds granted their members 'privileges',

15 Benjamin 2006, Thesis VII, p. 392.

16 See Stürmer 1979.

17 On Tieck's father, see Stadelmann and Fischer 1955, pp. 139–43.

18 Kocka 1990a, p. 154. On the 'decline' of the guilds, cf. Kluge 2007, pp. 389–446.

which, however, had to be 'paid for' (JTM, p. 74f.) through certain 'expenses' (JTM, p. 75), through an invested 'capital of time, studies, work and years of apprenticeship' (JTM, p. 77). Membership in a guild meant participation in a 'general security'; as a 'member of this closed estate', the guildsman was 'shielded' from the misfortune of economic insecurity (JTM, p. 75): according to a contemporary treatise by the political economist Karl Heinrich Rau, the guild system offered 'secure nourishment' through 'closing of trades', regulated 'price increases of products' and 'prevention of external competition'.[19]

Finally, an additional crucial factor is the control and limitation of internal competition. The guilds create broadly 'regulated markets' by limiting the sheer 'number' (JTM, p. 77) of applicants on the supply side.[20] In this way, the danger of social imbalances can be minimised. Rau cites the 'unequal distribution' of various trades as the first 'effect of freedom of trade'.[21] Summarised under the keyword 'overstaffing', the same phenomenon – ruinous competition within certain craft branches – was identified as the core of the 'crisis of the crafts' in the Vormärz, and especially as the crisis of the 'small masters', a crisis that had already caused urban pauperism before the actual take-off of industrial factory capitalism.[22] This nexus can also be seen as the central link in the mass 'conversion' of craftsmen into paupers; the freedom of trade thus becomes the motor of proletarianisation for the former 'bourgeoisie'.

Leonhard is well aware that things did not always go right in the past: 'The true abuses of the guild system, which ... are undeniable', could have been 'abolished without tearing down the venerable foundation itself' (JTM, p. 77). Tieck would later express a very similar opinion to Rudolf Köpke, his Eckermann: 'The *freedom of trade*, which has been so praised, belongs to these modern inventions. It is not the guilds that should have been abolished, but the perverse compulsion that prevailed in them. They were a very good institution, and could be reformed'.[23]

For Leonhard, the guilds also deserved a well-meaning reform because 'we' have them to thank for 'arts, prosperity and freedom'. The 'arts', the skills of the crafts, are protected by the guilds in that they ensure a proper training course and thus the '*maintenance of a thorough knowledge of the trade*' by apprentices

19 Rau 1816, pp. 48–63.

20 Müller, Schmidt, and Tissot 2011.

21 Rau 1816, pp. 98–102.

22 Cf. Meyer 1999, pp. 116–17. An early source on the craft crisis is Möser 1775, partial reprint in Bürger 1974, p. 74.

23 Köpke 1855, p. 244.

and journeymen, as Rau writes.[24] However, freedom of trade and the opening of all trades to practitioners without training inevitably leads to 'bad work'.[25] The 'present-day practice' of free, unregulated training would 'favour bunglers and bumblers'.[26]

The 'freedom' that Leonhard credits to the guild system, however, cannot be seen in the mere absence of centralised state supervision. Rather, with Rau, one must consider the 'wandering' that marks a decisive rite of passage in the course of a guild-organised life. It is first wandering, according to Rau, that provides for a truly free mind and should therefore be considered not only as an instance of (technical-artistic) *training*, but above all as an instance of *Bildung*, or 'culture' in an emphatic sense:

> It is not only the various peculiarities of the technical operations of the trades, the knowledge of which is acquired through wandering, although this in itself is to be rated very highly; the wanderer also becomes acquainted with life in general in its manifold branches, the advantages and infirmities that stand out here and there in bourgeois society. No wonder that the prejudices imbibed with the mother's milk are lost more and more with every step into the world, that the journeyman returns home more cultivated in head and heart, that he sees his conditions with a practised eye and knows how to move in them with skill. To what other circumstance could a greater share be attributed for the higher culture [*Bildung*] that one finds in the families of guild members in comparison with unguilded tradesmen or day labourers? Nor is this beneficial effect by any means confined to the person of the wanderer; it is communicated to the younger members of the household through instruction, storytelling, and the silent but powerful influence of the more mature, and in this way propagates itself, always nourished anew, throughout the entire estate.[27]

The wanderer gains in worldliness while losing everything parochial and narrow-minded, and can henceforth regulate his own affairs all the more confidently with prudence and foresight. In the process of cultivation 'in head and

24 Rau 1816, p. 73.

25 Rau 1816, p. 120.

26 Köpke 1855, p. 244. Rau also names the 'bunglers' as profiteers from the freedom of trade (Rau 1816, p. 120). See, for example, Epstein 2004; Epstein and Prak 2008; Lucassen, Moor and Zanden 2009.

27 Rau 1816, pp. 80–1.

heart', the 'beneficial effect' of wandering intertwines with the inner perseverance of the house in a way that initially seems paradoxical. For the house is an institution of storytelling – an establishment that depends on narrating and being narrated for its coherence and continuity, and quite tangibly, a place where stories are told.[28] It is precisely this limited, familiar space that, through its inherent power of transmission, provides the ideal medium for letting the 'younger members of the house' share in the world experience of the elders. Already in the house they get to know life and the world.

'*Wandering ceases*' – with this succinct, but disastrous statement against the background of his emphatic description of the advantages of wandering, Rau concludes his description of the effects of free trade on the individual. Since there was 'no longer any connection among the craftsmen', the exchange of journeymen also ceased; those who had not wandered themselves quickly lost sight of its 'beneficial effects' and became narrow-minded and self-sufficient.[29]

The sequence of years of apprenticeship and wandering characterises the course of development that every craftsman has to go through if he wants to become a full member of bourgeois society, because he is far-sighted and insightful, and not just a day labourer. Leonhard, too, is – once again – on the move. In the meantime, having long since become a husband and head of the household, he embarks on a 'second journey' (Rudolf Kassner), leaving his familiar circumstances and his marriage behind, becoming 'a stranger to himself' (JTM, p. 81) – not least in the erotic entanglements that await him at the Baron's castle – only to arrive at his house for the second time, now for good.

1.5 *Guild Representation*

Wandering is not only the only way for the guild journeyman to step outside their usual field of vision. The same movement – a movement of liberation from prejudice and ignorance through constant expansion of the wealth of experience – is also provided by the guilds to their local members. The freedom of wandering is conserved and cyclically renewed in a representational order that Leonhard finally explains to Elsheim, to himself and to us:

> Folk festivals, parades, processions, music and dancing in public on festive occasions, the transformation of common life into a poetic spectacle: it [the 'old world'] sought to satisfy all these innermost needs, leaving what existed and had been handed down, improving, adding, increasing

28 Cf. Riehl 1873, p. 242.

29 Rau 1816, p. 119.

> the shining appearance, and noble old men, fathers of the people, clergymen and princes did not consider it beneath their dignity to join in the rejoicing with all their heart, and to let good reason rummage among old reflections at home (JTM, p. 79).

Earlier, in the 'old world', the life of simple people, craftsmen and peasants, was structured by festive events; their 'common life' underwent a ritual conversion, a 'transformation' that arose from the 'innermost needs' and yet had to take place 'publicly' (JTM, p. 79). The 'transformation' starts with 'common life', with the 'prosaic and everyday', as Hegel puts it, and turns this 'prose of common life' (Hegel with Tieck) into a 'poetic spectacle': everyday things usually done naturally and automatically become something extraordinary that requires special care and attention, and also receives special attention from others.

Leonhard's quasi-ethnological observation of his own recent folk culture is based on a broad anthropological assumption about the nature of human 'drives':

> For man does not want to be just man (however often this was preached by Enlightenment thinkers a few years ago), nor does he want to be merely useful and gainful and a citizen, but at times to imagine something else beyond himself. This drive to put ourselves outside ourselves is one of the most powerful and indomitable, because it probably releases the deepest peculiarity in us (JTM, p. 80).

Later, Leonhard speaks of the 'drive to escape, to become alien to oneself and to encounter oneself again as another being' (JTM, p. 81). And so, in the old order, everyone was cyclically given the opportunity – once or 'more often in a year or month' – to 'be something alien' (JTM, p. 80).

For Leonhard, humans are by nature already theatrical beings. And for the third estate, it was the guilds in particular that provided the institutional framework for people to follow their drives, to step outside themselves and become different. The guilds *of all things*, one should stress, since according to the historical doxa, this institution functioned as force of perseverance, as a way of remaining completely within oneself.

The guilds organised 'frequently in jest and earnest, parades, games, representations of all kinds, allegorical or comic', where the 'master could become the head of his guild and brotherhood, the journeyman leader and champion, speaker and actor, even down to the apprentices, who could assert themselves among their peers' (JTM, p. 80). With their rituals of representation, the guilds give people the opportunity to step out of 'common life' and become something different, something 'outside themselves', even something 'alien'. But this other, stranger thing is not something *completely different*, it is not a disguise that is simply put on people. For people do slip into a role that corresponds to their position in 'common life', only this is transposed into a different order: it is the master who becomes 'head of his guild and brotherhood' – and not the journeyman – and as such he has to perform a certain ceremony. And one may assume that only the journeyman – and not the master or apprentice – can take on the role of 'leader', 'champion', 'speaker' or 'actor'. In these roles, then, he actually becomes something other, something 'alien'.

The craftsman does not remain 'just' a craftsman and thus tied into certain hierarchies, he *presents* or *depicts* this, in short: he represents. Immediately after this, Elsheim and Leonhard lament the *loss* of the opportunity and ability for public representation. Elsheim regrets that 'in recent times one can hardly find a person who can represent; even the diplomats who know how to do it are becoming increasingly rare'. The 'awkward, embarrassed, stuttering behaviour of our great men' is spreading everywhere;

in the end, 'all remaining representation withdrew' to the 'military posture in uniform'. (JTM, p. 81).

The intransitive use of the verb 'represent' indicates that in the 'old world' all facets of professional or working life were always already doubled from the outset, in two spheres at the same time: first in the sphere of 'common life', then in a sphere of presentation or representation, where the common is 'validated', that is, endowed with a social meaning, a justification and efficacy that is not already inherent to the activity and the position in which the activity is carried out.

The necessity of this doubling of working life in a sphere of representation arises not only from the theatrical drives of human beings, but also from a more tangible fact that Leonhard only touches upon in passing: through 'parades, games, representations' of the guild, people return 'to their ordinary occupation newly strengthened, healthier and more full of life, even comforted by it and with the near prospect of being able to take a bath in the fountain of youth again soon'. Apparently, it is only through the sphere of representation that people's everyday work acquires a higher determinacy; it is only through it that people learn that, despite their 'ordinary occupations', they themselves are not ordinary. Torn from the sphere of everyday life at regular intervals, they can only continue doing what they are used to do in a 'healthy and cheerful way' (JTM, p. 80).

With the confession made here, Leonhard's simple narrative of loss takes on a new twist: clearly, the step into freedom of trade that Leonhard laments is not simply the fall from an ideal, orderly world of meaningful, unalienated work into a hopeless world of 'mechanical and soulless' drudgery. It seems as if even in the 'old world' people suffered from their work, as though it had been ordinary and cruel before, and working people thus needed consolation. The difference between the 'old world' and 'recent times', however, is that there used to be stable orders and rituals of compensation that were firmly integrated into people's lives.

This turn of events makes Leonhard's critique of contemporary conditions all the more severe. For the imposition that freedom of trade holds in store for people now appears to be twofold: not only is work itself becoming ever more mechanical, soulless and stultifying under the dictates of the division of labour and profit orientation; the compensation that was still provided in the old order, guild representation, is also being knocked away at precisely the moment when it is needed most. Without it, people's need for compensation – which has increased anyway – becomes, as it were, free-floating and formless. Unrelieved by regulated representation, at the mercy of drunkenness, crime and sex, human beings become strangers to themselves *in their most crude form*, with no prospect of 'encountering oneself again as another being'. People lose their footing and orientation.

1.6 *Affect Politics from Above*

It is not only the elementary drive for representation that can no longer be experienced in a regulated manner in 'recent times' and therefore either atrophies or goes wild. For Leonhard, it is a complete misjudgement of human passions and drives in general that makes up the spirits and demons of the present. The 'wisdom of the old world' still knew 'that passions, folly, play, jest, pleasure and enjoyment are the elements that fight and unite in humanity, which only reason can balance', and must first be achieved through a process of confrontation – and cannot merely be posited in the abstract.

Instead of higher reason or 'wisdom', according to Leonhard, 'today' mere reason prevails, a 'helpless reason' that 'has never been able to put anything into effect and reality'. Instead of the expansion and enrichment that came from the old 'wisdom', this helpless but ruling reason merely achieves a general reduction, an *anthropological reduction*, as it were, aimed at 'weaning humanity off humanity'. Instead of affirming the heterogeneous affective nature of human beings, one finds everywhere only 'that new-fangled weaning' which ultimately 'leads to moral death and cold despair' (JTM, p. 79).

The reduction of human nature to reason – and the already reductive determination of what counts as reason – does not, according to Leonhard, arise of its own accord. It is enforced and reveals itself as an element of a specific, state-operated policy that, on closer inspection, does not present itself as universally human as it pretends to be in its appeal to reason. It turns out that it is the 'modern legislators' who 'have long regarded the human being as a being of reason, and all the more so the more he lives in a lowly estate'. That 'the human is merely human', as has been 'preached for some years by Enlightenment thinkers', elevates to the ideal a person 'without passions or stripped of them and educated to all the rational virtues, to diligence, earning money, and tireless work'. Leonhard now realises that this ideal, and with it the entire Enlightenment anthropology and educational emphasis, has a social *bias* – or, in the language of the late nineteenth century, a class character. After first being torn from the economic security and comforting representational order of the guild, the lower classes are now subjected to an ascetic heaven of virtue, which only humiliates them further. For it is not merely the lack of money that drags people down; it is the dependence on 'earning money' in general that forbids all 'unreasonable' impulses and finally turns people into what they least of all wants to be: 'merely human'.

In a small volte, Leonhard makes it clear that those virtues praised as 'reasonable' to the lower classes and considered common to all humanity are anything but socially innocent: 'The legislators tacitly reserve for themselves and their kind many pastimes and wasteful activities, of which they push the most decent under the heading "culture", which the common man can of course do without' (JTM, p. 78 f.). In a few words, Leonhard shows the dense web of ideological substitutions that lies behind the Enlightenment appeal to reason: the standards of efficient use of time and the associated 'virtues' apply only to those who are preached to, not to the preachers; 'culture' is not universal, but differs according to whether it is understood as a status-marking 'pastime' or as a model of disciplining ('stamping out', 'raising up'); and finally, the 'legislators' – and perhaps also the 'legislators of human reason' (Kant), the philosophers of the Enlightenment – are not as exclusively oriented towards the common good as might be assumed, but are driven by self-interest. They make the laws for themselves 'and their kind': for 'noblemen or businessmen', 'lords' and 'rich people' (JTM, p. 75 f.).

Finally, the virtues and values whose 'reasonable' character Leonhard exposes as ideological tricks are the same ones that, at the beginning of the nineteenth century, were or soon would be regarded as genuinely 'bourgeois': 'diligence', 'earning money' and 'tireless work'. These values are associated with a revaluation of work and the self-image of a new 'bourgeois' elite. This is the first and only elite in history that derives its identity-constituting pride not from the fact that it *no* longer has to work, but rather from the fact that it is constantly working. Franco Moretti has drawn attention to this with reference to Robinson Crusoe and Norbert Elias. In Tieck's work, this bourgeois ideology also appears as a deception: as the illusion of an ultimately idle upper class against the working masses, for whom the preached values only bind them more to work, and to whom the work ethic is to be implanted quasi-anthropologically via these values – *imagined* and *instilled*, one could say, in the wake of Leonhard's critique of the Enlightenment ideology of culture.

1.7 *Passions and Interests: Leonhard, Adam Smith and Albert O. Hirschman*

In a side note, Leonhard places his critique of the politics of affect in 'recent times' against a broader horizon that is also interesting in terms of the history of ideas. In passing, he claims that the newly much 'praised distribution of labour' is actually already an 'old invention' by which 'certain insignificant things, such as needles, nails and the like … could be supplied quickly and cheaply enough' (JTM, p. 76). Leonhard (and with him Tieck) thus identifies himself as a reader of Adam Smith, or at least as someone who has followed the German debates on Adam Smith since around 1800. For, as is well known, nail or needle production is used as an example of the productivity-increasing effect of the division of labour in the first chapter of Smith's *Inquiry into the Nature and Causes of the Wealth of Nations*, and this example crops up again and again in the German debates on Smith; it very quickly became a topos.[30]

In the contemporaneous German debate, all the social grievances that Leonhard criticised as consequences of the freedom of trade were often blamed on Smith himself as consequences of his theory. In this context, Leonhard's side-swipe at Smith would only provide further evidence of a common pattern of reception and criticism. In the context of the remarks on the reduction of the passions, however, the Smith reference can be read as an independent contribution by Tieck to the debate. For Smith's political economic *Wealth of Nations* is also based on a theory of the passions, thus connecting to his moral-philosophical *Theory of Moral Sentiments*, a text retrieved for twentieth-century social science through Albert O. Hirschman's study *The Passions and The Interests*.[31] At the centre of Smith's economic theory is the thesis of the 'invisible hand', in which the pursuit of private interest by all market participants leads quasi-automatically to serving the 'public interest'.[32] This thesis, however, about whose origin, scope and legitimacy much has been written since the publication of the *Wealth of Nations*, already presupposes – as Hirsch-

30 Cf. Smith 1976, pp. 13–24.

31 Hirschman 1997.

32 The classic formulation appears in a rather remote passage, in the second chapter of the fourth book, Smith 1976, p. 456.

man shows – a political-affective operation that first of all defines what can count as 'interest'. The category of interest was extremely ambivalent in the social-philosophical and economic theory of the seventeenth and eighteenth centuries – not least because it was always constructed as a counter-concept to the equally ambivalent 'passions'.[33] While Montesquieu, James Steuart and John Millar formulated the theory that economic interests could be used to curb the 'passionate excesses of the powerful' and therefore to 'improve the political order', Smith all of a sudden equates passions and interests in the *Wealth of Nations*.[34] How did this happen?

Before Smith could equate passions and interests, the passions and the concept of 'human nature' itself had to be narrowed and homogenised. Whereas human beings had previously been thought of as 'driven by, and often torn between, diverse passions', Smith declared economic greed, the lust for possessions, to be the root of all other passions. Hobbes and Rousseau had contrasted economic greed with the political 'craving for honour, dignity, respect and recognition'.[35] Smith now declares greed the sole operating principle of the 'need for recognition' – everyone wants to *possess* recognition as the highest good. Yet this means that recognition loses its autonomy and is degraded from a noble goal in its own right to a mere consequence of self-interest: an example, according to Hirschman, of Smith's brilliant irony.[36]

Hirschman's summary of Smith's reduction sounds almost like an echo of Leonhard's lament. Hirschman also sees in the reflection of Smith's theory that the step towards freedom of trade also and above all implies an intervention in human nature: whereas earlier 'passions, folly, play, jest, pleasure and enjoyment [were] the elements that fight and unite' together, today only the trinity of 'diligence, earning money, and tireless work' holds sway (JTM, p. 79). When discussing the reasons for Smith's reduction, however, Hirschman posits that Smith 'was concerned, far more than earlier writers, with the "great mob of mankind", that is, with the average person and his behaviour', but that, in contrast to princes and members of the aristocracy, these were less influenced by 'noble or ignoble passions', but rather merely moved by concern for 'subsistence'. Referring to Machiavelli and Hobbes, Hirschman suspects that for them '[t]he ordinary mortal was not thought to be so complicated' as the aristocrats with their urge for recognition.[37]

33 Hirschman 1997, pp. 7–66.
34 Hirschman 1997, pp. 67–113, especially p. 70.
35 Hirschman 1997, p. 108.
36 Cf. Hirschman 1997, pp. 109, 101.
37 Hirschman 1997, pp. 111–12.

Here, Tieck's Leonhard objects: 'ordinary people' with their 'ordinary professions' are not simply 'ordinary', they are only *made* 'ordinary' through the anthropological reduction to being 'merely human'; only by denying their traditional ways of stepping outside themselves and becoming something other are they left with nothing but the struggle to preserve their 'bare life' (JTM, p. 62) – and even this mere self-preservation becomes increasingly difficult in the new order.

Only a profoundly aristocratic ignorance can deny 'ordinary people' an affective nature beyond mere self-preservation, and it is precisely this arrogance that becomes historically effective when the disadvantage of 'ordinary' people in society becomes justified with reference to their limited desires. The fact that aristocratic ignorance is already revealed in the definition of what counts as a 'passion' becomes clear at the latest when Leonhard discloses his own alternative catalogue of passions, which does not just include the aristocratic-agonal affects of honour, thirst for glory and recognition, but above all simple, plebeian ones, such as 'folly, play, jest, pleasure and enjoyment' (JTM, p. 79), which, as Leonhard emphasises, would not have been considered 'ordinary' in the past.

The right to these passions and likewise the right to 'honour, dignity, respect and recognition' beyond aristocratic self-assertion were to shape the struggles of 'common people' in the further course of the nineteenth century. The struggle for these rights were at least as important as the struggle to secure one's livelihood; both struggles prove to be inseparable in the concrete situation. The fact that the passions – and, as will become clear, taste and education – are so strongly emphasised in the struggles of 'common people' will remain all the more irritating for the opposing side, the less they, the new commercial and moneyed aristocracy, can imagine that the 'common people', with all their misery, can think of anything else at all besides eating. The ignorance inherited from the old aristocracy will not disappear from the new one any time soon.

1.8 *Political Passions, Aesthetic Taste*

Tieck's Leonhard understands the break and anthropological reduction developed in Adam Smith's work and accomplished with the freedom of trade as irreversible. The romantic craftsman-poet harbours no illusions about the possibility of a simple return to a *status quo ante*. At the same time, however, the question arises of how to deal with a break that is both perceived and portrayed as an aberration.

Tieck sees art as a means of compensation – an art, however, that remembers its old closeness to craft and that must be reprogrammed after the demise of the old craft. In *The Master Carpenter*, this resetting of the task of art finds expression in a long conversation between Leonhard and Elsheim about the decline of taste, a conversation that takes place *before* the one quoted above about the social consequences of free trade, but which can only be understood in its full scope after that second one.

Having just set off on their journey, Elsheim elicits Leonhard's confession that he has become 'dissatisfied with [his] status, indeed almost with all of life'. The reason is both personal and social and leads back to Elsheim's old question as to why Leonhard, who had already gone through the world as a young man with 'open senses and a wide range of knowledge' and a 'love of all things cultured, did not rather prefer to be an artist'; whether Leonhard's 'profession is not perhaps also a mistake' (JTM, p. 55). Leonhard takes this provocation as an opportunity to ponder the order of art and craft, sensuality, usefulness and culture, as they existed 'in earlier times' and how they determined him to become a carpenter. Although interested in culture and art, he was not fit to be a 'scholar' because 'things interested [him] more than thoughts, words and forms'; to be an artist, he had always lacked the 'enthusiasm, that striving, flying spirit that can and may neglect and forget everything around it, that is at home in foreign worlds but not at home in ours'. Finally, Leonhard consciously – and coquettishly – characterises himself as simple: 'my mind, on the contrary, is limited and truly bourgeois, my zeal for work, utility, my desire for things that are useful and stand firm: all this convinced me early on that I was destined to be a craftsman' (JTM, p. 55).

However, and here Leonhard agrees with Elsheim to a certain extent, 'the carpenter is situated between the artist and the craftsman' (JTM, p. 55); carpentry shows a 'relationship to art … without wanting to be art' (JTM, p. 58). The carpenter's craft in particular thus brings out a 'drive' that Leonhard calls the 'beauty or artistic drive' and 'culture drive' (JTM, p. 56), which is closely related to that later discussed drive for representation. The 'artistic drive' impels human beings to 'hang a certain supplement of beauty around everything that his need requires, in addition to what is necessary'; every 'household item' is thus 'transformed into something higher by added ornament' (JTM, p. 55 f.).

Leonhard varies this idea in ever new formulations. A little later, for example, there is talk of the fact that 'everything empty must be disguised, everything expressing mere need must be transformed, and the mere necessity of it must be concealed' (JTM, p. 56 f.). The fact that the core of the matter must be 'disguised' or, later, 'surrounded' (JTM, p. 59), because it is actually *empty*, that 'necessity' moves from core to 'ornament' – Leonhard sums this up towards the end of his speech in an almost exemplary romantic, because ironic-paradoxical form: it is a matter of giving 'bare life a necessary ornament for its decorative dressing'. But when the 'ornament', the 'addition', the 'dressing' is recognised as 'necessary', this casts doubt on the whole distinction that Leonhard had previously exposed and repeated with almost provocative simplicity.

The distinction between 'need' and decorative shell is not entirely wrong: for Leonhard, too, 'need ... remains the first prosaic basis' of life, to which the shell is decoratively added (JTM, p. 57). However, the one-sided development of the latest taste is wrong: only the 'Hussite sensibility and the iconoclastic crudeness of our days' sharpen the distinction in such a way that finally the shell, the 'ornament', begins to be seen as 'superfluous and unreasonable' (JTM, p. 62), and thus as dispensable or even reprehensible – *ornament is crime* will later be the catchword. Rationalist iconoclasm isolates a bare functional core from which it wants to strip and discard everything superfluous. Leonhard problematises the distinction between what is necessary and what is superfluous when he shows that the superfluous is necessary and that only through the addition of the superfluous does the core remain functional.[38] The fact that the relationship between necessity and abundance is not as simple as rationalism believes generates the 'pleasant enigma' of this relation; the fact that it will never be possible to definitively clarify what is 'necessary' and what is 'superfluous' thus constitutes an essential charm of life itself.

Leonhard's critique of the rationalist flattening of taste in the present anticipates his critique of the rationalist politics of affect associated with the freedom of trade, which he will announce in the next long conversation with Elsheim. Just as the craftsman-artist was once responsible for giving a 'decorative dressing' to 'strict needs' and 'bare life', the guilds were responsible for providing the common and 'ordinary life' with a poetic representation that allowed people to step outside themselves and, precisely in this way, to stay completely with themselves (or, rather, to come to themselves for the very first time). Here, as there, a 'prosaic basis' is to be transformed into a 'poetic spectacle' or showpiece. Here, as there, the transformation follows a 'drive' that is suppressed or denied in the present, but which obviously has enormous social and human consequences if not followed or granted, as Leonhard reckons in his speeches.

Elsheim finds the social cause for the prevailing 'tastelessness' in 'a certain Enlightenment and absolute championing of the bourgeoisie' (JTM, p. 58). That the Enlightenment might have something to do with the incriminating developments is not so surprising. What is surprising, however, is that the

---

38 *Des Lebens Überfluss* [*The Abundance of Life*] is the title of another late novella by Tieck (1986), in which the relationship between necessity and abundance is systematically played out.

'bourgeoisie' are held responsible – after all, a little later, the 'bourgeoisie' are declared to be the custodian of the old, lost order, the abolition of which is now being held against them here.

Perhaps, however, the emphasis in Elsheim's argument lies not so much on the 'bourgeoisie', and possibly not even on the 'championing of the bourgeoisie', but on its 'absolute' character: that the representatives of the bourgeoisie believe themselves to be 'absolute'; that they think they have to isolate a 'bourgeois' culture (with absolutely bourgeois-sober values) and to be able to free it from any mediation with a notoriously aristocratic or plebian culture of extravagance – *this* is perhaps the real reason why the old culture, with its permeation of art and craft, abundance and need, was destroyed. And likewise, one could spin the thought further, the old guild culture was destroyed because a certain part of the bourgeoisie – the one that will later constitute itself as the modern bourgeoisie – wanted to free itself from this context of social mediation and determine itself 'absolutely': independent of those who are now relegated to the 'bottom' as people of lower status, of apprentice boys, journeymen, and servants. According to this reading, the 'absolute championing of the bourgeoisie' would be responsible for the human and social devastation of the present, because the associated demarcation, both downwards and upwards, thinks it can detach itself from the necessary mediation with these extreme positions of society. And so it might not be a coincidence that it is precisely the 'nobleman' Elsheim who demonstrates the inherent aggressiveness of the new bourgeoisie's self-definition as 'middle class', an aggressiveness of self-assertion qua exclusion that was quite alien to the old, 'true bourgeoisie'.

1.9 *Enclosing Class Struggle: Tieck's Guilds as Invention of Tradition*

For all the clairvoyance that Tieck's Leonhard demonstrates with regard to the actual socio-historical developments associated with the end of the guilds, his speeches must also be read as an ideological glorification of the guilds. Leonhard's reconstruction of the guilded past is as much projection as nostalgic construction. The guilds in Leonhard's speeches can be deciphered as an element of an overarching 'invention of tradition', as the invention of an idealised past intended to legitimise current political strategies and norms.

For instance, one should no longer overlook the fact that the 'genre portrait' of life in the house that Leonhard describes is put into the mouth of a head of household and guild master.[39] As such, he stresses the protective and shielding function of the guilds, which also benefits the apprentices and journeymen; all

39 Haupt 2002, p. 21.

the talk about the cohesion of the domestic-guild form of life implies in this context the unity and stability of the norms and values that guide the lives of all members of the household. Against this, one must object that the house and the guild are also places of a manifest conflict of interests; a few years after Tieck's *Master Carpenter*, Karl Marx will write of a class struggle between journeymen and guild masters.[40] Even in the carpentry trade or in Leonhard's beloved 'old bourgeois, Germanic, ornate Nuremberg' – which Tieck already contrasts with the bustling 'North America of Fürth' in his *Phantasus* – there was a major strike in 1788.[41] Master craftsmen and journeymen clashed because the craftsmen were hungry and 'pauverté stood watch at the doors of the houses with bayonet fixed', as a contemporary pamphlet put it.[42]

Leonhard strategically argues in a very flexible manner in his defence of the guilds, giving his speech a double thrust. In relation to the house and the guild – inwardly, as it were – he conceals existing conflicts in order to emphasise the *stability* of this order. Externally, directed at the state and the 'new legislators', he emphasises the guilds' *versatility*. Contrary to the state's position that the guilds were rigidly incapable of reform, Leonhard presents them as a thoroughly flexible and adaptable institution. The guilds were capable of change, according to Leonhard, and it would have been better to reform them. Precisely in light of the anomic conditions that only arose as a result of the abolition of the guilds, that is, pauperism and moral neglect, the guilds would have made quite an attractive offer of order. Not only were they responsible for the 'reduction of social risks', but also for the social 'pacification of urban society' in general; with 'support funds for the sick, invalids and

40 Marx and Engels, 'Manifesto of the Communist Party', MECW 6, p. 482: 'The history of all hitherto existing society is the history of class struggles. Freeman and slave, patrician and plebeian, lord and serf, guild-master and journeyman, in a word, oppressor and oppressed, stood in constant opposition to one another, carried on an uninterrupted, now hidden, now open fight, a fight that each time ended, either in a revolutionary re-constitution of society at large, or in the common ruin of the contending classes'.

41 Tieck 1985, p. 17. In the introductory framing narrative, the contrast between the two sister cities is further explained by saying that Fürth, with its 'mirror-grinding shops, button factories and all the clattering and rumbling trades' stands for everything 'useful, new, factory-like', while Nuremberg stands for that 'beautiful period of Germany' when 'the houses were still decorated from the outside with paintings of giants and old German heroes' (pp. 16–17).

42 Quoted in the monumental social-historical magnum opus of the journeyman locksmith and high-ranking SPD politician Rudolf Wissell 1981, pp. 161–2. On the desolate political, economic and cultural situation of Nuremberg at the end of the 18th century, see the travelogue by the Rhineland-Jacobin publicist Georg Friedrich Rebmann, *Kosmopolitische Wanderungen durch einen Teil Deutschlands of* 1793, in Bürger 1974, p. 64.

poor' and provisions for widows, they closed 'gaps in the public system of poor relief' and thus made a contribution that state institutions were often happy to accept.[43]

1.10 *The End of the Guilds and the Beginnings of the Labour Movement. 'Traditions' of Social History*

With the concept of 'invented traditions', Eric Hobsbawm asserts a strong contrast between 'traditions' and 'customs': where the former are characterised by invariance, the latter guarantee flexibility and adaptability. 'Customary or common law', Hobsbawm writes, 'still shows this combination of flexibility in substance and formal adherence to precedence'.[44] Following this strong asymmetry, 'invented traditions' have been repeatedly debunked in research, while 'customs' have been appreciated as part of the social basis and as a material cohesive force of society. If we look at the debates about the sense and nonsense of the guilds in the early nineteenth century, however, this juxtaposition must be symmetrised. For the defenders of the guilds emphasised in their 'invention of tradition' the perseverance *and* flexibility of the guilds, while their opponents, the economically liberal 'new legislators', also take an extremely flexible approach to the 'invented' tradition of the guild. Even after their official end, the guilds – and this most definitely means the guild orders and privileges of the masters – are used in a new form by the 'authorities' to 'discipline the dependent workers' and to 'bind the journeymen to rules and norms of living together' to ward off social unrest and labour disputes. Just as little as the state could tolerate the guilds as quasi-sovereign institutions (with their own legal and tax system), it could not completely dispense with their function of social order. The state's initially only weak ability to intervene, especially in the countryside – given the lack of police officers and the rudimentary administrative bureaucracy – had to be supplemented by the guilds' own justice system, which was now tolerated and even promoted, for example, to prevent the employment of unruly journeymen or to keep them on their toes by imposing penalties under guild law. With regard to the desired 'regulatory function of the guilds', both their defenders and opponents apparently agreed.[45]

Perhaps it is necessary here to draw a 'class line' (Jürgen Kocka) that runs across the pros and cons of the guilds. For even the journeymen – who are seen as a threat by the old masters *and* the new order and therefore become the

43 Haupt 2002, pp. 23–4.
44 Hobsbawm 2012, p. 2.
45 Haupt 2002, pp. 33–4.

target of state repression *and* guild control by the masters – pursue their own 'invention of tradition' in relation to the guild, or rather steal the 'invention' of the masters and put it to their own strategic use.[46] Kocka was the first to investigate the phenomenon, known from English and French social history, for the German-speaking world, that guilds and other organisational forms of the old trades must be seen as the nuclei of the early workers' movement, even though the latter was often characterised by a theory and rhetoric that was directed firmly against craft traditions. Kocka contrasts the 'claim' of the workers' movement to be a 'class movement' for 'all wage-dependent manual workers', 'including the large mass of unskilled day labourers and manual workers, agricultural workers and servants', with the fact that the early workers' movement was '*factually* ... a movement of *artisans*', in which 'journeymen craftsmen and other workers with a craft background made up the large majority'.[47] The fact that the early movement was strongly characterised by journeymen in its social structure was reflected organisationally in the adoption of certain guild 'forms of sociability', including the use of 'journeymen flags and symbols'.[48] Beyond that, however – and here Kocka opposes transferring 'protest research primarily oriented to Western European experience' onto German conditions – caution is advised when asserting more far-reaching continuities.[49] The 'organisations of the newly emerging workers' movement [could] not have been based on journeymen's organisations at all, either since there were none or because they were effectively controlled by the state authorities and the guilds'.[50] This finally leads Kocka to warn against overstretching the thesis of a continuity between the craftsmen's movement and the workers' movement, and finally to a conceptual restitution of the sharp separation between the two, which had previously been so convincingly called into question. Ultimately, Kocka maintains that the crafts movement was a 'defensive' movement, 'anti-modern', traditional and hostile to progress – in short, romantic – while the labour movement was a 'movement of emancipation and struggle for progress ... a product of modernity, offensive, anti-traditional and far removed from any glorification of the past, or critique of civilization'.[51]

---

46 Cf. Kocka 1986, p. 362: 'The authoritarian state vigorously helped to collectively break the back of the journeymen'.

47 Kocka 1986, pp. 340–1.

48 Kocka 1986, p. 354.

49 Kocka 1986, p. 368, fn. 61.

50 Kocka 1986, p. 353.

51 Kocka 1986, p. 375, cf. also p. 357.

In the end, the reader is left with the question of how to deal with the immediate contrast between Kocka's clearly pro-modern assessment and his own historical findings, which do not really conform to this evaluation. When Kocka states that 'backward-looking formations of tradition can obviously, under the right conditions of a proper challenge, generate downright radical, future-oriented movement energy', and that it is precisely in the guild traditions that the 'driving forces of the early workers' movement become visible, which it was hardly aware of itself and did not correspond to its self-understanding', then the historical problem reappears in this simple-sounding statement.[52] For how exactly does this transfer of energy ('movement energy', 'driving forces') come about if tangible-material, institutional-organisational channels can hardly be pinpointed? Obviously, we have to expand our conceptual tools in order to understand the transference between craft and guild traditions on the one hand and the early labour movement on the other, which Kocka merely states but does not explain.

To properly examine this historical process of transmission requires taking language, images and symbolic practices into account, in short, all the imaginary formations that serve as patterns and media of social identification; this 'imagery' – or, following Tieck, 'representations of all kinds' – not only confirms a given identity, but, as E.P. Thompson showed, also allows actors to step outside themselves and find themselves again in a new identity.[53]

If one wants to grasp the imaginary continuity expressed in a language shaped by craftsmanship, guild images and symbols, then one cannot reduce language to a secondary mimetic function. Social language 'reflects' not only 'modes of perception and patterns of interpretation', it not only provides 'information about how the social world is depicted in the minds of contemporaries', as Kocka postulates. Rather, language, especially 'imagery', often precedes the depiction of already existing conditions by suggesting, playing with and testing new 'modes of perception', and thus putting alternative 'patterns of interpretation' up for discussion. When the 'old terms no longer fit the new realities', this not only expresses itself in 'linguistic insecurities', but can also lead to increased poetic and political creativity and productivity of language.[54] This can be seen particularly well in the Vormärz.

In his study, Kocka fails to recognise this projective-constructive dimension of language – and thus does not do justice to the 'conceptual history' developed in Bielefeld, to which he nevertheless refers – when he writes, for example, of

52 Kocka 1986, p. 357.
53 Thompson 1966, p. 49.
54 Kocka 1986, p. 365.

'"left-wing" figures of thought and speech' behind which a 'right-wing' content can sometimes 'hide', since they are 'essentially defensive attitudes of protest'.[55] 'Imagery' in Thompson's sense, on the other hand, means

> much more than figures of speech in which ulterior motives were 'clothed'. The imagery is itself evidence of powerful subjective motivations, fully as 'real' as the objective, fully as effective, as we see repeatedly ... in their historical agency. It is the sign of how men felt and hoped, loved and hated, and of how they preserved certain values in the very texture of their language.[56]

In German social history, the juxtaposition of *tradition* and *progress* is structurally decisive: a juxtaposition in which it is always assumed that 'tradition' functions in a purely antiquarian way and does not itself progress. English social history, on the other hand, is based on a concept of tradition that is virtually equated with constant 'reinterpretation'. Already in the preface to *Culture and Society*, Raymond Williams names the possibility of 'reinterpretation' as the goal of any engagement with 'tradition'.[57] And Thompson wants to historiographically rescue William Morris's romantic anti-capitalism by extracting from its 'traditional, conservative, "regressive", "escapist" and "utopian" characteristics' the elements of a 'transformation' that first made possible a 'communist tradition' entirely independent of Marx and Marxism.[58] 'Binding tradition and class formation': it all comes down to freeing the terms of Kocka's relevant essay title from their dichotomous juxtaposition and understanding them in their complementarity.

---

55 Kocka 1986, p. 357.

56 Thompson, 1966, p. 49.

57 Cf. Williams 1960, p. v, where he names the initial impetus of his research: 'Our object then was to enquire into and where possible reinterpret this tradition which the word "culture" describes in terms of the experience of our own generation'. In *Keywords*, the conceptual and historical glossary to *Culture and Society*, Williams notes, in a clearly partisan way, the shifts in meaning of the term 'tradition': 'It is sometimes observed ... that it only takes two generations to make anything traditional: naturally enough, since that is the sense of tradition as active process. But the word tends to move towards *age-old* and towards ceremony, duty and respect. Considering only how much has been handed down to us, and how various it actually is, this, in its own way, is both a betrayal and a surrender. On the other hand, especially within forms of "*modernization* theory" (cf. *Modern*) *tradition* and especially *traditional* are now often used dismissively, with a similar lack of specificity' (Williams 2015, pp. 252–3).

58 Thompson 1976, pp. 90, 93.

Kocka, however, literally pushes aside Thompson's research (or William Sewell's similar studies of the French tradition) when he declares them unsuitable for German history.[59] In Germany, there was no 'revolutionary heritage' that could have been in harmony with a guild tradition; moreover, the German guilds from the outset were much more 'shaped by state authorities' than, for example, the French.[60]

This national enclosure of social history, which knows that everything always 'happens differently on this side of the Rhine',[61] is completely inappropriate for the situation in Vormärz. That 'beliefs in progress' among the early workers' movement are said to have spread 'on wanderings and journeys partly abroad', represents an almost droll trivialisation of the situation.[62] The early German workers' movement was a movement of German workers *abroad*, a movement across all European borders, and can therefore only be grasped transnationally from the outset; the phrase – admittedly coined later – 'journeymen without a homeland' must be taken literally in all its parts. Activists and authors of the early movement were painfully aware that there was no revolutionary tradition in the German territories to which they could connect, yet this was not an obstacle but rather an incentive for them to first create such a tradition – also by means of a partly consciously pursued and propagated import of French and English ideas. In a desolate present, marked by political repression and social depression, authors like Wilhelm Weitling and Georg Weerth discovered and created a counter-tradition of rebellious journeyman, which often draws on the specific idiom of German journeyman discourse, and which was to be revived in guild structures and self-organised journeymen clubs far from the state. The authors are partly aware of the fictional character of these constructions, but this does not detract from their effectiveness.

2 Journeymen Culture and the Workers' Movement: Wilhelm Weitling

In 1836, the wandering journeyman tailor Wilhelm Weitling reached Paris, the centre of a huge German exile community of journeymen craftsmen and bour-

59 Sewell 1980.

60 Kocka 1986, pp. 348–9.

61 Kocka 1986, p. 348.

62 Kocka 1986, p. 374.

geois liberals who had fled the repressive regime restoration in the German states. In the restless Paris of those years – French society was gripped by a veritable 'mania of revolt' after the July Revolution of 1830 – the German exiles also became radicalised.[63] The most determined among them, the journeymen craftsmen and bourgeois intellectuals around Jacob Venedey and Georg Fein, founded the League of Outlaws in 1834, which Weitling also joined in 1836.[64] Organisationally and programmatically, the Outlaws were close to those French clubs and societies that, after the victory of the bourgeois forces in the July Revolution, turned to the egalitarian and social revolutionary traditions of the French Revolution, such as those embodied by François Noël (called Gracchus) Babeuf and his Conspiracy of Equals. Filippo Buonarroti, a friend and disciple of Babeuf, initially fled to Italy after Babeuf's execution in 1797, only to bring back the revolutionary message to Paris in the 1830s.[65] The neo-Babouvists radicalised the debate, no longer merely demanding political participation rights or a fair distribution of land and wealth, but the abolition of all private property: communism took shape and immediately infected the German opposition in Paris.

Weitling, born in 1808 as the illegitimate son of a servant girl and a French occupation soldier, had never enjoyed higher education, having been apprenticed at fourteen.[66] While wandering (wandering educates!) he familiarised himself with the teachings and theories of the opposition movement; as an autodidact, he retained throughout his life an aversion to 'artificial phrases without content', which he saw everywhere in the elaborate works of philo-

63 Cf. Giesselmann 1993.

64 The organ of the League was *Der Geächtete. Zeitschrift in Verbindung mit mehreren deutschen Volksfreunden* [*The Outlaw: Journal published in conjunction with several German friends of the people*], Venedey 1834/35. In the twelve issues in total, texts by Börne and Heine were published alongside many anonymous texts. On the journalism of the German exile community, which shows the 'rudiments of an informal communication structure in the early German workers' movement', see Ruckhäberle 1977, p. 7. On the socio-historical background of the pronounced 'journeyman mobility' with the 'destination Paris' cf. Wadauer 2003, pp. 49–67.

65 For the central document of the entire movement, see Buonarroti 1836. Babeuf's teachings and their neo-Babouvist treatment were disseminated in the German Vormärz, for example, through the anonymous articles '*Babœufs Prozess* [Baboeuf's Trial]' and '*Analyse der Lehre Babœuf's.* (*Nach Buonarotti*) [Analysis of the teachings of Babœuf. (After Buonarotti)]' in Püttmann 1846a, pp. 102–136 and pp. 136–146.

66 For an overview, see the chapter 'Schulden als Beraubung: Eine Theorie des Pauperismus' in Suter 2016, pp. 154–170.

sophers and professional intellectuals; he also never warmed to 'the Hegel'.[67] Conversely, this did not stop him from hypertrophic projects of his own: he wrote a cosmology and drafted a universal language, which he sent to Wilhelm von Humboldt for examination.[68] Irritated comrades sometimes described the communist tailor as a 'handsome' well-dressed dandy in a 'coat of elegant cut' with a 'coquettishly trimmed small beard'.[69]

After Weitling's entry, and perhaps also driven by him, the League of Outlaws split along the class lines running through it; against the dominance of the bourgeois intellectual leading figures around Venedey, the proletarian social revolutionary wing of the journeymen workers now constituted itself as the League of the Just.[70] On behalf of the League, Weitling moved from Paris to Switzerland in 1841 to agitate and organise the local political-social subculture of wandering and native journeymen craftsmen. To this end, from 1841 onwards he published the *Hülferuf der deutschen Jugend* in Geneva, a journal which in 1842–3 would bear the title *Die junge Generation* [*The Young Generation*]. In the articles, which Weitling largely wrote himself, he drew on the experiences of wandering craftsmen to criticise the 'social disorder' of the present and to spread the principles of a 'well-organised society' that the League of the Just and other Babouvist and communist groups were trying to build.[71] Even the names of the journals can be read as a reminiscence of the journeymen movement, as the '"invention of journeymen" parallel to the journeymen's wanderings gave rise to the journeymen's societies as institutions of the youth movement'.[72] Through the Vormärz reinvention of the journeymen's political culture, one can trace how the idea of 'youth' became understood as a revolutionary and politically determined phase of life.

---

67 During his time in Zurich, Weitling met with the Russian revolutionary Bakunin for an hour a day to 'study the Hegel'. The teaching project failed. In the second hour already, 'we came to the word *spirit*. I didn't want to be led beyond it without the meaning of this word used here in the book being properly defined for me. I first wanted to know what *spirit* was. But Bakunin wanted me to follow him for the time being without this explanation. I tried, out of pure courtesy for Bakunin, but it didn't work. I felt that my mind was being led astray like this. And the study of Hegel's philosophy came to an end for me'; Wilhelm Weitling in the journal *Die Republik der Arbeiter*, New York, 10 May 1851, quoted in Lehning 1987, p. 62.

68 Weitling 1931a, 1931b, 1931c, 1991.

69 Thus the Russian revolutionary Pavel Annenkov writes in his report 'On the Meeting of the Communist Correspondence Committee in Brussels, 30 March 1846', cited in: Institute of Marxism-Leninism 1958, p. 270.

70 On the organisational structure and debate culture in the various forms of the League, see Christolova 2014, pp. 215–36.

71 *Hülferuf* 1841, No. 1, p. 21.

72 Kluge 2007, starting at p. 203, especially p. 210.

As Jacques Rancière put it, 'proletarian thought' is formed 'within the traditional framework of the estates for the purpose of defending crafts and skilled labour against the threatening order of capitalist industry and the division of labour'.[73] The progressive articulation and differentiation of this thought, however, leads to an exhaustion of its own conditions of emergence; 'proletarian thought' emancipates itself from its roots in the guilds and finally distances itself sharply from them. Weitling had to experience this process first-hand. He wrote a manifesto for the League of the Just, published in 1838–9 under the beautiful title 'Humanity as it is and as it should be' – it lasted for ten years.[74] In 1847, the League of the Just renamed itself the League of Communists; Karl Marx and Friedrich Engels wrote its new manifesto. Weitling now became the victim of that 'process of emancipation' in which the new movement breaks with its social, historical and intellectual conditions of emergence. At the moment when Marx and Engels – who both despised any craft romanticism – take over the League, Weitling himself is pushed to the edge of the movement and finally personally excluded by the new heads. In the transition to organised communism, the journeyman becomes outlaw again.[75]

In the following section, Weitling's poetry of class – his contribution to the imaginary self-invention of class – will be examined in three different forms: first, his contribution to a poetry of political language, his creation of an alternative political discourse from the spirit of the old journeyman's language; then his contribution to the (re)creation of artistic forms of expression of class from the spirit of old journeymen songs; finally, Weitling's contribution to an institutional self-creation of the young journeyman's movement, his re-creation of journeyman's association through a changed self-narrative. On all three levels, one can see how class formation takes place not as a break but as a transformation of the journeymen traditions from which it derives.

73 Rancière 1978, p. 147.

74 Weitling, 1971, pp. 142–77. *Humanity* is a genuine product of proletarian nights. Weitling: 'I wrote it at a time when I had to work as a journeyman tailor every evening until 10 or 11 o'clock and every Sunday until 12 noon' (Weitling 1907, pp. 58–59).

75 The sources are compiled in Instituten für Marxismus-Leninismus 1970, pp. 301–9. Marx's and Engels' comrade Moses Hess summed up the outcome of the conflict when he wrote to them: 'His distrust of you has reached its highest peak. You've done a great job on him, and now you wonder why it's him. I don't want to have anything more to do with the whole story; it makes me want to puke, shit in all dimensions' (Hess 1959, pp. 155–56). Hess probably already suspects here that he himself will be the next to have to jump over Marx's and Engels' organisational blade.

2.1 *Journeymen Language*

In the article 'Asking, Begging, and Fencing', published in the second issue of *Hülferuf* in October 1841, Weitling attacks the prevailing system of bans on begging.[76] Sooner or later, as Weitling knows from his own experience, every craftsman – every wandering journeyman – inevitably comes into conflict with the 'begging laws' and the 'begging bailiffs' (BBF, p. 20 and p. 22) of the towns or countries he passes through. Anyone who stays in a town for only a few days cannot take up permanent work, and many trades are also seasonal; in order to 'eke out a living on the journey', the young craftsmen often have no choice but to beg. Not only the 'writer of this essay knows examples of young strong craftsmen' who felt compelled to take this step, but his readers would also know these examples or have already done so themselves (BBF, p. 20). Begging is part of wandering, and so whoever bases their economy (partially) on wandering journeymen, but forbids begging, is hypocritical or malicious – according to Weitling's initial thought.

The original aspect of Weitling's essay is that he uses the 'disorder' of society as an occasion for a discussion of the politics of language. For what does 'begging' really mean anyway? And what distinguishes 'begging' from 'asking'? Weitling's essay begins with a few things taken for granted and asks about their implications: are we not 'all Christians', and is not 'the highest and greatest commandment' of Christ to 'love one's neighbour'? And must not every Christian therefore follow the sentence: 'Ask, and you shall receive'? Shouldn't a society that sees itself as Christian also give to all who ask? In the present day there are 'gaunt figures wrapped in rags', 'made unfit for work by exhaustion, illness or old age', who 'ask passers-by with uplifted hands for a gift' (BBF, p. 18 f.). And what does society do? It changes the state of *affairs* by changing the *words*:

> The society that lets the commandment of love be preached has found no other means of putting an end to the tiresome, disgusting asking and demanding of the necessary needs of life than to transform the expression *asking* into *begging*, in order to make the contrast between the love and unity of the *Christian* law, and the hatred and isolation of the *political* law less obvious (BBF, p. 19).

However, as Weitling shows, it is not just a question of *what* is said, but also of *who* says it. The character of speech acts is determined by the political and social framework of the utterance:

76 *Hülferuf* 1841, No. 2, pp. 18–25; hereafter cited in the body of the text as BBF with page number.

> When we speak of the *desires* of the rich and powerful, in relation to the poor, we no longer call it *asking* but *demanding, ordering, commanding, calling*. The poor, however, in their relationship to the rich, *ask* when seeking a small favour, and *beg* when it is a question of extending their existence (BBF, p. 19).

The 'rich and powerful', the 'manufacturers of law' (BBF, p. 18) – the manufacturers of laws of manufacture – know about the power of words. With their linguistic-political manoeuvres, they disguise the obvious and create (legal) facts that make life hell for the poor. For the begging laws do not eliminate any of the causes for why people feel compelled to beg: 'If we now examine the goal of these begging laws, we find everywhere that it is not achieved: for after a while these unfortunates are let off again as naked and helpless, indeed even more helpless than before' (BBF, p. 19). Only an improvement of the social situation, an abolition of poverty through the creation of sufficiently well-paid work, could ultimately eliminate begging. The peculiarity of Weitling's approach is that he has no illusions about the enforceability of this demand through concessions by the 'rich and powerful' – after all, the measures would be tantamount to a self-abolition of their 'privileged idleness and free play'. Instead, Weitling relies on the self-help of the underprivileged in the unruly, rebellious tradition of the travelling journeymen.

Weitling attempts to wrest the power of definition away from the 'rich and powerful' by means of an equally linguistic-political feint, which comes from the arsenal of the journeymen's speech – the language of the Walz or journey. Using the example of a 'young craftsman' who 'in the winter of 1830 … was forced by the police, according to existing non-Christian but police laws, to leave the city because he was a stranger and … had no work with any guild master', Weitling introduces the third title-giving term of his essay after 'asking' and 'begging': 'fencing' (BBF, p. 21). For it was to this 'fencing' that the poor craftsman finally sought 'his refuge', and a long footnote explains what this was all about:

> Fencing! How do you like that expression? Compare it with begging and asking. The first was invented by the craftsmen, the second by the police, and the third by Christian love. Fencing, struggling one's way through the difficulties of life, that is the meaning of the word (BBF, p. 21).

In Walz speak, as in thieves' argot, 'fencing' simply means 'begging', even if the etymology is disputed.[77] Weitling, however, is not so much concerned with the

77 Cf. Wolf 1985, pp. 92–3.

purely denotative-descriptive function, but with the 'flavour' of the word: its connotations and social-affective content. And it was precisely this that the journeymen were concerned with when they created the word, according to Weitling:

> Since asking and begging offends a man's dignity, and neither the one nor the other occurs in a well-organised society, because it is the duty of all to secure the needs of each, and the duty of each to help meet the needs of all, the young journeymen, since iron necessity sometimes leaves them no other choice in order to live, have transformed the expressions asking and begging, which insult pride and the sense of honour, into fencing (BBF, p. 21).

Where 'no other choice' remains, the choice of words can still mark a difference, which in turn can impact the whole: the very word 'fencing' grants a way out of the prison of police language. The language of the police itself represents a form of violence that intrudes on the inalienable 'dignity', 'pride and sense of honour' of human beings. The language of 'Christian love' is also defenceless against this violence, because it too sees the poor person from the outset only as a passive object of external help and is therefore unable to oppose his transformation into an object of external discipline. Only the language of the craftsmen puts the poor back into the position of a subject with the power to act, who can actively assert his needs against the adversity of circumstance.

In the case of the 'young craftsman' who gave rise to the whole digression, 'fencing' had a thoroughly desperate-aggressive flavour: after endless harassment by the police, and seeking an 'opportunity' to 'say goodbye to humanity with a bloody warning', he 'put a bread knife in his pocket with the firm resolution to run it down the throat of the first henchman who stopped him'. This example, born of 'frenzied despair', is surely intended to serve as a 'bloody warning' sign for the 'rich and powerful' and their cronies. Only by chance does the desperate man escape the scaffold (BBF, p. 22).

Weitling urges his readers to learn from the example of their journeyman brother:

> Certainly, we do not posit fencing as a moral act, but as an emergency remedy. Morality itself commands man to choose, if he has only the choice to die, to steal, or to fence. Where the powerful voice of self-preservation speaks, all other feelings are silent, and the weakest become foolhardy (BBF, p. 23).

'Self-preservation' takes precedence over 'political' or 'police law'; where morality and the Christian law no longer apply, only a *right of necessity* exists, which every individual, even and especially the 'weakest', can and may assert. Legal philosophical considerations of this kind can be found in many places in the Vormärz, as different legal systems overlap and areas of legal indeterminacy arise.[78] Weitling's reflections on the right of necessity take on a flavour all its own, which in turn is fed by a reference to the journeymen tradition. Weitling develops the problem, which is certainly recognised in its general social relevance, strictly *ad personam*. It is the individual 'police servant' who confronts the individual craftsman and enforces the begging laws against him; it is the individual 'police slave', who spices up his sinister service with an excess of 'brutality', 'drudgery and oppression', against whom Weitling's attack is directed. The abstract, social relationship becomes a scene in which individuals confront each other, individuals could always choose differently if they wanted to. There are strong affects provoked in this social conflict, which Weitling also mobilises in his essay: if 'the heart of the executing officer' necessarily 'petrifies' at work, as Weitling insinuates, and the officer nevertheless sticks to his business, then one cannot help but eventually feel 'aversion and disgust' for each individual policeman (BBF, p. 20).

2.2 *Journeymen Song*

In the last issue of *Die junge Generation* from May 1843, there is a 'speaking song', which is formally based on journeymen or Walz songs.[79] The song consists of ten stanzas, in each of which 'One' advances for five lines, with every fifth line formulating a question, followed by the phrase 'Right? Hey? Well?', then in the sixth line, 'All' answer 'Yes!', with 'One' concluding the stanza in the seventh line with an exclamation and cheer 'with Ho, Hop and Hopsala!'

The alternating call-and-response pattern is reminiscent of workers' songs, although the very first stanza makes it clear that the singers are actually happy to have 'escaped from the workshop and meagre fare'.[80] Instead, the song describes and celebrates 'a feast' centred on wine, which is generally shared unequally – 'But we usually get the very worst? Right? Hey? Well?' – and the 'feast' essentially consists of the 'workers' today securing their fair share of the goods:

---

78 On the 'right of necessity' as a right 'in extreme danger and in collision with the rightful property of someone else', see Hegel 1991, § 127, p. 154.

79 *Die junge Generation*, No. 5, 1843, pp. 73–6.

80 Formally, Weitling's 'speaking song' is based on traditional journeymen's songs, such as those collected in Schade 1865.

One: Yes, we are there too, and we want to live
As well as any moneybags after all,
The very best juice of the German vines,
We love and we pretend;
The wine is also there for the workers? Right?
Hey? Well?
All: Yes!
One: I think so too! With Ho, Hop, Hopsala!

In the traditional journeymen's songs, as in Weitling's, work is a point of repulsion rather than an object of positive identification; what unites the journeymen is the rejection of work and the hierarchical conditions in which it is carried out. The shared point of reference for the journeymen is drinking together, which also appears in other songs of the time as an act of resistance:

Journeymen, join with me
And let the work be done!
Let the work be done!
We want to drink wine and rum,
and have lots of merry fun,
Yes have fun, yes have fun.[81]

Or:

In Frankfurt lived a master,
who kept journeymen in two and threes.
The first one said 'I feel, I do not feel well'.
The second was drunk,
The third was full.

'Journeymen, journeymen! It stays between us:
We want to let the master do the work,
And go for a little walk,
to the cool red wine,
And see the pretty girls'.[82]

81 'Gesellen Trinklied' in Schade 1865, p. 173.
82 'Die lustigen Gesellen' in Schade 1865, p. 219.

Weitling not only gives his 'speaking song' a structure reminiscent of the old, traditional forms; he also takes the old, rebellious content and systematises it with regard to a 'common cause'. His journeymen's song, communistically appropriated as it were, takes wine as an occasion to expose and accuse the unjustly organised production and distribution: 'To the servant who painstakingly, faithfully tends the vineyard, / To him the wine is rightfully due', and yet it is appropriated by the 'rich dogs' who have contributed nothing to its cultivation and harvest.

Ultimately, however, Weitling makes it clear that wine is 'only a secondary matter' – an allegory of the discrepancy between the promise of happiness and its poor fulfilment. But it is not for material well-being that 'we' hunger and thirst – 'too much' wine, after all, 'is unhealthy'! – but for 'justice', for 'recognition' and 'wisdom', for *culture* and *knowledge*.

The last (regular) stanza brings together the alternating song form with the egalitarian content. In the first stanzas, the structure of the dialogical instruction and enlightenment is consistently based on the internal hierarchy of the journeymen, determined by the principle of seniority – thus the lead singer addresses the others as 'little boys'. In the last stanza, however, this collective of the young and inexperienced is released by the lead singer into maturity when he compels them to break with the automatisms of their own song structure:

One: We will pluck from the tree of knowledge
And taste the fruit's sweetest core.
And adorn ourselves with flowers of noble wisdom,
And so flee the earth from star to star,
Then shall we die as fools?
Hey? Well?
All: No!
One: I say amen to that, with ho, hop and hopsala!

The poet also knows that a 'Yes!' is always more likely to come out of everyone's lips than a 'No!' and accordingly sends an alternative version of the last verse, marked as an aside ('NB'.), in case 'All' would have answered 'Yes!' as usual and rhyming: 'No, you cursed yes men! If you always want to sing "Yes", then you won't get any further in life than the backwater of ***. *No, no*, you must say'.

Enlightenment, 'knowledge' and 'wisdom' begin with a clear and unflinching negation; only through the repeated 'No!' can the workers 'flee the earth' to which they seem chained and build another world. In the end, the process of self-liberation through self-enlightenment in Weitling's work is sealed by a conscious break with the aesthetically invoked form of the traditional journeymen's song; for Weitling, however, the break can only be made with precisely this tradition. If, as Heinrich Bosse writes, Tieck's *Wanderings of Franz Sternbald* is already about an 'overcoming of craftsmanship' through culture, then one can add with Wilhelm Weitling that such an overcoming can only be had through a stylisation of the institutions of craftsmanship itself.[83] Tradition is preserved in its negation, negation remains dependent on tradition. A break that actually does away with the whole tradition of craftsmanship and makes a *tabula rasa* of the workers' movement will eventually eject Wilhelm Weitling himself from the movement.

2.3 *Journeymen Association*

Reports from the life of the 'Association of Young Germans in the Trades' in Geneva occupy a large space in Weitling's *Hülferuf*. The association is introduced in the very first article of the first issue, after a long editorial, while the second issue reports on its 'monthly general meeting'.[84] Both the chairman, Mr Mersch, and the 'treasurer', Mr Bonnet, are identified as craftsmen: the first is a carpenter – without stating his status – and the second is a master shoemaker. The association has existed since November 1839, with a fluctuating number of members, 'depending on the ratio of those who have left and those who have arrived'. On average there are ninety members (HVG, p. 7). The fact that travelling funds were paid to departing members from the association's treasury also makes it clear that the association recruited its membership not insignificantly from young craftsmen, from travelling journeymen (cf. HVG, p. 11 ff.).

The reports focus on the internal organisational form of the association, and here in particular the question of finances arises in detail; the first article resembles a statement of accounts, especially at the beginning. The association earns its income by collecting 'registration fees' as well as 'extraordinary and monthly contributions'. The total income of the first two years, 3,600 francs, was mainly used on the maintenance of a rented clubhouse (including 'heating and lighting') (HVG, p. 7).

The fact that the association appears to be just about financially viable, but does not manage to generate surpluses for further investments, is now taken by some of its members as an opportunity to propose a far-reaching reform of

83 Bosse 2012, p. 126. On the history of the bourgeois transformation of journeymen songs, see Bosse 1999.

84 *Hülferuf* 1841, No. 1, pp. 7–16, and No. 2, pp. 25–8; hereafter cited in the body text as HVG with page number.

the financial and organisational form; the report of the general meeting of the association even speaks of an 'old' and a 'new' order. The adoption of the new order was finally decided unanimously (HVG, p. 25 f.).

At the centre of the proposed 'new order' is the idea of 'establishing an association tavern'; the clubhouse is to be transferred from private management to 'self-managed' (HVG, p. 8). Up to now, a landlord has been running the clubhouse on extremely favourable terms: the association pays him half the rent, provides heating and lighting costs and leaves him the entire income from catering the guests who, as association members, form a regular clientele. The self-governing 'association tavern' should put an end to this. Finally, 'the entire surplus shall go to the association instead of a family, as it is now' (HVG, p. 8). It soon becomes clear that the 'association tavern' is more than just a jointly run pub; for Weitling, it becomes the symbol of a self-managed collective economy in general – communism as pub project.

As the discussion progresses – Weitling combines visionary foresight with a penchant for meticulous attention to detail ('50 Centimes') – the surpluses that inevitably result from the collectivisation of the farm are now calculated. When it comes to ideas for how to spend the 14,400 francs that would now accumulate each year, it becomes apparent that the 'new order' essentially remains an old, well-known one. The money should be mainly used for social and sociopolitical tasks that earlier were the responsibility of the guilds and journeymen's associations. Journeymen 'were the most vulnerable of craftsmen, since they usually had no family'.[85] In case of illness, the guilds and especially the journeymen's unions took over their care and provision. The guilds did not feel responsible when journeymen were unemployed or wandering, and there was no provision for old age. Here, especially in the later eighteenth century, when the journeymen period was officially still regarded as a purely transitory stage on the way to mastery, but de facto had increasingly become the end point of many careers, only the journeymen's unions stepped in with their 'chests': funds from regularly collected contributions from the members, with which the associations contributed to the expenses of wandering or provided assistance in old age. In many cases, the journeymen's chests also served as strike funds.[86]

85 Kluge 2007, p. 325.

86 While the 'chest' was originally just the container in which files, regulations and statutes were kept together with the cash register, it later became the *pars pro toto for* the entire guild. Even later, and especially in the case of the journeymen's chests, a reverse semantic movement can be observed: the chest now only denotes the till and what is financed with it, in the sense of 'health insurance', 'social security'; cf. Kluge 2007, pp. 23–4.

Weitling does not mention a strike fund, although he certainly has it in mind; explicitly mentioned – and calculated down to the centime – are travel funds, support in cases of unemployment and incapacity for work, as well as a pension system that could be built on top of the 'association tavern'. Through skilful 'calculation and interest on the capital to be obtained in this way', a kind of old-age and nursing home, an integral 'pension institution for workers' could even be created; its conceptual form, however, is to be 'given in another paper' (HVG, p. 11).

With the proposed reform of the 'association tavern', Weitling pursues an institutional-organisational reinvention of the guild tradition, and by concentrating on the concerns of travelling journeymen and 'journeymen-workers', whom Weitling explicitly counts among the 'working classes' (HVG, p. 10), he connects directly to the tradition of the autonomous self-organisation of journeymen. He seeks this connection, however, under completely different circumstances, under the intensified socio-political conditions of a largely realised market economy. That Weitling's utopian sketch of his new association social fund already has to prove its market-based economic viability sharply marks the social-historical distance between the old, guild order and its reinvention in the Vormärz.

Weitling's calculations are initially aimed at establishing a basic material security for the members of the association through social security and pension funds. This is only the first step, however, since ultimately it is a matter of 'bringing the physical *and moral* condition of the working classes to a peak of prosperity' (HVG, p. 10 [emphasis added]). For Weitling, the physical well-being of the workers is ultimately only a symbol of a much broader one: with a well-organised collectivised 'association tavern', the association could 'give the world an example of the cultural level of the German worker' (HVG, p. 10). The association should not miss the opportunity to realise such a model and thus also to work towards the 'political emancipation' of the workers:

> Are you still hesitating? Do you want the present and future generations to say: he also did not believe, did not see with open eyes, did not hear with open ears, for he fought against the system of unification for the sake of separation (HVG, p. 10).

The stages of culture and emancipation, for which the association should set an example, are not only evident in the decisions, but already in the way the decisions are made: 'A motion that would have been laughed at and ridiculed by many a great gentleman was discussed in the German craftsmen's association with a calmness that would have done honour to any parliament'. In their culture of discussion, the workers not only prove equal to established parliamentarians, they even surpass them foresight. For the 'democrats of today, who only gaze at the wil-o'-wisp of the political question and do not want to see the star of the social question, could have been cured of their sick conviction here [in the club of the German craftsmen's association]' (HVG, p. 26). The very form of self-organisation on a *social* basis elevates the craftsmen's association above all forms of purely *political* organisation; for the latter separates itself from the 'social' dimension of its activity and thus inevitably comes into difficulties. Today's democracy, with its exclusive concentration on the 'political question' – the question of democracy and parliamentarism – thus remains a mere symptom of a system based on the 'separation' of different social spheres.

Weitling's broad understanding of politics, which no longer separates the 'political' from the 'social question', also finds expression in his holistic concept of *Bildung*. This indeed includes the purchase of a hitherto only 'rented forteppiano' and the constant 'enlargement of the small library' (HVG, p. 7). '*Bildung*', however, should not be just a sub-domain, as in the existing system of separation, but a comprehensive way of life, a social form of existence based on 'union' and 'interweaving' – not least that of body and mind, of being and consciousness, or with Brecht, of food and morals. In response to the (anticipated) accusation that the self-managed takeover of food and service would turn the political association into a mere 'caterer's or eating club', Weitling counters:

> To live, you have to eat. And to eat well and cheaply, you have to eat together. Nothing has a more powerful effect on the moral formation of the members of the association than the joint provision of a part of material needs, the interweaving of the interests of the individual into the interests of all (HVG, p. 15).

Even in everyday – and, it would seem, lowly – matters such as food, the communist motto of *Hülferuf* and *Die junge Generation*, which precedes every issue, proves itself: 'Against the interest of individuals, insofar as it harms the interest of all, and for the interest of all, without excluding any individual'.

The meaning Weitling assigns to *Bildung* corresponds in the English debate of the time, as Raymond Williams has shown, to the term 'culture'. Using the textile metaphor of 'interweaving', Weitling already alludes to the motif of a connection between the two terms, which will only become theoretically viable in the twentieth century, when 'culture as text' or as 'webs of significance' is spelled out. Absolutised and freed from any companion ('*culture* as such' in contrast to 'culture *of* something'), 'culture' becomes the epitome of 'a whole way of life, material, intellectual and spiritual'.[87] The emergence of such a comprehensive concept of culture is only intelligible, Williams shows, as a reaction to the development of industry and the market system. In this way, culture becomes the 'court of appeal' for a critique of the present and an imaginative resource for the construction of alternatives.[88] The source of the new, critical concept of culture according to Williams is the English Romantic movement, and as this chapter has shown, this also applies to the German Romantic movement.

3 Georg Weerth and the Break with Guild Traditions

In Weitling, the concept of *Bildung*, or culture in the broadest sense, still exhibits a universal appeal that counteracts the autonomous, separatist tendencies of the journeymen tradition. For Weitling, there is still a 'world' – and there is still *a* 'world' – as an overarching entity (and as a human 'court of appeal' in Williams' sense) in which the example of the Geneva workers can be noted and appreciated.

In Georg Weerth (1822–56), the overarching universal claim has disappeared. He already moves in a world that is no longer *one* in its horizon of meaning, but rather permeated by a deep division into different class spheres: on the one side that of the workers, on the other that of the bourgeoisie. Yet Weerth, 'the German proletariat's first and most important poet', as Friedrich Engels would later call his friend and comrade who died young, explicitly placed himself in the tradition of craftsmen and wandering journeymen.[89] Unlike Weitling and most of the other protagonists of the early movement, however, he was not a craftsman himself. He came from a Westphalian clergy house and began a commercial apprenticeship at the age of 16 in a textile shop in Elberfeld in the southern Ruhr area. After stations in Cologne and Bonn, he moved in 1843 to Bradford in Yorkshire, a central hub of the wool industry's global value network. Further stations in his career were Brussels, Paris, Cologne again, Spain, Portugal and finally the New World, where he travelled throughout the USA, Mexico and Brazil on behalf of various textile trading houses. He died in 1856, aged 34, of malaria in Havana, Cuba, where he is buried. What Weerth shares with the wandering journeymen is the experience of homelessness and restlessness; he

87 Williams 1960, p. xiv.
88 Williams 1960, p. 37.
89 Engels, 'Georg Weerth', MECW 26, p. 109.

too is 'without a homeland' in the best sense.[90] Perhaps for this reason, Weerth uses the tradition of journeyman poetry and songs as his material and at the same time subjects them to a radical transformation.

In an anthology of 'social poems' already mentioned in the Introduction, published in 1847 by Weerth's friend Hermann Püttmann under the title *Album of Original Poetry*, Friedrich Sass, Percy Shelley, Wilhelm Weitling, Ferdinand Freiligrath, Anastasius Grün, Heinrich Heine, Hermann Overbeck, Ludwig Seeger and several others appear, all of whom were prominent in the socialist poetry scene of those years. In it, Weerth presents a whole cycle of 'journeymen songs'; the poem that prefaces Engels' late appreciation of Weerth also comes from this cycle.[91] Even Engels, one of the fathers of 'scientific socialism', who in his later years contributed a great deal to the establishment of a linear historical narrative of the workers' movement, in which the theoretical and practical early forms of the movement were only appreciated as pre-forms and thus downgraded to mere 'precursors', seems to have found the connection between 'journeymen songs' and a poetry of the proletariat still plausible in 1883.[92]

The five poems of Weerth's cycle, 'The Farewell', 'On a High Mountain', 'In the Green Forest', 'Three Beautiful Journeymen' and 'Around the Cherry Blossom', follow the cycle of wandering: the dialectic of sorrow and euphoria of liberation associated with departure ('Farewell, you dull city! / Now rejoice, whoever has a free / happy life!'; 'The Farewell', pp. 5–6); the look back at childhood and the expectation of return ('O bloom on, you roses, / without hardship and adversity; / Until I see you again / Well over a year and day!'; 'On a High Mountain', pp. 7–8); finally the camaraderie with other journeymen on the road ('So they sang in the forest; / The green grass flashed. / The sounds of stream and quarry / Treble, tenor and bass'; 'In the Green Forest', pp. 9–10).[93] Only the last two poems step out of this popular-romantic idyll, free of all social or class struggles, and approach a confrontation with a master and a landlord in a manner already familiar to us. First of all, it concerns the possibility of seducing the master's wife and daughter ('The first spoke to the master, / The second greeted the wife, / The third kissed the

90 On Weerth's biography, see the 1910 work of his niece Marie Weerth (2009), and Füllner 2006.

91 Cf. Füllner 2012.

92 Engels' *Socialism: Utopian and Scientific* of 1880 (MECW 24, pp. 281–325) provides the template for this linear self-understanding of the workers' movement.

93 The poems of the cycle are quoted in the body of text according to Püttmann 1847, pp. 5–14.

daughter, / With eyes so sweet and blue'; 'Three Beautiful Journeymen', p. 11), as well as the poor hospitality and excessive working hours ('And beat like nightingales, / And pricked with needles, / And sewed the trouser flies / Till about starlight'; p. 11). The last poem, 'Around the Cherry Blossom', which Engels prefixes to his short homage to Weerth, radicalises this manner to a point that is arguably beyond the bounds of any traditional craftsman's song:

Around the Cherry Blossom

At the time when the cherries blossomed,
In Frankfurt we did stay.
At the time when the cherries blossomed,
In that city we did stay.

Up spake mine host, the landlord:
'Your coats are frayed and worn'.
Look here, you lousy landlord,
That's none of your concern.

Now give us of your wine,
And give us of your beer,
And with the beer and wine,
Bring us a roast in here.

The cock crows in the cock-stop,
Out comes a goodly flow,
And in our mouths it tastes
Like urinatio.

And then he brought a hare
In parsley leaves bedight,
And at this poor dead hare
We all of us took fright.

And when we were in bed,
Our nightly prayers reciting,
Early and late in bed
The bed-bugs kept on biting.

It happened once in Frankfurt,
That town so fine and fair,
That knows who did once dwell
And who did suffer there. (pp. 13–14)[94]

After the bumpy, repetitive introduction, the landlord's words, which do not announce an exchange of pleasantries, are still marked as speech and thus distanced at the same time. The following third line of the second stanza responds directly with an insult ('You lousy landlord') and then in the fourth line with a break in communication: 'That's none of your concern!' The landlord is addressed directly here, the completed speech act is not quoted, performed or narrated, like that of the landlord, but expressed directly, without any marking of distance, for example, by inverted commas. The affront is not stated but carried out by removing the common linguistic level from the utterances of the landlord and the 'we'; the speech acts no longer have a common framing. The third stanza then switches to the pure performance of the command; through the insistent repetition of the imperative 'give' (and the repetition of the demanded 'beer' and 'wine'), the communicative situation now finally presents itself as irreconcilable.

In stanza four, which follows the sequence of commands without a marked change of situation or setting, the demanding party's calculation seems to have worked out: beer and wine fall into a 'goodly flow'. When the landlord brings the demanded 'roast' in stanza five, however, the situation changes: the uncanny itself seems to come to the table in the form of the 'dead hare'.[95]

If one wants to interpret this symbolically, then it could – as a fertility symbol – also stand for the vagrant sensuality and sexuality of the craftsmen themselves; indeed, the preceding poem reminded us of this. Engels will praise Weerth's poetry as an 'expression of natural robust sensuality and carnal lust' – without, of course, considering that in the poem he himself mentions, these feelings become victims of themselves in a certain sense.[96] Sensuality is slaughtered, one's own physical lust consumed. In the sixth stanza, the setback is revealed: in the 'bed' are only 'bed-bugs' – and not, for instance, the wife or daughter of the landlord, whom one might have hoped to find there as a continuation of earlier adventures. The landlord may have allowed himself to be temporarily bossed around by the journeymen, but this will not have

94 Translated by Engels in 1883, MECW 26, p. 108.

95 Strictly speaking, the break already takes place at the end of the fourth stanza: that beer and wine taste like urine does not bode well.

96 MECW 26, p. 111.

changed the social disparity between those who 'dwell' in the 'fine and fair' town of Frankfurt and those who 'suffer' there.

The pessimistic conclusion of the poem, however, can no longer relativise the completed break – 'That's none of your concern!' Weerth leaves no doubt in any of his texts that such a rupture is necessary. In the short story, 'The Flower Festival of the English Workers', the completed break with the world of the 'bourgeoisie' is finally presented as a prerequisite for the real development and emancipation of the sensuality and passions of the workers.[97]

The text begins with the narrating 'I' (hereinafter referred to as 'Weerth' for the sake of brevity) receiving a visit from his friend Jackson as the evening bell rings, a friend who will be described in the last paragraph of the text as a militant member of the Chartists, the first great mass movement of English workers (BF, p. 274).[98] Jackson is 'a handsome man, about forty or forty-five years old', and outwardly a little eccentric: he wears a green waistcoat, a black tailcoat with a red tulip in the buttonhole, brown breeches with white stockings and clunky hobnailed boots. Jackson's appearance is directly contrasted with the image of the 'returning workers' who roam the alleys of the 'factory town' after the end of their shifts. The children 'creep silently and sadly towards their freedom, for a day of the most strenuous work has paralysed their feet, bruised their arms, confused their minds, and fatigue, like a nightmare, rides on their poor souls'; the 'men and women' also have their heads down, 'their eyes staring at the pavement' (BF, pp. 266–67).

The contrast between Jackson's effervescent vitality and the grey world of work structures the whole vignette. Jackson has invited Weerth to leave town with him and stop at the 'Old Mutton Shoulder', an inn not far from town. The short walk is portrayed as an exodus from the factory town, the sphere of work and oppression:

> Jackson took giant steps. In ten minutes, we had already left the dank city behind us. The dank city! Eternally shrouded in the thickest coal vapour. So that half a mile from the first houses you don't even notice a roof.
>
> Only on Sunday does it suddenly get light, up above the city; but not in the hundred thousand heads down there! –

---

97 The autobiographical sketch was first printed in the journal *Der Gesellschaftsspiegel*, which, with the silent collaboration of Engels, was published in twelve issues by Moses Hess in Elberfeld in 1845/46. Weerth's 'Flower Festival of the English Workers' is quoted in the body of the text as BF with page number, according Weerth 1975/1976, vol. 1, pp. 266–74.

98 On Chartism, see also Weerth's 'Geschichte des Chartismus von 1832. Feargus O'Connor', in Weerth 1975/1976, vol. 1, pp. 275–87.

> But on that evening, which was not a Sunday evening, a few hundred slender factory chimneys spewed their last smoke towards the sky. From halfway up the hill, we could barely distinguish any house down in the valley. Total darkness below, but the most glorious evening up on the hill! (BF, pp. 267–8)

The exodus from darkness into light is not an individual one. It takes place, as will be shown, with many others who will first gather together on the hill outside the city. The exodus is reminiscent of the *Secessio Plebis* in ancient Rome, not only in its spatial disposition; the first and most famous of these led the plebeians to the Mons Sacer, where they gathered to subsequently demand the installation of a tribune of the people in an organised manner. The next *Secessiones* also aimed at institutional reforms in favour of the plebeians.[99]

The exodus of the English workers can be instructively contrasted with that of the Roman plebeians. The English workers do not demand social reform – indeed, they flee not only 'from the filth of the towns, from the smoke of the factories', but also 'from the waves of a people's assembly, from the rage of a mob' (BF, p. 268). But they do not flee from collectivity in general into individual escapism; rather, they organise a festival beyond the world of work (which also includes assemblies and mobs), *extra muros*, as it were: a 'flower festival'. The narrator then succinctly explains what this is all about – he is well aware that the very word 'flower festival' is extremely improbable in the given context, and he savours the implied surprise of the reader in the directness of his presentation:

> Every labourer who has rescued from the filth of the towns, from the smoke of the factories, from the haze of the brandy houses – but also from the waves of a people's assembly, from the rage of a mob, the tender sense,

99 The classic account of the first *Secessio Plebis* is Livy 1919, Book 2, Paragraphs XXXII and XXXIII, pp. 321–9. In England in the 1840s, Livy's history had quite a new reception. In 1845, Friedrich Engels referred to Kersal Moor in northern England, where workers' meetings were regularly held, as the 'Mons sacer of Manchester'; Engels 1844, *The Condition of the Working Class in England*, MECW 4, pp. 295–583, here p. 347. In Rancière 1999, starting at p. 23, there is a critique of the fable by which Menenius Agrippa affirmed the subordinate position of the plebeians, and thus 'prevailed upon the minds of his hearers', as Livy writes. Rancière notes, however, that by leaving, the plebeians made themselves into 'beings who may very well make promises and draw up contracts', beings who 'speak *like* patricians' (p. 25). The reason for Rancière's treatment of Livy is that as early as 1829 the counterrevolutionary writer Pierre-Simon Ballanche reinterpreted ancient history in the mirror of its present. The spectre of the *secessio* was omnipresent in the European Vormärz.

> the love of a flower, seeks a small spot either next to his home or in the garden of some friend, which he carefully cultivates with hoe and spade, which he fertilises even more carefully, which he tries to protect against all adversity with slats and sticks, and to which he entrusts his dearly bought flower seeds, his tulip or hyacinth bulbs.
>
> Then, when spring arrives, these flower-loving workers agree on a day to show each other the results of their gardening. The tulip is usually chosen for the first meeting, the buttercup for the second, and the aster and dahlia for the third and last. In addition, each person pays a shilling into a common fund, from which the costs incurred, such as the rent of the hall in which the flowers are exhibited, fees for the flower judges and other things, are paid. The rest of the money is used to buy a gift for the person with the most beautiful flower. These flower shows or flower festivals are held three times a year by the workers in many parts of England, but especially in the northern provinces (BF, p. 268).

Now the organisation of a flower show – even by workers – may seem banal to us today, and perhaps this impression already existed in the Vormärz; in contrast, Weerth emphasises the thoroughly non-trivial implications of the event. Firstly, he shifts the main contrast of the whole text, that of darkness and light, of oppression and elevation, onto the individual participants themselves, who are now examined more closely: 'But what people! … people on whom poverty had gnawed silently for a long time, who perhaps only just crept out of the factories with their sunken heads, where they worked for twelve hours, where a rattling machine for twelve hours long sung them the jubilant song of industry, and their own dirge'. These people, 'just slaves, poor devils, street urchins and lumpen', now become 'flower fellows'. They cherish their love of flowers and gather around a crude table in a disreputable tavern, 'on which the most beautiful tulips sat resplendent in many small glasses' (BF, pp. 268–9).

Secondly, Weerth emphasises that the collectively cultivated love of flowers among the workers originated from themselves and was organised by themselves. The exhibitions, says Weerth, 'are not under any higher protection. This love of flowers developed purely from the people. The bourgeoisie, as with so many other things, knows nothing, so also nothing of this poetic passion of the workers' (BF, p. 268). Precisely that which one might consider universally human and to which one might appeal – in the sense of 'culture' or '*Bildung*', for example – in order to proclaim a common basis for all people, becomes in Weerth's case the occasion for a final separation of the classes. And one may even doubt that the bourgeoisie could have such a passionate 'love of flowers' at all. The flower passion of the workers is not harmless; it must prove itself under difficult circumstances and be fought through; if this resistance and contrast are lacking, then the 'love of flowers' threatens to turn pale and wilt.

The autonomy of organisation continues in the competition through the specifics of collective discussion and decision-making. The final decision on the winner of the competition is made solely by two 'flower judges' (BF, p. 269), appointed and paid from the funds of the 'communal treasury'. These two old codgers calmly inspect and sniff the tulips, and finally 'come to an agreement about the most beautiful tulip. This was done in front of the whole flower society' (BF, p. 271). Although the two judges are undisputed 'flower authorities' (BF, p. 269), their decision-making must nevertheless be transparent and *coram populo*, if not collective. One can perhaps even see a political model in this. In any case, the public does not freeze in reverent silence in the face of the two luminaries, but participates loudly in the deliberation process (BF, p. 272). After the 'choice of [one] judge seems to meet with no approval at all', and the audience 'grumbled', 'some laughed and others mocked', the most delicate thing decides: the tulip, which has the least to show in its visual appearance, has a subtle but distinct 'violet scent'. The general cry of 'Violet scent!' that then permeates the tavern finally decides the *Concours*. The award-winning breeder is – of all people – the militant labour leader Jackson.

The form of workers' autonomous organisation that Weerth describes has no explicit reference to the tradition of guilds and journeymen's associations – unlike Weitling's Geneva Association or Weerth's own poems. Only the pure form of self-organisation on a professional basis could be referred to here. The organisation of the 'flower fellows' seems more justifiably to be interpreted as a forerunner of the workers' clubs and associations which, as the century progresses, will become an integral part of that proletarian counter-society that emerges with the establishment of the workers' movement.

What legitimises placing the 'Flower Festival' in the tradition of the guilds is solely the cultural-affective need to which the guilds – as Tieck depicts them – and journeymen's associations – in Weitling's version – form a response. The 'Flower Festival of the English Workers', as Weerth depicts it, stands in this line because here too, in this text and in the event that the text describes, one finds that human beings cannot live by bread alone – even and especially when bread is difficult to find. The special point of Tieck's *reinvention* of the guilds was that he did not break them down primarily in terms of their economic or socio-political protective and insurance function, but rather in terms of their representational function. In the 'representations of all kinds' provided by the guilds, the whole human being could express himself, along with all the passions and drives considered dysfunctional for socio-economic self-preservation, which are thus supposed to be cut off. The urge to step outside oneself and become something different, the drive for beauty or culture, which seeks to envelop useful things with beautiful ornaments that go beyond necessity and solely towards taste – all this, according to Leonhard, should retain its significance especially for people of lower status. They in particular – comforted by art and representations – should always be allowed to do more than simply reproduce their 'bare life'.

Weerth's 'Flower Festival' can also be read with this in mind. Weerth's first aim is to show that there is still a 'poetic passion' in the downtrodden and oppressed workers of northern England. They indulge in alcohol not simply because they are incapable of anything else (vicious version of pauper-hatred) or because they want to forget their misery (philanthropic version), but because drinking is part of the celebration, and the celebrations of the English workers are – 'poetic celebrations'. Thus the 'simple flower festival is all the more important because it has sprung from the people without any external cause' (BF, p. 274): it is not a defensive reaction, nor compensation, nor protest, but an expression of a poetic need that exists also among workers. *This* is the politically explosive message of the 'Flower Festival':

> Therein lies proof that the worker, alongside his political development, has still preserved in his heart a treasure of warm love for nature, a love which is the source of all poetry and which will one day enable him to carry a fresh literature, a new mighty art through the world. (BF, p. 274)

For Weerth, the class formation of the workers does *not only* take place as a political struggle; Weerth in no way negates or neglects the socio-political struggles of his time; on the contrary, these are consistently present in this text and others. The role of political struggle and political organisation are by no means denied; they are, however, relativised and placed in relation to a resource that remains closed to politics alone, but on which it nevertheless remains dependent. For Weerth, this other resource lies in the ability of the English workers 'to celebrate such splendid poetic festivals in spite of all tyranny'. This source of energy for proletarian politics feeds not only on hatred of one's living conditions and those responsible for them, but on love, 'love for nature'. This love 'in his heart' protects the worker from being poisoned inside by the life he is forced to lead.

The 'love for nature' is at the same time the 'source of all poetry' – and thus of a *poetry of class* in a double sense. On the one hand, Weerth has in mind a completely new, 'fresh literature, a new mighty art', to be created by workers and for workers (BF, p. 274). On the other hand, to build on Weerth's poetic argument, it is also about the poetic development of the working class – its emergence and self-emergence, its formation *as a class*. Weerth shows that political self-organisation alone is not enough for the class to create itself. The *poetry of class* – in the sense of its constitution or formation – cannot only be achieved through struggle and consciousness-raising, but also and again and again ('three times a year', says Weerth) through *poetry*: through beauty, passion, extravagance ('exuberance is beauty', says William Blake), through taste, education, nature, *culture*. This is the secret message that was passed along from Romanticism to the journeymen's clubs of the Vormärz and into the early workers' movement. This long-lost message, articulated over long stretches in an imaginary reference back to the guilds and journeymen traditions, must be taken up today and deciphered if we wish to rethink the emergence of the working class and its organisations.

CHAPTER 2

'We? Tricky Question!' on the Search for Class Identity in Proletarian Journals

> The deeds of the romantics were journals.
>
> CARL SCHMITT[1]

∴

In October 1848, Wilhelm Weitling intervened in the revolution occurring in Berlin. After falling out with Marx in the League of the Just in 1846 and, together with his followers, being expelled from the organisation, Weitling went to New York, where he took up a position as an editor of the socialist *Volks-Tribun* [*People's Tribune*], a weekly newspaper founded by former fraternity member turned communist Hermann Kriege. The slogan 'Up with labour! Down with capital!' was writ large on the front page of the newspaper.

After the outbreak of the revolutions in Europe, Weitling hurried back to the old continent and, after a stopover in Cologne, where he again quarrelled with Marx, ended up in Berlin in autumn. Upon arriving he published *Der Urwähler* [*The Primal Voter*], a new 'weekly paper'. The paper's subtitle, 'Organ of the Liberation League', is fictive – Weitling had indeed founded a 'Liberation League' during his time in New York, but no such organisation existed in Berlin. Weitling financed and edited the four issues of the paper largely on his own. Even as the course of events progressed, he remained completely isolated. Instead of the 'hundred thousand subscribers' which the opening article of the first issue demanded, *Der Urwähler* received a mere one hundred and fifty.[2] After the counter-revolutionary coup d'état in November 1848, Weitling was deported from Berlin by General Wrangel on 21 November. Weitling continued his agitational activities for several months in Hamburg before returning to the USA in 1849, disappointed.

---

1 Schmitt 2011, p. 36.

2 'Bless us with a hundred thousand subscribers and we promise you any victory you desire in the next elections', the first issue pompously states, *Der Urwähler*, No. 1 (October 1848), p. 3. The journal appeared in four issues in Berlin from October to November 1848.

 | DOI:10.1163/9789004685536_004

Weitling's interventions in *Der Urwähler* come across as outspoken from the very beginning, with the headline of the second article already promising substantial answers before immediately branching out into more and more questions:

> What reforms do we want?
>
> We? Tricky question! What don't we want? Who are we? Indeed, all of us. Which all? All of us in the party? All of us in the city, in the province, or in Germany? Does it include all *Bürger*, or only all the working classes? Is it only all shoemakers, all tailors, machinists, printers, or does it include everyone? Do all tradesman and craftsman belong to this all, or only some? What about the nobility, the army? Does it include the landowners or the factory owners, the poor or the rich, or both together?[3]

By deflecting the question about the goal of the reforms and reformulating it as a question about the 'we', Weitling illuminates a fundamental political dimension normally obscured by the presuppositions of day-to-day politics: the question of political subjectivation. Before a group can find its common interests and formulate demands so as to then be able to represent them politically, it must first identify itself as a group as such. Weitling exposes the mystification involved in thinking that interests and political 'desires' alone are capable of achieving this: prior to any question of how to frame political interests and demands in a way that would make them recognisable and representable, a preconception of the 'we' must be given at the very least.

The passage following the previous one reads:

> Where shall I pause to list all the individuals who constitute the we in question above? To answer this question, I will turn to the examples society provides us with. What a multitude of various associations, criss-crossing and fighting each other, each representing particular desires![4]

What 'multitude' is this? In his catalogue of questions, Weitling once again lays out the divisions in Vormärz society, running through all the principles which grounded different models of political subjectivation or different modes of possibly constituting a 'we' in the Vormärz: territory, profession, class, and status.

3 *Der Urwähler*, No. 1, pp. 3–5, here p. 3.

4 *Der Urwähler*, No. 1, p. 3.

The majority of Weitling's cascade of questions is concerned with spelling out the social distinctions within the category of *'Bürger'*: does 'all of us' really mean 'all *Bürger*', or is it 'only all the working classes?' Are workers the antithesis of the *'Bürger'*, or does the term include the latter as well? The open universality of 'all of us', which was mentioned earlier ('Indeed, all of us'), obviously requires limitations in order to assert a 'we' in the first place.

The questions continue: if the 'we' is supposed to extend to the 'working classes', does it really include 'all the working classes', or only some trades and crafts which can be distinguished and singled out? In any case, the shoemakers, tailors, machinists and printers mentioned are not just any trades – they formed the most active segments of the revolutionary craft-workers of the Vormärz period. Although shoemakers and tailors were traditional trades, they underwent a brutal process of proletarianisation very early on, and thus made up the nucleus of the crisis of craftsmanship and urban pauperism. The machinists, on the other hand, were among the new, highly skilled workers who took pride in the fact that what they produced was important to the process of industrialisation. Finally, because of the requirements of their trade, printers were the intellectuals among the workers. Both the misery experienced by workers in one trade and the superior position of those in another fed the revolutionary fervour that eventually drove them to the barricades and the forefront of the revolution.[5]

The next question invokes the well-nigh paradigmatically ambiguous figures of 'the tradesmen and craftsmen', whose class belonging remained controversial in the Vormärz. Do they belong to the 'working classes', or rather to the 'bourgeoisie' (in a delimited, exclusive sense)? Small shop owners had been denounced as henchmen of the counterrevolution as early as the July revolution of 1830 in Paris, an accusation which was also heard amidst the tumult of the March revolution in Berlin. But at the same time, several protagonists of the early workers' movement worked as sales clerks and commissars themselves, and at the very least many of the movement's abounding journal projects were driven by leaders with a commercial training: Friedrich Engels, Georg Weerth, Ferdinand Freiligrath.

With the mention of the 'nobility' and the 'army', Weitling recalls the powers of the old order, who began the massive operation of mounting their forces just weeks after the publication of the article. The proclamation of a state of siege in Berlin and other Prussian cities on 12 November 1848 spelled the end

---

5 On the possibility of deriving the intensity of 'working class militancy' from the social position of various trades, see the debate between Rancière, Sewell and Christopher Johnson: Rancière 1983; Sewell 1983; Johnson 1983.

of the revolution for the time being. Finally, the 'landowners' and 'factory owners' bring to mind figures of both the new and old power, whose will for reform was certainly of an entirely different nature than that of the 'working classes'.

In these passages, Weitling displays the boundless potential of the political 'we'. At the end of his catalogue of questions, Weitling names the ultimately decisive opposition for him, as the sequel to the article will show: do 'the poor or the rich' form the 'we' of reform – 'or both together?' Even though it appears at the height of his provocation, this relativising follow-up question cannot go unanswered.

Before taking up the different answers to the question of who made up the 'we' capable of changing society, one should pause to appreciate the openness of Weitling's question. In his impartiality, he provides an adequate summary of the debates of the Vormärz as they appeared in the culture of journals and yearbooks, which will be examined below. Weitling was right to leave his question open-ended, since the society of the time was in motion; it was a highly dynamic society in transition, one that could only be conceived as the result of different tendencies 'criss-crossing and fighting each other'.

The journals of this period test out various proposals concerning the conditions and possibilities for constituting a political 'we'. In the process, one can observe conceptual history at work in the journals. Crucially, this work of linguistic and conceptual politics is carried out in public: *who are we, and who are you?* From the very beginning, the question of who one speaks to and from what position is political, and for that reason it can only be settled publicly.

1 Negations: 'Bourgeois' and 'Intellectual Prolatarians'

Who is this 'we'? In the beginning is the *negation*: no, we are not proletarians! Arnold Ruge, the editor of the *Anekdota zur neuesten deutschen Philosophie und Publicistik* [*Anecdotes on the Latest German Philosophy and Journalism*], a yearbook project that was intended to push the Young Hegelian school in the direction of becoming a 'party' or a political group, insisted on this point in 1843.[6] Contributors to the *Anekdota* included the crème de la crème of the Hegelian left, such as Bruno Bauer, Ludwig Feuerbach, Friedrich Köppen, Karl Nauwerck, and Ruge himself.[7] Anyone who claimed that they

6 Ruge 1843.

7 The names of those listed are mentioned named on the title page of the journal along with 'a few unnamed' (among whom Marx had long been suspected).

were only 'a few proletarian individuals' contributed to the 'sham', which ultimately hindered the emergence of a truly free press in Germany.[8] Why is that so?

The *Anekdota* was founded in response to the ongoing censorship of the *Halleschen Jahrbücher für deutsche Wissenschaft und Kunst* [*Halle Yearbooks for German Science and Art*] and the *Deutschen Jahrbücher für Wissenschaft und Kunst* [*German Yearbooks for Science and Art*]; the journal tasked itself with remedying the 'woes of censorship' and working towards 'an honest freedom of the press'.[9]

Like his colleague Feuerbach, Ruge was also a habilitated philosopher who was denied a teaching post at the university for political reasons. After the equally politically motivated demotion of Bruno Bauer from his position as chair of Protestant Theology at the University of Bonn in 1842 (and the suspension of his *venia legendi* for life!) – Friedrich Wilhelm IV led a bitter struggle against the 'dragon seed of Hegelian pantheism' from the very beginning of his term in office in 1840 – the heads of the Young Hegelian movement were all barred access to university positions. The relegation of the Arabist Nauwerck followed in 1844, and Bauer's confidant Karl Marx, who was a few years younger, abandoned his attempts to gain habilitation prematurely. In light of this turn of events, the political struggle waged by the Young Hegelian party became much more self-referential than it had been in its initial years: the *Anekdota* first deals with 'censorship', 'freedom of press', 'educational freedom', and 'political freedom' before turning to philosophy and theology. The journal's aspirations were scientific, and its creators and contributors understood themselves as the true representatives of science, a pursuit which was no longer possible in German universities.

To declare the press to be the only true outlet for science and criticism lends an enormous value to the concept of the press. For Ruge, a true Hegelian, working in the press is no everyday task – i.e. journalism – but rather a privileged manifestation of spirit. If spirit can no longer encounter and realise itself in

8 See Ruge 1843, Vol. I, 'Die Presse und die Freiheit [The Press and Freedom]', pp. 93–116, here p. 111.

9 Unpaginated, two-page 'preface' to the *Anekdota*, Ruge 1843, Vol. I. The *Anekdota* were published by the Literarisches Comptoir in Winterthur near Zurich. The publishing house was founded in 1840 by the German liberal Julius Fröbel in order to specifically publish literature that had been banned in Germany. It quickly became the leading publisher of Vormärz literature and journalism. In 1845–6, the young Gottfried Keller also published his first literary works in the publishing house of his friend Fröbel. On Fröbel and his publishing house, see Grab 1987, pp. 217–56. The history of the yearbooks has recently been comprehensively documented by M. Hundt 2010.

science, as Hegel had intended, then the press must transform from a 'discussion of the people to itself' to a 'discussion of universal spirit with itself'. The press, as an 'organ of collective thought', must be able to act freely and without any hindrances, since otherwise 'public reason' itself will be obstructed and an 'explicitly self-reflective human species' as a whole becomes impossible.[10] Indeed, these are the consequences of 'censorship' and the 'police state'.[11]

In the wake of this immense loading of the press and the press-writer, Ruge considers it necessary to counter the personal vilification afflicting the proponents of the Young Hegelian movement in a decisive manner: no, what is said about these '*innovators* among writers' is not true. They are *not* 'only a few prolatarian [*sic*] individuals, propertyless, ill-willed troublemakers and deluded idealists, who will never win over the prudent masses, who are intent on quiet earnings and a dutiful life'.[12] In order to effectively counter this slander, 'a historical turnaround is needed' through which 'the concept of the *free citizen* … will be born alongside that of the *free writer*, and the sham which claims that the free writers were only free because they were *bourgeois* prolatarians [will] cease'. Finally, specifying further, Ruge states that he and his comrades-in-arms should not be regarded as '*intellectual* prolatarians' either.[13]

There are several things worth noticing in these passages. For instance, the apparently not yet standardised use of language – prolatarian instead of proletarian – points to a not yet standardised social configuration: the word 'prola/etarian' is used here more as a pejorative or a disparaging accusation than as a description of a real class position. Placed alongside the 'ill-willed troublemakers', Ruge's 'prolatariat' even begins to resemble Hegel's 'rabble'.

However, if one attempts to read Ruge's characterisation of the 'prolatarian individuals' in a reasonably unbiased manner, it must be admitted that these accusations are indeed a fitting description of the author himself and his colleagues, especially those he wins over at the same time for his new project, the *Deutsch–Französische Jahrbücher* [*German-French Yearbooks*]. For they are all 'propertyless', which is why they have to take on jobs as 'free writers'; they can also be called 'ill-willed troublemakers' as long as one is not willing to confuse the prevailing calm with a reasonable order; and it is partially justified to call the Young Hegelians 'deluded idealists' insofar as theirs is an idealism which, in its contrived over-articulation and with its short-circuits between the current

10 Ruge 1843, Vol. 1, 'Presse', pp. 96–7.

11 Ruge 1843, Vol. 1, 'Presse', starting at p. 102.

12 Ruge 1843, Vol. 1, 'Presse', p. 111.

13 Ruge 1843, Vol. 1, 'Presse', p. 112. A few years later, Ruge's 'prolatarians' will appear in Wilhelm Heinrich Riehl as 'proletarians of intellectual labour', cf. Riehl 1866, pp. 312–49.

political (and by all means also individual) situation and the history of world spirit, sometimes threatens to tip over into the ridiculous or the unintentionally comical. Indeed, the polemics of Max Stirner and Karl Marx, which appeared a little later, attest to the fact that the group was perceived this way by its contemporaries.[14] And finally, that 'the prudent masses, who are intent on quiet earnings and a dutiful life', kept their distance from the philosophical extravagance of the Young Hegelians rather than letting themselves be infected by it, is a historical fact that even Ruge was forced to concede.

One can thus confidently read Ruge's defence against the accusation of representing merely 'prolatarian individuals' as a *negation* in the Freudian sense, wherein *everything negated is in fact true*; and like every negation, Ruge's also provides a special clairvoyance often lacking in positive self-descriptions. The fact that 'free writers' can only rightly be called 'free' because they are 'bourgeois prolatarians' already anticipates the irony which Marx will use to describe the 'double' freedom of the wage labourer in *Capital*: the 'free writer' is only conceivable as a proletarianised writer, one who may live 'free of everything', but must therefore also surrender himself to the market, for better or worse.[15] Ruge himself, like so many of his generation, was familiar enough with this way of life. Precisely because he could not (or did not want to) hold office as a scholar, that is to say, take up a permanent post as a professor, he had to become a 'intellectual prolatarian' and distinguish himself as a journalist until finally, in old age, he kowtowed intellectually to the new Hohenzollern Empire – as did Bruno Bauer, however, much more quickly – and was rewarded with an annual honorary salary by Bismarck in 1877.

By way of negation, Ruge sees with astonishing clarity the future of the 'proletaroid intelligentsia' (Max Weber) that had been shaping the political and journalistic debates with great persistence since the Vormärz began (and up to the present), especially concerning class issues. Again and again, these debates will revolve around whether the proletarianised intellectuals are able to situate themselves as 'prolatarians' – the 'a' may be left as a marker of a socio-cultural *différance* – among other proletarians of different backgrounds, or whether they cling to a hard (and here that means above all cultural) difference in an effort to distinguish themselves from the 'rabble'.

Taking a look at the intellectuals of his time, Ruge sees very clearly that the process of proletarianisation also threatens to create divisions. For example, the dismissal of the 'free writers' as 'intellectual prolatarians' by interested

14 Cf. Stirner 2018; Marx and Engels 1845, *The Holy Family*, in: MECW 4, pp. 5–211.

15 Marx 1976, p. 272. Translation revised.

parties was 'eagerly nourished ... because this tears apart the world of writers and scholars into two hostile camps'.[16] The designation 'prolatarian' was degrading for some and provoked fears of being demoted in others. This insight reveals Ruge's implicit awareness that in societies organised in a market form, the profession of writing, whether intellectual or not, is *always* subject to the omnipresent threat of rabbleisation. Thus every 'free writer', every intellectual without a permanent post is and remains a 'virtual pauper'.[17] Tieck was also familiar with the dangers of proletarianisation and pauperisation, not only because he was the son of a craftsman who had experienced the dark side of the emerging freedom of trade in his childhood, but rather due to the fact that he was a 'free' proletarianised professional writer who received payment for his writing by the line and was only able to escape this precarious mode of existence from time to time by taking refuge with his friends from the ranks of the old aristocratic elites. Of course, Tieck could and would never fully accept that he himself belonged to those proletarian strata whose emergence he himself so clear-sightedly observes in his writing. After 1841, over the course of his final years, Tieck's 'bourgeois prolatarian' life was supported by an honorary salary from Friedrich Wilhelm IV.

2 Ascension: 'We' Want to Be *Bürger*

The 'foreword' to the *Deutschen Bürgerbuch für 1845*, edited by Hermann Püttmann, begins with a conceptual and political reflection on 'the word "*Bürger*" in the title of this book'. What seems to be important is not only who is called a *Bürger*, but who uses the term. The word

> can be defined in many ways, or rather the predicate '*Bürger*' has been applied to various classes or fractions of humanity in the state: the representative of the so-called middle class in Germany, the *loyal subject* or one who obeys submissively, for example, is sometimes euphemistically called a *Bürger* by the authorities, while the students call him a philistine, the military call him a conformist, the aristocrats call him a scoundrel and others call him other things. He is the *bourgeois* of the French, the inept member of the existing order whose first duty and highest purpose is passivity.[18]

16 Ruge 1843, Vol. I, 'Presse', pp. 112–13.
17 Marx 1993, p. 604.
18 Püttmann 1845, 'Vorwort', pp. III–VIII, here p. III.

Unlike the 'bourgeois', Püttmann will not champion the 'republican *citoyen*', as Ruge did in modelling the 'free writer' on the '*free citizen*'.[19] According to Püttmann, although the 'citoyen' may appear to be a 'better species', it is already historically obsolete, even in France: 'In Germany we are not familiar with this figure, nor do we have any desire to get to know him'. It can be assumed that the distinction between *bourgeois* and *citoyen* does not suit the needs of the *Bürgerbuch*, since Püttmann has recognised that both sides of the distinction complement each other – whoever demands the *citoyen* cannot escape the *bourgeois*.[20]

To counteract the vast array of existing conceptual and political entanglements, the *Bürgerbuch* proposes a definition of the word '*Bürger*' that emerges from an analysis of the present political situation and then uses it unflinchingly for its own ends:

> What we need, what *we* want to call a *Bürger* for the time being, is the *educated person* who wants to become an *active member* of a *social arrangement*, based on *free morality*, in a union of all for all, in which the whole protects the whole.[21]

What is modestly presented as an 'explanation' intended to 'prevent misinterpretations of the term' is ultimately a socialist-communist party programme *in nuce*. Somewhat later, the *Bürgerbuch* will openly identify as a 'socialist yearbook'.[22]

Clearly, this deliberate act of naming – 'what we want to call a *Bürger*' – designates a political subject that is at odds with the usual segmentations, with the 'various classes or fractions of humanity within the state'. Precisely because of its ambiguity, the word '*Bürger*' seems to lend itself particularly well to this act of designation – far more so than the word 'prola/etarian' at any rate, which was too derogatory as a term. The word '*Bürger*', despite all its echoes of conformist narrow-mindedness, still has enough genuine potential to lend a sense of dignity that would validate the new socialist cause as well. At the same time, however, the very act of naming is intended to give the word a new meaning.

---

19 Ruge 1843, Vol. I, 'Presse', p. 112.

20 In his text 'On the Jewish Question' published in the *Deutsch-Französische Jahrbücher*, Marx elaborated on the explosive contradiction of this distinction: whoever affirms the 'citoyen' must not only accept the 'bourgeois' as a subject, but also the capitalist 'bourgeois' who socially and economically undermines the political equality of the 'citoyens' (Marx 1844, 'On the Jewish Question', MECW 3, pp. 146–74).

21 Püttmann 1845, 'Vorwort', pp. III–IV.

22 Püttmann 1845, 'Vorwort', p. VII.

From this point on, one could say, the word '*Bürger*' should evoke the principles of a socialist society in every speaker and listener; however, this redefinition of the term should also supplant the implications of the 'loyal subject' and the 'free market citizen'.

The desire to upgrade one's position as a speaking subject ('what *we* want to call a *Bürger* for the time being') may also be due to a concrete desire for those working in journalism to redefine themselves. Unlike the Young Hegelians, the creators and contributors of the *Bürgerbuch*, who were on average ten years younger, had long since ceased to have to face the high-strung expectations of the educated classes. Hermann Püttmann, Moses Hess, Karl Heinzen, Wilhelm Wolff, Georg Weerth, Friedrich Engels and Ferdinand Freiligrath all dropped out of university, were expelled for political reasons or never attended in the first place: Weerth and Freiligrath, for example, completed commercial apprenticeships. Some, such as Karl Grün or Ernst Dronke, did graduate, but never made an effort to pursue a university career, and instead worked as journalists or freelance writers. Proletarianisation – the necessity of securing one's own existence through wage labour and paid writing – is a constant factor for these people. Thus, on the one hand, there is the desire to advance 'upwards', to ascend to the bourgeoisie, at least in terms of self-designation; on the other hand, however, the independence and freedom of the 'free wage labourers' – and wage-writers – asserts itself as a desire to carry out this nominal ascension *on their own terms*. They do not want to be subsumed under the blanket term '*Bürger*' without first recalibrating it to their own political standards: 'what *we want* to call a *Bürger* for the time being'.

The struggle for the power to name is clearly part of the *invention* of the bourgeoisie's own tradition, the invention of a counter-tradition of anti-bourgeois bourgeoise. The latent self-destructive potential of this constellation will emerge within the workers' movement in the decades that follow, for example, when the 'respectable' parts of the proletariat join the 'civic militias' during the revolution and take up arms against their less submissive class brothers and sisters.

Even at the time, the attempt made by those involved in the *Bürgerbuch* to use political and journalistic concepts to cut across old fronts by redefining themselves as '*Bürger*' of the Vormärz opposition was already seen as a failure. In a letter to Marx, Moses Hess, one of the journal's most important contributors and behind-the-scenes masterminds, got upset about the 'stupid mishmash' that the *Bürgerbuch* presented to the readers.[23] Due to the 'strange

23 Hess to Marx on 17 January 1845 from Cologne, Hess 1959, p. 105. The same letter shows that the *Bürgerbuch* was distributed with a circulation of three thousand copies.

assortment' of material, most reviews were unable to detect a unified political line, instead criticising the fact that the liberal-bourgeois tendency of authors like Jacob Venedey or Karl Heinzen did not fit in with the clearly socialist programme of Hess or Weerth, thus in retrospect the *Bürgerbuch* can even be seen as a 'farewell between [these] two currents'.[24]

Hess promises Marx that he will exert his influence with Püttmann so that he will soon only produce '*pure* socialist' books – which indeed happened that same year.[25] By publishing the *Rheinischen Jahrbüchern zur gesellschaftlichen Reform* [*Rhenish Yearbooks on Social Reform*] in 1845 and 1846, Püttmann launched a direct competitor to his own *Bürgerbuchern* of 1845 and 1846. The *Jahrbüchern*, however, openly and uncompromisingly promote the 'doctrine of communism', that 'wisdom of life which has finally become practical' and which 'must incorporate all doctrines of the past', as the 'Foreword' demands.[26]

Engels, shrewd tactician that he was, spares himself any distress over the indecisive character of the *Bürgerbuch*; for him, it fulfilled its task by showing communist agitators 'how far one can go without being locked up or thrown out' under conditions of censorship and repression.[27] In the same letter, Engels discloses to Marx his plans for his own journalistic project, the *Gesellschaftsspiegel* [*Mirror of Society*], which he planned to publish shortly thereafter together with Hess. In this journal, the appeals to bourgeois culture will serve as a cover to smuggle the real cause to the reader under the table, so to speak.

3 Activation: What 'We' Should Be

Between May 1845 and July 1846, twelve issues of the *Gesellschaftsspiegel* were published by '[Julius] Baedeker, the communist bookseller' in Elberfeld.[28] Moses Hess was the editor.[29] Friedrich Engels was directly involved in at least the conceptual design and publication of the first issues, although his name is listed only as an author, not as someone responsible for the publication. For

24 The quotations are taken from a contemporary review in the *Trier'sche Zeitung* on 7 and 13 March 1845, quoted in Pelger 1975, p. XXVI.

25 Hess 1959, p. 105.

26 Püttmann 1845/1846, 'Vorwort', Vol. I, pp. III–VI, hier p. IV.

27 Engels to Marx, 20 January 1845, MECW 38, p. 16.

28 Engels to Marx, October 1844, MECW 38, p. 5.

29 As early as the end of 1845, Bädeker reprints the first six issues of the journal unchanged in a single volume, the cover of which names 'M. Hess' as editor. Hess's name is not on the cover of the individual issues however.

example, authorship of the articles 'On the Condition of the Working Class in England' in issue three and 'The Moral and Spiritual Condition of the Working Classes in England' in issues four and five are attributed to him. These pieces are modified excerpts from Engels' epoch-making book *The Condition of the Working Class in England*, which was also published in 1845.[30] The publication of book and journal must be seen as parallel endeavours, complementing each other in the campaign to popularise communism in Germany. The lectures given by Hess and Engels must also be understood within this context.[31] On the one hand, the journal was intended to publicise Engels' book, and on the other hand, to supplement and complete the results of Engels' investigations in England with investigations of a similar nature in Germany. Engels' book was tremendously important not only for the study of living and working conditions in the Vormärz period, but also for the development of empirical social research based on participant observation and for the establishment of the literary genre of empirically supported documentation of social conditions. In all these different fields, the *Gesellschaftsspiegel* can be seen as a mere supplement to Engels' work. However, there is one aspect of the journal which exceeds Engels' other literary outputs both conceptually and in terms of results, that is, its decidedly activist and agitational disposition. Empirical observation and reporting is distributed among many individuals; the journal is planned as a collective research project.

While the journal was still in its planning phase, the founders sent out a two-page prospectus penned by Hess.[32] Hess describes the intention behind the new journal, asserting that the project not only plans to research and document the 'condition of the working classes', as is written in the prospectus, but also to politicise and change those conditions. The subtitle makes this double objective clear: *Organ for the Representation of the Propertyless Classes and for the Clarification of the Social Conditions of the Present*. The journal will also show – not so much in what it *preaches* as in what it *does* and how it does it – that the goal of 'representation' always presupposes a certain 'clarification' of social conditions, and that such a 'clarification' must be seen in itself as a form of 'representation'. 'Clarification' (in the sense of investigation, enlight-

30 MECW 4, pp. 295–583.

31 Cf. the anonymous contribution 'Versammlungen in Elberfeld [Meetings in Elberfeld]', in Püttmann 1845/1846, Vol. I, pp. 35–97.

32 In the book edition of the first six issues of *Der Gesellschaftsspiegel*, the prospectus was prefixed to the first issue, unpaginated. The references to the German are given below as Hess 1845/1846, [I] and [II], and translated as 'To the Readers of and Contributors to the *Gesellschaftsspiegel*' in MECW 4. pp. 671–4.

enment) and 'representation' are linked by a *certain form of presentation*, or a particularly configured representation. It is no coincidence that the prospectus so thoroughly details the forms of presentation and modes of writing that the new journal intends to test out.

The comprehensive programme which unifies 'representation' and 'enlightenment' – or, in the words of Hess's early biographer Theodor Zlocisti, 'arousing and organizing' – is already revealed in the title of the prospectus: 'To the Readers and Staff of *Gesellschaftsspiegel*'.[33] The first paragraph makes clear that the 'and' here functions as an appellative and not an additive:

> The noble striving to hasten to the aid of suffering humanity, which, to the credit of the 19th century, manifests itself everywhere at the present time, has not yet in Germany a central press organ giving publicity on the one hand to the evils which must be remedied, and on the other to the proposed or already implemented measures for their redress, and casting light on their success or failure. We hereby submit to the public the first issue of such an organ, and hope that every friend of humanity will feel prompted to support the *Gesellschaftsspiegel* with appropriate reports.[34]

Behind the classical humanist mask of a 'noble striving', the concern becomes very concrete: the 'evils in our social life' are to be given 'publicity' so that the reader can familiarise himself with them and at the same time get an idea of the relief measures that are already being implemented. The journal explicitly aims to 'help the *associations* which are being formed to eliminate the social evils', but the most important, *central* function of the journal lies in its role as a repository of struggles. The 'evils' are being fought 'everywhere at the present time' by such associations and perhaps also by individual 'friend[s] of humanity' who would benefit from knowing more about each other. The various efforts need a 'central organ' that brings together the local initiatives – 'networks', one would say today – and initiates a collective learning process. The public is not addressed as a passive 'audience', but as a cast of potential collaborators. Whether the journal and its creators really live up to the high standard they set themselves will be discussed at the end of our examination of the *Gesellschaftsspiegel*.

As the prospectus progresses, it becomes clear why the *Gesellschaftsspiegel* relies on this kind of cooperation: if the aim is to explore the 'condition of

33 Zlocisti 1921, p. 179.

34 Hess 1845/1846, Prospectus, pp. [1]. MECW 4, pp. 671–674, here, p. 671.

the working classes', then this is certainly meant in a 'micrological and socio-empirical' sense.[35] The goal is to shed light on the tiniest minutiae of the living spaces of the '*large towns*' and their '*disreputable areas*'; furthermore, attention will also be paid to 'every single instance of oppression of the workers' in the '*industrial and factory districts*' where the 'working classes' are employed.[36] The 'correspondents' will provide the 'most accurate reports on this subject giving names, places and dates':

> If in factories working hours are too long or night work is resorted to, if workers are obliged to clean machines in their spare time, if factory-owners are brutal or tyrannical towards their workers, lay down tyrannical working regulations, pay wages in goods instead of money – we shall especially fight this infamous truck system wherever and in whatever forms or disguises it occurs – if workers are forced to work in unhealthy premises or to live in unsatisfactory lodgings belonging to the factory-owner – in a word, whenever any act of injustice is committed by the capitalists against the workers, we ask everybody who is in a position to do so to inform us on this score as soon and as exactly as possible.[37]

The twelve issues of the journal meticulously cover the points mentioned above. Each issue is divided into two sections. The first, editorial section contains three to five longer articles printed in block and sometimes signed by individual names. This section also includes political analyses, theoretical discussions, reports from different countries and regions, reviews and updates on the activities of the various workers' and aid associations. The first article of each issue is entitled 'The Social Conditions of the Civilised World', the first of which was written by Hess.[38] The editorials of the following issues are written by other authors and often include summary translations of benchmark foreign-language texts on the social situation of the time, such as Eugène Buret's standard work from 1840, *De la misère des classes labourieuses en Angleterre et en France*.[39]

35 Mohl 1971, p. IV.
36 Hess 1845/1846, Prospectus, [I]. MECW 4, pp. 672.
37 Hess 1845/1846, Prospectus, [I]/[II]. MECW 4, pp. 672–3.
38 Hess 1845/1846, No. 1, p. 1.
39 Hess 1845/1846, No. 1, pp. 3–9; No. 2, pp. 35–39. Buret's work placed the pauperism debate of the 1840s on a new empirical basis; the data that Buret compiled in his two-volume work was repeatedly quoted and utilised up to the revolution, for instance, in Marx's Paris Manuscripts. Marx 1844, *Economic and Philosophical Manuscripts*, MECW 3, pp. 229–346, here p. 244. and pp. 256–7.

The second section of each issue, titled 'News and Notes', is printed in two columns in smaller type. This section contains short texts sent in by readers which indicate the place and date from which they originate, but appear anonymously – in part to protect the authors from political repression. These texts report on the condition of the *local* working classes. In the first issue, this particular section offers a case history about the distressed weaver Karl Klaus from Barmen, news about the 'truck wage system' in Solingen, 'extortion' in Cologne and the 'trade in notarial auction deeds' on the Rhine, the 'consequences of parental hardship' in Trier, the 'revision of poor relief' in Düsseldorf, on 'poverty in the Hunsrück' and 'coal mining' in Essen, on the new hunting laws in Silesia, on the 'abolition of corporal punishment in penitentiaries', on an 'association for promoting education for craftsmen' in Hamburg, and on 'workers' unrest' in Bohemia.[40] The topics covered here will be varied and enriched in the following issues, with a focus on the housing question, wage disputes, the judicial and prison systems, organisational issues (news from workers' associations, strikes, unrest) and economic policy issues (customs tariffs and free trade, sales crises, servants' and craftsmen's regulations), in addition to discussions on the problem of emigration.[41]

The 'News and Notes' section deals with a whole range of different proletarian forms of life grouped by country. 'Germany' is followed by 'France' and 'England', sometimes 'Switzerland' and 'America'. The foreign news articles are often translations of press reports. In the *Gesellschaftsspiegel*, the scope of what fits under the topic 'condition of the working classes' is obviously not so narrowly defined, and the subject of the 'working classes' (in the plural) is also still broadly defined. In addition to wage labourers in factories and cottage industries, the category of working classes also includes small farmers and winegrowers, servants, domestic workers, prostitutes, day labourers, craftsmen (journeymen and small master craftsmen) and inmates of penitentiaries and poorhouses. Rather than being theoretically derived, the internal plurality of class determination in 'News and Notes' comes from a process of summation. This open-ended method for determining the subject matter at hand – which is also found, for example, in Weitling – corresponds to an openness of additive linguistic determination, which proceeds by gathering an assortment of terms. In the preface to *The Condition of the Working Class in England*, Engels had already announced that he will 'continually use the expressions workingmen

40 Hess 1845/1846, No. 1, [pp. 1–14], the '*Nachrichten und Notizen*' [News and Notes] are not paginated.

41 On the new prison in Cologne, see Hess 1845/1846, No. 2, [pp. 33–6].

and proletarians, working class, propertyless class and proletariat as equivalents'; the same terminological elasticity prevails in the language used in the *Gesellschaftsspiegel*.[42]

Even in retrospect, it is remarkable that an author like Moses Hess, who until then had mostly published lofty philosophical texts, delves into the minutiae of the empirical day-to-day struggles of the working classes with great patience and without any plan for all of the material to culminate in some theoretical or political output.[43] It is precisely this empirical and local orientation that makes the *Gesellschaftsspiegel* the only project of its time capable of delivering on the promise of creating a 'proletarian public sphere' which contains a diversity of voices that corresponds to the real heterogeneity of the Vormärz proletariat, yet which nevertheless remains *one* public sphere.[44] The journal's particular ability to live up to this promise is due to the fact that its creators manage to withdraw completely into the empirical accounts they themselves collected without sacrificing the larger vision of the overall project. Considering this delimitation, one could almost speak of a certain humility on the part of the theoretically versed, philosophically savvy authors vis-à-vis a reality which they themselves did not yet have a grasp of and which they only became acquainted with through their project. Wolfgang Essbach gave an emphatic summary of the promise:

> For a moment, and perhaps the year 1845 is this moment, it seems as if Hess and Marx might be satisfied with a proletarian public sphere. It seemed as if theory had been submerged in a great chorus of proletarian voices, as if the hope had been fulfilled that this proletarian public sphere would succeed in abolishing the political limitations of the bourgeois public sphere and its party system to make way for an even more comprehensive community of communication.[45]

42 Engels 1844, MECW 4, p. 304. In the *Gesellschaftsspiegel*, too, there exists the 'working class(es)' in singular and plural, as well as 'worker(s)' and 'proletarian(s)', along with the 'propertyless class(es)', again in singular and plural.

43 Parallel to the *Gesellschaftsspiegel*, Hess published the treatise 'Über das Geldwesen' [On the Essence of Money] in the first volume of the *Rheinische Jahrbücher*, which presents a first, already very far-reaching attempt to apply Feuerbach's theological critique to political economy.

44 On the importance of the *Gesellschaftsspiegel* in the constitutive phase of the labour movement, see Na'aman 1978, starting at p. 39, and Mehring 1963, pp. 170–5.

45 Essbach 1988, p. 279.

This moment should not be underestimated; in the history of proletarian (counter-)public spheres in Germany, an experiment like the *Gesellschaftsspiegel* must be regarded as a significant and long-forgotten 'opportunity not taken'. At the same time, however, one cannot help but regard the experiment a failure; not because constraints arising from censorship and financial hardships led the journal to be discontinued after one year, since this happened to all journal projects of the time, and usually much more quickly. A more accurate conclusion would be that the project and its specific orientation was continually confronted with internal limits pertaining to outdated ideas of authorship and who it was addressed to.

The journal's open-ended and at the same time detail-obsessed approach to its subject matter corresponds to a strange cluelessness in determining the addressee: the journal states that 'everyone' can become a contributor through 'communication'. Almost helplessly and quite conventionally, the last paragraph of the prospectus finally specifies the addressees by asking 'especially the pastors, school teachers, doctors and civil servants for friendly cooperation in the interest of the cause'. Parallel to the appeal to the old pastoral elites, the speaker's position developed in the journal also threatens to lapse into that of an *advocate*. In any case, the 'working classes' themselves are never addressed as possible readers or collaborators, but are instead treated as an object of concern. The perspective of the *Gesellschaftsspiegel* thus remains that of an outsider: it is the view of a doctor who analyses 'the diseases of the social body' and takes scrupulous care not to get infected by his patients.

Essbach notes that 'the resurrection of theory as a particular institution' took place precisely 'at the moment of its going underground', and then describes historically how 'Brussels became a centre of the exile community, where Marx, Hess and Engels joined forces'. This

> communist 'Correspondence Committee' that the three of them founded in Brussels at the beginning of 1846 is nothing less than the germinal form of a new type of political party. The secret society is still the predominant form at this time. The 'Correspondence Committee' draws up directives which every communist has to follow, while itself being tasked with writing reports on different situations and sending them to the central office. The aim of the committee is to steer the convictions within the international communist movement. It is now no longer a question of disseminating the spirit through mere *participation* in the proletarian public sphere, but of disseminating the spirit through a *power structure behind* the public sphere.[46]

46 Essbach 1988, p. 279.

This account by Essbach makes use of an obvious and clearly deliberate anachronism: as of 1846, there did not yet exist *the* global communist movement, that is to say a movement which would be steered centrally as the Comintern (including Lenin's 'party of a new type') will do in the 1920s and as the neo-Leninists in the K-groups of the 1970s will imagine in their fantasies of omnipotence. It remains true, however, that even in the analytical perspective and speaker position of the *Gesellschaftsspiegel* – and not only in the secret institution in Brussels – a sovereign distance is forged, one which prevents the formation of a universally inclusive 'we' in Weitling's sense. The creators and writers of the journal never count themselves amongst the 'working classes' with whom they are concerned; they do not attempt in the least to construct a 'we' that would bring together the subject writing with those described in the journal. Even the newly recruited reader/collaborator, who are included *as collaborators* in the 'we' of the journal creators, perhaps for this very reason never themselves belong to the 'working classes' which form the object of their reports. It also seems – at least the often paternalist tone of the reports seems to suggest – that the large majority of those who responded to the invitation to collaborate were actually the pastoral elites, who were addressed directly.

Just as the *Gesellschaftsspiegel* contests the possibility of a neutral, impartial representation of social conditions by tying 'clarification' to 'representation', it in turn erects an opaque surface behind which the critics of the conditions hide. A political subjectivisation of the 'working classes', whose lives the *Gesellschaftsspiegel* constantly evokes, does not take place. The proletariat remains a mute object, since the creators of the journal are not willing or able to understand themselves as proletarians.

4 Affirmation: 'We' Who Raise Our Voices

At the end of this short review of proletarian journals, which attempted to determine the revolutionary 'we' of the Vormärz, we come back to the beginning. Weitling's 'tricky question' from the revolutionary period – the question concerning the real 'we' of the revolution – can be most concisely answered by making reference to the first articles from Weitling's first journal project from 1841, the *Hülferuf der deutschen Jugend*. Within the thriving journal scene of the 1840s, a theoretical and organisational process of division and escalation takes place. For example, in 1846 Püttmann programmatically titled the editorial of *Prometheus* – his next, by that time third journal project in two years – 'Friend and Enemy': here, determining the 'we' only becomes possible through demarcating and declaring an enemy.[47] In retrospect, however, this process of division allows a certain radicality to emerge, one which makes the universally inclusive programme and transversal, motley subject constitution of the *Hülferuf* distinct.

On the title page of the first issue of the *Hülferuf* there is a short, untitled text that anticipates the gesture of mobilisation found in the *Gesellschaftsspiegel*:

> We call upon every German day-labourer, peasant, worker, master, artist and scholar who wishes to add his good will and practical experience to send us news postage-free about the craftsmen's state of education, the conditions of work and wages, to include how much their needs cost, and to accompany this report with advice on improving the situation of the workers.[48]

The addressees and possible contributors named in this passage – in the next article they too will be addressed as 'collaborators' – are situated much lower on the social hierarchy than the intellectuals addressed by the *Gesellschaftsspiegel*, and it also does not consist of '*Bürger*' in the usual sense of the term.[49] By beginning with day labourers, Weitling manages to construct a series of addressees that climbs up the social ladder, but which nonetheless remains bound to the lowest positions of society. As a prototypical proletarian subject without any security stemming from status or tradition, the day labourer provides the paradigm of the series; the masters are mentioned in the sequence alongside artists and scholars, all who appear quite naturally in this arrangement as 'prolatarian individuals'. When the short text ends by stating that even 'reports from physicians ... on the harmful effects of the various trades on the health of the workers' would be 'very welcomed' by the editors, the physician is understood here as a local specialist with a specific valuable perspective, and no longer as a generally privileged reader/collaborator.[50]

This text operates through a complex interweaving of collective economic and political denominations which also characterise the entire programme of the *Hülferuf*: the 'we', which calls on people to 'send us news postage-free', is already identified and socially marked in the journal's subtitle: *Der Hülferuf der deutschen Jugend. Herausgegeben und redigiert von einigen deutschen Arbeitern* [*Cry for Help of German Youth: Published and Edited by Some German Workers*].

47 Püttmann 1846b, 'Freund und Feind' [Friend and Enemy], pp. 3–25.
48 *Hülferuf* 1841, No. 1, p. 1.
49 *Hülferuf* 1841, No. 1, p. 6.
50 *Hülferuf* 1841, No. 1, p. 6.

But the 'workers' now also appear in the list of addressees, between peasants and craftsmen/masters; 'workers' thus designates at once a segment of the class that is at issue, in addition to the class in its entirety. The category 'workers' serves as an operator of universalisation, it refers to 'all', 'all of us': 'we have addressed all working classes, indeed all classes of society; this proves that our voice has been heard by all, and that its benefit has been recognised'. The universalisation is finally articulated in biblical imagery: 'Christ also learned a trade, that of the carpenter, and his apostles were labourers'. But in following Christ and his apostles, we are all 'diligent labourers in the Lord's vineyard'.[51]

The first article of the first issue can be considered the lead article of the whole enterprise: 'Call to All Who Belong to the German Language'.[52] The text, which combines Weitling's egalitarian, early Christian millenarianism with an almost casual pragmatism, can be understood best starting at the end. Along with a clear self-identification, there appears a possible identification beyond existing class and status barriers:

> [T]his is the first German workers' journal. It will soon be followed by others, until all individuals devote themselves to both intellectual and physical work, manual labour and the sciences, and the distinction between scholars, craftsmen and peasants becomes increasingly blurred.[53]

Finally, in the last paragraph of the text, Weitling also imagines a day when the 'national borders ... will collapse': a day when the 'son of Man' and 'the kingdom of saints living in communion' will have arrived.[54]

What makes Weitling unique is his method of proceeding towards the end times in small, successive stages consisting of immediately concrete tasks. Thus, that longed-for world beyond the basic separation of manual and intellectual labour already seems reachable *today*: 'artists and scholars' form the last links in the chain that begins with the day labourer and continues through the worker. Some of these links are addressed again in the 'Call', and are invited to subscribe to the journal, with the invitations explaining to each group once more why they in particular should see themselves as the addressees of the journal:

---

51 *Hülferuf* 1841, No. 1, p. 6; p. 2.
52 *Hülferuf* 1841, No. 1, pp. 2–6.
53 *Hülferuf* 1841, No. 1, p. 6.
54 *Hülferuf* 1841, No. 1, p. 6.

> That's why whoever shares the same grievances and toils of work should subscribe to our journal. It is the language of the brother to the brother, the mutual exchange of thoughts and feelings, the proof of our maturity and the awareness of our dignity.[55]

Those who share 'the grievances and toils of labour' with 'us' are workers just as we are, our collaborators, our brothers-in-arms. The fraternity is organised by the circulation of words, 'thoughts and feelings', and this proves its 'maturity'. Earlier, the 'Call' makes a great scene of speaking out: 'We too wish to have a voice in the public debates about the woe and weal of mankind; for we, the people in blouses, jackets, smocks and caps, we are the most numerous, useful and vigorous people on God's wide earth'. The idea repeats in different forms, since only through repetition can the new and unheard assert itself:

> We too wish to have a voice, for we live in the nineteenth century and we have never had one before.
>
> We too want to have a say in public opinion, so that we may be known, for we have truly always been misunderstood up to now.[56]

Speaking out ultimately appeals to a paradoxical natural law, which underscores the degenerate nature of the present state of society: 'We want to have a voice, because we already have one by nature, and man does not live by bread alone, but by every word, etc'. They must raise their voices publicly because only in this way can the *natural* ability to speak realise itself *socially*. By raising their voices, the workers remove themselves from the state in which they have found themselves '[s]ince time immemorial': a state in which 'others have always spoken for our, or rather their own interests'. Now it is time to 'mature' and put an end to 'this despicable, boring tutelage'. Seizing one's *own words* and one's *own maturity* against the *tutelage of another* – that is the linguistic-political prerequisite of a politics of the first person which Weitling proclaims: 'Whoever wants to judge the conditions of workers correctly must himself be a worker, otherwise he can have no understanding of the toils involved'.[57]

55 *Hülferuf* 1841, No. 1, p. 4.

56 *Hülferuf* 1841, No. 1, p. 3.

57 *Hülferuf* 1841, No. 1, p. 4. On the 'seizure of words' as a genuinely political gesture, see Rancière 1999. For Rancière, the crucial historical scene is that of Blanqui in court in 1832: 'Asked by the magistrate to give his profession, Blanqui simply replies: "proletarian". The magistrate immediately objects to this response: "That is not a profession", thereby setting himself up for copping the accused's immediate response: "It is the profession of thirty

The mistrust and hatred towards the 'despicable tutelage' is also taken up again in the call for subscriptions when the 'intellectuals' are finally addressed.

> Subscribe to our paper, you poets and scholars, doctors, professors, etc., for you have helped us think what we write. You are our masters in intellectual work, we are your apprentices; but you only ever work for others. You have not wanted to work for us; or have you not been able to? Enough, we are compelled to work for ourselves and to devote our evening hours, which remain free to us after the day's toil, to intellectual work. But with that, your tutelage also ends.[58]

The first thing that stands out is the list of addressees: while the 'artists and scholars' on the title page still formed the end of a series that began with the day labourer and remained subordinate to the labourer within the given paradigm, here the series begins with 'poets and scholars' and ends with 'professors'. At the end, the paradigm is more concerned with the intellectuals in civil service rather than the 'free', 'prolatarianised' intelligentsia. The relationship to the salaried intelligentsia – who 'only ever work for others' – is ambivalent: the intellectuals are helpful as long as there is a division between intellectual and manual labour; their merit as 'masters' for the 'apprentices' can still be formulated in the language of craftsman training. In terms of forming political camps, however, the 'for others' also signals the betrayal contained in the fact that those knowledge competencies have primarily been at the service of the rulers ('You have not wanted to work for us').

The workers instead must now do everything themselves, manual labour all day long, and intellectual labour all night. The 'proletarian nights' are too precious to spend sleeping; the worker uses his nights to become something more, something different, so as not to remain a mere worker. He becomes a worker who devotes his 'night watch' to transgressing the social divide which binds him to the 'grievances and toil' of physical labour, leaving the 'intellectual labours' to the 'poet and scholar'.[59] This worker delegitimises this social divide by no longer adhering to the division of time, to the 'normal round of work and repose', of day and night.[60] 'Turning the world upside down begins around

---

million Frenchmen who live off their labor and who are deprived of political rights". The judge then agrees to have the court clerk list proletarian as a new "profession"' (Rancière 1999, p. 37).

58 *Hülferuf* 1841, No. 1, p. 5.

59 *Hülferuf* 1841, No. 1, p. 5.

60 Rancière 1989, p. viii.

the evening hour when normal workers should be tasting the peaceful sleep of people whose work scarcely calls for thinking', writes Jacques Rancière.[61] In effect, this makes the intellectuals, or their superior position with respect to the common worker, superfluous. The 'difference becomes blurred', as Weitling writes, and this corresponds more and more to the objective developments taking place: in this case, Weitling is reacting to the fact that after the 'educational revolution [*Bildungsrevolution*]' (Heinrich Bosse), public educational institutions produced an overabundance of educated people, and thus intellectuals become workers – 'prolatarians'. They are forced to think and write 'for others', but they can choose *for whom*: one choice leads to lonely night hours and perhaps to the brotherhood of workers, the other leads to the professor's chair.

As if to support this alternative, another type of intellectual has been listed and called upon to subscribe:

> You, deep thinker who devotes his day and night shifts to the life of humanity, subscribe to our journal. We can only offer a simple, genuine language; but the language is German, not ornate, it comes from the heart and for the heart.[62]

The 'deep thinker' is not the one who 'only ever thinks and writes for others', but the one who thinks for the cause of 'humanity'. This, in addition to the fact that he also gives up his night hours – the word 'night watch' occurs twice in this article – connects him with the workers, who approach him with a straightforward, everyday language. The thinker, in turn, will benefit from this encounter with the workers insofar as he can finally drop all bourgeois pretentiousness, all ambitions of distinguishing himself and finally act as a human being among human beings.

In what follows, Weitling still addresses the 'great and powerful' people of society as potential subscribers and supporters, but from the outset he is sceptical that such a cross-class reconciliation in the sense of an original Christian-universal 'communion' can still be achieved. Weitling's militant egalitarianism – as the very first article of the *Hülferuf* shows – nevertheless follows the programme of a 'traversal of differences', as Alain Badiou wrote with respect to Saint Paul.[63] The various calls to subscribe to the *Hülferuf* all start out by listing existing social differences: *we are not yet equal*, he insists. In the end,

61 Rancière 1989, p vii.
62 *Hülferuf* 1841, No. 1, p. 4.
63 Badiou 2003, pp. 98–106.

however, the differences are marked out only to be traversed again in a universalising movement that begins by producing the universal, the common and equal ('we all') instead of simply taking it for granted.

Finally, the universalising movement can be discerned quite clearly in a final appeal, which remains remarkable even if it has no real consequences in the journal: 'Subscribe, you women and girls, for this journal is also dedicated to you; you (or the great majority of you) also share our situation; indeed, yours is often even worse than ours'.[64] The 'woman question' is posed here in such a way that it cannot be answered independently of the class question. Weitling marks the class difference that also delineates the group of 'women and girls', as well as the gender difference within the proletarian camp. In the second case, however, the difference only represents an intensification in the experience of a fundamentally shared 'situation', while the first case represents a basic difference: a proletarian woman and one from the 'higher classes' share nothing, a proletarian man and a proletarian woman, on the other hand, share a great deal, even if the woman ultimately has it 'worse' than the man. What 'worse' means here, and to what extent 'we' (proletarian men) are possibly partly to blame for this worse situation of women, is not answered here – nor in the following issues of *Hülferuf* or *Jungen Generation*. However, the invocation of 'women and girls' at least opens up a gap into which a proletarian feminist movement can step. In France, for example, Flora Tristan made the first attempt at such a movement the year before with her *Promenades in London, or The Aristocracy and Proletariat of England*.[65] In 1843, she will make clear the connection between the 'women's' and the 'social question' in her manifesto *L'Union Ouvrière*:

> Thus, workers, it is up to you, who are the victims of real inequality and injustice, to establish the rule of justice and absolute equality between man and woman on this earth.
>
> Give a great example to the world, an example that will prove to your oppressors that you want to triumph through your right and not by brute force. You seven, ten, fifteen million proletarians, could avail yourselves of that brute force!
>
> In calling for justice, prove that you are just and equitable. You, the strong men, the men with bare arms, proclaim your recognition that

64 *Hülferuf* 1841, No. 1, p. 5.

65 Translated as 'The London journal of Flora Tristan, 1842, or, The aristocracy and the working class of England' in Tristan 1982.

> woman is your equal, and as such, you recognize her equal right to the benefits of the UNIVERSAL UNION OF WORKING MEN AND WOMEN.[66]

Such a 'Union universelle des ouvriers et ouvrières' in Flora Tristan's sense will not exist in Germany for a long time.[67] It is significant, however, that Weitling raised the issue openly in his time. His concept of class and his attempts to define proletarian identity – who are 'we'? – are highly permeable and comprehensive, without homogenising those included through their inclusion. The assembling gesture of Weitling's concept allows for differences within the assembled collective without questioning its collectivity. Shortly thereafter, theoretical and political concepts of class that rely on a more rigid management of difference will begin to take hold. These exclusive class concepts, which know and determine exactly who belongs to 'us' and who does not, will also have an impact on gender relations: *if 'you' – proletarian woman and sister – do not quite agree with 'us' – the proletarian men and brotherhood – then 'you' are against 'us', 'you' are a traitor in your own house who should no longer find a place in our ranks*. This, or something like this, summarises the position that will later shape the workers' movement for decades to come.

---

66 Tristan 1983, pp. 87–8.

67 Here the role of Louise Otto-Peters must be mentioned, who already in the Vormärz linked the 'social' and 'women's question' together. She later founded the *Frauen-Zeitung* [*Women's Newspaper*] in 1849 and the *Allgemeiner Deutscher Frauen-Verein* [*General German Women's Association*] in 1865. On Otto-Peters' Vormärz novel *Schloss und Fabrik* [*Castle and Factory*], see the sections 'The Family Romance of the Proletarian' in the fourth chapter and 'The Machine Breakers' in the seventh chapter of this book. Clara Zetkin analyses the early feminists of the Vormärz from the perspective of the already constituted socialist women's movement, see Zetkin 1971, especially the second chapter 'Die Forderung der Frauenemanzipation in der deutschen Revolution 1848/1849 [The demand for women's emancipation in the German Revolution of 1848/1849]'.

CHAPTER 3

Counting the People: Class Statistics

The emphatic openness of the concept of class, as expressed in the *Gesellschaftsspiegel* and *Hülferuf*, is only one side of the coin. Alongside this, and sometimes opposed to it, many theorists and activists of the early proletarian movement sought to pinpoint more precisely who belonged to the working class – and who did not. In order to do so, class theorists turned to social statistics, which became increasingly widespread as a political and socio-technological science and praxis in the Vormärz. The idea that class relations within society can be calculated and represented as numerical relations, that classes can be *counted*, and that revolutionary change in society can be initiated on a mathematical basis – this is the great promise of class statistics, announced in the pamphlets and journals of the 1830s and 1840s.

Ever since 'class' began circulating as a way for people to categorise themselves within society, it has also functioned as a type of social 'set theory' (Essbach). As an instrument of classification, 'class' maintains an inextricable relationship to countable sets and thus to the principle of countability in general. After the July Revolution, Saint-Simonians spread the concept of class throughout Europe with a formula that inscribed quantification within it: 'la classe la plus nombreuse et la plus pauvre'. Heinrich Heine, who as a sympathiser of the Saint-Simonians translated their political-social vocabulary into German in his essays and correspondence, thus making it widely available for the German public, identifies 'the larger and poorer class' as the subject of the most recent literature in his 1836 essay *The Romantic School*.[1] Readers can find mention of the 'the poorest and most numerous class' – a translation which is closer to the original French and puts more emphasis on numerical countability – in German texts dating back to the early 1830s.[2]

At the same time, it quickly became clear to writers and activists of the Vormärz that the mere countability of classes would never be sufficient: bare numbers must be made meaningful and presentable in order to be effective. To this end, numbers and tables were often supplemented by descriptions, stories and poems. Thus, even where the specifically modern prose of numbers and tables promises unambiguity and clarity, a poetry of class will once again make its appearance.

1 Heine 1976, vol. 5, pp. 357–504, here p. 468.

2 See *Hülferuf* 1841, No. 1, p. 39; Weitling 1974, pp. 241, 252.

 | DOI:10.1163/9789004685536_005

1 Statistics and Social Agitation: *The Hessian Messenger*

In 1834, a subversive pamphlet distributed anonymously under risky circumstances in the Grand Duchy of Hesse made history with its explosive mix of statistics and social revolutionary agitation. The author of *The Hessian Messenger* [*Der Hessische Landbote*] is Georg Büchner, who, as a medical student on a semester abroad in Strasbourg in 1831–2, caught the revolutionary virus that gripped France after the July Revolution of 1830. In Strasbourg, Büchner was introduced to the neo-Babouvist secret societies, and *may have* – the practices of secrecy continue to this day – joined the local section of the *Société des droits de l'homme*, the successor to the *Société des amis du peuple* founded by Blanqui, which was persecuted and disbanded after a failed attempt at insurrection. In any case, we know that Büchner met the young Saint-Simonian A. Rousseau in Strasbourg, who as a prophet of revolution was on his way to the underdeveloped East. At some point, Büchner will hear him speak of the 'poorest and most numerous class'.[3] Back in Giessen, Büchner founded his own 'Society of Human Rights' in 1834, which was responsible for *The Hessian Messenger*. The most important member of the society, apart from Büchner, is the pastor Ludwig Weidig from Butzbach, who heavily revised Büchner's first draft of the *Messenger*.

The Hessian Messenger is considered one of the most important political pamphlets of the Vormärz period.[4] Opening with the battle cry 'Peace to the huts! War on the palaces!', the pamphlet launches a scathing critique of the political and social conditions in the Grand Duchy of Hesse and all of Germany; it is a downright (and literal) 'reckoning' with the 'gentry' and the government.[5] This reckoning is backed up by statistics and numerical data, provided in the form of a table in the second paragraph of the text:

> In the Grand Duchy of Hesse there are 718,373 inhabitants, who each year pay 6,363,364 gulden to the state, as follows:

1)	Direct taxes	2,128,131 gulden
2)	Indirect taxes	2,478,264 "
3)	Crown lands	1,547,394 "

3 See Rancière 2003, pp. 41–3.

4 On the medium of the pamphlet, see Ruckhäberle 1975, and more recently the chapters 'Der Hessische Landbote' and 'Die Nachrichtentechnik der Flugschrift' in Patrick Fortmann 2013, pp. 46–55 and pp. 71–77.

5 Schaub 1977, p. 362.

4)	Regales	46,938	"
5)	Fines	98,511	"
6)	Sundry sources	64,198	"
		6,363,363 gulden[6]	

In a fascinating essay, Gerhard Schaub identifies and examines the source of this data: it comes from the *Statistical Topographical Historical Description of the Grand Duchy of Hesse* by the 'Grand Ducal Hessian Surveyor' Georg Wilhelm Justin Wagner, published by Leske in Darmstadt between 1829 and 1831. The fourth volume, entitled 'Statistics of the Whole', contains the figures listed.[7]

It was thus not the statistical data itself that lent *The Hessian Messenger* its revolutionary force, since that had already been published and was well-known. What must be examined instead is the absolutely unique manner of presentation of the statistical material. An investigation of this sort, as undertaken below, will reveal Büchner's potent rhetorical loading of the material at hand.

The first sentences after the above table reads: 'This money is a tithe of blood squeezed from the body of the people. Some 700,000 human beings sweat, groan and starve because of it. It is extorted in the name of the state, the extortioners cite the government, and the government claim it is necessary for maintaining order in the state'. And shortly thereafter: 'To live in order is to starve and be flayed' (MBA 2.1, p. 6).

Thanks to Wagner, the *Messenger* lists successively which ministries and institutions are allocated what expenses, down to the last gulden: the 'Ministry of Justice and the Interior' 1,110,607 gulden, the 'Ministry of Finance' 1,551,502 gulden, the military 914,820 gulden, and so on. These figures are then followed by highly impassioned explanations of how this money is taken from the 'body of the people' only to their further detriment and for the benefit of the 'gentry' and their lackeys (MBA 2.1, pp. 6–9). The shortest of these paragraphs is telling:

---

6 Büchner, *Der Hessische Landbote*, MBA 2.1, p. 5. Quotations from the *Hessischer Landbote* are marked in the body of the text with the abbreviation MBA 2.1 and the page number. For the English translation of *The Hessian Messenger*, see Büchner 1993. In the table, the sum of the total tax revenue mentioned first does not match the sum added up. If one actually adds up the individual items, a third value is added. It seems that the authors, unless one simply wants to count them among the proverbial *innumerate humanists*, did not really care about exact figures in their political arguments.

7 Wagner 1831. The 'list of subscribers', printed in the first volume, sorted by districts, on pages VII to XVI, lists 'Dr. Weidig, Rector' (p. XV) in Butzbach in the district of Friedberg. Büchner probably borrowed the work from him.

> For pensions: 480,000 gulden.
>
> For this the officials are put comfortably out to grass when they have served the state faithfully for a certain period – that is, when they have been zealous henchmen in the regular round of exploitation and oppression known as law and order (MBA 2.1, p. 7).

In his essay 'Statistics and Agitation', Schaub not only shows that Wagner's *description* is undoubtedly the source of the statistical material in the *Messenger*, he also clearly demonstrates that using statistics for the purposes of political agitation was hardly novel in 1834. In addition to French precursors, Schaub identifies two Palatine sources in particular which prefigured Büchner's statistical and political argumentation, namely the speeches of the liberals Friedrich Schüler and Philipp Jakob Siebenpfeiffer, which were delivered in Zweibrücken on 5 and 6 May 1832 and published together that year as 'Flugschrift 5' [Pamphlet 5] under the ironic title *Our Luck* by Johann Georg August Wirth's Deutscher Pressverein [German Press Association]. In their speeches, Schüler and Siebenpfeiffer use somewhat caustic diction to compare the expenses 'squeezed' from the population of the Palatinate, which was part of Bavaria at the time, with the expenditures that flowed primarily into the military and almost exclusively into the Bavarian heartland. The two Palatine speakers take aim at the extravagance of the court in Munich in particular, along with the horrendous spending on 'dance halls and picture galleries and libraries and monasteries and princely castles'.[8]

The choice of words is remarkably similar to Büchner's. For example, the sentence, 'What a hundred day labourers, if they find steady work, earn in a whole year, the court consumes in a single day' could have easily appeared in the *Messenger*.[9] Yet Büchner's pamphlet does not stop at making a scandal out of the tax burden and expense budget. Another essential aspect is the biblical rhetoric that, with its sometimes excessive intensity, goes beyond any bourgeois appeal to moderation from the outset. In the *Messenger*, the religious register does not give rise to the 'sigh of the oppressed creature', as Marx will later describe in his Young Hegelian critique of religion, but rather to a cry of rage.[10] The biblical language of the *Messenger* accounts for the matter at hand, such as the tax burden on the poor and the extravagance of the rich, no longer according to the 'soft' liberal attributes of 'appropriate/inappropriate', but rather by means of the hard, intransigent opposition of 'good/evil'.

8 Schaub 1977, p. 354.
9 Schaub 1977, p. 354.
10 Marx 1844, MECW 3, p. 175.

In any case, a tax reform alone will no longer appease the indignation expressed in this language.

But even the political-theological parlance which draws on 'tax statistics and ... the Bible' as its two rhetorical 'sources of invention' is not entirely unique: the contemporaneous pamphlets and manifestos of the early French communist movement or even the journeymen's movement organised by Weitling a short time later also express a similar linguistic spirit.[11] The unsettling effect that *The Hessian Messenger* continues to evoke today is due to something else, namely the social and political 'set theory' the *Messenger* brings into play.

It is not (only) the juxtaposition of statistical figures and biblical language that vexes the reader, but also that in *The Hessian Messenger*, and already on the mathematical-statistical side, the set-theoretical basis on which any numerical-statistical argument can be grounded is cast aside. This kind of statistical argument, which Schüler and Siebenpfeiffer also perform, only works with fixed social parameters by which the columns of numbers can be sorted by income and expenses: 'citizens' and 'government', 'taxpayers' and 'spenders'. It requires, in a nutshell, a coherent and self-contained *partition of the social*.

Exactly such a partition is missing in *The Hessian Messenger*. Even before the table listed above, the first paragraph presents an utter jumble of 'large group designations' to which the subsequent numbers are supposed to be assigned.[12] These group designations suggest a simple social binarism in keeping with the biblical rhetoric, but one which is not semantically upheld:

> In the year 1834 it might seem as if the Bible stood convicted of lying. It might seem as if God created peasants and craftsmen on the fifth day, and princes and gentry on the sixth, and as if the good Lord said to the latter, 'Have dominion over every creeping thing that creepeth upon the earth', and counted peasants and burghers amongst the worms. The life of the gentry is one long Sunday, they live in fine houses, wear elegant clothes, have over-fed faces and speak their own language; but the people lie before them like dung on the fields. Behind the plough go the peasants, but behind the peasants go the gentry, driving them on together with the oxen, stealing the grain and leaving them the stubble. The life of the peasant is one long work-day; strangers devour his land in his presence, his whole body is a callus, his sweat is the salt on the gentry's table (MBA 2.1, p. 5).

11 Schaub 1977, p. 373.
12 Essbach 2005, p. 727.

At first, the juxtapositions seem to be clear: 'peasants and craftsmen' are juxtaposed with 'princes and gentry'; later, the 'princes and gentry' are reduced to 'the gentry'. In the very next sentence, however, the 'peasants and craftsmen' become 'peasants and burghers', whereby the relationship of the craftsmen to burghers remains in question: are they identical, or do they have to be added together? If one takes the 'gentry' to designate the second estate, then peasants, craftsmen and burghers together would form the third estate. In the following sentences, however, the peasant alone represents this side of the distinction; the craftsman and burgher have disappeared in the parallelism formulated as '[t]he life of the gentry is one long Sunday' and '[t]he life of the peasant is one long workday'. Instead, a third term has been inserted between the parallel terms, which will later prove to be an almost 'floating signifier': 'the people'. 'The people' are also juxtaposed with the 'gentry', without the relationship of the people to the peasants being clarified. Later, the 'poor' are placed on the side of the non-gentry, which does not have its own positivity (MBA 2.1, p. 6).

Finally, a fundamental distinction cuts across the social divisions, one that will increasingly come to the fore throughout the course of the pamphlet: the distinction between human and animal. In the passage quoted from the beginning of the *Messenger*, the animal-human distinction still clearly serves to allegorise relations of domination with reference to the biblical creation myth. A later, more ambiguous formulation will raise the question of belonging to the human species in general.

Following the presentation of the table cited above, 'the people' are equated with 'human beings': 'This money is a tithe of blood squeezed from the body of the people. Some 700,000 human beings sweat, groan and starve because of it' (MBA 2.1, p. 5). By giving an (approximately) exact calculation of the number of 'human beings' who pay the given amount of taxes, the pamphlet suggests that 'the people' are countable. The principle of countability is used again shortly thereafter to define the state: 'Now what kind of a mighty thing is this: the state? If a number of people live in a country, and regulations or laws exist which all must follow, then they are said to form a state'. The countability of a 'number of people' populating a certain area – the quantifiability of a *population* – serves the rhetorical function of defetishising the 'mighty thing' that is the state. In the very next sentence, however, a new fetish is constructed: 'The state is therefore *everyone*; the state is regulated by laws which ensure the well-being of *all*' (MBA 2.1, p. 6).[13] The Rousseauian concept of a 'will of all' or 'well-being

13 On the editorial-historical dispute as to whether it should correctly read 'will of all', see MBA 2.1, pp. 225–6.

of all' initially appears to be universally inclusive; but by tying 'all' back to 'the people' via the '700,000 human beings', while at the same time identifying 'the people' with the peasants, craftsmen and burghers of the first paragraph, the 'gentry' are excluded from the 'welfare' and 'will of all'. This exception has been a firm aspect of the revolutionary tradition ever since Sieyès posed the question 'What is the third estate?', and answered with: 'Everything!'[14] In the *Messenger*, however, the 'gentry' and the prince are not only excluded from the ranks of the nation, but also from humanity as such, via the series *people – human beings – all*. By naming the '700,000 human beings' – and we know this includes us '*all*' – whom the prince harnesses to his plough, and by assigning the prince and his wives and children to a 'superhuman race' (MBA 2.1, p. 8, emphasis added), the groundwork is laid – with all irony – for portraying the prince and the 'gentry' as *in*human and *sub*human races:

> The prince is the head of the leech that crawls all over you, the ministers are its teeth, the officials its tail. The hungry bellies of all the high and mighty gentlemen to whom he gives the top offices are cupping-glasses with which he bleeds the country dry. The L at the foot of his edicts is the mark of the beast that is worshipped by the idolaters of our epoch (MBA 2.1, p. 8).

In this passage – and there are several of them – one ought not to see a 'hard', completely serious, i.e. literal dehumanisation of the 'gentry'. A more accurate reading would consider it a strategic reversal that aims to counter the real dehumanisation of 'the people' by the 'gentry'; that the people are only 'cattle' for the gentry is something the *Messenger* emphasises repeatedly from its very first page. If the 'gentry' have long since made a habit of 'robbing' the 'poor' of all elementary 'human and civil rights', then the *Messenger* threatens to now, conversely, relegate the 'gentry' to a place beyond the boundaries of the species. Belonging to the human race thus becomes, at least rhetorically, a question of political power. To make this point, Büchner demonstrates with his characteristic rigidity what it means to use *totalising* concepts of a political *set* which aim at the whole ('the people', 'human beings', 'all'), and then how, by means of these 'political concepts, … divisions are introduced into the concept of humanity'.[15] The consequences of such an operation are fatal, as Carl Schmitt will note a hundred years later:

---

14 See Sieyès 2003, 'What is the Third Estate?', pp. 92–162.
15 Essbach 2005, p. 729.

> To confiscate the word humanity, to invoke and monopolize such a term probably has certain incalculable effects, such as denying the enemy the quality of being human and declaring him to be an outlaw of humanity; and a war can thereby be driven to the most extreme inhumanity.[16]

Büchner certainly cannot be blamed for the consequences of this manoeuvre so easily, especially since playing with the 'limits of being human' has a counterpoint in the *Messenger*.[17] The second part of the pamphlet subjects the concept of the people to a decisive transformation in which the people as the epitome of the mute, poor, disenfranchised and 'nameless' (Maud Meyzaud) becomes the people as the bearer of a sovereignty which the *Messenger* recognises: *the people as sovereign*. By way of the romantic construction of a German people's emperor, 'who used to be freely chosen by the people', a new conception of the people is introduced as an electing body: 'the choice of the people' is declared to be the source of legitimacy of every 'rightful authority'. However, the electing people as a constituent power undermines the people as a totalising entity, for in the part of the *Messenger* that theorises sovereignty, the will and 'welfare of *all*' now becomes countable: 'Supreme authority resides in the will of all or of the majority'. The 'will of all' is thus delegated to 'representatives of the people' who are 'elected by everyone'. The representatives 'express the will of those that elected them, hence the will of a majority of them corresponds to the will of a majority of the people' (MBA 2.1, p. 9). A utopia of countability replaces the 'grand' metaphysics of political wholes. The sovereign are the many – 'a number of people', as was said – who decide by the principle of majority rule: the term 'majority' expresses this unequivocally. The people no longer have to be totalised (*all* or none), but this detachment from the 'grand' metaphysics of totalities is bought (or swindled) by entanglement in a 'small', clandestine metaphysics, according to which *speaking for* inevitably leads to *not speaking*. If the representatives speak for the people, then the will they express should correspond to the will of the people, who for that very reason no longer have to speak themselves.

This relativisation, casually expressed in the phrase 'will of all or of the majority', unmistakably affects the whole. This does not remain without consequences in the *Messenger*, and the setback follows immediately. Only a few paragraphs later, the people, which has only just become divisible and countable, is totalised again in the name of another totality: now 'the entire German

16 Schmitt 2007, p. 54.

17 See the title of the volume containing Essbach's essay, *Grenzen des Menscheins* [*Limits of Being Human*], Stagl and Reinhard 2005.

people' must 'win freedom' (MBA 2.1, p. 11). As a 'German' people, however, it can only be defined by its language: it is a people that God 'united through a single language into a single body' (MBA 2.1, p. 12). Here the text is brought full circle: the 'body of the people' from the beginning has become the 'single body' of the German people. In this circle, however, all variants of what 'the people' could mean appear: the nameless, *lowly people* that first became the *people of popular sovereignty* now culminates in the *national people*. To be countable or representable in numbers is only one of these variants. Whenever this democratic-sovereign variant is brought into play, a seemingly irresistible counter-attack is launched, emphasising the uncountability and indivisibility of the *single, whole people*. Numerical statistics can only ever capture one of these two aspects, and each time it does so it can only bring about its own negation; that is to say it aims to capture a totality that can never be had in numbers. Statisticians know this, or rather, at least the statisticians of the Vormärz knew this, who were still struggling with the new knowledge afforded by the practice of statistics. As if to demonstrate the inevitability of the alternation between divisibility and countability on the one hand, and wholeness and indivisibility on the other, the pendulum swings back once again at the end of the *Hessian Messenger*, and the countability of the people appears once more in its purest form as an 'arithmetical argument'.[18] 'There are perhaps 10,000 of them in the Grand Duchy, and 700,000 of you; and the ratio of the people to their oppressors is the same in the rest of Germany' (MBA 2.1, p. 13). 'Ye are many – they are few', proclaimed Shelley's *Masque of Anarchy* in 1819, while Occupy Wall Street in 2011 shouted 'We are the 99 percent'.

The ultimate paradox that the *Hessian Messenger* puts forth is whether there exists a fixed 'number of the people' and whether it would be possible to determine this number statistically without causing a setback in the conception of the whole. No solution is offered. The complaint that the *Hessian Messenger* 'preaches complete anarchy', as voiced by moderate radical Sylvester Jordan, refers not only to the social revolutionary content of the writing, but above all to the heterogeneity and incalculability of the categories which arrange its content.[19] This heterogeneity and inconsistency, however, cannot be solely attributed to Weidig's interventions in Büchner's draft; even if Weidig had abstained from replacing 'rich' with 'gentry', the resulting system of calculation would not have been any more consistent.[20] Nor can the

18 Schaub 1977, pp. 356–7.

19 Hauschild 2013, p. 94. On Jordan's role in preparing the November edition of the *Landbote*, see MBA 2.1, pp. 173–7.

20 According to co-conspirator August Becker, Weidig's central intervention seems to have consisted in the aforementioned replacement.

inconsistency of the set-theoretical basis of the *Messenger* be levelled against Büchner or Weidig as an inadequacy of their text. Quite the opposite: by not even attempting to conceal the fractures in its construction, or rather, by allowing the conflict-ridden collaboration of the two authors to reveal these fractures in the first place, the *Hessian Messenger* makes itself pervious to the objectively unclear social-historical situation to which it responds. On the one hand, the text brings the problem of political address to the fore: to whom can a writing like the *Hessian Messenger* really address itself? On the other hand, it becomes clear that the social-historical strata which needs and desires revolution cannot be determined easily without contradiction. Büchner and Weidig had vastly different responses to these two problems – *class in itself* and *class for itself* – which are interrelated but not identical, and Büchner was even at odds with himself in this regard.

Even from today's standpoint, the extremely heterogeneous conglomerate of different class fractions and class strata found in the state of Hesse and in large parts of Germany in 1834 still does not lend itself to a consistent conceptualisation: urban merchants, the educated middle class, craftsmen, wealthy peasants, but also that 'class of small farmers, day labourers and nomadic agricultural workers, all of whom own little to no property', with which Büchner is particularly concerned.[21] In addition, there are the 'proletarians of intellectual labour', among whom the important Vormärz oppositionist Wilhelm Schulz included his friend Büchner after Büchner's death.[22] All of these groups have little or no material interests in common, and this is something no revolution can do without, as Büchner had insisted to Gutzkow.[23] The situation becomes utterly confusing if we add the 'lowlifes' to this list, whom Büchner later dramatises in his *Woyzeck*: 'urban plebeians, *murdered by work*, not infrequently on the verge of alcoholism or madness; ragged small farmers, hucksters, journeymen, soldiers, coachmen, servants, guards, boot cleaners, showmen, executioners, prostitutes, beggars, petty crooks'.[24]

21 Hauschild 2013, p. 236.

22 According to Schulz, Büchner 'on his deathbed' pointed out 'the deeper, social reason for his premature death': '"Had I been able to live in the independence that wealth gives, I might have made something right of myself"' (Schulz 1985, p. 67).

23 See the letter of (presumably) 1 June 1836, in which Büchner insists that '[o]ur time … is purely *materially*' oriented and therefore can only be revolutionised out of material interests (MBA 10.1, p. 93).

24 Hauschild 2013, p. 245; the italicised passage in the quote comes from the second scene of the first act of *Danton's Death*. On the class basis of the *Hessian Messenger*, see Hörmann 2012.

After the July Revolution, the *question of revolution* can only be formulated as a *social question*, which in turn must be posed as a *class question*, as Büchner had learned in Strasbourg. After suffering failure with the *Hessian Messenger* – or at least experiencing this experiment as a failure – Büchner sees himself condemned to take up an *attentiste* or wait-and-see attitude, perhaps even a 'revolutionary attentism' (Dieter Groh). In a letter to his brother Wilhelm from 1835, he writes:

> A close acquaintance with the happenings of the German revolutionaries abroad has convinced me that there is not the slightest hope in this country either. There reigns a Babylonian confusion among the people that will never be resolved. Let us hope for the future![25]

Here, Büchner provides a motif that will be echoed by the laments of German revolutionaries for (at least) the next fifteen to twenty (if not 150) years: *time will help us*, because, over time, class relations and revolutionary battle-lines will be clarified – or so it is hoped. In the *meantime*, the statisticians among the revolutionaries will try, again and again, to quantitatively survey the unclear intermediate strata and mixed class relations of society.

2 Statistics in the Service of Revolution: *Gesellschaftsspiegel*

From the late 1830s onwards, the problem of pauperism prompts a turn to social statistics in order to account for misery, at least in the advanced countries. Thus, the *Gesellschaftsspiegel* not only translates passages from Buret's *De la Misère des classes laborieuses en Angleterre et en France*, it also resorts to social statistics to enhance its own critique. In doing so, the authors of the *Gesellschaftsspiegel* become particularly intent on providing new and adequate ways of presenting social statistics that would allow it to be used in the critique of society.

2.1 *Rhetoric of Facts: Statistics and Description*

Already in its second section, the prospectus for the *Gesellschaftsspiegel* reflects on how to present its critique along with various approaches that the journal intends to try out. Here it is stated that 'general descriptions, monographs, statistical notes and particularly interesting cases' are to be published, followed a

25 Letter from Strasbourg to Wilhelm Büchner 1835, MBA 10.1, pp. 72–3.

few lines later by 'descriptions, statistical data, certain striking facts', followed by 'descriptions and news pertaining to statistics, medicine and other matters'. Finally, the spectrum of possible modes of representation is decisively expanded when it is stated that the *Gesellschaftsspiegel*,

> in this representation [of material misery] it will not confine itself to statistical notes and accounts of real facts taken from life; it will open its columns to fiction in prose and in verse, but only to such as depicts life *truly*. Descriptions *based on* life will be no less welcome than descriptions *taken from* life.[26]

For the publishers of the *Gesellschaftsspiegel*, description and fiction seem to be perfectly compatible; their common element is the 'life' of society, to which all the modes of presentation used in the journal are committed. The 'fictions' – as 'descriptions *based on* life' – are nevertheless not entirely dissimilar to the 'descriptions *taken from* life', and thus one can assume that 'description' (plain and simple) refers to all those aspects of 'representation' that have an affinity with literature and 'fiction': textual procedures that guarantee a particular representation's fidelity to life ('as depicts life *truly*'), something 'statistical notes' alone cannot guarantee. If one considers 'note' to be an antonym or complementary term, then 'description' refers to a representation with a certain amount of breadth and detail, to a space given to the representation, which the 'note' as a short, mnemonic notation, as an abbreviation, does not claim. Moreover, the term 'note' does not specify in which notation system it is written. When the third paragraph of the prospectus announces that a major topic will be 'reports on the numerical relation of the needy classes, the propertyless classes in general, to the propertied', it explicitly suggests a mode of representation based on numbers and tables.[27]

The entire question concerning the mode of representation, however, is not an end in itself, but placed from the outset in the service of a fundamentally fact-based orientation. The prospectus announces that the *Gesellschaftsspiegel* will 'stand exclusively on the ground of fact, and carry only facts and arguments based directly on facts, arguments the conclusions from which are also obvious facts'.[28]

Despite their fact-based orientation, the publishers of the *Gesellschaftsspiegel* are obviously aware that there is no substantial difference between the

26 Hess 1845/1846, Prospectus, [II]. MECW 4, p. 673. Translation revised.

27 Hess 1845/1846, Prospectus, [I]. MECW 4, pp. 671–72.

28 Hess 1845/1846, Prospectus, [I]. MECW 4, p. 671.

'fact' as *factum brutum* and its formulation in thought ('argument'). 'Facts' are the basis of every argumentation, but when formulated as arguments, they form a new 'ground of fact'. It is worth noticing that it is not only the dichotomy of fact and thought which is called into question here, but also the juxtaposition of fact (and factual reasoning) on the one hand and linguistic-rhetorical composition on the other. The formation of intellectual arguments should result, as a matter of logical necessity, not only in new facts and factual connections, but also in '*obvious* facts' (emphasis added). That is to say, facts that can lay claim to evidence: the 'immediate certainty of what appears vividly or what is necessary for thinking'.[29] By resorting to the tradition of rhetorical *evidentia*, the journal's explicitly emphasised fact-based orientation encompasses the whole spectrum of what is meant by 'description', since in ancient rhetoric *evidentia* functions as the epitome of linguistically 'putting something before our eyes', of detailed descriptive visualisation, of artistically enhanced vividness. 'One fact followed the other, like stones to stones. And the stones began to talk' – is how Hess's biographer Theodor Zlocisti summarises the practice of representation in the *Gesellschaftsspiegel*.[30]

The publishers of the journal claimed that letting the facts speak for themselves – 'speak' in a rhetorical sense, as crafted speech intent on effect – was not a trivial feature of the journal, but its distinguishing characteristic. This is made clear by the series of articles entitled 'Rapid Progress of Communism in Germany', which Engels published in the winter and spring of 1844–5 under the pseudonym 'An old friend of yours in Germany' in the *New Moral World*, the newspaper of the English *Owenites*. In the second article, dated 8 March 1845, the 'old friend' announces a new monthly journal which the 'Messrs Hess of Cologne, and Engels of Barmen' would publish. The character of the journal is described as follows: 'This periodical will contain *facts* only, showing the state of civilised society, and preaching the necessity of a radical reform by the eloquence of facts'.[31]

2.2 *Exaggeration and Distance: the Style of Criticism*

The rhetoric of facts in the *Gesellschaftsspiegel* has a clear purpose: to prove the necessity of radical reform. The journal aims to gather incriminating evidence

29 Kemmann 1996, p. 33.

30 Zlocisti 1921, p. 179.

31 Engels 1845, 'Rapid Progress of Communism in Germany', MECW 4, p. 235. In an earlier article in the *New Moral World* of 21 November 1843, Engels described his comrade Hess as 'in fact, the first Communist of the party' (meaning the Young Hegelian group). See Engels 1843, 'Progress of Social Reform On the Continent', II, MECW 3, p. 406.

to build a major case against the present state of affair, and to convince readers of the necessity of overcoming current social conditions. Producing this effect, in turn, depends on the rhetorical and literary treatment of the facts, expressed by the term 'description' [*Schilderung*] in the prospectus, which is also important in the history of statistics. Yet, the authors of the journal cannot seem to agree on what exactly 'description' means. The range of different writing styles used to make the statistical-empirical material understandable is remarkable. Put simply, there is a tendency for the (presumably more experienced) writers in the editorial section to strive for a 'dry tone', while the amateur writers in the second section of the journal – where readers can publish contributions from their regions and cities – often overshoot the mark rhetorically. Precisely because of this stylistic heterogeneity, the *Gesellschaftsspiegel* can be seen as a laboratory for experimenting with different modes of writing that would eventually be used in the workers' and socialist movements in the nineteenth century and beyond.

In the more elaborate contributions from the first section, the authors themselves often reflect on the status of 'description' in their texts, while also exploring the limits of this concept. In his series of articles, 'The Situation of Weavers and Spinners in Ravensberg', Otto Lüning, a Gütersloh publicist and doctor for the poor, offers rich statistical material on the social situation of textile workers in East Westphalia.[32] The treatment of the data follows the same pattern used in the *Gesellschaftsspiegel* when the goal is to make the reader aware of the social situation in more remote and especially rural regions. These articles – one might also think of Hess's series of articles on the winegrowers along the Ahr – open with idyllic descriptions of the landscape and an appeal to the (urban) reader to follow the author on a 'hike' into the areas described:[33]

> If you, dear reader, are a friend of beautiful landscapes, historical memories and poetic pleasures, then join me on a breezy, clear late summer or autumn day on a hike over the hilltops and the ridge of the Teutoburg Forest where Hermann defeated Varus. If you look north, you can see a wide, flowering, fertile plain. This plain looks like a large, beautiful garden, like a park in the grandest style.[34]

---

32 Lüning was one of the great journalistic project makers of the Vormärz. The weekly *Das Westphälische Dampfboot*, which he edited, existed for three and a half years (1845–8).

33 [Moses Hess], 'Die Ahr in den Pfingsttagen 1845', in: Hess 1845/1846, No. 3, pp. 114–116; No. 4, pp. 157–60.

34 Lüning, 'Die Lage der Weber und Spinner im Ravensbergischen', in: Hess 1845/1846, No. 3, pp. 126–30; No. 4, pp. 153–7; No. 5, pp. 187–91; No. 6, pp. 203–8, here No. 3, p. 126.

But after just one and a half pages, the idyll is broken:

> So far, dear reader, you will have certainly taken to our region. But if you are nothing more than a gentle nature lover, I advise you to go no further than Bielefeld, which lies picturesquely, prosperously, nobly at the entrance to a gorge; here you will surely be convinced of the 'blessing' of our 'flourishing industry'. But above all, as you ramble through the countryside beware of straying too far from the path and entering into the huts, where you may well find scenes that, although they read quite nicely in the *Mystères de Paris*, in reality afflict a sensitive heart too rudely; under many a roof which shone so kindly to you from the trees last night, you would find a kind of misery that would spoil the beautiful impression that the landscape made on you yesterday.[35]

Lüning employs a narrative of disillusionment which, in dissuasion, calls on us to not trust appearances and to look beneath facades. This must be considered a rudimentary form of ideology critique that traces a 'reality' behind appearances. However, the reality of rural pauperism which Lüning describes can only be uncovered by straying off the main roads and by persistently and patiently engaging with the inhabitants of the huts – that is, by wandering, as the first folklorists of the time did as well.

In the opening of his article, dramatised by the contrast between the romantic facade and the miserable reality, Lüning not only makes extensive use of various techniques of literary description himself, he also indicates the limit of literary representations of social misery by mentioning Eugène Sue's *Mystères de Paris*. After a few paragraphs describing the misery of the huts, he then names this limit explicitly: 'These are not exaggerations, and the *numbers* I provide below will prove it better than the most eloquent descriptions'.[36] Eloquent 'descriptions' may be useful in guiding the reader towards understanding; but they only form one pole of the continuum of possible modes of representation. When it comes to really 'proving' what is shown, Lüning advises us to move to the other pole: we must use 'numbers'. Only numbers are above suspicion of dishing up 'exaggerations' to the reader, which, conversely, probably also means that 'descriptions' certainly have a tendency to exaggerate, to rhetorically embellish reality.[37]

35 Lüning, 'Spinner', No. 3, pp. 127–8.
36 Lüning, 'Spinner', No. 3, p. 128.
37 Sue himself claims to have penetrated 'into the huts of the unfortunate' in the preface to the *Mystères*: Sue 2015, p. 3.

The royal road to an effective and convincing critique of the existing society can only lead through the interplay of statistical data and 'descriptions'. The effectiveness of this interplay seems to depend on finding the right balance, for which there can be no fixed rules. It is left to the writer's own sense of style to determine whether his 'descriptions' capture the life of society – and thus are able to change it – or whether his critique, through too much 'description', falls into that 'idealising sentimentality' already castigated in the prospectus and most adequately represented by the successful author Sue, according to the writers of the *Gesellschaftsspiegel*. This sentimentality

> indeed displays hypocritical sympathy for the sufferings of humanity when these eventually develop into a *political scandal* – as we saw all the newspapers and journals overflowing with so-called socialism in connection with the Silesian *disturbances* – but as soon as the disturbances are over, it *quietly* lets the poor go on starving.[38]

The search for an appropriate style of critique also preoccupies Karl Marx in his article 'Peuchet: On Suicide'. This article in the seventh issue comprises thirteen pages, of which only two are authored by Marx himself: an introduction and a short summary. The rest is Marx's own, slightly modified translation of a section of the 1838 posthumously published memoirs of the French politician, journalist and statistician Jacques Peuchet, who died in 1830.[39] Peuchet, as Marx's introduction informs us, emerged as a scholar with two major works, a five-volume *Geographie commerçante* published in 1800 and 'Statistics of France' published in 1807. Marx cites Peuchet's comments on suicide as an example of the '*French* criticism *of society*' and, above all, praises its superior style of writing. According to Marx, the French are able to criticise 'the contradictions and unnaturalness of modern life', and not only in its individual aspects or 'in the relationships of particular classes'. Rather, the French criticise modern life in its totality, a 'criticism of the existing property, family, and other private relations, in a word of *private life*'. In the various revolutions and counter-revolutions of the past decades, the French have learned that the totality of life is political and must therefore also be subject to political critique.[40] Peuchet thus does not see suicide as a merely private or even intimate affair, but as a 'symptom of the faulty organisation of our society': 'The classification of the various causes of

---

38 Hess 1845/1846, Prospectus, [II]. MECW 4, p. 674.

39 Marx 1846, 'Peuchet: On Suicide' in MECW 4, pp. 597–612, originally published in Hess 1845/1846, *Gesellschaftsspiegel*, No. 7, pp. 14–26.

40 MECW vol. 4, p. 597.

suicide would be the classification of the *very defects of our society*'.[41] Although Peuchet repeatedly emphasises the connection between suicide, pauperisation and unemployment – 'for at times when industry is at a standstill and in crisis, in periods of dear food and hard winters, this symptom is always more conspicuous and assumes an epidemic character', a description that applies to Paris of the 1840s as much as to Greece of the 2010s – his examples nevertheless emphasise other phenomena that are at best indirectly related to concrete economic facts. Marx places the victims of another of the 'tyrannies' at the centre of his excerpt: the victims of the tyranny that persists '*in the family*' even after the great revolutions.[42] In three of the four cases presented, it is women who become victims of social circumstances and kill themselves: the daughter of a tailor kills herself because her despotic father publicly shames her on the basis of false accusations; a young woman from Martinique kills herself after her frantically jealous husband drives her to despair; the 'young niece of a Paris banker' kills herself because her uncle impregnates her and she cannot find a doctor to perform an abortion. The episode with the young woman from Martinique is framed in terms of colonial history: the despotism of the man, a rich 'creole', is portrayed as stemming from the regiment of a slaveholder, with slavery in turn depicted as a special form of private property. For Peuchet (and Marx), private property combines the economic characteristics of the capitalist money economy, colonial slavery and the disenfranchisement and oppression of women:

> The unfortunate wife was sentenced to the most intolerable slavery, and this slavery was only enforced by Monsieur de M … on the basis of the *Code civil* and the right of property, on the basis of social conditions which render love independent of the free sentiments of the lovers and allow the jealous husband to surround his wife with locks as the miser does his coffers; for she is only a part of his inventory.[43]

In writing about Peuchet, Marx highlights both the ability of the French to discover and criticise the political in the private sphere as well as the particular style of criticism employed. Peuchet's 'accounts' (like those of all French criticism) contain 'the warmth of life itself, broadness of view, refined subtlety, and bold originality of spirit, which one will seek in vain in any other nation'.[44] For

41 MECW 4, p. 598 and p. 610.

42 MECW 4, p. 604.

43 MECW 4, p. 607. On the gender dimension of Marx's article, see Anderson 1999. On the place of the early text in Marx's thinking on gender relations, see Brown 2012, pp. 44–8.

44 MECW 4, p. 597.

Marx, it is the abundance of personal 'political experiences' gained through introspection – Peuchet is a 'practical man', as Marx emphasises – combined with a certain cosmopolitanism, which seems to be important in Peuchet's writing.[45] One could contrast this with the stale air found in the study-rooms of German criticism, which Marx repeatedly chides. In addition to the familiarity with practical experience, however, Marx also praises a certain detachment ('subtlety', boldness) that abstains from making any direct moral evaluation.

Marx's characterisation of Peuchet's style of writing, like so many of his early polemical (and sometimes laudatory) words about others, must be read first and foremost as an effort to develop his own writing style. Marx, too, strives for a detached stylistic ideal that signals more than it states sympathy for the suffering. Such a style is on display in the succinct conclusion to the article on suicide. Here Marx includes a *table* from Peuchet's book without comment, as an anti-climax, so to speak. In the end, for Marx, only the numbers speak, and in their barrenness they are obviously *also* meant to say something for which there are no longer adequate words, or at any rate, no words that would not betray the matter at hand through exaggeration. The last section of the table lists the 'motives' of the suicides. After 'passionate love, domestic quarrels and grief – 71 [cases]; illness, weariness of life, unsound mind – 128; misbehaviour, gaming, lotteries, fear of accusations and punishments – 53; misery, poverty, loss of position, loss of job – 59', there remain 60 cases undetermined. For them, the table lists – and this ends Marx's article – 'motives unknown'.

2.3 *Fiction and Correction: Statistics of Prostitution*

Marx's ideal of an abiding critique that takes numbers not only as evidence of empirical statements but also as a sign of the unfathomable, aims to make the poetic-literary aspect of 'description' gradually disappear. The text on suicide must certainly be read as a part of this tendency, perhaps even an extreme case of the maxim 'critique through presentation' which characterises Marx's major systematic works after 1857.[46] Marx then makes use – as he already tested in the Vormärz – of a *poetics of de-poeticisation*: a poetics that uses all artistic

45 MECW 4, p. 597. Translation modified.

46 In a letter to Lasalle on 22 February 1858, Marx expresses this ideal: 'The work I am presently concerned with is a Critique of Economic Categories or, if you like, a critical presentation [*Darstellung*] of the system of bourgeois economy. It is at once a presentation [*Darstellung*] of the system and through the presentation a critique of the same'. MECW 40, p. 270. Translation revised.

means possible to specifically not let its products appear as poetically formed constructions. Bluntly put, Marx wants nothing to do with a 'poetry of class' – and yet he still belongs to it.

In the *Gesellschaftsspiegel*, however, other, more wide-ranging formats are prevalent. A set of articles about prostitution demonstrates how different forms of representation can interact, such as numerical-tabular statistics, their critical contextualisation and finally genuine poetry – 'descriptions *based on* life', as the prospectus puts it.

The two-part article series from issues nine and ten, '*Schicksale weiblicher Dienstboten, in Briefen*' [Fates of Female Servants, in letters], likely authored by Hess himself, presents a fabricated exchange of letters between the servants Gertrude and Maria. A footnote to the title fictionalises the author as a mere editor: 'A friend has permitted us to publish here for the first time the above account from real life, which is taken from very interesting memoirs intended for later publication. The editors'.[47]

In the letters, the reader learns details about the everyday life and working conditions of young servants, and offered a glimpse into the lives of other domestic servants and craftsmen who work in the home. In addition to the recurring complaints about hard work, excessively long working hours, poor accommodation and lack of supplies, as well as harassment by the ladies of the house, the description of (threatened or carried out) sexual assaults by the house masters and other domestic servants takes up a great deal of space. Both inside and outside their workplace – especially during periods when they are without employment, when they live on the streets or in asylums – the young women see themselves condemned to always be perceived by others as prostitutes: job advisors and pension providers turn out to be brothel keepers, shady mistresses turn out to be former prostitutes who have maintained contacts in the milieu, house masters and colleagues offer money:

> How utterly despicable it is to offer a girl money for her love! And what silliness! You wouldn't believe it until you see it. And yet this infamy seems to prevail throughout the world. Priests, husbands, waiters, innkeepers and guests have already offered me money to love them.[48]

That those higher up constantly insinuate or accuse their servants of being prostitutes becomes clear at the latest when the demure, respectable mis-

---

47 [Moses Hess] 'Schicksale weiblicher Dienstboten, in Briefen', in: Hess 1845/1846, No. 9, pp. 80–91; No. 10, pp. 114–133, here No. 9, p. 80.

48 Hess 1845/1846, No. 10, p. 125.

tresses keep suspecting their servants of wanting to seduce their sons or husbands, in addition to insulting the women's proletarian friends and lovers as 'vagabonds', 'thieves and scoundrels' and, implicitly, their pimps.[49]

The correspondence also describes the women's survival strategies, their concepts of honour, and the tricks they use to turn adverse circumstances to their own advantage. This frees both women – to some extent – from their role as victims and places them in an independent subject position. Finally, the (albeit vague) political hope arises that 'soon everything will look different' – if only 'thousands were like us' and 'all the maids ... stuck together faithfully'.[50]

Through these fabricated autobiographical documents, the living conditions of the servants are presented in a highly condensed form; their personal circumstances are typified and made comprehensible in a concise manner. Such typification sometimes contains caricatural or even stereotypical features: the accusations of sexual assault in particular read like made-up male fantasies. As if to correct this inherent tendency of fiction to exaggerate, the question of prostitution is taken up once again in issue 11 of the *Gesellschaftsspiegel*, this time statistically. The article, '*Die Prostitution in Berlin und ihre Opfer. Nach Amtlichen Quellen Und Erfahrungen*' [Prostitution in Berlin and its Victims, According to Official Sources and Experience], is a review of the eponymous book which appeared anonymously in Berlin in 1846.[51] Subsequently, the notorious Vormärz political investigator for the Berlin police and later Prussian chief of police, Wilhelm Stieber, was identified as the author, but the reviewer did not know this at the time of writing.[52] For him, 'an unnamed Prussian official, probably a police officer' is the author. Even if, as the anonymous reviewer complains, the work is 'understandably less valuable' than its French counter-

49 Hess 1845/1846, No. 9, p. 90.

50 Hess 1845/1846, No. 10, p. 123 and p. 133.

51 [Anonymous] 'Die Prostitution in Berlin und ihre Opfer', in: Hess 1845/1846, No. 11, pp. 142–52. For the full title of the reviewed work, see Stieber 1846.

52 Wilhelm Stieber was in charge of monitoring the political opposition in Berlin since 1845. After going too far, even by the standards of the time – he was accused of mistreatment and falsifying evidence – he was dismissed from the service. Reinstated after the revolution, he led the investigation against the League of Communists. Karl Marx sharply attacked Stieber for this in his 1853 paper 'Revelations Concerning the Communist Trial in Cologne'; among other things, he again accused Stieber of falsifying evidence and perjury (MECW 8, pp. 395–457). At Bismarck's personal behest, Stieber was then appointed head of the entire Prussian secret and political police in 1867. After the founding of the Reich in 1871, he was thus able to draft the (Anti)Socialist Laws. Stieber did not live to see the failure and repeal of the (Anti)Socialist Laws in 1890; he died in 1881, filthy rich – he owned several tenements in the proletarian quarters of Berlin – and highly honoured. On Stieber's biography, see Schoeps 1977.

part, 'Parrent-Duchatelets', Stieber's book nevertheless contains 'some statistical notes' that provide a 'not entirely worthless contribution to the knowledge of our social conditions'.[53] Though 'his statistical data' contain the 'only content of the book of any value … even this is to be used with caution'.[54]

The review first begins with an extensive account of the statistical material in Stieber's book, but it also contextualises the figures, questions the basis of the survey and takes the author's political intentions into account. For example, the reviewer disputes the book's claim that there were only 10,000 prostitutes in Berlin on the grounds that only women aged 17 and over were recorded in the study. The reviewer suggests that the reason why the presumed police officer celebrates the closure of sanctioned brothels by the authorities as a great success and claims he can detect a decline in prostitution is only because unofficial 'corner' prostitution is less visible and thus less dishonourable for the city officials. Criminalising prostitution, however, has only exacerbated the misery of prostitutes, their ruinous competition and dependency on pimps.[55]

This touches on a crucial point that threatens to compromise the validity of the entire statistical presentation: prostitution, especially criminalised, unofficial, temporary prostitution, only becomes accessible and quantifiable when it collides with official authorities. Stieber's book deals with this problem in the chapter on *'Dirne im Gefängnis und im Kampf mit der Polizei'* [The Prostitute in Prison and in Conflict with the Police]. 'Of course, it is easy to explain', according to the reviewer, 'why the author glosses over this "conflict" so rich in tragic and outrageous situations and deeds': because as a policeman he is biased and can only ever represent one side of the conflict – his own. Here, the reviewer concludes, other perspectives and other forms of representation must intervene. If officer Stieber's bias distorts the depicted situation to such an extent that it becomes unrecognisable as a whole, then the tales told by the police become useless; then more 'police stories' are needed 'which fill in the gaps left by the author'.[56] These 'police stories' are most definitely Ernst Dronke's fictional *Polizei-Geschichten* [*Police Stories*], which are reviewed by Friedrich Schnake just after the Stieber review in the same issue of the *Gesellschaftsspiegel*.[57] One of the *Police Stories*, 'Die Sünderin' [The Sinner], is

53 This refers to the work of Parent-Duchâtelet 1836.

54 Hess 1845/1846, No. 11, p. 151.

55 Hess 1845/1846, No. 11, pp. 144–5 and pp. 148–9.

56 Hess 1845/1846, No. 11, p. 150.

57 F. [Friedrich] Schnake, 'Die Polizeigeschichten und "aus dem Volke" von Ernst Dronke', in: Hess 1845/1846, No. 11, pp. 152–5. The review refers to Ernst Dronke, *Polizei-Geschichten*, 1846, and Dronke, *Aus dem Volk*, 1846, collected in Dronke 1981.

even printed in the *Gesellschaftsspiegel*, just after the review. This was most likely intended to supplement and correct the biased and necessarily incomplete figures and statistics in Stieber's book.[58] Whether the 'social novella' as a form will have the last word remains to be seen; the presumption, however, that this too will eventually have to be supplemented by 'hard' empirical evidence is present from the beginning. In his review, Schnake also complains that Dronke's narratives sometimes seem exaggerated due to an excessive desire for stylisation.

The fact that the desired forms of representation in the *Gesellschaftsspiegel* are not consistently followed can be seen in some of the kitsch descriptions of prostitution in the journal. Following the second part of the 'Fates of Female Servants', in which the two servants always appear as subject to their own fate, there is a poem by Püttmann in the tenth issue that systematically discredits Hess's claims as well as those of the entire series of articles on prostitution. As for the poem, at best it is unintentionally funny. It begins: 'By the coffin of an unfortunate woman. An elegy by Püttmann': 'You are dead, Mary sleep well! / Long ago it is, when you sweetly / Grew up in the neighbour's house, / A shimmering sylph, / A rose transformed by light'. The path of the sylph is then mapped out: the impoverished father is imprisoned for debt, the mother dies, the 'rich and merciful' take over their role and rob the orphan of 'the rest of the old state: / Lace bonnet, little silk dress'. The *'orphan!'* is then employed as a 'maid': 'A maid. How terrible, / Without your own, a foreign will / Submissive to another's whim, / Submitting to another's lust of sin, dumb and dull, always silent / Bowing to another's wrong'. Marie and Gertrude, Hess's protagonists and heroines, never appear like this. In the case of the weak-willed and mute Mary, the inevitable happens: she falls in love with her young master, who takes advantage of her and then: 'Out the door with laughter'. The last resort is prostitution: 'At last you gave yourself to sin, / A sad prostitute'.[59] Püttmann's reproach against the 'rich cannibals' ends up incapacitating the poor female victim entirely, who – one could maliciously insinuate – was actually destined to become the submissive, miserable housewife and house slave of the proletarian boy next door, from whose perspective the poem speaks. This, too, is part of the *poetry of class*.

58 [Ernst Dronke,] 'Die Sünderin', in: Hess 1845/1846, No. 11, pp. 155–63; also in Dronke 1981, pp. 235–49.

59 Hess 1845/1846, No. 10, pp. 134–6.

CHAPTER 4

Miserabilism and Critique: from the Poverty of Literature to the Poverty of Theory

During the Vormärz, 'la classe la plus pauvre', the poorest class, often assumed the form of absolute impoverishment. Pauperism would not recede from the political-theoretical imagination until the 1850s. The search for remedies against the immiseration of ever wider circles of the population became the first testing ground of social policy.[1]

The *poetic* question of how social misery can be portrayed without feeding on misery, that is, without humiliating those who suffer even more through the depiction, was already widely discussed in the Vormärz. What is always negotiated in these debates is the possibility of a political-theoretical *critique* of social misery that avoids miserabilism – the mere continuation of misery in poetic or theoretical form.[2]

1 Ludwig Tieck and the Wolves of London

On a trip to London in 1817, which was supposed to merely acquaint him with the current English performance practice of his beloved Shakespeare, Ludwig Tieck found himself confronted with modern mass poverty. He later addressed the shocking social divide in his 'fairy-tale novella', *Die Vogelscheuche* [*The Scarecrow*]:

> When we are in London, we know that many thousands wake up (if they have slept) not knowing how and what to eat for breakfast, or even for lunch. The furious hunger drives them around, and we even meet these raging wolves without knowing them, who are ready to bite, and none of them can touch even a morsel of what is laid out in a thousand places, because they lack even the smallest coins to buy anything. Even more: in the streets, where everything is in flux, the richest silver and gold dishes,

1 An early, impressive account of pauperism can be found in Engels 1839, 'Letters from Wuppertal', MECW 2, pp. 7–25. An innovative theorisation of pauperism comes in two memoranda by Alexis de Tocqueville 2007, and a collection of material in Jantke and Hilger 1965.

2 On the concept of miserabilism, see Suter 2016, p. 170.

 | DOI:10.1163/9789004685536_006

> priceless gems, are placed outside. No walls of Ehrenbreitstein, Jericho or the Dresden Green Vault protects these treasures; a thin, fragile pane of glass separates the jewel from the foot of the passer-by. The pinkie toe could shatter the almost air-thin screen with one push – often the street is empty, with no one in the rich shops. A kick, a grab would give the hungry man what he needs to buy a meal, a room, a host and the host's home – and yet nothing of the sort happens. Must not a Bedouin of the desert see the miracles here! What then is the invisible spirit wall that protects these jewels? A ten-year-old boy from London will say: there is nothing incomprehensible, that goes without saying. To a soldier who recently bore witness to the sacking of various towns, what I call miracle would only seem a foolish prejudice, if the miracle word 'subordination' did not build the ghostly wall in front of his desire.[3]

For all the striking vividness of the roaming, starving 'wolves', Tieck does not stop at the mere depiction of poverty. He also – and *already* – penetrates the structural conditions of poverty. It is not only external mechanisms that prevent the 'hungry' from satisfying their hunger. In the scenario of the shop window, Tieck makes clear that it is the 'subordination' to the fully enforced commodity form *as a general form of inversion and thought* that produces the 'miracle' by which people would rather starve than violate the 'sacred laws of property'. And so, Tieck, as he reports to Köpke, is repelled by the 'commercial and factory life of the modern world', which he first experiences in full bloom in London.[4]

At the same time, however, Tieck alludes to a possible way out of the dilemma of hunger and property, one whose basic possibility he would have also discovered in Britain at the latest: for the 'soldier who recently bore witness to the sacking of various towns' could have been one of the 12,000 soldiers dispatched to the Midlands and Northern England in 1811–12 to put down the widespread food riots and the broadly organised Luddites. Tieck would have at least noticed the after-effects of this de facto occupation of the country by its own troops during a trip to Stratford-upon-Avon – Hobsbawm emphasises that the soldiers 'greatly exceeded in size the army which Wellington took into the Peninsula in 1808'. The rebels of north England showed how easily the 'sacred laws of property' could be ignored – and that glass panes are the least of what was broken in the food riots. But they also illustrated how brutally the powers

3 Tieck 1988c, p. 491.

4 Köpke 1855, Vol. 1, p. 375.

of order take revenge. That the force of the riots could also infect the soldiers deployed to suppress them was already heavily debated at the time.[5]

As mentioned, Tieck alludes to all of this only implicitly. And just as casually, and typically romantically, he refers to the possible deep connection between mass poverty and the hunger revolts. For on his journey through England, Tieck is bitterly disappointed by a nature that appears 'tailored', that has lost all 'character of originality': 'industry had robbed it of its dense, poetic fragrance'.[6] This 'tailored' nature is 'contained', divided by hedges and fences, created by the extensive *enclosures* that Parliament passed in countless *Inclosure Acts* at the end of the eighteenth and beginning of the nineteenth century. Only through these acts were the rural residents driven out, cut off from their livelihoods and thus proletarianised and pauperised: 'tailored nature', 'commercial and factory life' and 'furious hunger' are three aspects of one and the same thing, which Tieck, the hopeless romantic, instinctively traces.[7]

Tieck's depiction of this connection was hardly noticed by the public at the time, probably because of its marginality in the work of an increasingly marginalised author. Tieck's younger contemporaries had to first slowly approach the various possibilities of an adequate literary representation of poverty and destitution. Whether literature could do more than merely reflect misery – whether it could also potentially contribute in its own way to analysing and representing the social conditions that produce poverty – was highly controversial among the writers and literary critics of the time.

2 German Misery, German Verse: Engels as Narrative Theorist

Friedrich Engels, for example, takes aim at the socio-critical literature of his time in the polemic 'German Socialism in Verse and Prose'. In a series of articles from the *Deutsche-Brüsseler Zeitung* of autumn 1847, Engels first addresses Karl Beck, whose *Lieder vom armen Mann* [*Poor Man's Songs*] are ridiculed as the

5 Hobsbawm 1967a, p. 8. Hegel stated in his 1821/1822 lectures on the philosophy of right, no doubt with regard to the social unrest of the time: 'The most despicable rabble, which phantasy cannot even imagine, is thus in England' (Hegel 2005, p. 223). The most comprehensive and best overall account of the Luddite Revolt is Reid 1986.

6 Köpke 1855, Vol. 1, p. 376.

7 On the history of the *Inclosure Acts*, see Clark and Clark 2001 (the spelling *i/enclosure* was not yet standardised at the end of the eighteenth century). On the connection between enclosures and proletarianisation, see Linebaugh 2008, especially pp. 46–93, as well as the classic account of 'So-called Primitive Accumulation' in Marx 1976, pp. 871–940.

'poetry of true socialism'.[8] For Engels and Marx, 'true socialism' was the nickname for a specifically German, 'petty-bourgeois' tendency of early socialism, which rejected existing conditions on purely moral grounds and – precisely for this reason, according to Marx and Engels – could not rise to a real analysis of capitalist conditions.

Engels accusation against 'true socialism' becomes clear in his polemic against Beck: according to Engels, the 'poor man' from Beck's title can only appear as a 'little man'. But by depicting the power of the 'great men' – the songs begin with a directly addressed accusation 'To The House of Rothschild' – the 'little man' would only be made smaller and even more powerless.[9] The fixation on the 'power of a big capitalist', however, testifies to nothing other than the 'ignorance of the connection between this power and existing conditions'.[10]

Instead of a 'connection' that understands the social reality of power and powerlessness, of wealth and poverty as a necessary relation or, even more sharply, as a contradiction, Beck and the 'true socialists' are only able to represent a mere juxtaposition of various aspects in the form of an 'on the one hand … on the other hand':

> The most common kind of socialist self-complacent reflection is to say that all would be well if only it were not for the poor on the other side. This argument may be developed with any conceivable subject-matter. At the heart of this argument lies the philanthropic petty-bourgeois hypocrisy which is perfectly happy with the *positive* aspects of existing society and laments only that the *negative* aspect of poverty exists alongside them, inseparably bound up with present society, and only wishes that this society may continue to exist *without the conditions of its existence*.[11]

Engels' mockery of Beck's 'cowardly petty-bourgeois wretchedness' still applies in large part – one can say in passing – to the present 'critique of capitalism' revived since the financial crisis of 2008. Instead of arriving at the structural conditions of the crisis, this criticism is limited to the 'negative sides',

---

8 Engels 1847, 'German Socialism in Verse and Prose', MECW 6, p. 235; Beck 1846. The Austrian poet, journalist and philosopher Karl Isidor Beck (1817–79) published around ten volumes of poetry between 1838 and 1870, as well as dramas, novels and short stories He circulated at times amongst *Jungen Deutschland*, acquainted himself with Georg Herwegh and clashed with Prussian censorship during the Vormärz. In the *Österreichisch Biographisches Lexikon* 1957, p. 61, Beck is described 'as one of the earliest poets of the proletariat'.

9 MECW 6, p. 235; Beck 1846, pp. 1–32.

10 MECW 6, pp. 240, 235.

11 MECW 6, p. 246.

the 'power' and 'greed' of the bankers, who are accused – as Beck reproached the Rothschilds – of being 'not socialist philanthropists, not enthusiasts for an ideal, not benefactors of mankind, but just – bankers'.[12] The Vormärz poet, like contemporary critics, does not see that all 'criticisms of Rothschild [and his contemporary successors] are transmuted into the most slavish flattery' because 'he is extolling Rothschild's power [and his contemporary successors] as the most cunning panegyrist could not have extolled it'.[13] Without addressing the conditions that produce the disparity between power and powerlessness, between wealth and poverty – because then one might have to explain why one does not actually intend on changing anything about these conditions – the persistence of all the bad, negative sides of contemporary society is only attributed to the moral depravity and 'greed' of the powerful:

> After our poet has so far versified the romantic and ignorant fantasies of a German petty bourgeois concerning what is within the power of a big capitalists if only he were a man of good will, after he has puffed up the fantasy of this power as far as it will go in the puffed-up dizzy grandeur of his mission, he gives vent to the moral indignation of a petty bourgeois at the discrepancy between ideal and reality …[14]

The political and theoretical impotence of 'true socialism', its inability to grasp an overarching connection in society, necessarily turns, Engels concludes, into a 'complete inability to tell a story and create a situation'. This narrative impotence is 'characteristic of the poetry of true socialism. True socialism, in its indeterminacy, provides no opportunity to relate the individual facts of the narrative to general conditions and thus bring out what is striking or significant about them'.[15] Engels, who would later appear again and again as a poetologist of literary realism and who, early on, criticised *Junges Deutschland*, presents here implicitly and *en passant* a narratology of his own, against whose standards he measures the literary products of the 'true socialists'.[16] A narrative is told – this much has been clear since the ancient poets – by linking or connecting, and without linking, there is no narrative. For Engels, however, narration does not coincide with the proverbial 'linking of events', nor with the linking

12 MECW 6, p. 235.
13 MECW 6, p. 240.
14 MECW 6, p. 240.
15 MECW 6, pp. 244–45. Translation revised.
16 See Engels 1842, 'Alexander Jung, "Lectures on Modern German Literature"', in: MECW 2, pp. 284–97.

of things of the same order of magnitude or reference. Rather, narration only takes place when *individual* things – the 'facts of the narrative' – are related to something *universal*, 'to general conditions'. The relation of individual facts is then *mediated* through general conditions, and not just among themselves. It is only through this mediation in a universal that it becomes possible to 'bring out what is striking or significant about' the individual facts – and perhaps also of the general conditions: this remains grammatically open in Engels (possibly intentionally so). *Significance* is defined here as something striking, surprising, not simply as something to be tacitly presupposed; and it is precisely this striking aspect that Engels identifies as the effect of narration. The individual is not to be subsumed under the general, nor is the general to be merely illustrated by the individual. Rather, their *connection* should be made striking, instantly lucid: only then can a story be told in a sophisticated sense, and this, according to Engels, is precisely what 'true socialism' cannot do in its 'prose and poetry'.

For Engels, the prerequisite for the narrative mediation of the individual and the general is *determinacy*, and thus the 'indeterminacy' of 'true socialism' makes it incapable of providing a narrative representation of the world. The 'poetry of true socialism' is unable to tell a story not only because it cannot link the individual to the general, but also because it cannot distinguish between the two at all. Only that which is differentiated can be linked. In the 'outlook' of the 'true socialists', however, all orders of reference become mixed up. That is why the only order they can establish is an 'arid and boring catalogue' into which they sort 'isolated instances of misfortune and *social cases*', that is, the details *as details*, without reference to that which makes them details, individual cases of an overarching context.[17]

In his polemic, Engels masterfully overlays the (failed) poetic representation of social 'misère' attempted by the 'true socialists' on top of the intellectual representation of the poetic and theoretical 'German misère', in which the 'true socialists' themselves are stuck and of which, according to Engels, they are a symptom. In his poems, Beck himself reveals 'being trapped in the German petty-bourgeois misery', being 'entangled in German misery', as he 'sings of the cowardly petty-bourgeois wretchedness, of the "poor man", the *pauvre honteux* with his poor, pious and contradictory wishes'.[18]

Engels does not see a *poetic* way out for the poor little man Beck. If the 'German misery' is so all-encompassing, then only one way out remains, which Engels unapologetically suggests to poor Beck:

17 MECW 6, p. 245.
18 MECW 6, pp. 245, 235, 248.

> Beck has incontestably more talent and at the outset more energy too than most of the German scribbling fraternity. His great lament is the German misery, amongst whose theoretical manifestations also belong Beck's pompously sentimental socialism and Young German reminiscences. Until social conflicts in Germany are given a more acute form by a more distinct differentiation between classes and a momentary acquisition of political power by [the] bourgeoisie, there can be little hope for a German poet in Germany itself. On the one hand, it is impossible for him to adopt a revolutionary stance in German society because the revolutionary elements themselves are not yet sufficiently developed, and on the other, the chronic misery surrounding him on all sides has too debilitating an effect for him to be able to rise above it, to be free of it and to laugh at it, without succumbing to it again himself. For the present the only advice we can give to all German poets who still have a little talent is to emigrate to civilised countries.[19]

3 Striking Stereotypes: Ernst Dronke's 'Rich and Poor'

'True socialism', especially in its literary form, gave Engels no rest. Already in a longer piece from the spring of 1847, entitled 'The True Socialists', which was actually intended for publication as part of the *German Ideology*, but was then consigned to the 'gnawing criticism of the mice' for almost a hundred years, Engels deals successively with some already familiar journalists (Otto Lüning, Hermann Püttmann) in order to then follow up with a biting polemic against a number of literary figures, some of whom were to appear (again) as his comrades a little later.[20] Mention should be made of Ferdinand Freiligrath and Ernest Dronke, who would become Marx and Engels' co-editors at the *Neuen Rheinischen Zeitung* during the revolutionary period.[21]

The mockery and reproaches that Engels dumps on Dronke are largely the same as those with which he targeted Beck. But where he presents Beck in

19 MECW 6, pp. 248–9.

20 'The manuscript [*The German Ideology*], two large octavo volumes, had long ago reached the publishers in Westphalia when we were informed that owing to changed circumstances it could not be printed. We abandoned the manuscript to the gnawing criticism of the mice all the more willingly since we had achieved our main purpose – self-clarification'. Marx 1859, 'A Contribution to the Critique of Political Economy: Preface', MECW 29, p. 264.

21 Engels 1847, 'The True Socialists', in MECW 5, pp. 540–81. For a biography of Dronke, see Frost 1989.

detail with individual failed verses and stylistic gaffes, Engels proceeds more summarily towards Dronke: his novellas – published in 1846 in the two collections *Polizei-Geschichten* [Police Stories] and *Aus dem Volk* [Among the People] – are 'touching' and written in 'the most good-natured fashion' and in this way depict 'poignant conflicts' between simple people and the law; but all in all, they are merely 'lachrymose descriptions of German philistine misery'.[22]

According to Engels, the moralistic sentiment of the novellas results from a 'total lack of imagination and considerable ignorance of real life'. But where there is neither imagination nor a sense of reality, morality must intervene, and so '[the novellas] serve only to foist Herr Dronke's socialist ideas on people in whose mouth they are completely inappropriate'. But because the novellas are so badly composed aesthetically, their political thrust is also inverted: Dronke 'believed that this was socialist propaganda; [he] has never for a moment reflected on the fact that such lamentable scenes … [are] not *socialist*, but *liberal* propaganda'.[23]

In setting out to examine Engels' criticism of Dronke's prose, one must first of all agree with him to a very large extent. In *Reich und Arm* [Rich and Poor], for example, the first and longest novella in the collection *Aus dem Volk*, the unrelated juxtaposition of social spheres criticised by Engels is already apparent in the very title. Dronke does not contrast the 'negative side' of immiseration with a 'positive side' of an intact bourgeois culture, as Engels at least sees in Beck; in Dronke's work, the socially 'negative side' of poverty is instead overlaid on the 'positive' side of an intact working class morality.

In the novella, we meet Marie, a sixteen-year-old 'working-class girl', who, after the death of her parents, lives alone and impoverished in the attic of a run-down house in a bad neighbourhood behind Berlin Palace. She sews shirts for a 'big shop' on Friedrichstrasse, whose owner constantly squeezes the piece rate from the 'little seamstress'.[24] Her boyfriend, Paul Hofacker, works as a cotton printer in a large factory in the city; he is hardworking and modest and takes Marie for walks every Sunday. A friend of the seamstress, Alwine, has chosen a different path: she is a 'grisette' and lets an aging aristocratic bon vivant, Baron Herzberg, support her. A friend of Herzberg's, Baron Max von Rothenburg has his eye on Marie. Alwine now wants to bring her friend to the Baron in order to rescue her from poverty. After the landlord throws Marie out of her

22 MECW 5, p. 572.

23 MECW 5, p. 572.

24 Dronke, 'Reich und Arm', in: Dronke, 1981, pp. 13–90, here p. 24.

room for outstanding rent, she agrees and becomes Rothenburg's mistress, with some resistance. Paul finds out, condemns his former girlfriend's 'weakness' and breaks off all contact.[25]

After some time, Paul chooses a 'young girl' from the neighbourhood as his bride, they celebrate the wedding, and soon thereafter three children follow. With the wedding and children, however, there begins the descent of this 'working-class family' – the title of the fourth section of the novella, in which a genuine passion tale of the family unfolds. Because of the pregnancies and then the children, Josephe, the young woman, has to give up her 'service jobs', with which she had previously contributed to the family income. As the money runs out, she takes up work again and locks the small children in the flat while she is away. On one such occasion, the two-year-old eldest child fatally burns himself on the stove; the mother suffers a shock and cannot return to work again. Paul asks his 'factory owner', the Baron von Bernheim, for an advance on his wages to pay for the medical expenses for Josephe and the child, as well as for a few days off to tend to his terminally ill child. The factory owner refuses. The child dies while Paul is working at the factory.

After Paul tries to borrow money from a usurer, which fails because he refuses to enter a false guarantor in the promissory note – the section is called 'An Honest Man' – the final and precipitous fall of Paul Hofacker and his family begins, which Dronke hardly needs three pages to describe: incapacitated by a haemorrhage, Paul tries to earn a living as a day labourer. He now leaves 'honest society' for the good of his family: 'They were in the last, most helpless realm of misery and unhappiness, where the warranted *police hunt* begins'.[26] As an underemployed casual labourer, Paul is repeatedly picked up and drawn into the spiral of prison and workhouse. After a court sentences him 'as vagrant and workshy' to six months hard labour followed by 'three years confinement in a correctional house', Paul's fate and that of his family is finally sealed: 'Paul listened to his sentence with dull indifference. He did not ask himself what he had done; he did not care. After all, by being locked up, he escaped the worries and miserable picture [*Jammerbild*] of his family!'[27]

One last 'miserable picture' brings Marie and Paul together again at the Charité hospital. Paul had been transferred there from the 'correctional house' with a fever and learns that his wife and children had 'long since died in poverty'. Marie's life also took a downhill path. Quickly abandoned by Rothenburg, and after several other rich lovers, she finally ended up in a 'house of sin'. 'No longer

25 Dronke 1981, p. 39.
26 Dronke 1981, p. 83.
27 Dronke 1981, p. 84.

profitable enough', she is thrown out on the street by the madam and picked up by the police: 'Since she was ill, they sent her to Charité first; after recuperating, she was to start her sentence in the workhouse'. Marie still hopes she can 'change her life' after the workhouse by marrying a lover. Paul mocks her and her unshakable hopefulness and dies the following night.[28]

That this tale of poverty and descent does indeed testify to a certain 'lack of imagination' and an 'ignorance of real life', as Engels claims, can be corroborated by the fact that essential elements of the story are highly stereotypical: the 'miserable scenes' or 'miserable pictures' – Engels and Dronke use almost the same phrase but with opposing thrusts – appear in such a similar way for a whole series of 'social novels' and 'social novellas' of the time. For example, the little seamstress, the grisette or cleaning lady, always with one foot in prostitution, was already imported as a stereotype from French to German literature.[29] Dronke himself contributed to its establishment as a 'realistic' social figure, not least with his 1846 book *Berlin*, as Engels specifically points out.[30]

4 The Family Romance of the Proletarian

The crucial structural principle of 'Rich and Poor', shared by numerous social novels and novellas of the Vormärz, consists in a familialisation of the social problem of mass poverty: social misery is cast in forms of kinship that are intended to enable and guarantee the immediate sympathy and compassion of the readers, even if they have no personal experience that connects them to the narrative. The bonds of kinship are then effectively consumed – in the literal sense – in the course of the narrative. If there are 'alimentary structures of kinship', as anthropologist Claude Meillassoux has pointed out, then miserabilist literature also generates moments of shock through the fact that family providers can no longer fulfil their function – neither as paternal breadwinners nor maternal nurturers.[31] And so, the starving child, the desperate father and, finally, the *Pietà*, the emaciated proletarian *Mater dolorosa*, become the icons of this miserabilist 'picture of misery'.[32]

28 Dronke 1981, p. 87.
29 See Wachenhusen 1855.
30 See Dronke 1987, especially the section 'Die Grisette', pp. 33–4, where it says: 'Almost all working women have an "affair"'.
31 Meillassoux 1981, p. 50.
32 Otto-Peters 1996, p. 132.

One might call this kind of literature 'petty-bourgeois' since the appeal to the family-coded affects of empathy and compassion firstly presupposes that very code as binding, and secondly, the appeal only reaffirms the code as a tribunal – regardless of whether the family structures in the stories collapse or triumph over adversity. Throughout his life, Engels attacked the patriarchal family and the ensuing bigotry around it, both theoretically, as an anthropologically versed historian who, following the work of Lewis H. Morgan, researched *The Origin of the Family, Private Property and the State*, and practically, in his relationships with the Irish proletarian sisters Mary and Lizzie Burns, which were not guided by any moral standard.[33] He must have been repelled by the invocation of those very bourgeois patriarchal values omnipresent in miserabilist literature. Such values, whose historical specificity Engels sought to reveal, are declared anthropological constants in this literature, the eternal human antithesis of the bad society, and thus made unassailable and unintelligible as a historical formation. To carry Engels' verdict further, the social critique within miserabilist literature turns out to be, against its own intentions, not 'socialist' but 'liberal' – *liberal* since it insists on the integrity of the private sphere and wants to keep it free from external, political-economic influences. Whoever chooses the private sphere – the family, feelings, the natural – as their tribunal affirms *nolens volens* the distinction between the private and non-private, thereby leaving the functioning of the non-private – business, economy, politics – untouched.

Following Tieck, one could say that 'the family' is just as much a decaying product of the 'whole house' as the modern bourgeoisie is of the 'true bourgeoisie'. The house still represents an overarching institutional unity of the spheres of production and reproduction. In the house, different classes – lords and servants, masters and journeymen – are brought together. Only in this way can the house become a site of class struggle (as in Marx), but it can also present the ideal image of a successful class reconciliation (as in Tieck). The family, on the other hand, is socially homogeneous and harmonious in its hegemonic self-narrative. In the social novellas and novels of the Vormärz, all family members belong to the same class. Gender and generational differences can become conflictual, but only as a consequence of external factors hostile to the family. The family is by definition not political; it therefore always appears in the narratives as a victim of the socio-political conditions that break into it and shatter its happiness.

33 Engels' great late work of 1884 can be found in MECW 26, pp. 129–276.

A high point of bourgeois family ideology in the social literature of the Vormärz is the Christmas festival, already given attention in Engels' review of Beck. The 'philanthropic petty-bourgeois hypocrisy' of 'true socialism' shows itself 'in the most trivial possible way … in connection with Christmas'. Engels cites Beck's corresponding poem:

> O day that gently edifies men's hearts,
> You would be gentler still and doubly dear –
> Did there not lodge in *poor* children's hearts
> Whose orphan gaze surveys the festive
> Rooms of their rich playmates,
> Envy and the seeds of sin,
> Along with rabid blasphemy!
> Yes … more sweetly would the children's merry cheer
> Sound to my ears in the Christmas candlelight,
> If only in damp caverns destitution
> Were not shivering on putrid straw.[34]

On Christmas, the unjust coexistence of 'rich and poor' can be symbolised by the equally innocent and socially undivided wishes and aspirations of children, who hold no responsibility for all the misery that will soon separate them socially, and in fact already does. The unfulfilled desires of the poor children, whose hearts are already beginning to be eaten away by 'envy', can no longer be accommodated even in the protective sphere of the family. The festival of love and family thus serves as a contrasting foil against which the distortions of 'modern society' stand out all the more sharply – not least because the poor no longer know what to do with the beautiful festival. In Louise Otto-Peters's novel *Schloss und Fabrik* [*Palace and Factory*], the young daughter of a factory owner, Pauline, decides to 'give presents on Christmas morning to the poor children', after finding out that her father's employees are forced to live in poverty and misery.[35] Against her father's resistance, she carries through her philan-

---

34 MECW 6, p. 246.

35 Otto-Peters 1996, p. 68. The committed women's rights activist Louise Otto-Peters not only advocated for a *women's right to earn a living* – the title of her perhaps best-known pamphlet from 1866 [*Das Recht der Frauen auf Erwerb*] – but also repeatedly emphasised the responsibility of bourgeois women in particular to combat the negative consequences of industrialisation. In the character of Pauline, she paints a cautionary portrait that shows where middle-class commitment leads when the narcissism of wanting to help is not rationally controlled.

thropic plan and finally has the children line up on Christmas morning in the 'brilliantly decorated hall of the factory building' to distribute the presents. The desired effect, however, does not appear:

> But these were pale, thin children, scantily clad in unclean rags, whose small hands and half-crippled limbs were already accustomed to hard work, whose faces showed how often their small mouths with their colourless lips had to ask for bread in vain, how in those dull, downcast eyes there was an expression of animalistic, mute acquiescence. These small, pallid children had stared strangely at each other as they had been led to the shimmering Christmas trees and then given the warm skirts and shoes with red apples and rattling nuts. They had accepted the gifts without thanks and rejoice, almost without joy – and only following a rough instinct had they brought the fruit to their mouths – the daily misery and the constant work made them so completely powerless of any emotion, Pauline had to cry aloud when she saw these unhappy little ones gathered around her – but she wept not out of quiet emotion, as she had probably imagined, but out of deep, endless sorrow, which she thought must cut all the way through her soft heart.[36]

The desired reconciliation at the celebration of love goes wrong; class antagonism not only pervades the stomach, it burrows deep in their hearts. When love and emotion no longer allow rapprochement, then the chances of a peaceful understanding between the classes as a whole are dim – this is the warning message of the miserabilist Christmas festivities.[37]

In *Reich und Arm* [*Rich and Poor*], we find another key element of familial imagination that structures the 'social novellas' and novels of the time, shaping their ideology: namely, that the ideally opposed protagonists of the antagonistic classes, the rich capitalist and the rebellious worker, are in fact related, or, more directly, they are brothers. Ernst Willkomm's bulky *Weisse Sclaven* [*White Slaves*] has such an 'exceedingly convoluted plot', not only because three brothers appear on the side of the capitalists, each of whom embodies a distinct kind of capitalist (Adrian von Stein, the sadistic factory despot; Aurel, the versatile global merchant; Adalbert, the disinterested coupon cutter), but because Martell, a fourth and illegitimate half-brother, appears as a labour leader on strike in Adrian's textile factory and represents the interests of his

36 Otto-Peters 1996, pp. 76–7.

37 See also Willkomm 2013, the chapter 'Des Armen Weihnachten' [Poor Man's Christmas], pp. 438–48.

class-brothers against his biological brothers.[38] The fact that Martell and the three von Stein gentlemen are brothers is revealed only in the course of the plot and none of the four know about the relation. Martell is the son of poor Marianne, who was raped and later murdered by the von Stein patriarch, Magnus von Boberstein, a tyrant of the old estate. Separated from his biological father, Martell grows up in poverty with a wet nurse and ends up having to work as a hired hand to the son of his mother's rapist. In the chapter 'Adrian and Martell', the two brothers meet for a showdown, a final 'duel' in which Adrian perishes.[39]

The double figure of hostile brothers also structures *Rich and Poor*, for the worker Paul is the brother of Baron von Rothenburg. Paul, the firstborn, is abducted at the age of four and raised by the village fool Betty Hofacker. Max, on the other hand, remains 'heir to the barons' estates'. Part of the novella's makeshift tension stems from the fact that Paul and Max are brought together as the story progresses, while the reader anticipates a dynamic revelation. But it never comes. Paul and Max meet briefly at Alwine's, after the poor brother had to learn from her that his great love, Marie, has now become the kept mistress of Max, of all people: 'These rich people take everything from us, our love, all our enjoyment of life. At best, they allow us to eke out a miserable existence through endless work, so that hunger does not drive us against them'.[40] Unlike in Willkomm's *White Slaves*, there is no anagnorisis of the brothers in *Rich and Poor*. In the end, the carriage carrying Rothenburg and his bride (who is, of course, the daughter of the Baron von Bernheim, a factory owner who had previously tormented Paul) to Anhalter Bahnhof on their way to their honeymoon nearly collides with the hearse carrying Paul's body to the pauper's grave. At the corner of Friedrichstrasse and Kochstrasse, the two carriages are forced together by a reckless overtaking manoeuvre of Max's coachman, and both begin to swerve: 'but then the silver-clad coachman struck his horses with an angry curse, and the carriage dashed off. The hearse overturned from the force of the blow and was righted by passing workers'.[41]

'The triumph of the rich should strike the poor even in death'.[42] The hostile, class-antagonistic brothers can be understood as a variant of the model of 'constricted spaces' that will emerge paradigmatically (and admittedly, in reverse orientation) in the love concepts of later realism. Dronke, Willkomm and oth-

38 Adler 1998, p. 204.
39 Willkomm 2013, starting at p. 650.
40 Dronke 1981, pp. 38–9.
41 Dronke 1981, p. 85.
42 Dronke 1981, p. 90.

ers must narratively limit the open social space of the new class society, which is characterised by a contingency of positional assignments difficult to comprehend. The (misunderstood) juxtaposition of wealth and poverty, happiness and misery, life and death must be made plausible and vivid as a juxtaposition of things that are actually similar, which are only driven apart and set against each other by an incomprehensible 'fate':

> This was the end of things.
>
> The two brothers, born of the same circumstances, but separated from each other by a strange fate, by the insurmountable chasm of society, each came to an end, as the conditions of different circumstances entail. One got everything, while the other failed. The former robbed the latter of his love; he found salvation in the danger where the latter lost it; and even in the enclosure of his domestic hearth [the 'liberal' critique!], the one found the stage of his happiness, while it became ruin for the other. The rich ... triumphed; the poor ... succumbed to misery. Growing up in the same circumstances, both might have experienced a happier, but certainly more evenly distributed and fairer lot.[43]

Where Engels wants to theoretically mediate the juxtapositions in a historical-genetic context of mutual constitution and let them emerge from each other, in Dronke's case blind fate becomes the power that connects and separates; fate, however, primarily befalls families or generations. *Rich and Poor* also relies on a narrative of generational succession, and in the complicated texture of Willkomm's novel we can trace the 'much-interwoven tangle of crimes committed long ago' that 'enmeshed' all participants 'with magical power', down to the second and third generations.[44] The history of the 'original accumulation of capital' in Lower Lusatia, and thus the history of class formation in general, unfolds in Willkomm's novel as a mythical family history of rape, robbery, repudiation, reconquest and revenge. The essential injustice, however, and the sheer coincidence with which the market 'hovers over the earth like the fate of the ancients, and with invisible hands allots fortune and misfortune to men' – this profound and impersonal injustice of systematic contingency of the capitalist economy is made both visible and invisible through the narrative of the family.[45] The narrative insertion of the family into the backdrop is ideology and ideology critique in one.

43 Dronke 1981, p. 90.
44 Willkomm 2013, p. 383.
45 Marx and Engels 1845, *German Ideology*, MECW 5, p. 48.

5 Relentlessness

Starting from this ambivalence, a modest attempt can perhaps be made to save the honour of miserabilist literature and especially of Dronke, who was specifically reproached by Engels. To this end, one will first have to agree with the central accusations made by Engels, and Dronke himself agrees – to a certain anticipatory extent. Thus, Dronke accepts Engels' reproach that his novellas are ultimately *Tendenzpoesie* [*tendentious poetry*] which 'serve only to foist Herr Dronke's socialist ideas on people in whose mouth they are completely inappropriate'.[46] Already in the preface to the collection *Aus dem Volk*, Dronke takes the wind out of the sails by outlining the program of a literature that sees itself openly and offensively as a poetic 'means' to a political 'end':

> The *following* pages have no other purpose than to provide episodes from real life, and thus mainly to present the contrasts and inadequate guarantees of the *human* justification of contemporary society. These pages have a 'tendency' at their basis: it is true. I have not written these novellas in order to 'write novellas'; I am not stingy with the honour of being a 'fiction writer'. Rather, I have draped the 'tendency', which could undoubtedly be brought before the public in a pamphlet, a critique or a history of contemporary society and the like, in the garb of the novella only because in this *form* of tracing real life the truth of those conditions comes most clearly and most eloquently before the eyes and thus has a greater effect than abstract treatises.[47]

That the accusation of crafting *Tendenzpoesie* was not particularly original at the time, but rather to be expected, is already made clear here by the fact that Dronke repeatedly places 'tendency' in quotation marks. Indeed, distancing oneself from *Tendenzpoesie* is one of the obligatory gestures of literary self-assurance in the Vormärz (and beyond). When Dronke in his preface takes up *and affirms*, meta-rhetorically as it were, the discourse of language as the clothing of thought and, further, that of poetic language as a particularly artful dress, then Engels' *critically* intended revelation of Dronke's literature as merely the more or less artful coating of the author's thoughts misfires. That the content of the novella could just as well find its place 'in a pamphlet, a critique or a history of contemporary society' is almost coquettishly formu-

46 MECW 5, p. 572.
47 Dronke 1981, 'Vorwort', p. 10.

lated; that, however, literary dressing is supposed to be particularly suitable for placing this content 'clearly and eloquently before the eyes' of the reader corresponds to a classical rhetorical tradition: nothing else is meant by *evidentia*, which can be interpreted as a metatrope of literary speech in the first place. As has been shown, the makers of the *Gesellschaftsspiegel* – among them Engels – also invoked this tradition at the same time when they announced that they would include 'poetry' in their magazine, as long as it gives a '*faithful* portrayal of life' and presents social circumstances as 'evident facts'.

Dronke urges us to judge his novellas only according to his own programme: 'the "art form" according to the rules of aesthetics may be taken as a yardstick in the works where this ["art form"] is the end: here it was the means'.[48] So if we now take the 'true, unvarnished view of the contemporary contrasts of life' as the 'yardstick', then we may indeed glimpse here the beginnings of a whole 'new genre of artistic writing', as Engels scoffs.[49] The essential characteristic of this literature is that the focus is not on *narration*, but on the *description* of social conditions and circumstances. Engels also understood this correctly, without, however, hitting the crucial point. When Engels criticises Dronke's novellas for 'lachrymose descriptions', which instead of real storytelling can only notice 'pictures of the conflicts in modern society' – then this must be taken just as literally as Dronke's own talk of 'miserable pictures': we are dealing here with a mode of writing that repeatedly solidifies itself in literary images, depictions and tableaux.[50] The mere juxtaposition, which for Engels prevents 'narration' in the full, proper sense, produces instead a series of images that should not be judged by narrative criteria such as tension, probability or resolution, but rather by the accuracy of representation. Dronke's novellas thus actually prefigure – not alone, but to an astonishing degree – a new, realistic or, more precisely, social-realist literature, whose novelty is apparent both in its 'material' and in its specific treatment of the material.[51] In the literary-political debates of the 1850s, 'realism' will be fought through as the new binding paradigm, but the winning party around Julian Schmidt and Gustav Freytag will again very strongly prize 'narrative' as the genuine potency of literature. The descriptive *juxtaposition* will be rejected and devalued by the 'bourgeois' propagandists Schmidt and Freytag, just as much as the socialist Engels.

---

48 Dronke 1981, p. 10 (addition by the editor).

49 MECW 5, p. 570.

50 MECW 5, p. 572.

51 MECW 5, p. 570.

The very first page of the first chapter offers an example of Dronke's descriptive-realistic craftsmanship.[52] The description of social stratification in a Berlin tenement building with the inverted coupling of floor and social status captures with extreme precision all groups and subgroups of the Vormärz proletariat. The brief outline of the crisis of the crafts and especially the crisis of the 'small master craftsmen', which Dronke 'dresses' in a flashback story of the impoverishment of Marie's father, a poor tailor, can hardly be surpassed in terms of concision. Even figures on the 'overstaffing' of handicrafts find their place here ('Berlin counts about three thousand self-employed tailors').[53] In addition, there are facts that are no longer known, at least today, and are hardly dealt with in contemporaneous sources either – that, for example, the garrisons maintained 'workers divisions' that were repeatedly 'dismissed for longer periods' in the event of insufficient employment, and then flooded the local labour markets as cheap labour.[54]

Such detailed, realistic depictions of social conditions frequently give rise to moments that Engels' critique cannot challenge. At times, Dronke's scenes of misery are condensed into a few terse sentences, after which the author obviously finds it difficult to maintain even a makeshift pace of narrative. After detailing the figures of the compensation scheme for Marie's domestic labour and the systematic wage suppression of the textile merchants, the first chapter, for example, reads: 'And that was her life day after day, without variety, without prospects. What enjoyment does the girl receive for her work? When she dies, can she not rightly ask whether she ever lived at all?'[55] The bitter punchline, that Marie of course can no longer ask anything at all after she has died, *and that no one else will ask about her either*, is played by Dronke without dragging it out. 'Dying early without having lived', says Tieck's Leonhard, a formula that describes precisely the *modus vivendi* (or *moriendi*) of Dronke's characters.[56]

The ideology of the bourgeois family in the novella serves as a contrasting foil for the misery of proletarians, as well as a tribunal. The fact that the value system of the family does not necessarily have to be affirmed – even if negatively – but, conversely, is sometimes proverbially hounded into oblivion, proves itself again and again, especially toward the end of the passion tale of

52 Dronke 1981, p. 19.
53 Dronke 1981, p. 22.
54 Dronke 1981, p. 22.
55 Dronke 1981, p. 24.
56 Tieck 1988b, p. 75.

Paul and his family. Even the description of the first period after the wedding can hardly be surpassed in terms of its bleakness:

> Thus, they lived in alternating, unsteady circumstances, both separated in a toilsome struggle for their meagre existence. Where was their domestic happiness? They saw themselves almost exhausted by the exertions of the day, glad that the night was there, where they could seek rest in slumber. Their persistent labour, which robbed them of the enjoyment of a peaceful life, helped them to nothing; it hardly protected them any longer from the ultimate extreme want, and at most sustained them to a doubtful existence of insecure, sad misery.[57]

If 'domestic happiness' still appears in the background as a (crossed out) ideal, it retreats further and further until finally – at least in the darkest parts of the novella – it disappears altogether. The fact that he has married and brought children into the world ultimately becomes the very embodiment of Paul's misery: 'If only I didn't have you!' What, against the background of a patriarchal image of the family, can only be understood as an expression of fatherly joy and fatherly pride, becomes for Paul the utopian unreality of a lonely, familyless existence in which he could somehow make his way alone and perhaps even find happiness:

> 'If only I didn't have you!' he murmured with gloom, with a glance at his own poor resources. 'If I got rid of you, left you! That alone could still save me, and create a better lot for me! Your fate is decided, what do you want from life? I cannot help you, only perish with you, you drag me with you if I stay with you! But alone – me, I! At least I can perhaps then still be happy!'[58]

Of course, Paul does not leave his family. Dronke concludes, perhaps ironically, that the 'power of sweet habit' continued to 'bind' Paul to his own family. The family appears only as a curse; but whether this negatively (and uncritically) merely upholds the promise of the bourgeois family once more, as one might say with Engels, becomes increasingly questionable.

At the end, shortly before Paul's death in the poor ward of Charité hospital, the 'family's sky of values' finally darkens entirely in an image of complete tran-

57 Dronke 1981, p. 54.
58 Dronke 1981, p. 82.

scendencelessness.[59] After Paul tells Marie that his wife and children have died, she, the notorious optimist, tries to cheer him up with the thoroughly conventional prospect of a heavenly reunion: 'God will reunite you in eternal life'. Paul's reply is short and unrelenting: '"I don't want to know about any more life", said the sick man sullenly. "I'm tired of being flayed"'.[60]

'We poor people ... I believe that if we went to heaven, we would still have to serve thunder'.[61] Where Woyzeck still plays the game of imagination (*what would it be like up there?*), for Paul the mere offer of such a game becomes an imposition. Not only does he not want to be 'flayed' in heaven, he also does not want to be flayed here and now by a prospect that would exceed his naked and imminent end. Dronke always escapes the kitsch, the clichés and tastelessness of miserabilism when his language becomes laconic; when the desire to represent misery eschews the embellishment of that misery; when familial patriarchal values as a tribunal are replaced by the simple things of life, reproduction, and death. The fact that there is no longer any spark of hope to be found, that Dronke, in his best moments, instead succeeds in stripping the misery of any prospect of a consoling (or avenging) otherworldly beyond – that is what comprises the greatness of this literature.

In this way, Dronke even goes beyond Engels. As differentiated and accurate as his criticisms are over long stretches, Engels' positive counterproposals remain crude. One could have guessed already in the 1840s that the 'proud, threatening, and revolutionary proletarian' of whom Engels would like to read would have been just as kitschy or even kitschier than Beck's 'poor man' or even Dronke's bleak figures.[62] Engels' fantasies of revolutionary violence in which a horde of angry proletarians punish, 'by means of lamp-posts', those miserabilist writers who had previously made literary capital out of their social misery, seem no less unintentionally comic than the poetic outpourings of the 'true socialists' he mocked.[63] Even in these fantasies, the misery of the present is legitimised by revenge in the future, which appears as its reward.[64] Dronke's profane relentlessness already went further.

59 Koschorke et al. 2010, p. 7.

60 Dronke 1981, p. 87.

61 Büchner 1993, *Woyzeck*, scene 6, my own translation. Georg Büchner, *Woyzeck*, MBA 7.1, p. 63.

62 MECW 6, p. 235.

63 MECW 5, p. 572.

64 Cf. Engels: 'When things reach the stage when the German proletarians settle their accounts with the bourgeoisie and the other propertied classes, they will, by means of lamp-posts, show the knights of the pen, the lowest of all venal classes, how far they are proletarians' (MECW 5, p. 572).

6 Mystères – Misère

The quintessence of Engels' critique of Dronke and other 'true socialists' is that they did not really *understand* the world they intended to realistically portray and could therefore only present it as a mere juxtaposition of unconnected facts, which ultimately entailed no *critical penetration* but at best a *moral scandalising* of the state of the world, a critique not limited to second or third-rate German poets. Engels and Marx applied it equally to the most prominent and widely read contemporaneous representatives of French social literature and social theory: Eugène Sue and Pierre-Joseph Proudhon.

Sue's *Les Mystères de Paris* was first published in ninety instalments in the liberal *Journal des débats*, between June 1842 and October 1843, before the novel appeared as a book in late 1843. It immediately became an international best-seller and its own seminal genre. In Germany, a first translation appeared as early as 1843. By 1848, at least ten imitations had come on the market, each purporting to explore the *Mysteries of Berlin* [three versions!], *Königsberg, Vienna, Hamburg, Amsterdam* and *Brussels*. In Sue's many hundreds of pages, the Grand Duke Rudolph of Gerolstein goes incognito in the Paris underworld. Together with his faithful servant Murph, he rescues fallen damsels from the clutches of their pimps and leads even hardened, violent criminals back to the right path, sometimes by brutal means – the 'schoolmaster', for example, is blinded by Rudolph so that he may find repentance through blindness. In contrast, Rudolph, as a nobleman, gets acquainted with the high society of Paris – and Sue's novel thus presents both, dive bars and ballrooms, to the curious eye of the reader.

Marx already dealt with Sue in his first book, *The Holy Family* (written together with Engels), at first, however, only from the side, as it were, mediated by a polemic against an (again, at best third-rate) German adept of Sue, the 'critical critic' and Young Hegelian Szeliga-Wischnu.[65] The latter had referred to Sue in an article and elevated the title of Sue's novel to a 'critical' concept: 'Herr Szeliga conceives all present world conditions as mysteries. But whereas *Feuerbach* disclosed *real mysteries*, Herr *Szeliga* makes *mysteries* out of real *trivialities*. His art is not that of disclosing what is hidden, but of hiding what is

65 Marx and Engels 1845, *The Holy Family, or Critique of Critical Criticism. Against Bauer and Company*, MECW 4, pp. 5–212. In The *Holy Family*, Marx and Engels complete the final break with the young Hegelian party, which they dispose with through the figure of their mastermind Bruno Bauer and his disciples. 'Szeliga' is the pseudonym of the Berlin officer and journalist Franz von Zychlin.

disclosed'.[66] In his detailed, dissecting (and, at least for today's readers, often agonising) polemic, Marx at first only opposes the mixing of the spheres of literature and theory, which Szeliga offensively propagates, for example, when he postulates that 'if the *Critic* wished, he could also be a *poet*'.[67] Sue himself is not yet targeted here by Marx; Marx even appreciates that everything which appears to the dumb German Szeliga as a genuine metaphysical *mystery* is to be understood in Sue as rather an aesthetic refinement. The confrontation between the rabble and the 'haute volée', between the gutter and the boudoir, should not be understood as a misunderstanding and thus truly mysterious juxtaposition, but rather as an effective contrast that evokes an aesthetic thrill in the reader: 'M. Eugène Sue has counted on the timid curiosity of his readers in all his novels', claims Marx, and he has also provoked and served this curiosity to the best of his ability.[68] Where Marx already consigns Szeliga to ridicule, he spares Sue (for the time being) and credits this man of letters with an aesthetic calculation, while the (would-be) theorist must be credited with merely a category error, as an embarrassing confusion of art and science.

However, the fact that Sue knows how to make aesthetic – and as a best-selling author, also economic – capital out of misery and especially out of the stark difference between misery and wealth in the manner described above must, sooner or later, provoke Marx to criticise Sue himself.[69] Since Sue's social world, in all its confusion and depravity, is structured by the simple juxtaposition of good and evil, Sue's superhero Rudolph can also only perform the task of '*rewarding the good* and *punishing the wicked*' in his own way.[70] The 'morally coerced gratifications' initiated by Rudolph have consistently disastrous consequences for the gratified.[71] The strongman Chournier is raised to be a specimen of 'moral bulldogishness' who takes a stabbing for his master.[72] The former prostitute Marie, who had always remained 'joyful and unaffected', becomes '*enslaved by the consciousness of sin*' through Rudolph's education, for whom the 'continual hypochondriacal self-torture' becomes 'the self-purpose of her existence'.[73]

66 MECW 4, p. 56.
67 MECW 4, p. 55.
68 MECW 4, p. 57.
69 Cf. *The Holy Family*, Chapter VIII, 'The Earthly Course and Transfiguration of "Critical Criticism", or "Critical Criticism" as Rudolph, Prince of Geroldstein (by Marx)', MECW 4, pp. 162–209.
70 MECW 4, p. 188.
71 Bachleitner 1993, p. 166.
72 MECW 4, p. 165.
73 MECW 4, pp. 171, 174.

Marx reveals the social and judicial reform projects integrated by Sue in his novel as a collage of the 'most pitiful off-scourings of socialist literature', especially of Fourierian provenance.[74] Finally, with particular devotion, Marx analyses two projects that play a prominent role in Sue's work: a 'Bank for the Poor' and the agricultural 'model farm at Bouqueval'. Here, Marx simply calculates their economic unfeasibility, for instance: 'The difference between the Critical Bank for the Poor and the mass-type savings-bank is therefore that the worker loses his interest and the Bank its capital', and later, 'The Bouqueval model farm is nothing but a fantastic illusion; its *hidden fund* is not the *natural* land of the Bouqueval estate, it is a magic purse of Fortunatas that Rudolph has!'[75] The fact that Marx attacks Sue's projects not from a literary but an economic point of view indicates how they are clearly not literary fantasies but set pieces of contemporaneous socialist theorists. This is Marx's actual concern: when Marx lunges at Sue, he aims for Proudhon.

Since the appearance of *What Is Property?* in 1840, Proudhon emerged as one of the leading figures of the French socialist movement. The blast of 'La propriété, c'est le vol!' ('Property is theft!'), found on the very first page of his book, is also omnipresent in the German socialist literature of the 1840s.[76] While Marx was initially close to Proudhon's views for a few months – the writings on property in particular represented for Marx a bridge from German philosophy to modern political economy – there is already an estrangement in the course of 1846 that finally culminated in Marx's second book in 1847: *Misère de la philosophie. Réponse à la philosophie de la misère de M. Proudhon*, or *The Poverty of Philosophy: Answer to the 'Philosophy of Poverty' by M. Proudhon.*[77] Proudhon had presented his second major work in 1846, *Système des contradictions économiques ou Philosophie de la misère*, in which he now provided his philosophical-economic theses in the guise of a Hegelianised dialectic.[78] This ambitious mode of presentation forms the starting point of Marx's polemic, in which he shows that Proudhon is not in fact at all familiar with Hegel's thought and that Proudhon's dialectic is at best a malapropism of the original. In truth, Marx primarily uses the confrontation with Proudhon's ideas on political eco-

74 MECW 4, p. 196.

75 MECW 4. pp. 199–200

76 Proudhon 1994.

77 Marx 1847, *The Poverty of Philosophy*, MECW 6, pp. 105–212. First published in French, the German translation by Karl Kautsky and Eduard Bernstein, with a preface by Engels, was not published until 1885 by Dietz in Stuttgart.

78 Proudhon 1888. A first German translation of the *Système* by Karl Grün and Wilhelm Jordan was published as early as 1847 under the title *Philosophie der Staatsökonomie oder Notwendigkeit des Elends by* Leske in Darmstadt.

nomy to systematically develop his own reflections in the field for the first time. Marx presents his criticism of Proudhon to a large extent as a critique of language. In doing so, however, Marx not only deals with the matter itself – the 'critique of political economy', as it will later be called – but also with the problem of possible ways of presenting criticism. In the *Poverty of Philosophy*, Marx seeks to overcome miserabilism in theory as well, implicitly elaborating his own ideal of 'critique through presentation', which he will later name as such.[79]

Like the 'critical critic' Szeliga, Marx also reproaches Proudhon for transfiguring facts – that are either obvious or demand explanation – into 'mysteries'. Already in a brief preliminary remark, Marx mocks Proudhon's high tone: Proudhon's *Système* presents itself 'not just a treatise on political economy, an ordinary book; it is a bible. "Mysteries", "Secrets Wrested from the Bosom of God", "Revelations" – it lacks nothing'.[80] Just as Szeliga could see only 'mysteries' everywhere because he had fallen for Sue's aesthetic calculus, so Proudhon must see mysteries everywhere because he neither understands the economic authors (whom he embarrassingly attempts to criticise at every turn) nor comprehends Hegel, whose terminology he employs everywhere. Against 'the profound mystery of opposition and contradiction', which Proudhon already identifies in the distinction between exchange value and use value, Marx upholds the strict and austere logic of David Ricardo, who analysed this distinction with all desirable clarity – to the point where it no longer reveals itself as a logical problem, but as a *social contradiction*.[81] Even from the point of view of the critique of language, Ricardo remains the measure of all things for Marx in the field of political economy:

> Doubtless, Ricardo's language is as cynical as can be. To put the cost of manufacture of hats and the cost of maintenance of men on the same plane is to turn men into hats.[82] But do not make an outcry at the cynicism of it. The cynicism is in the facts and not in the words which express the facts. French writers like M.M. Droz, Blanqui, Rossi and others take

79 See the subsection 'Exaggeration and Distance: The Style of Criticism' in the third chapter of this book.

80 MECW 6, p. 110.

81 MECW 6, p. 115.

82 Marx had just quoted a passage from Ricardo: '*Diminish the cost of production* of hats, and their price will ultimately fall to their new natural price, although the demand should be doubled, trebled, or quadrupled. Diminish the cost of subsistence of men, by diminishing the natural price of the food and clothing by which life is sustained, and wages will ultimately fall, notwithstanding that the demand for labourers may very greatly increase' (MECW 6, pp. 124–5).

> an innocent satisfaction in proving their superiority over the English economists, by seeking to observe the etiquette of a 'humanitarian' phraseology; if they reproach Ricardo and his school for their cynical language, it is because it annoys them to see economic relations exposed in all their crudity, to see the mysteries of the bourgeoisie unmasked.[83]

The critique of language is not a matter of taste, but represents one of the core functions of critique in general: every critique of ideology begins as a critique of language. Those who recoil from the 'cynical language' of English political economists and instead take refuge in the '"humanitarian" phraseology' of 'French writers', also forgo exposing the 'facts' themselves and instead hide behind 'words'. It is the task of critique to commit *treason*. It must renounce false loyalties to the power of the 'bourgeoisie' and divulge its trade secret: that the emperor is naked, that there are no 'mysteries'. The 'mysteries of the bourgeoisie' are to be replaced by naked proletarian truth without any false shame. All moral evaluations are thus revalued: since the facts themselves are cynical, it is necessary to name them just as cynically. Those who think they have to speak in a 'humanitarian' way – in quotation marks! – only make themselves accomplices of the real cynicism of conditions.

In this critique of the French school of political economy, Marx and Engels' critique of miserabilist literature is repeated. The latter, too, used a 'humanitarian' language precisely in order to shield itself from real insights into the origin and nature of the lamented misery. What miserabilist literature lacks, therefore, is the courage to use a 'cynical language' that rises to the level of the prevailing cynicism of reality.

Yet another line of argument from Engels' literary criticism can be found in Marx's polemic against Proudhon: where the poets of 'true socialism' can only present isolated elements of social life and then merely file them away according to a moral sorting system, Proudhon too can only ever isolate 'two sides' of everything, 'one good, the other bad', without being able to grasp both as *moments* of a contradiction in movement.[84] Where the 'true socialists' of literature fail in narrative, the 'true socialists' of theory fail in dialectics.

The fact that Proudhon is not a great dialectician is for Marx only a nuisance, since everywhere he claims the opposite. The application of dialectics to questions of political economy, which Proudhon alleges to have accomplished, becomes Marx's life's work. Meanwhile, the mockery continues:

---

83 MECW 6, p. 124.

84 MECW 6, p. 167.

> Let us see now to what modifications M. Proudhon subjects Hegel's dialectics when he applies it to political economy.
>
> For him, M. Proudhon, every economic category has two sides – one good, the other bad. He looks upon these categories as the petty bourgeois looks upon the great men of history: *Napoleon* was a great man; he did a lot of good; he also did a lot of harm.
>
> The *good side* and the *bad side*, the *advantages* and the *drawbacks*, taken together form for M. Proudhon the *contradiction* in every economic category.
>
> The problem to be solved: to keep the good side, while eliminating the bad.[85]

With tables in which he sorts Proudhon's arguments according to 'good' and 'bad sides', Marx takes his mockery to the extreme, since the 'dialectical movement', whose reconstruction matters, can in no way be grasped in the form of a table – that much is clear for Marx.[86] With the table, Marx wants to demonstrate that Proudhon's theory can only isolate individual facts, where it should instead proceed through the conceptual reconstruction of a *living process* and the reconstruction of necessarily interdependent relations.[87] Where dialectics liquefies thinking in general by depicting 'the coexistence of two contradictory sides, their conflict and their fusion into a new category', Proudhon's petty-bourgeois rubric thinking leads to an eternalisation of now static, ossified moments.[88] All categories of political economy, whose historicisation, according to Marx, should be at stake – value, money, division of labour, competition – appear in Proudhon as 'eternal law' or 'eternal necessity'.[89] In other words: 'The sequence of categories has become a sort of *scaffolding*. Dialectics has ceased to be the movement of absolute reason. There is no longer any dialectics but only, at the most, absolutely pure morality'.[90]

Once again, moralising about prevailing conditions overtakes their conceptualisation. But where there is no conceptualisation, there are no concepts; and 'where ideas fail', as Goethe's Mephisto already knows, 'words come in very handy'. In the end, with Proudhon, there is only the 'mere word' and 'rhetorical form'; the entire dialectic degenerates into a mere 'manner of speaking'.[91]

85 MECW 6, p. 167.
86 MECW 6, p. 168.
87 Cf. MECW 6, starting at p. 145.
88 MECW 6, p. 168.
89 MECW 6, pp. 179, 191.
90 MECW 6, p. 169.
91 MECW 6, pp. 179, 173, 168. Translation revised.

7 Misery in Relations: Production, World Market, Needs

If Marx really wants to go beyond Proudhon, then he must put all the categories that Proudhon isolates and ossifies back into 'motion' and present them as relations. Marx now puts misery into relation in three ways:

a) First, Marx points out that poverty can only be meaningfully defined in relation to wealth, and more precisely, that both, poverty and wealth, have to be understood as results of social relations of production. Social poverty and social wealth are produced, thereby reproducing the class relation at the same time. Relations of production, however, demonstrate their 'dual' character in this,

> that in the selfsame relations in which wealth is produced, poverty is produced also … that these relations produce *bourgeois wealth*, i.e. the wealth of the bourgeois class, only by continually annihilating the wealth of the individual members of this class and by producing an ever-growing proletariat.[92]

Poverty and wealth, however, do not stand in a reciprocal relation simply because of limited resources. Even with constantly expanding social production, the opposition is produced and reproduced in an equally expanded manner: the production of poverty *and* wealth emerges from a relation of exploitation that is directly linked to the social form of wage labour (and not, for instance, to excessively low wages).[93] With figures showing the increase in the productivity of social labour in Great Britain between 1770 and 1840, Marx makes it clear that intensified exploitation does not represent a contradiction to expanded production, but rather that the two are mutually dependent. According to these figures, in 1840 twenty-seven times more was produced each working day than seventy years prior:

> According to M. Proudhon, the following question should be raised: why was not the English worker of 1840 twenty-seven times as rich as the one of 1770? In raising such a question one would naturally be supposing that the English could have produced this wealth without the historical conditions in which it was produced, such as: private accumulation of

92 MECW 6, p. 176.

93 Louise Otto-Peters poignantly writes that the factory gives 'bread and misery alike', Otto-Peters 1996, p. 71.

> capital, modern division of labour, automatic workshops, anarchical competition, the wage system – in short, everything that is based upon class antagonism. Now, these were precisely the necessary conditions of existence for the development of productive forces and of the surplus left by labour. Therefore, to obtain this development of productive forces and this surplus left by labour, there had to be classes which profited and classes which decayed.[94]

b) The fact that poverty (and wealth) cannot be determined individually, but only in social relations, implies for Marx that national and individual standpoints do not suffice. A meaningful determination of social misery in the present, according to Marx in 1847, can only be made against the backdrop of the world market and the global division of labour: even if material poverty in England decreases in phases, we would still have to speak of 'the millions of workers who had to perish in the East Indies so as to procure for the million and a half workers employed in the same industry in England three years' prosperity out of ten'.[95] If capitalism is a relation of production whose production of wealth 'depends entirely on the world market, on international exchange, on an international division of labour', then we must also assume a global production of misery, a world market of misery.[96]

An examination of the global context also reveals the relationship between wealth and poverty as an *intra*-class relationship, as a relation and potential clash of interests within the 'global working class' (Marcel van der Linden).[97] Due to competition, which cannot be separated from the division of labour and the market, prosperity for one fraction of the global proletariat is always accompanied by the poverty of another fraction. That the relations between North and South have become more flexible since Marx's time, and that it is no longer clear from the outset who will win and who will lose within global competition, does not change the structural connection. The fact that the world market and the international competition of workers was already perceived and accepted as a challenge to literature in the Vormärz period will be encountered again below in Willkomm's *Weisse Sclaven* [*White Slaves*].

c) Finally, social misery must be put in relation to needs. Accordingly, one can only speak of misery or poverty when needs are permanently unmet. But what

94 MECW 6, p. 159.
95 MECW 6, p. 160.
96 MECW 6, p. 187.
97 See Linden 2008.

are needs? To Marx, Proudhon simply presupposes human needs in an abstract and ahistorical manner, without attending to the 'genealogical details' of their emergence.[98] Instead, needs must be interpreted as socially produced and thus historically variable. Since human beings in modern societies inevitably have needs that presuppose the division of labour and exchange, Proudhon would have to also regard exchange and the division of labour as unquestionable givens.[99] In his theory of value, based on the juxtaposition of use value and exchange value, Proudhon supposes a 'struggle between two as it were incommensurable powers'. Use value is based on need, while exchange value (or simply 'value') is based on 'estimation' or convention. In this way, however, Proudhon promotes a false ontologisation of use value and thus of need:

> Most things have value only because they satisfy needs engendered by estimation. The estimation of our needs may change; therefore the utility of things, which expresses only a relation of these things to our needs, may also change. Natural needs themselves are continually changing. Indeed, what could be more varied than the objects which form the staple food of different peoples![100]

There are no natural needs, Marx emphasises, that are not always already socially and thus historically determined. '[A]ll history', he says later on, 'is nothing but a continuous transformation of human nature'.[101] Needs are produced within a system in which they can only appear as demand and consumption, which are themselves productive and part of a social relation of production.

This means that consumption should be regarded as part of a class relation. Additionally, what appears as a 'natural need' is fundamentally shaped by class relations. Class society 'dictated its orders to consumption' by already adapting the qualitative nature of products to class-conditioned needs:

> Cotton, potatoes and spirits are objects of the most common use. Potatoes have engendered scrofula; cotton has to a great extent driven out flax and wool, although wool and flax are, in many cases, of greater utility, if only from the point of view of hygiene; finally, spirits have got the upper hand of beer and wine, although spirits used as an alimentary substance are

98 MECW 6, p. 113.
99 MECW 6, p. 112.
100 MECW 6, p. 117.
101 MECW 6, p. 192.

> everywhere recognised to be poison. ... Why are cotton, potatoes and spirits the pivots of bourgeois society? Because the least amount of labour is needed to produce them, and, consequently, they have the lowest price.[102]

Far from appealing to any pre-social nature, under capitalist conditions the very form of needs – and not their mere non-fulfilment – constitutes misery: 'in a society founded on *poverty* the *poorest* products have the fatal prerogative of being used by the greatest number'.[103]

Now one could counter that potatoes are still better than *no* potatoes; but it is precisely this kind of calculation that Marx accuses Proudhon of making in the first place. To think in this way would mean 'accepting the present state of affairs; it is, in short, making an apology ... for a society without understanding it'.[104] To fix 'natural needs' in present society by setting a subsistence level is always also to fix how much a person has to earn at least in order to reproduce their existence. In this way, however, the (pre)supposition of natural needs serves to depress wages; for the wage is measured by what the worker needs to restore their labour power. But the lower this mark is set, the greater the profit of the capitalist, and the greater the misery of the workers.

8 Poverty and Quality of Life: Disposable Time

Whether the situation of the 'working classes' had 'improved' or rather worsened overall as a result of industrial capitalist development was already for Marx a 'very debatable question'.[105] This dispute not only determined the debates of the time, but also the historiographical debates about the period. In his articles 'The British Standard of Living, 1790–1850' (1957) and 'The Standard of Living Debate: A Postscript' (1964), Eric Hobsbawm looks back on a discussion that had already been going on for thirty years.[106] After a 'pessimistic' school dominated the debate since Marx, according to which the industrial revolution had fairly disastrous consequences for the standard of living of the labouring poor, an 'optimistic' school of economic historians appeared on the scene, starting in the 1920s with John H. Clapman and T.S. Ashton,

102 MECW 6, p. 133. Scrofula is a skin disease in the neck area associated with rashes and tumours.
103 MECW 6, pp. 133–4.
104 MECW 6, p. 134.
105 MECW 6, p. 160.
106 Hobsbawm 1967b; 1967c.

which claimed exactly the opposite, with statistical evidence on real wage development. The task of the generation of historians including Hobsbawm and E.P. Thompson did not consist in simply restoring the dominance of the 'pessimist' school, but rather in changing the question entirely: is economic – 'economic (in the narrowly quantitative and material sense)' – core data really sufficient to adequately capture the standard of living of a population group, or is it not rather necessary to include 'social' and 'cultural' aspects?[107] And if the latter is true, how can these 'soft', socio-cultural factors be determined?

At one point in his *Young Master Carpenter*, Ludwig Tieck refers to the English 'standard of living' debate that was already unfolding in the early nineteenth century.[108] As already cited in Chapter 1, Leonhard states that 'factories and the much-lauded division of labour are already an old invention', useful for the production of 'certain insignificant things, such as needles, nails and the like', because only in this way could they be 'supplied quickly and cheaply enough'. What upsets Leonhard, however, is that the factory system is also spreading to areas where the division of labour is inappropriate. His example is historically significant: 'and whether even in this case the benefit is so great that everyone can carry a bad, useless watch in his pocket, I leave undecided, since the truly good works are sold in London and Paris more expensively even now than they ever were in the first days of their invention'.[109]

The fact that suddenly 'everyone' feels they must own a watch, clock or timepiece, can on the one hand be taken as an example of a 'revolution of standards'.[110] Whereas the possession of a watch had long been considered the privilege of 'the gentry, the masters, the farmers and the tradesmen', as E.P. Thompson writes in his ground-breaking essay, 'Time, Work-Discipline, and Industrial Capitalism', from 1790 onward, a standardisation of this utilitarian and decorative object set in, and it became increasingly common for simple farm workers, handweavers and manufacturing workers to also acquire a watch.[111] The timing may not be coincidental, for 'a general diffusion of clocks and watches is occurring … at the exact moment when the industrial revolution demanded a greater synchronization of labour'.[112]

In the course of the industrial revolution, the division of labour, as well as the wage system, required a standardised measure of time. The 'new time-

107 Hobsbawm 1967c, p. 143.
108 On this debate between poets and historians, see Speck 2001 and Griffin 2010, pp. 144–61.
109 Tieck 1988b, p. 76.
110 Kocka 1986, p. 373.
111 Thompson 1967, p. 67.
112 Thompson 1967, p. 69.

discipline' was finally 'internalised', which leads Thompson to speak of a 'radical restructuring of man's social nature and working habits'.[113] Now this anthropological transformation corresponds to the anthropological reduction that Tieck's Leonhard laments: for the imposition of the new industrial or factory time does not take place in a vacuum, but must be understood as an attack on other, traditional divisions and ideas of time. The 'attack upon popular customs, sports, and holidays' that Thompson describes, the restructuring of the previous 'irregularity of the working year, punctuated by its traditional holidays, and fairs' and the struggle against 'Saint Monday' describe the same restructuring of the social time regime that Leonhard also deplores.[114] With the rhythm of the festivals, the cyclical guild order of life disappears, which, according to Leonhard, had given existence its dignity and meaning in the old days. Where the 'new legislators' set their sights on the 'old traditional games, songs, jokes and drinking', the 'folk festivals, processions, music and dancing', there soon remained, according to Leonhard, nothing of life but 'bare life'.[115]

For Thompson, the proliferation of watches is a simple example of the capitalist production of needs: the urge to own one's own watch is one of those 'needs which industrial capitalism called forth to energize its advance'.[116] Through the spread of watches, the new time regime stabilises itself as an everyday consciousness of time, which in turn increases the discipline of working time. Alongside this, the necessary mass production of new watches devalues watchmaking as a highly specialised handicraft and transforms it into a largely mechanised industry.[117]

It is precisely this connection, that people's own disciplining becomes an external need that they think they can satisfy by acquiring a watch, that outrages Tieck's Leonhard. For Leonhard, the 'bad', industrially produced watches that 'everyone' now thinks they have to show off are materially condensed symbols of a bad era and time regime; it is a time that no longer gives people a foothold and has itself become a commodity, so to speak. People sell their labour power for a limited time in order to indulge in a 'stultifying', 'completely mechanical and soulless business', and in their (wage-bought!) watch, they then look upon the objectification of their lifetime in material form. With a bad watch, one could say, man carries his own alienation 'in his pocket'. The mater-

113 Thompson 1967, p. 91.
114 Thompson 1967, pp. 84, 76.
115 Tieck 1988b, p. 62.
116 Thompson 1967, p. 69.
117 Tieck 1988b, p. 75.

ial symbol of the watch already illustrates with Tieck many features of that whole complex Marx will later analyse as the 'fetish-character of the commodity'.[118]

While the proliferation of watches could be seen – positively – as a sign of a developed wealth of needs among the lower classes and a symptom of the democratisation of luxury, Leonhard again notes the tension that asserts itself beneath the social surface. For not all watches are the same, and the 'truly good works' – *and the truly good time*, one can add – are kept by the rich for themselves, just as they also 'tacitly reserve for themselves many pastimes and idle times' for the purpose of 'culture', which is exactly what they no longer want to grant to the 'lower classes'.[119]

Drawing on the historical discussion of the establishment of the industrial capitalist time regime, Thompson attempts at the end of his essay to pose the question of what today, in a phase of the dismantling of industrial capitalism, could be an index of a true quality of life – beyond the standards and values of industrial capitalism itself. Such an index could be *truly* free time: time that would be exempt from the 'Puritan time-valuation, a commodity-valuation'.[120] Finally, Thompson dreams of new 'arts of living' that would be necessary for valuing time differently and yet bring the newly valued time into harmony with the requirements of a 'highly-synchronized automated industry', which in turn remains indispensable for the continued production of 'free time'. Humanity must therefore

> combine in a new synthesis elements of the old and of the new, finding an imagery based neither upon the seasons nor upon the market but upon human occasions. Punctuality in working hours would express respect for one's fellow workmen. And unpurposive passing of time would be behaviour which the culture approved.[121]

An image of utopia treads softly here, one Marx already outlined in the rough draft of *Capital* – and then, not by chance, dropped from the final version. If sociality were no longer produced indirectly and unconsciously by comparing

118 Cf. Marx 1976, pp. 163–77.

119 Tieck, 1988b, pp. 78–79; Thompson 1967, p. 69, confirms in social historical terms the fact that prompts Leonhard's complaint: 'Although some very cheap – and shoddy – timepieces were beginning to appear, the prices of efficient ones remained for several decades beyond the normal reach of the artisan'.

120 Thompson 1967, p. 95.

121 Thompson 1967, p. 96.

and exchanging the value of 'socially necessary labour time', but directly and consciously, then, according to Marx, the entire economy would dissolve into an 'economy of time'. The provision of 'disposable time' would then become the goal of social production: 'For real wealth is the developed productive power of all individuals. Then wealth is no longer measured by labour time but by disposable time'.[122]

Perhaps we are dealing here with an updating of the 'ancient dream of the idle man'.[123] Certainly, Marx and Thompson are drawing on elements of a 'romantic anti-capitalism' that has always rebelled against the 'religion of labour' – following Georg Lukács and Paul Lafargue – and waged a 'struggle for leisure'. The 'imagery' of Romanticism can help pose the question of wealth and poverty not only in terms that are already shaped from the outset by currently prevailing determinations of value; it is precisely in the 'escapism' of Romanticism that lies its heightened social-critical potency.[124] For even if the retrospective imagination of a guild-representative time regime, of which Tieck's Leonhard indulges, is ideologically overdetermined, it nevertheless demonstrates that 'free time', which emanates from the individual, does not necessarily have to be an individualistic time, but can also be a *shared time*: collectively shared, as in the time of festivals and processions, or intimately shared among friends, as in the seemingly endless conversations which Tieck lets us join in the *Young Master Carpenter* and countless other novellas of his late period.

Time as free time, as *disposable time*, is the hollow form in which everything can take shape, in whose name individual and collective subjectivity is formed: taste, education, lavishness, nature, culture. Without *disposable time*, there is no poetry, especially no poetry of class. But without the poetry of class, there is no *disposable time* either. The formation of a conscious and combative class is the leading precondition for its self-abolition in a realm of free time. The class must first struggle for what makes it possible as a class, and at the same time struggle for what will make it superfluous as a class, as a working class.[125] The complex arrangement of transcendentals of self-abolition – the condition of possibility of class is at the same time the condition of its superfluity: *disposable time* – can only be had *in* and *as* struggle. Class struggle, as a process of the constitution and destitution of classes in general, is always also a *struggle for*

122 MECW 29, p. 94.

123 Priddat 2005, p. 129.

124 Thompson 1967, p. 96.

125 Cf. Bloch 1995, the chapter 'Eight-hour Day, World in Peace, Free Time and Leisure', pp. 885–924, especially the last section, 'Leisure as imperative, only half explored goal', pp. 920–4.

time; it is a struggle for the fact that 'certain persons or certain classes have more time than others – and this is', as Jacques Derrida knew, 'finally the most serious stake of political economy'.[126] For the working class, however, the struggle *over* time is always also a struggle *against* time. And this was already felt and symbolically executed by the combatants of the July Revolution of 1830: 'On the first evening of fighting', as Walter Benjamin recounts, 'it so happened that the dials on clocktowers were being fired at simultaneously and independently from several locations in Paris'.[127]

126 Derrida 1992, p. 28.

127 Benjamin 2006, Thesis XV, p. 395.

CHAPTER 5

Wage Labour and Slavery: Unfulfilled Promises of Freedom

> Slavery, serfdom and wage labour are historically and socially different solutions to a universal problem, which remains fundamentally the same.
>
> FERNAND BRAUDEL[1]

∴

With the triumph of capitalism, the lives of ever more parts of the population became more dependent on wage labour, a condition still recognised as scandalous in many places during the Vormärz, attested to by the widespread use of the phrase *labouring poor*.[2] Observers at the time saw clearly that the regime of wage labour not only brought immiseration along with it, but that wage labour changes the very nature of social relations themselves. The individual and society are now said to be connected solely through the infamous 'cash nexus' (Thomas Carlyle); every other form of bond is suspected of being antiquated and backwards. Defenders of the old forms are now suddenly regarded as romantics, blind to reality.[3]

---

1 Braudel 1984, p. 63.

2 On the concept of the 'labouring poor', see Marx 1976, p. 925: 'The expression "labouring poor" is found in English legislation from the moment when the class of wage-labourers becomes noticeable. This term is used in opposition, on the one hand, to the "idle poor", beggars etc., and, on the other, to those workers who are not yet plucked fowl but rather the possessors of their own means of labour. From the statute book the expression passed into political economy, and was handed down by Culpeper, J. Child, etc to Adam Smith and Eden'.

3 The exact phrase 'cash nexus' is not found in Carlyle's work. However, in his 1840 book *Chartism*, a firm endorsement of the early labour movement, he describes his present as 'these complicated times, with Cash Payment as the sole nexus between man and man' (Carlyle 1840, p. 66). In *Past and Present*, his great 1843 text on the state of the nation, Carlyle repeatedly quotes himself with this formulation in different variants; Carlyle 2005, pp. 149 170, 186, 188, 189. In this quote, he clearly relates the cash nexus to wage labour as a social form: 'We have profoundly forgotten everywhere that *Cash-payment* is not the sole relation of human beings; we think, nothing doubting, that *it* absolves and liquidates all engagements

 | DOI:10.1163/9789004685536_007

Paradoxically, the complete novelty of this situation led many at the time to use old, familiar terms and topoi – an old *imagery* – in order to make sense of what was new in the first place. With the advent of wage labour, slavery once again became a topic in many places; 'free' wage labourers were suddenly referred to as 'white slaves' in literature and journalism.

1 Allegories of Class: 'Steam King' and 'White Slaves'

Engels was the one who brought the talk of 'white slaves' from England to Germany. In his 1845 work, *The Condition of the Working Class in England*, he agrees with the 'philanthropic Tories' who 'gave the factory workers the name white slaves', and he justifies this choice by quoting a poem from Edward P. Mead, a poet close to the Chartists:

> There is a King, and a ruthless King;
> Not a King of the poet's dream;
> But a tyrant fell, white slaves know well,
> And that ruthless King is Steam.
>
> He hath an arm, an iron arm,
> And tho' he hath but one,
> In that mighty arm there is a charm,
> That millions hath undone.
>
> Like the ancient Moloch grim, his sire
> In Himmon's vale that stood,
> His bowels are of living fire,
> And children are his food.
>
> His priesthood are a hungry band,
> Blood-thirsty, proud, and bold;
> 'Tis they direct his giant hand,
> In turning blood to gold.

---

of man. "My starving workers?" answers the rich Mill-owner: "Did not I hire them fairly in the market? Did I not pay them to the last sixpence the sum covenanted for? What have I to do with them more?"' (Carlyle 2005, p. 149). Engels dedicated an extremely favourable review to *Past and Present* in the 1844 *Deutsch-Französische Jahrbücher*, 'The Condition of England. *Past and Present* by Thomas Carlyle, London, 1843', in MECW 3, pp. 444–68.

For filthy gain in their servile chain
All nature's rights they bind;
They mock at lovely woman's pain,
And to manly tears are blind.

The sighs and groans of Labour's sons
Are music in their ear,
And the skeleton shades, of lads and maids,
In the Steam King's hell appear.

Those hells upon earth, since the Steam King's birth,
Have scatter'd around despair;
For the human mind for Heav'n design'd,
With the body, is murdered there.

Then down with the King, the Moloch King,
Ye working millions all;
O chain his hand, or our native land
Is destin'd by him to fall.

And his Satraps abhor'd, each proud Mill Lord,
Now gorg'd with gold and blood,
Must be put down by the nation's frown,
As well as their monster God.[4]

Mead and Engels capture the physical and political-social power of industry in a monstrous allegory. 'King Steam' appears as the cannibalistic 'monster God' of the Old Testament, ruling over people and the world through a 'priesthood' who ruthlessly use the power of their idol for their own enrichment[5] – 'in turning

4 Engels 1845, *The Condition of the Working-Class in England*, MECW 4, pp. 474–7. The original title of the poem is 'The Steam King' and includes two more stanzas. It is reprinted in Scheckner 1989, pp. 287–8. The poem appeared on 11 February 1843 in the weekly newspaper *The Northern Star*, the most important organ of the Chartists. The ambitious translation is by Engels himself, who repeatedly translated poems of the English labour movement into German, but also German poems into English, for example Heine's 'Schlesische Weber' [Song of the Silesian Weavers]. Engels' translation of Heine's poem appeared on 13 December 1844 in *The New Moral World*, the newspaper of the Owenites, Engels 1844, 'Rapid Progress of Communism in Germany', MECW 4, p. 232.

5 Mead 1843, 'The Steam King' in Scheckner 1989, p. 288.

blood to gold'.[6] The biblical imagery that fuels Mead's 'Chartist imaginary' pits the idol and its priests against the 'nation' whose 'frown' will eventually bring about the overthrow of the false God and the restoration of the true God.[7] In this respect, Mead's poem also shares a messianism typical of Chartist poetry.[8] The poem itself becomes a 'call for action'.[9]

2 Point of Comparison: Weitling's 'Politics of Slavery'

It is in the second part of Wilhelm Weitling's *Garantien der Harmonie und Freiheit* [*Guarantees of Harmony and Freedom*] from 1842 – probably the most elaborate blueprint of a system for early German socialism – that we find the outlines of a large-scale plan for a communist 'reorganisation of society', for the establishment of a society of equals. In the first part of the pamphlet, Weitling provides a grand historical-philosophical narrative intended to clarify the 'origin of social evils'.[10] Starting from an 'original state of society', he reconstructs the genesis of a world of inequality, one in which labour, wealth, and power are all unequally distributed.[11]

Weitling's account of the prevailing inequality is systematically oriented around the concept of property. After the 'emergence of movable' and 'immovable property', the true fall of man according to Weitling's narrative occurs with the 'emergence of slavery', for in slavery, 'the concept of property extends to humanity itself', thus institutionally cementing the inequality between people. Weitling dramatises the onset of slavery as a kind of anthropological-civilisational break: with it, humanity ceased to be an 'image of God'. There was

6 The personification of the ritual sacrifices of children, which appears in the Old Testament under the name 'Moloch' in the form of a sinister king, has been known in the British tradition since Milton's Moloch, the 'horrid King besmear'd with blood / Of human sacrifice, and parent's tears' (Milton 1832, Book I, lines 392–3, p. 25).

7 On the Chartist 'politics of form', see Loose 2014.

8 Cf. Sanders, 2009, pp. 205–223.

9 On the activist aspect of Mead's poem, cf. Hughes 2010, p. 120. Hughes also emphasises here that the 'biblical allusion' of the child-eating Moloch was motivated by the excessive use of child labour in modern industry.

10 Weitling 1974, pp. 9–120.

11 For Weitling, the original state is less a real historical condition than the construction of a contrasting foil against which the 'evils of the present' can be more sharply drawn: 'What a gap between then and now! What a changed state of society in our civilised countries today!' (Weitling 1974, p. 10).

no longer one humankind, but 'two kinds of human beings, those who work and those who do not work. Masters and slaves'.[12]

Weitling emphasises the importance of slavery for two opposing but complementary reasons: on the one hand, with the advent of slavery, the last memory of that 'primordial state' had vanished in which the happiness of one was unthinkable without the happiness of the other – happiness as the happiness of equality.[13] On the other hand, however, the conceptual elaboration of slavery allows Weitling to scandalise the present state of society by describing it as still subject to slavery. 'Could human beings sink lower?', Weitling asks, and his answer is: yes. For humans can still submit to money, the 'invention' of which leads to a final corruption of the social body.[14] In Weitling's narrative, money does not appear primarily as a medium of social exchange, but as a generator and stabiliser of social inequality, as a means of command over social labour: it is only through money that the 'outrageous difference of classes in society' – the epitome of all 'social evils' – finally comes to light.[15]

By way of a 'then' and 'now' schema, Weitling outlines the modern, money-mediated exploitation of labour in terms that are entirely distinct from that of slavery: while the slave was transformed 'by the concept of property into a captured, exchanged or inherited good' and as such reduced to the status of cattle, today human beings 'no longer have any value at all, not even that of cattle'. In the past, the slave owner at least had to treat his property with enough care so as not to completely spoil it for use, whereas now modern workers

> are tormented to death in order to take advantage of their strength; and when they then become ill, old and weak, they are chased out of the workshop, out of the factory and out of the house, so as to no longer have to feed them, while outside they line up in hordes and crowds for the torture caves, from which one victim after another staggers as soon as their strength is exhausted.[16]

Weitling objects to work in modern workshops and factories for two reasons: first, because of its material content. For Weitling, work is mere drudgery, and workplaces appear as 'dark Satanic Mills' as in the writings of William Blake.

12 Weitling 1974, p. 42.
13 Weitling 1974, p. 10: 'Only the satisfied are happy, and only those who can have everything that everyone else has is satisfied.'
14 Weitling 1974, p. 41.
15 Weitling 1974, p. 55.
16 Weitling 1974, p. 49.

And second, because of its social form.[17] The first is always assumed as the background experience of work and is not explained any further. Thus nowhere does Weitling give an apology for wage labour the way the later workers' movement will do. Nonetheless, Weitling continues to analyse the social form of labour, and how the 'invention of money' changed it.

He shows how the introduction of money is accompanied by a sublimation and internalisation of that compulsion without which the organisation of social labour cannot function: 'In the past, people were made slaves by force; now they sell themselves'.[18] For Weitling, the modern worker is still a slave; he sells himself and his work to others and in doing so makes himself a slave to money.

By way of this central claim, Weitling's political account follows a representational scheme that I would like to call, following Quentin Skinner, the 'politics of slavery'. The fact that even at the time, people still lived in a 'state of slavery' under the reign of money makes the abolition of the rule of money appear as an 'act of self-liberation' by an enslaved people that dreams of 'regaining their birthright of freedom'.[19] Weitling takes advantage of the fact that slavery is widely recognised as an injustice in order to equate the modern rule of money with slavery on the one hand – *there has been little progress on this front*, he claims – while at the same time emphasising that the modern rule of money is far more socially pernicious than slavery. For 'the outward evil' of slavery today hides in the 'shadow of contracts and laws', while the state of slavery 'in many respects persists in even worse degrees'. With 'this colourful masquerade of fraud, injustice and deception', however, there is always the risk of self-deception.[20] For this reason, the workers must constantly be made aware of the coercive character of the social form, and a rhetorical updating of historical phenomena serves this purpose. By accusing the workers of a slave morality, Weitling intends to foster a self-confident and combative attitude among his audience. As long as 'man does not have what others can have to satisfy his needs' – and here we may do well to include spiritual needs – 'he *cannot* and *must not* be satisfied; for that would be the satisfaction of a slave or a beaten dog'. Money, after all, undermines any possible sense of 'honour': 'The natural, manly soul turns into the soul of a dog!'[21]

---

17 The 'Preface' to Blake's 1804 epic *Milton* reads: 'And was Jerusalem builded here, / Among these dark Satanic Mills?' (Blake 1988, p. 95).

18 Weitling 1974, p. 52.

19 Skinner 2008, p. 287.

20 Weitling 1974, p. 50.

21 Weitling 1974, pp. 11, 52.

With his rhetorical 'politics of slavery', Weitling holds a mirror up to modern workers in which they certainly do *not want* to recognise themselves. The negative image of the slave is supposed to lift them up, and so Weitling finally shouts provocatively to the reader: 'And you too! Slave! Crawling through dust! What? That gaze you so timidly and fearfully cast down before your master, dare you turn it boldly towards heaven? Shall heaven be reflected in thy shame?'[22]

3 The 'Semblance of Liberty' and Real Slavery: Engels

The ambivalence that characterises Weitling's discussion of slavery – on the one hand, an analytical distinction between wage labour and slavery, on the other hand a polemical-agitational equating of the two – comes to a head in Engels' various reports from England in the mid-1840s.[23]

Engels makes clear conceptual distinctions between slavery, serfdom and 'free' wage labour. Like Weitling, he starts with the 'money system' and gives a systematic account – one which is much more forceful than Weitling's – of money's power to objectify. Here Carlyle's cash nexus becomes the midwife of Engels' conceptual differentiation:

> The abolition of feudal servitude has made 'cash payment the sole relation of human beings'. Property, a natural, spiritless principle, as opposed to the human and spiritual principle, is thus enthroned, and ultimately, to complete this alienation, money – the alienated, empty abstraction of property – is made master of the world. Man has ceased to be the slave of men and has become the slave of *things*; the perversion of the human condition is complete; the servitude of the modern commercial world, this highly developed, total, universal venality, is more inhuman and more all-embracing than the serfdom of the feudal era; prostitution is more immoral and more bestial than the *jus primae noctis*.[24]

The difference between being a slave of men and a slave of things, which turns on just one word in this formulation, is a difference in the whole. Many years

22 Weitling 1974, p. 43.

23 Engels 1844, 'The Condition of England. I. The Eighteenth Century' and 'The Condition of England. II. The English Constitution', series of articles in *Vorwärts!* (Paris), 31 August to 19 October 1844, MECW 3, pp. 469–513; Engels 1845, *The Condition of the Working-Class in England*, MECW 4, pp. 295–583.

24 MECW 3, p. 476.

later, an entire tradition of sociological theories of modernisation will be constructed around this difference – personal relations of dependence on the one hand and objectifying structures on the other. Not only Engels but also Marx will elevate this difference to the *differentia specifica* of the capitalist social formation in their later work. *Wage Labour and Capital*, a series of articles published by Marx in the *Neue Rheinische Zeitung* in April 1849, can be read as a summary of his Vormärz critique of political economy.[25] In this series, Marx singles out the existence of 'free labour' as the defining feature of the capitalist economy. Capitalism can be historicised precisely through this characteristic:

> Labour was not always a *commodity*. Labour was not always wage labour, that is, *free* labour. The *slave* did not sell his labour to the slave owner, any more than the ox sells its services to the peasant. The slave, together with his labour, is sold once and for all to his owner. He is a commodity which can pass from the hand of one owner to that of another. *He is himself* a commodity, but the labour is not *his* commodity.[26]

The slave is a commodity, the wage labourer owns a commodity that he can sell: his labour, or more precisely, labour power. The decisive difference is between *having* a commodity and *being* a commodity. The serf, on the other hand – the other major figure of unfree labour – is not a commodity that could pass from the hand of one owner to that of another; rather, he is essentially immobile, he 'belongs to the land and turns over to the owner of the land the fruits thereof'. That is why he does not receive a 'wage from the owner of the land', and must instead pay him 'a tribute'. 'The *free labourer*, on the other hand', Marx continues, 'sells himself', but not 'once and for all', like the slave, but 'piecemeal': for certain periods of time. Finally, the wage labourer 'belongs neither to an owner nor to the land, but eight, ten, twelve, fifteen hours of his daily life belong to him who buys them'.[27]

As noted, Marx's more rigorous differentiations come later. In 1845, in Engels' *Condition of the Working Class in England*, the later terminological distinctions between slavery, serfdom and 'free' wage labour are all present, but Engels

25 Marx 1849, *Wage Labour and Capital*, MECW 9, pp. 197–228. The set of articles goes back to a series of talks Marx gave in December 1847 while still in exile in Belgium at the German Workers' Association in Brussels.

26 MECW 9, p. 203.

27 MECW 9, p. 203.

continues to rhetorically explore the similarities between the various labour regimes in order to create a scandalising effect resulting from the discrepancy between the almost identical *description* of social relations with opposite social *content*. However, a long series of antitheses then leads him straight back to finding an *equality* (or at least similarity) of the social forms under investigation:

> Let us compare the condition of the free Englishman of 1845 with the Saxon serf under the lash of the Norman barons of 1145 ... The serf owed his master the *jus primae noctis*, the right of the first night – the free working-man must, on demand, surrender to his master not only that, but the right of *every* night. The serf could acquire no property; everything that he gained, his master could take from him; the free working-man has no property, can gain none by reason of the pressure of competition ... The lord of the soil could not separate the serf from the land, nor sell him apart from it, and since almost all the land was fief and there was no capital, practically could not sell him at all. The modern bourgeois forces the working-man to sell himself. The serf was the slave of the piece of land on which he was born, the working-man is the slave of his own necessities of life and of the money with which he has to buy them – both are *slaves of a thing*. The serf had a guarantee for the means of subsistence in the feudal order of society in which every member had his own place. The free working-man has no guarantee whatsoever, because he has a place in society only when the bourgeoisie can make use of him ... The serf sacrificed himself for his master in war, the factory worker in peace. The lord of the serf was a barbarian who regarded his villain as a head of cattle; the employer of workers is civilised and regards his 'hand' as a machine.[28]

The rhetorical effect of this sequence lies in the continual inversion of well-established expectations: where the bourgeois self-image claims progress for itself – progress from slavery via serfdom to free (wage) labour, for example, and thus progress from barbarism to civilisation – Engels, in playful, nimble rejoinders, detects stagnation at best, if not regression. In the end, he gives a concise summary of the whole development by labelling it an *ideology* of progress – as the progress of a cover-up:

28 MECW 4, p. 473. Translation revised.

> In short, the position of the two [the serf and the free working-man] is not far from equal, and if either is at a disadvantage, it is the free working-man. Slaves they both are, with the single difference that the slavery of the one is undissembled, open, honest; that of the other cunning, sly, disguised, deceitfully concealed from himself and every one else, a hypocritical servitude worse than the old.[29]

Through the rhetorical juxtaposition of slaves, serfs and free workers, the freedom of the latter becomes revealed as a transparent 'semblance of liberty'.[30] However, as Engels points out, it is a thoroughly *necessary* semblance, a semblance which necessarily emerges from the functioning of the factory system and which remains necessary for its functioning: only through the 'semblance of liberty' can the factory system supply itself with cheap labour power without having to offer any additional guarantees for the workers, for example, if they are unable to work due to illness or because they have to look after sick family members.[31]

Behind the semblance, however, Engels exposes a layer of reality where factory owners rule despotically over their workers. Engels writes in no uncertain terms of a 'slavery in which the bourgeoisie holds the proletariat chained'; the whole subsection is given the concise title 'Slavery'. Here Engels delves into the immediate process of production, where 'all freedom in law and in fact ends'.[32] In 1845, Engels is one of the first to present this outright, 'shameful tyranny' of the factory owners to his readers with great urgency: the 'employer is absolute lawgiver' who dictates the entire life rhythm of his workers, who must 'eat, drink and sleep at command'; if they show up ten minutes late for work, a quarter of their daily wages is withheld from them in a rigid system of punishment; they can be fired at any time, while they themselves have to give a week's notice if they wish to quit; the work itself, especially the 'supervision of machinery', is 'not work, but tedium, the most deadening, wearing process conceivable'. The 'life' of the factory worker is 'condemnation to be buried alive in the mill'; the workers themselves are constantly 'degraded to machines', Engels repeats.[33]

Engels emphasises in particular the close interconnection between wage labour and time discipline. That the struggle for genuine freedom proclaimed

---

29 MECW 4, pp. 473–4.
30 MECW 4, p. 379.
31 MECW 4, pp. 379–80.
32 MECW 4, p. 467. Translation revised.
33 MECW 4, pp. 466–9. Translation revised.

by Marx will ultimately be defined as a struggle for free time, for disposable time, seems already prefigured in Engels' scandalising description of the command wielded by the – all too often manipulated – 'despotic bell' and factory clocks to which the workers' entire lives are subject 'from the ninth year to their death'.[34] In this context, the struggle for genuine freedom – and the struggle against the mere 'semblance of liberty' – can only be understood as a struggle against the clock and against time.

4 Class Slavery

At the beginning of the chapter on 'Competition', Engels writes that the 'proletarian is, therefore, in law and in fact, the slave of the bourgeoisie'.[35] Implicit in this simple sentence is a social 'set theory' that Engels will elaborate only a few pages later. He correlates two elements of different kinds: the individual 'proletarian' – and one could add, *each* individual 'proletarian' – is not the slave of an individual bourgeois, but of the 'bourgeoisie' as a class. The individual 'worker', he writes a little later, is 'in law and in fact, the slave of the property-holding class'. It is this condition of enslavement *to a class* that comprises 'the only difference as compared with the old, outspoken slavery'.[36]

In *Wage Labour and Capital*, Marx conceptually develops Engels' polemical provocation. Marx argues here that the wage labour relation cannot be conceived as Robinsonade and individual, i.e., as a relation between single individuals who enter into a contract so that one can sell the commodity labour power to another. Instead, the wage labour relation must be conceived as a *social relation*, that is, as a relation between *classes*. As soon as an individual worker enters the labour market, the class relation appears in force: a 'free worker' can leave 'the capitalist to whom he hires himself whenever he likes', just as the capitalist can dismiss the worker 'whenever he thinks fit'. The fundamental compulsion to earn one's living, however, remains: 'But the worker, whose sole source of livelihood is the sale of his labour, cannot leave the *whole class of purchasers, that is, the capitalist class*, without renouncing his existence. *He belongs not to this or that bourgeois, but to the bourgeoisie, the bourgeois class*'.[37] That the 'bourgeois class' only considers the individual worker as part

34 MECW 4, pp. 467–68.
35 MECW 4, p. 376.
36 MECW 4, p. 379.
37 MECW 9, pp. 203.

of a class and not an individual is shown by the fact that the worker's wages are not calculated according to individual subsistence needs, but only with a view to securing the existence of the working class as a whole. The minimum wage to be paid must indeed replace the '*cost of labour*', but:

> This wage minimum, like the determination of the price of commodities by the cost of production in general, does not hold good for the *single individual* but for the *species*. Individual workers, millions of workers, do not get enough to be able to exist and reproduce themselves; but the *wages of the whole working class* level down, within their fluctuations, to the minimum.[38]

If the wage labour relation is no longer understood as an individual but as a class relation, then although the individual capitalist still appears as a despot of factory discipline, he nevertheless functions as merely an executor and ultimately – as described in *Capital* – as 'capital personified' or the 'personification of capital'.[39] This means that critique can no longer take aim at the individual capitalist, who after all could run his factory better – as Marx accuses Proudhon of wishing – but ultimately at *the system* as such. If the proletarian is a '*slave* of labour for gain', as *The Holy Family* boldly states, then critique must declare war on the entire system of labour for gain.[40] One could sum up Marx's claim by saying that the critique of the system must rise to the level of the objectification and reification of personal relations diagnosed in the system itself. This claim, however, which Marx will only fulfil in his later critique of political economy, in *Capital* for example, must oppose all forms of romantic anti-capitalism. Marx already began distancing himself from this form of criticism in the Vormärz period. The romantic conception of anti-capitalism, Marx and Engels repeat again and again, is based only on *outrage* and insists on criticising the system *from the outside* – for example, from the standpoint of an ideal past or some proletarian natural law. Marx, on the other hand, maintains an *immanent* standpoint of critique. As a result, Marx will strive to overcome romantic anti-capitalism – that of his early companions and that of his own early approach – not only for stylistic reasons (as we have seen in his article on suicide, for instance), but also for theoretical and systematic reasons. He will not succeed; the revolutionary pneuma of an ultimately moral

38 MECW 9, pp. 209–10.
39 Marx 1976, pp. 254, 423–24, 739.
40 MECW 4, p. 113.

indignation also pervades the systematic work of the 'mature' Marx and even lends it a final consistency.

5 Why '*White* Slaves'?

During the Vormärz, the new social regime of 'free' wage labour was compared with slavery, and as a result, 'free' wage labourers were referred to as 'white slaves'. Discussions during this period primarily emphasised slavery as an unfree form of labour. At the same time, however, colonial and postcolonial slavery, which was still ubiquitous on a global scale in the Vormärz, was also taken into account, although mostly only implicitly. The scandalising effect of the talk of 'white slaves' draws a considerable amount on the widespread knowledge of 'Black' slavery and the enslavement and abduction of 'Black' Africans.

The talk of 'white slaves' in England, from which Engels and others took the phrase, occurred in clear connection to (post)colonial slavery: since the end of the eighteenth century, a strong abolitionist movement existed in England, which eventually reached all the way to Parliament via uprisings, strikes, signature collections and petitions.[41] After an initial prelude in the House of Commons in 1792 and the worldwide shock caused by the slave revolt in Haiti, the international slave trade was banned in both houses of the British Parliament in 1807. The Slavery Abolition Act of 1833 finally declared all slaves in the British Empire free, providing generous compensation for the former owners – but not the former slaves.[42]

When debates erupted in England in the late 1830s and early 1840s around working conditions in factories, such as child labour, and when the 'philanthropic Tories' and other opponents of pure laissez-faire policies referred to factory workers as 'white slaves', they were trying to take advantage of the uproar sparked by the debates around (Black) slavery, which had not yet completely died down. In the German context, where no comparable debate took place, the talk of 'white slaves' had a significantly different effect. While in England the scandal was that 'free born Englishmen', that is to say, free white Englishmen, were subject to the same working and living conditions previously recognised as intolerable for Black slaves, in the German context the reference

41 On the genesis of abolitionism 'from below' out of the labour struggles and uprisings of a multi-ethnic 'Atlantic proletariat' throughout the eighteenth century, see Linebaugh and Rediker 2000, pp. 229–67.

42 On the history of the abolitionist movement, see also the standard work by David Brion Davis 1999, as well as 2014.

to (colonial and postcolonial) slavery often led to a trivialisation of the latter. Engels, caught between the English and German references, writes in his *Condition of the Working Class in England* that the English factory workers were 'worse slaves than the Negroes in America, for they are more sharply watched', which probably did not reflect the reality of slavery.[43] Research on the rigid labour regime of plantations in the US South and the Caribbean, for instance, suggests the opposite.[44]

Weitling goes a step further and ridicules the English abolitionist debate by equating it with campaigns to 'prevent cruelty to animals'. For him, the 'abolition of slavery' by the 'philanthropic English' is simply 'comedy' and hypocrisy that only highlights the scandal of modern wage slavery: 'In faraway countries they forbid the slave trade, while their own is teeming with unhappy slaves dying of hunger by the thousands!'[45] In contrast to the proletarian, who is constantly threatened with starvation – 'In former times, no one, not even the slave, had to worry about this' – the slave was at least 'assured that he would always receive shelter and food from his harsh master'.[46] The idea that the owners would somehow treat their slaves with care and attention, simply because they considered them property, must again be doubted from a historical point of view. This assertion seems to have sprung more from propaganda of the time than from any knowledge or even genuine interest in actual slavery.

There are, however, some instances in the Vormärz where the comparison of modern wage labour with (post)colonial slavery did bring about a valid theoretical connection between both regimes of labour. One example is when Weitling declares it 'sheer mockery' to identify the '*partial* liberation of Blacks' with the *total* 'abolition of slavery'.[47] In many cases, as Weitling knew, former slaves often remained entirely dependent on the same masters and tied to the same material form of labour as before, only now they could formally be called free wage labourers.[48] These insights into the connection between wage labour

43 MECW 4, pp. 468–9.
44 Cf. Zeuske 2002; Zeuske 2004.
45 Weitling 1974, p. 50.
46 Weitling 1974, p. 51.
47 Weitling 1974, p. 51 (emphasis mine).
48 Buck-Morss also claims a functional connection between the liberation of slaves and the regime of wage labour: 'The success of the abolitionists, ending British slave trade in 1807, coincided with the birth of the idea of "free" labor, destined to become its own form of labor discipline, as earlier legislation protecting British workers was systematically eliminated.' In a footnote, Buck-Morss cites E.P. Thompson's observation that by 1809, just two years after the prohibition of the slave trade in Britain, 'all the protective legislation in the woolen industry … was repealed' (Buck-Morss 2009, p. 97).

and slavery, which the metaphorical talk of slavery grants for wage labour, nevertheless remained peripheral in the Vormärz. More often than not, actual (post)colonial slavery was trivialised by its metaphorical use.

6 Theory as Mystification: the Cult of the Industrial Worker and Global Critique

Paradoxically, the same ambivalence caused by the *metaphorisation* of wage labour as slavery also appears wherever there occurs a rigid *conceptual* distinction between the two. Precise conceptual differentiations in particular seem to produce a logic which ultimately mystifies rather than illuminates the structural relations at hand. Marx, who drew the sharpest conceptual distinction between wage labour and slavery, illustrates this problem in a particularly succinct manner.

In his theory, Marx proceeds with ideal types *avant la lettre*. In a methodological confession at the end of the third volume of *Capital*, he writes that he is 'only out to present the internal organization of the capitalist mode of production, its ideal average, as it were'.[49] In drawing the conceptual distinction between serfdom, slavery and wage labour, however, Marx increasingly presents the comparison of *ideal types* as valid *empirical description*. In empirical terms, all three forms of dependent labour almost never appear in their pure form; this can already be seen in Vormärz journals such as *Gesellschaftsspiegel* and their reports on the new forms of labour across the still unknown continent.

The confusion between empirical description and the construction of ideal types deepens when the conceptual juxtaposition is given a temporal dimension and presented as a historical course of development. The famous beginning of the *Communist Manifesto* assigns slavery and serfdom to 'earlier epochs of history' and sharply distinguishes them from the present.[50] Linked to this is the thesis that class antagonism in the present is simplifying and moving towards a clear opposition of 'bourgeois and proletarians', the latter being identified in passing as 'the modern working class', mainly employed in 'large-scale industry':[51] 'Of all the classes that stand face to face with the bourgeoisie today, the proletariat alone is a really revolutionary class. The other classes decay

49 Marx 1991, p. 970.

50 MECW 6, p. 482.

51 MECW 6, p. 490. Translation revised.

and finally disappear in the face of large-scale industry; the proletariat is its special and essential product'.[52]

Marx thinks in ideal types, he thinks historically, and, combining both, he thinks in terms of historical *tendencies*. For him, history must always be conceived as a process of development, the meaning of which can only be deciphered from its peak, from its most advanced formation. All three modes of thinking are facets of a heuristic, which for Marx, deliberately or inadvertently, become cornerstones of a politics that conceives historical progress as a necessarily avant-garde project. From an empirical point of view, all the elements that contribute to the precise conceptual definition of wage labour as a social form can be found most readily in the industrial worker. However, no theoretical deduction follows from this which would automatically make the industrial worker the spearhead of the *political* struggle for liberation from wage labour – this conclusion springs from other, *class-political* preconditions.

The metaphor of slavery for (wage) workers highlights their dependency and lack of self-sufficiency. This status is usually less attractive and possibly more difficult to politically organise than the blue-collar pride of a productive working class identified with modern industrial labour, who often appear as the very embodiment of technical progress. The executors of the industrial revolution will complete the social revolution – this is Marx's promise.

The reverse side of this emancipatory promise is an 'exclusionary thinking' that can only perceive all those parts of the proletariat not integrated in advanced 'large-scale industry' as atavisms, as impurities of the ideal type, to whom the best that can be promised – at least according to the historical 'tendency' – is the prospect of soon being pulverised between the two 'pure' class camps of bourgeoisie and industrial wage labourers.[53] The vanguard of industrial workers is thus distinguished from a rear-guard of formally unfree or irregularly employed workers who, in the face of the sheer necessity of survival, must somehow make ends meet, but not in the progressive sector of 'large-scale industry'. Anyone who moves 'up' from this conglomerate (and earns a living as a freelancer or small independent worker) is suspected of having become 'petty bourgeois', while 'below' the 'lumpenproletariat' awaits: whoever could

52 MECW 6, p. 494. (Translation revised). The historical idea of development, with its sharp emphasis on the difference between 'free' and 'unfree' labour, serves not only in Marx but in the entire thinking of the 'West' to classify other forms of society that are allegedly based on 'unfree' labour as 'backward'. On the 'invention of backwardness in Western economic and philosophical thought', see Stanziani 2008, p. 29.

53 Linden and Roth 2014a, p. 13.

not (or did not want to) enter into organised wage labour became the target of this accusation, the epitome of conceptual and socio-political cleansing.[54] The intellectuals – the 'intellectual prolatarians' – were very familiar with *both* accusations.

There are historical reasons for the theoretical favouring of industrial labour and the political privileging of industrial workers as a class: both were based on the overwhelming evidence of a hitherto unseen development of productive power, which virtually exploded in the first half of the nineteenth century and continued for many more decades thereafter. It is no coincidence that 'acceleration' becomes the central term in self-descriptions of the era.[55] The accelerated development of productive forces corresponds to the productive power of an industrial working class which alone is capable of setting the colossal assemblage of machinery in motion – or bringing them to a halt, if its 'strong arm wants', as the Vormärz poet Georg Herwegh wrote in his later party song of the Social Democrats.[56]

To the extent that Marx's theoretical and political preference for the industrial working class as the subject of revolutionary change can be explained historically, it must also be subject to historical critique. In recent years, a globally oriented social history of labour, or Global Labour History, has presented a critical rejoinder to Marx.[57] From a global perspective, it appears highly doubtful that 'freedom' (free disposal over one's own labour power, voluntary ability to enter into contracts, freedom of movement) can serve as a paradigm of modern labour relations; even in modern times, 'free wage labour' must be seen 'as an exception rather than the rule'.[58] Parallel to the implementation of free wage labour in the metropolises, Global Labour History argues that the increasingly market-oriented global economy of the nineteenth century was consistently characterised by all kinds of unfree labour relations: first and foremost, Atlantic slavery. Parallel to the enslavement of millions of Africans, hundreds of thousands of Europeans were taken to the colonies to work in debt bondage, in indentured servitude or as convicted delinquents. The Atlantic world market

54 See the infamous clause in the 'Manifesto of the Communist Party', according to which the lumpenproletariat is conceived as 'that passively rotting mass thrown off by the lowest layers of old society' (MECW 6, p. 494).

55 Cf. Koselleck 2000.

56 Herwegh 1886. The 'Bundeslied' was written in 1863 for the founding of the General German Workers' Association.

57 Lucassen 2008.

58 Cf. Brass, Linden and Lucassen 1997, p. 5.

from the sixteenth century to the beginning of the twentieth can rightly be described as an integrated 'world market for forced labour'.[59]

7 The Universality of Proletarianisation

> The generalized separation of worker and product has spelled the end of any comprehensive view of the job done, as well as the end of direct personal communication between producers. As the accumulation of alienated products proceeds, and as the productive process gets more concentrated, consistency and communication become the exclusive assets of the system's managers. The triumph of an economic system founded on separation leads to the *proletarianization of the world.*
>
> GUY DEBORD[60]

∵

In the Vormärz, 'free' wage labour – especially its 'pure form' in industrial labour – had not yet achieved hegemony over other forms of dependent labour. Instead, heterogeneous forms of dependent labour coexisted alongside one another. Ahlrich Meyer summarises their diversity:

> This class of the labouring poor consisted of beggars and vagabonds searching for work, day-workers in the country, impoverished farmers and sharecroppers, weavers of the proto-industrial cottage-industry, domestic servants and city-handymen, seasonal migratory workers, railroad-construction workers, proletarianised craftworkers, the manufacturing and factory-proletariat and, last but not least, those that Marx named the 'lumpenproletariat', the *classes dangereuses* – men, women and children, altogether an extensively mobilised class on a labour market that, for the first time, also took on a European dimension through processes of migration.[61]

---

59 See Manning 1990, p. 102. The talk of 'white slaves' is not only metaphorical. In the seventeenth and eighteenth centuries, more than 300,000 'whites', mainly Irish, were indeed brought to America as slaves, cf. Jordan and Walsh 2008.

60 Debord 1995, § 26, p. 21.

61 Meyer 2014, pp. 260–1.

Moses Hess undertakes a far-reaching attempt to reconstruct a convergence of the various forms of dependent – free and unfree – labour when he shows that, under prevailing social conditions, every activity must become 'gainful employment', every labour 'wage labour'. In his ground-breaking essay 'Ueber die Noth in unserer Gesellschaft und deren Abhülfe' [*On Hardship in our Society and its Remedy*] from the *Deutschen Bürgerbuch für 1845*, Hess describes a society whose only source of unity lies – paradoxically – in universal 'egoism' and the 'competition' of all against all.[62] In such a society, 'gainful employment' and 'wage labour' become the generalised form of social survival, since the present economic system keeps 'people and their products ... separate from each other – and both perish'.[63] Only the (labour) market and money (in the form of wages) can reunite people with their products; the market – or 'huckster system' for Hess – becomes the universal mediator through which social universality is created in the first place: 'Wage labour or gainful employment is therefore no longer restricted to certain circles; the third estate, the business or merchant class, becomes the *general* estate, and all barriers within it fall away'.[64]

In a remarkable passage, Hess diagnoses that the mere compulsion to be gainfully employed does not in any way determine how exactly the individual acquires the money necessary for survival. The compulsion to earn money is instead a socially hollow form in which every theoretical-historical teleology towards a specific norm (as Marx suggests) is suspended – as long as the general commercial basis of 'egoism' and 'competition' is not questioned:

> The contradiction of the human being, of the human species with itself, is here universal, and this universal shape contains all earlier, one-sided forms. Here man is robber, slave, serf, swindler, usurer, wage-labourer and beggar all at once. In our world of hucksters, from North America to Russia, all the political and social forms of domination and servitude, which history presents in succession, flourish at once, from the beastlike of African slavery to the godlike of theocracy.[65]

With the concept of a '*world* of hucksters' (emphasis added), Hess has in mind a system indeed conceived at a global scale, a 'modern world system' in which different regimes for employing and exploiting labour coexist and even 'flourish'.

62 Hess 1845, pp. 25–26, 29, 31.
63 Hess 1845, p. 25.
64 Hess 1845, p. 32.
65 Hess 1845, p. 26.

The various 'political and social forms of domination and servitude' do form a historical 'succession' for Hess, but this is not a developmental movement which begins from a backward pole and advances towards a more progressive one: 'African slavery' and 'theocracy' are both at best starting points, but by no means end points of a history of progress. And the 'beastlike' form of 'African slavery' was at the time celebrating its resurrection in 'North America' of all places. The fact that precisely those places where progress has advanced the most are also particularly regressive – especially with regard to slavery – came as no surprise to Hess, having read his Tocqueville; nevertheless, the observation can be regarded as challenging a simple narrative of progress.[66]

In the 'world of hucksters', everyone must 'earn money' in order to survive; in the modern world, everyone is forced into 'wage labour or gainful employment' – Hess uses 'or' in its inclusive sense.[67] But he also denies this equation again when, in the passage just quoted, he includes wage labour as one form *among others* in a seemingly arbitrary list of all possible forms of gainful employment. All people must 'earn money'; but only some become 'wage labourers'. Alternatively, one can also become a 'slave', a 'serf', a 'robber', a 'usurer' or a 'beggar': what characterises these roles is that one person can alternate between all of them over the course of their life. Many of the social novellas and novels of the Vormärz period describe just this.

The distinction between 'passive' and 'active' proletarianisation, mentioned in the Introduction, can be used to conceptualise the almost imperceptible difference that appears in the quoted passage from Hess: 'passive' proletarianisation applies to all those who are deprived of any possibility for a secure, gainful subsistence outside of the market. 'Passive' proletarianisation means the 'destruction of the previously dominant forms of labour and subsistence', the dissolution of all non-capitalist forms of material reproduction.[68] Accordingly, all those who are at the mercy of the market (the 'world of hucksters')

66 Hess cites the first volume of Tocqueville's *De la démocratie en Amérique*, published in 1835, as early as 1837 in his *Heiligen Geschichte der Menschheit. Von einem Jünger Spinozas* [*Holy History of Mankind. By a Young Disciple of Spinoza*], Stuttgart 1837, reprinted in Hess 1961, pp. 1–74, here p. 47. Tocqueville's observations on the political and social effects of slavery in the American Free States, found in the last chapter of the first volume of *Démocratie*, can thus be assumed as background knowledge for Hess. See Tocqueville 2000, 'Position That the Black Race Occupies in the United States; Dangers to Which Its Presence Exposes the Whites', pp. 548–82. The chapter ends with one of Tocqueville's famous aporias: 'If you refuse liberty to the Negroes of the South, they will end by seizing it violently themselves; if you grant it to them, they will not take long to abuse it' (p. 582).

67 Hess 1845, p. 32.

68 Offe 1984, p. 92.

and have to hire themselves out to it, for better or worse, can be called 'proletarians'. 'Active proletarianisation', on the other hand, means the transformation of the 'passively' proletarianised into wage labourers, their placement into conditions of 'free' wage labour. In this passage, Hess makes it clear that at the given stage of economic and industrial development in the German Vormärz, there can be no question of an automatic progression from 'passive' to 'active' proletarianisation and thus of an exclusive role for 'free' wage labour: the forms of existence of slaves, serfs, robbers, usurers or beggars still appear here as equally plausible 'alternatives, both past and present, to "active" proletarianisation through wage labour'.[69]

The distinction between 'passive' and 'active' proletarianisation – or, in class terms, between the proletariat and the class of wage-labourers – can be conceived in two stages which do not necessarily follow one another, but neither do they exist without one another. In the debates of the Vormärz, both stages are repeatedly lumped together. In terms of class politics, the appeal of a position that allows its class subject – the class of wage-labourers – to be identified with the progress of the productive forces has already been named as a possible reason for this conflation. Based on the distinction between active and passive proletarianisation, one could imagine that an *active* class position has greater appeal compared to a merely *passive* one. Among others, Marx identified the proletariat's active role in shaping progress, a claim happily accepted by the entire workers' movement of the later nineteenth century, at least in its mainstream tendencies. One part of the proletariat, the active, productive industrial workforce, was then ascribed qualities that were inherently positive, such as 'freedom' and material creative power. Submission to wage labour and the experience of total heteronomy was thus ideologically reversed. To put it bluntly: labour, *of all things*, was suddenly supposed to make people free.

In the drafts of *Capital*, the socio-historical conditions of 'passive' proletarianisation are put into terms that present the experience of such proletarianisation even more drastically and vividly. 'Labour capacity denuded of the means of labour and the means of life', it states,

> is therefore absolute poverty as such, and the worker, as the mere personification of the labour capacity, has his needs in actuality, whereas the activity of satisfying them is only possessed by him as a non-objective capacity (a possibility) confined within his own subjectivity. As such, con-

69 Offe 1984, p. 93.

> ceptually speaking, he is a pauper, he is the personification and repository of this capacity which exists for itself, in isolation from its objectivity.[70]

The freedom of wage labour does not yet offer any positive possibilities for identification; rather, it becomes recognisable as mere freedom to 'absolute poverty': 'free to quit, free to starve'.[71]

Eduard Gans had already observed this in Paris 1830: 'Isn't it called slavery when you exploit a human being like an animal, even if he would be free to die of hunger otherwise?'[72] In the Vormärz, the relentless compulsion that forces this freedom was consistently described as slavery – or in Willkomm's words, the 'slavery of freedom'. If we understand the talk of slavery as a paraphrase of 'passive proletarianisation', then it represents a universal structural feature of all modern societies. In order to describe the inescapable compulsion to take on wage labour, Marx could not completely dispense with the peculiar suggestive power of the word 'slavery'. In *Wage Labour and Capital* he writes of the 'slavery of the workers'.[73] Later he will occasionally use the term 'wage slavery', which openly admits the 'difficulty fixing a dividing line between free labor and forced labor'.[74] The use of the word 'slavery' ultimately proves indispensable if the coercive character of proletarianisation is to be kept visible in language, precisely where this coercion threatens to become invisible behind the ideological rhetoric of 'freedom' – *freedom of contract, freedom of trade, free wage labour*.

---

70 Marx 1861–63, *Economic Manuscripts*, MECW 30, p. 40.

71 Linebaugh 2006, p. 11.

72 Gans 1995, p. 100.

73 MECW 9, p. 198.

74 On 'wage slavery', see Marx 1871, *The Civil War in France*, MECW 22, pp. 307–59, here p. 335. On the 'difficulty fixing a dividing line between free labor and forced labor', see Stanziani 2008, p. 29.

CHAPTER 6

Representing the 'Labouring Poor'

1 The Possibilities of Literature: Ernst Willkomm's *White Slaves or the Sufferings of the People*

Recent labour history suggests no longer rigidly opposing 'free' and unfree labour, but rather proceeding from a 'maze of labour relations and modulations', from a continuum that stretches 'between the two poles of slavery and free labour'.[1] In the Vormärz, literature was perhaps better able to portray such a continuum than theory, which had to first stake clear front lines in order to provide any sharply defined terms at all. In Ernst Willkomm's novel *Weisse Sclaven oder die Leiden des Volkes* [*White Slaves or the Sufferings of the People*], the term 'white slaves' is used to disclose two continuums at once: a diachronic one that links modern 'free' labour with submerged forms of unfree labour such as serfdom and slavery, and a synchronic continuum that ties 'free' wage labour in Central Europe to forms of unfree labour in other parts of the world, such as plantation slavery in America.

Historically, the novel presents a wide time span: the main action takes place in 1832, a long internal narrative flashes back to the time of the French Revolution.[2] At the end of the eighteenth century, Count Boberstein's castle stood in a remote corner of the Lower Lusatian Heath; in 1832, an industrially operated 'cotton spinning mill' stands on the castle's site.[3] The novel locates the 'white slaves' of the title in both timelines: the serfs of the Count in the first, the wage labourers of the factory in the second. The historical step from serfdom to the status of 'free' labourers follows the progress of village inhabitants over generations. At the same time, the 'masters' are identical in terms of family: the factory is run by the sons of Count Magnus von Boberstein, whose crimes led to disaster at the end of the long flashback. After the count rapes Rose, a young peasant woman from the village, on her wedding night, the serfs rise up and burn down the castle. The sons of the criminal Magnus, who now call themselves only 'Messrs von Stein' – Adrian, Aurel and Adalbert – found a company

1 Linden and Roth 2014b, p. 457.

2 The internal narrative is found in Willkomm 2013, pp. 58–291; the beginning of the plot is dated '179*' (p. 58).

3 Willkomm 2013, p. 298.

 | DOI:10.1163/9789004685536_008

years later and rebuild the castle as a factory. The sons and daughters of the rebellious serfs, now formally free, are employed as workers in the factory.

The 'white slaves' of the first timeline are directly and physically at the mercy of their master. As a sign of their serfdom, they wear a 'leather strap' around their foreheads, a 'slave ring', which one of the protagonists, the old Sloboda, who was born in bondage, compares in retrospect to the branding of sheep.[4] The landlord exercises jurisdiction and carries out corporal punishment. Finally, the count claims the *jus primae noctis*, although this is already controversial, as shown by the outrage after Rose's rape. The peasants regularly perform 'compulsory labour and domestic services' for the count. In addition, servants are selected every year to work in the castle. Young women are constantly subject to assaults by the lords and older servants.[5]

The historical continuity of enslavement is pronounced by the old Leberecht, also born in bondage:

> I hate the selfish Count from the bottom of my heart, because perhaps with more consciousness and sweeter pleasure than his father, he is turning us poor freedmen back into wretched slaves who must blindly, without will, obey his beck and call if they are not to sink into nameless misery![6]

In the middle of the novel, the title 'White Slaves' returns as the heading of a chapter that drastically – and with the usual means of miserabilist literature – illustrates enslavement through 'nameless misery'.[7] After a 'major wage cut', hunger ravages the 'factory village'. Riots break out and a work stoppage ensues; the workers demand more pay. Adrian, the factory owner, rejects the workers' demands. In his response, he sums up the new form of slavery: 'Anyone who thinks they are neglected by me can leave! I hold no one, force no one to serve me! Dear God, what more do you want? No king and no emperor moves more freely on God's wide earth than my workers!' The workers themselves perceive the alleged freedom as merely a 'joke', which they themselves, however, find 'very bitter'.[8] A little later, Leberecht pointedly describes the bitter irony of freedom as the 'slavery of freedom', the 'most despicable slavery' of all.[9]

4 Willkomm 2013, p. 16.
5 Willkomm 2013, p. 83, and the chapter 'Die Gesindestube' [The Servant's Quarters], pp. 114–128.
6 Willkomm 2013, p. 383.
7 Willkomm 2013, pp. 413–26.
8 Willkomm 2013, p. 419.
9 Willkomm 2013, p. 400.

The plight of the workers, however, does not only result from the mere structure of the wage-labour relation. Rather, Adrian deliberately used the situation of 'passive proletarianisation' after the abolition of serfdom to ensnare the villagers in a system of debt. He freely admits this to the protesting workers:

> I accepted everyone kindly and recruited as many as I could employ. But I made it clear that anyone who wanted to find and keep a job with me would have to settle on my own land. At first, some of them were surprised by this demand, but when I offered to give them a piece of land free of charge and to advance money at a low interest rate for the construction of a small house, everyone agreed. I caught the freedom fighters like mice. They jumped into my trap in droves, and that's how the spinning village over by the lake came into being. As my debtors, these fools were in my power from the very beginning.[10]

'Free' labour turns out to be disguised debt bondage: 'We had no weapons against you', the labour leader Martell tells Adrian, 'because we were poor, depended on you, stood in your debt books, in a word, we were your servants in body and soul, your white slaves!'[11]

Adrian knows that his workers are at his mercy and demands absolute submission: 'I wish and command obedience! To the one who blindly obeys I will be a kind master!'[12] By emphasising the total dependence of the workers on their master, the novel places the situation of the wage labourers in a historical continuity with serfdom; the formal-legal difference in status is ignored. With the systematic indebtedness of the workers, which subsequently has to be worked off, the novel identifies a practice common in early industrialisation that practically and even legally undermines an essential element of the formally free status of wage workers: their freedom of movement and free choice of occupation. These and other practices of effectively tying workers to an employer were repeatedly scandalised at the time in the *Gesellschaftsspiegel*. Beyond the anecdotal and concrete historical significance in the German Vormärz, David Graeber has also shown that a systematic indebtedness of workers and capitalists forms the unacknowledged centre of all capital accumulation: without indebtedness there is no original accumulation of free capital and

10 Willkomm 2013, pp. 433–4.
11 Willkomm 2013, p. 683.
12 Willkomm 2013, p. 425.

no original accumulation of free labour.[13] 'Freedom' is a derived category that presents itself in continued metalepsis as cause of those social relations whose functioning it simultaneously obscures.

Synchronically, too, the novel displays a social continuum in which many forms of dependent and unfree labour are arrayed. Through Aurel, who is introduced as a Hamburg sea captain, seamen and sailors come into view. With 'impressment', labour history uncovered one of the roots of modern dependent labour, the violent recruitment of sailors for war and merchant fleets of the early modern period, and discovered one of the origins of modern labour discipline in the brutally regulated everyday life of seafarers.[14] More than this, the novel records the cruel history of modern seafaring – idyllically disguised – in the figure of Gilbert. This young 'son of an Englishman and a Creole woman' from New Orleans is Aurel's servant. Completely 'destitute' after the early death of both parents, the boy is taken in by the captain 'out of sheer good nature', and is completely at his mercy in return. With the 'good nature' of the experienced sea captain, Aurel also takes care of the boy's upbringing, whose origins continually make themselves felt in a disturbing way:

> Although Aurel loved the boy like a child, he had no leniency with him on duty. Violations of discipline, of which Gilbert was often guilty in the beginning, sometimes out of carelessness, sometimes out of obstinacy and recalcitrance, were punished by Aurel with the same severity as the meanest sailor. Several times the spoiled boy of the idle Creole woman saw his blood flow until his obstinacy bowed to the implacability of the strict captain.[15]

The global dimension of transatlantic slavery, alluded to by Gilbert's mother, is further linked to the plot. Captain Aurel connects Adrian's remote cotton mill to the 'transatlantic world' and thus to the world market.[16] The brothers establish a trading house in Hamburg which handles the cotton trade and organises the distribution of the spun cotton to the corresponding 'manufactories'. The raw cotton is initially sourced from Louisiana, before the von Stein brothers

13 Cf. the section 'So What is Capitalism, Anyway?' in Graeber 2011, pp. 345–55, where he succinctly states: 'It is the secret scandal of capitalism that at no point has it been organized primarily around free labour' (p. 350).

14 Cf. Linebaugh and Rediker 2000, especially the chapter, 'Hydrarchy: Sailors, Pirates, and the Maritime State', which characterises the warship and merchant ship of the early modern period as the 'prototype of the factory' (pp. 143–73, here p. 150).

15 Willkomm 2013, pp. 305–6.

16 Willkomm 2013, p. 298.

proceed to operate their 'own plantation … on the *Red River* in Arkansas'. The brothers are not only cooperating with slave owners, as plantation owners they have become slave owners themselves; 'white' and 'Black' slaves are subject to the same masters.[17]

With reference to the abducted African slaves of the cotton plantations, the first word of the novel's title now receives its counterpart. The talk about 'white slaves' is not only about exposing the 'freedom' of modern wage labour as poorly disguised slavery; it is also about relating this slavery to a knowledge of those *Black* slaves who are never directly named in the novel. The title *White Slaves* presupposes such knowledge and scandalises the fate of the title characters against the background of this knowledge. At the same time, however, the novel shows – if only in passing – that the fates of the white and Black slaves are functionally related: not only are they subject to the same master, they are also part of the same global production chain, elements of the same world system.[18]

Marx sums up this connection in the *Poverty of Philosophy*, one of the few places in the Vormärz where he addresses transatlantic slavery, the 'direct slavery … of Blacks in Surinam, in Brazil, in the Southern States of North America':

> Direct slavery is just as much the pivot of bourgeois industry as machinery, etc. Without slavery you have no cotton; without cotton you have no modern industry. It is slavery that gave the colonies their value; it is the colonies that created world trade, and it is world trade that is the precondition of large-scale industry. Thus slavery is an economic category of the greatest importance.[19]

The question remains as how to represent such economic categories and their global significance in literature. If 'structures as such are either impossible to narrate or can only be narrated in a very pale manner', as Albrecht Koschorke remarks, then Willkomm first makes the superstructure of the capitalist world system apparent by locating it in a small village in a remote – not to say godforsaken – region.[20] From there, he unravels the global networks of value creation; he thus reconstructs the world market 'from below', from the local to the global. In turn, Willkomm intimately portrays the socio-economic transformation process, which reshapes the serf-based agrarian economy into

---

17 Willkomm 2013, p. 299.
18 On the 'Atlantic recomposition of textile labor-power', see Linebaugh 2014, pp. 89–90.
19 MECW 6, p. 167. Translation revised.
20 Koschorke 2018, p. 54.

a commodity-producing economy, and thus ties it to the life cycle of the villagers and their masters. Historical change becomes vivid in the natural process of birth, growth and decay; caesurae and radical changes – such as the rebellion of the serfs and the burning down of the castle – become palpable as violent intrusions into this process.

Literature finds its function in tying abstract, systemic connections to the reader's background experience by *figuring* these connections, that is, by letting them appear as figures and clashes with other figures. Literature depicts how large, global connections affect individuals and shape their experiences; it shows how abstract phenomena such as 'competition', 'the world market' or 'economic crisis' befall individuals in real life. The figurative achievement is facilitated if it can fall back on figurative constellations which, for their part, do not need to be explained and whose emotional value can be taken for granted. This is undoubtedly the case with the figurative constellation of the family. Willkomm also illustrates how well-worn conventions of representation can be used to make the hitherto unseen and unimagined – a capitalist world system, for instance – visible. Through the depiction of three young capitalists, the von Stein brothers, who know how to profitably transform their inherited power, Willkomm demonstrates that the economic power of capital does not emerge out of nothing, that the 'original accumulation of capital' can only ever be a 'so-called' accumulation, as Marx will write, because in many places it builds upon old power structures. In socio-historical terms, too, industrialisation was not necessarily linked to a replacement of the ruling elites – for example, in the sense of a replacement of the nobility by the 'aspiring bourgeoisie' – as the historical doxa assumes. In many cases, it was the nobles themselves that pursued industrialisation and profited from it. Mead's 'Mill Lords', who are not (only) to be understood allegorically, already expresses this, as does Willkomm when he makes the generational chain of the (Bober)Steins his protagonists.

But the familial narrative, whose possibilities Willkomm knows how to use in an innovative way, keeps him – as we have seen – on tracks that can at best be described as stereotypical. The logic of the narrative seems to dictate that the constellation of the three capitalist brothers, for instance, must be further exaggerated by a secret sibling relationship between the brothers and the labour leader Martell; and this already improbable relationship is then surpassed by ever more proliferating (family) relations that are ultimately almost impossible to understand. In the end, the pure will to intrigue reigns supreme.[21]

21 Magnus rapes three women who also play a role in the novel, and two of the three children born of these rapes – Martell and Klütken-Hannes – are involved in the novel's plot.

If, according to Engels, the quality of 'social' literature is measured by the extent to which it is able to 'relate the individual facts of the narrative to general conditions and thus bring out what is striking or significant about them', then one cannot help but describe Willkomm's novel as a success.[22] At the same time, the novel is ruined by the very means that ensure its quality: where narrative familialism weaves its web, kitsch and cheap thrills are never far away.

2 Engels and the Invention of Social Reportage

Engels attributed a general narrative weakness to contemporary 'social' literature. The reason why the 'general conditions' of class society can no longer be *narrated* may be that these relations can no longer be *experienced as general* by the individual; the system has decoupled itself from experience and the possibility of experience. This was, after all, Marx's main point in his argument with Proudhon and in his theoretical construction of the contradiction of *Wage Labour and Capital*: in the individual's experience, 'general conditions' are necessarily inverted. Since it is not individuals who confront each other in the capital relation, but classes, the whole of this relation can only be perceived by classes, not the individual; 'class experience' is therefore never that of the individual, but constitutes itself in a break with it. Talk of 'class experience' will never be able to completely free itself from a metaphorical or even ideological admixture: anyone who claims to express class experience in terms of 'we' must first have appropriated this position, and this appropriation requires legitimisation in any case. In the historical sequence, the aporia of the impossibility of experiencing class society by the individual will lead to the deployment of authorities that are supposed to function as legitimate subjects of class experience. A central authority will be the party, which will ultimately – as Georg Lukács will put it – *impute to itself* the experience of class *as class* and the class consciousness that develops from it.[23]

The aporia contained here cannot be grasped sharply enough: the moment the individual is set free as an individual and can only find a superior unity in the collective figure of the class, he simultaneously loses access to experience and to the fundamental ability to experience his social relations and conditions. The *condition prolétarienne* must do without experience for the individual proletarian – not by chance, but by structural necessity.

22 MECW 6, pp. 244–5.
23 Cf. Lukács 1971, p. 51.

And that is why it must also do without narration: 'Where has it all gone? Who still meets people who really know how to tell a story?' asks Walter Benjamin in his aptly titled 1933 essay, 'Experience and Poverty'.[24] In the Vormärz, it becomes clear that poverty consumes experience – and the poverty of experience consumes its narratability. One solution is to *stop telling stories*.

Now, 'modernity's much-lamented poverty of experience' and the end of narrative derived from this diagnosis have been questioned with good arguments from the perspective of a 'general theory of narrative'.[25] And indeed, one cannot deny that even in texts that present themselves as post-narrative, there is nevertheless a story being told in the sense of a general cultural-semiotic and anthropological operation. But if we still want to take Engels' diagnosis of a 'complete inability to tell a story' in capitalist modernity seriously, then we will have to specify what Engels means (and what he does not mean) by 'telling'.[26] It may be helpful here to look for counter-terms. In the next section ('The Reporter in the Field: "The Big Cities"'), for example, I will propose *narration* as a counter-term to description, *narratio* as counter-term to *descriptio*. Engels describes rather than narrates, and he organises his descriptions not in stories but in tableaus and small scenes. In this context, my heuristic juxtaposition of 'description' and 'narration' does not necessarily coincide with that of 'depiction' and 'poetry', which in the *Gesellschaftsspiegel* are seen as continuously merging into one another. There it was about the fictional status of the texts, here it is a question of how they are organised. (Fictional) poetry can be as descriptive as narrative, and the same applies to (factual) depictions. Nevertheless, there is – already in the history of concepts and rhetoric – a close elective affinity, if not identity, between 'depiction' and 'description', for example with regard to the root of both in the ancient description of images, the *ekphrasis*. In the following, the heuristic juxtaposition of narration and description serves only to clarify poetological tendencies.

In this chapter, however, a modification in the position of the speaking-writing 'I' must first be considered. This 'I' renounces narrative generality, it drops any distanced, sovereign attitude, and thus also abandons the claim to establish a coherent space of fiction. The 'I' of the text appears on the scene as limited, and becomes an *observer* who communicates only his observations; the writing-reporting observer thereby marks himself as a mere informer, as messenger and medium: he becomes a *reporter*.

---

24 Benjamin 2005, p. 731.
25 Koschorke 2018, p. 54.
26 MECW 6, p. 244.

Engels plays a crucial role in the invention of social reportage. Even before his ground-breaking work on *The Condition of the Working Class in England*, he caused a sensation with his 'Letters from Wuppertal', which appeared in Gutzkow's *Telegraph für Deutschland* in 1839.[27] Berthold Auerbach refers to an important precursor in 1846 in *Schrift und Volk* when he cites *Sketches by Boz* as an example of a literature that elevates 'the conditions of the lower people' back into the purview of poetry.[28]

Published in 1836 by the still unknown Charles Dickens, whose name was not given, *Sketches by Boz. Illustrative of Every-Day Life and Every-Day People* was a collection of small prose pieces which intended 'to present little pictures of life and manners as they really are'.[29] The pictorial element, already mentioned in the title of the collection, is expressed in the individual prose pieces in an art of description obsessed with detail, the explicit aim of which is to present the object of the description as vividly as possible to the reader. Concerning the 'beadle', the church servant of the described 'parish', it says:

> See him again on Sunday in his state-coat and cocked-hat, with a large-headed staff for show in his left hand, and a small cane for use in his right. How pompously he marshals the children into their places! and how demurely the little urchins look at him askance as he surveys them when they are all seated, with a glare of the eye peculiar to beadles! The church-wardens and overseers being duly installed in their curtained pews, he seats himself on a mahogany bracket, erected expressly for him at the top of the aisle, and divides his attention between his prayer-book and the boys. Suddenly, just at the commencement of the communion service, when the whole congregation is hushed into a profound silence, broken only by the voice of the officiating clergyman, a penny is heard to ring on the stone floor of the aisle with astounding clearness. Observe the generalship of the beadle. His involuntary look of horror is instantly changed into one of perfect indifference, as if he were the only person present who had not heard the noise. The artifice succeeds. After putting forth his right leg now and then, as a feeler, the victim who dropped the money ventures to make one or two distinct dives after it; and the beadle, gliding softly round, salutes his little round head, when it again appears above the seat, with various double knocks, administered with the cane before noticed,

27 MECW 2, pp. 7–25.
28 Auerbach 2014, p. 76.
29 Dickens 1995, p. 7.

> to the intense delight of three young men in an adjacent pew, who cough violently at intervals until the conclusion of the sermon.[30]

The invitation to 'see' and 'observe' reveals the aim of this prose: to make things visible. The dramatising word 'suddenly' creates the impression of a simultaneity of observation. As the text itself implies, the necessary familiarity with the *object of observation* is given by the fact that the *subject of observation* is part of the described world. The first chapter of the collection is called 'Seven sketches from our parish', the observer is part of the neighbourhood in question. The exact position of the observing subject, however, remains unmarked; only never in doubt is his – mostly ironically articulated – solidarity with the poor people of the neighbourhood against the pompous caprice of the small and big authorities and dignitaries.

Engels also adopts a similar standpoint of speaking and writing in his 'Letters from Wuppertal'. The reports from Barmen and Elberfeld focus on the desolate situation of the poor and pauperised as well as the 'obscurantist' double standards of the educated and propertied classes, who were (and probably still are) strongly organised in free churches and reformed sects.[31] The knowledge offered to the enlightened, foreign readership is that of an *insider*, who can nevertheless distance himself far enough so as to perceive and emphasise the ridiculousness of it all. In his later reports from England, Engels changes the standpoint of speaking and writing, which makes these texts social reportage in the full sense of the word. In *The Condition of the Working Class in England*, Engels reveals himself as an *outsider* who has gone inside the situation in order to bring the outside readers a knowledge of the inside.

Engels' claim to introspection is already stated in the subtitle of the book: 'from personal observation and authentic sources'. One of the subtleties of Engels' writing style is that he first makes this claim, which is intended to confirm his credibility above all with the reading *outsiders*, in an address to the *insiders*. The book is preceded by a two-page dedication 'To the Working Classes of Great Britain', written in English and also printed in English in the German first edition, which begins with the exclamation and call 'Working Men!'

In this dedication, Engels summarises everything that make his text a reportage and in turn illustrates its innovative standpoint:

---

30 Dickens 1995, pp. 18–19.

31 MECW 2, pp. 7. Here the congregations in Wuppertal are called the 'Zion of the obscurantists'.

> Working Men!
> To you I dedicate a work, in which I have tried to lay before my German Countrymen a faithful picture of your condition, of your sufferings and struggles, of your hopes and prospects. I have lived long enough amidst you to know something about your circumstances; I have devoted to their knowledge my most serious attention, I have studied the various official and non-official documents as far as I was able to get hold of them – I have not been satisfied with this, I wanted more than a mere abstract knowledge of my subject, I wanted to see you in your own homes, to observe you in your everyday life, to chat with you on your condition and grievances, to witness your struggles against the social and political power of your oppressors.[32]

The claim to draw 'a faithful picture' is based on introspection and participation. The observer comes into the 'homes', lives and talks with the workers, participates in their 'sufferings and struggles' and learns about their 'hopes and prospects'. This leads to – and simultaneously is only made possible by – the observer abandoning any pretension of neutrality and locating himself as a partisan in the field of observation: he wishes, as he writes to the workers, 'to witness your struggles against the social and political power of your oppressors'. He testifies in his person that everything was as he reports it, he certifies this, and at the same time he appears as a witness for the prosecution in that great (court) trial which Hegel, Marx and Engels called world history. As a 'witness' for the prosecution he has collected 'sufficient evidence' with which he can break the ideology of the 'middle class'. After all, it is a matter of 'doing justice to an oppressed and calumniated class of men'.[33]

Engels' method can be understood as *participant observation*. This designation is anachronistic only insofar as the methodological concept of participant observation will be systematically elaborated only later and then named as such; but the 'ethno-sciences' in which this method is used – folklore, ethnography, ethnology – are quite contemporaneous inventions. When Engels writes that he visited the workers in their 'homes' in order to learn about their 'everyday life', he also plays on an already established *literary* topos that refers back to the ethnological field. In the preface to his *Mystères de Paris*, Eugène Sue compares himself to James Fenimore Cooper and makes a similar claim of exploration for himself and his work:

32 MECW 4, p. 297.

33 MECW 4, pp. 297–8.

> We have all read the legendary work of the American Walter Scott, James Fenimore Cooper, whose pages describe the brutal ways of savages, their quaint and poetic language, the countless tricks they use to pursue or flee their enemies … For our own readers, we are going to attempt to depict some episodes from the lives of French savages who are as far removed from civilization as the Indians Cooper so vividly depicts. And these barbarians are all around us. We will spend time with them in the dens in which they get together to plan murders and robberies, in the holes where they divvy up their victims' spoils among themselves.[34]

Engels also uses the topos of an exploratory journey to that continent of poverty and neglect which is to be discovered in the 'bad quarters' of the cities. However, in contrast to and perhaps also as a criticism of Sue, he tries to avoid any exoticisation of the 'savages'. For Engels, the English workers are not 'strangers' or 'savages', but representatives and forerunners of the universalism of '"One and Indivisible" Mankind', which has not yet been realised anywhere else – not even and especially not among the educated, 'civilised' classes. In the dedication, Engels marks a significant difference between the directly addressed workers and the English middle class:

> A foreigner to *them*, not to *you*, I hope. Though my English may not be pure, yet, I hope, you will find it *plain* English. No working-man in England – nor in France either, by-the-by – ever treated me as a foreigner. With the greatest pleasure I observed you to be free from that blasting curse, national prejudice and national pride … I found you to be more than mere *English*men, members of a single, isolated nation, I found you to be *Men*, members of the great and universal family of Mankind, who know their interest and that of all the human race to be the same. And as such, as members of this Family of 'One and Indivisible' Mankind, as Human Beings in the most emphatical meaning of the word, as such I, and many others on the Continent, hail your progress in every direction and wish you speedy success. Go on then, as you have done hitherto. Much remains to be undergone; be firm, be undaunted – your success is certain, and no step you will have to take in your onward march, will be lost to our common cause, the cause of Humanity![35]

34 Sue 2015, p. 3.

35 MECW 4, pp. 298, 301.

Engels does not only draw his knowledge of the life of the English workers from 'personal observation' and from his familiar contact with them. He has also prepared himself conscientiously as a 'participant observer' by studying all 'authentic sources', all 'official and non-official documents' and also by reading all the 'voluminous reports' of the 'commissions of inquiry', which are otherwise just gathering dust 'on the shelves of the Home Office'.[36] That he has access to all these documents and that he has the time to study all these sources stems from the fact that Engels himself is *not a* worker, even though he shows solidarity with them. Engels, the observer, moves in both worlds – in that of the workers and in that of the 'middle class' – with great ease, and it is precisely the possibility of switching that enables his privileged position as an observer:

> Having, at the same time, ample opportunity to watch the middle-classes, your opponents, I soon came to the conclusion that you are right, perfectly right in expecting no support whatever from them. Their interest is diametrically opposed to yours, though they always will try to maintain the contrary and to make you believe in their most hearty sympathy with your fates. Their doings give them the lie.[37]

The position of the reporter is a peculiar non-position. The reporter is a world changer untied to any place or social world, but who can always view *one* world from the perspective of another and thus relativise both. What applies to classes also applies to nations. After the dedication to the English workers, the 'Preface' addresses the German readers. Engels acts as a mediator between England and Germany and again exposes narrow-minded, one-sided lies of life by refracting them in the mirror of the other: 'In the meantime, however, the established fact of wretched conditions in *England* will impel us to establish also the fact of wretched conditions in *Germany*'. Conversely, Engels' German philosophical education helps him grasp English misery in its *totality*, so that he can proudly claim that 'even in England there exists as yet not a single piece of writing which, like mine, takes up *all* the workers'.[38]

The reporter's placeless position allows for a form of critique that does not have to theorise its standpoint further, but which can nevertheless appear as decisive and well-founded. At the same time, nothing guarantees the reliability of the reporter's judgements except his own assurance of having *really been there*. His self-grounded authority and shady position make it plausible to think

36 MECW 4, pp. 297–8.
37 MECW 4, p. 298.
38 MECW 4, p. 303.

of him as a kind of *trickster*. The trickster, who as a threshold figure brings different worlds, cultures or societies into contact, in no small part by deceiving both sides, appears in the mid-nineteenth century in both ethnological and political discourse.[39] It is said to have been the later Tory Prime Minister Benjamin Disraeli of all people who called his Whig opponents tricksters in the British Parliament; incidentally, with his 1845 novel *Sybil*, Disraeli himself proved to be a kind of literary threshold explorer between the *Two Nations* and the two classes.[40] The backlash was not long in coming: in the years that followed, Disraeli was repeatedly accused of being a trickster himself, and the antisemitic tinge of this accusation cannot be denied.[41]

Without wanting to generalise too much, we can say that the reporter structurally places himself in a position that constantly and even necessarily exposes him to the suspicion of being a fraudster or forger – and this precisely where he wants to expose fraud, forgery and lies. Suspicion is part of the reporter's professional ethos *and* professional risk.

3 The Reporter in the Field: 'The Great Towns'

> It is a kind of duty to see and smell such places now and again, especially smell them, lest you should forget that they exist; though perhaps it is better not to stay there too long.
>
> GEORGE ORWELL[42]

So how does social reportage depict the lives of the *labouring poor* without falling into the trap of miserabilist social romanticism? Engels' chapter on 'The Great Towns', which according to Tristram Hunt is the 'philosophical and journalistic spine of the whole book', can serve as a test case here.[43]

The 'great towns' or big cities come into Engels' focus because the 'industrial proletariat' has its home there. And that is why, according to Engels, in the 'great towns' the characteristics of the modern social order can be seen 'carried out to its utmost extreme'.[44] The first thing that stands out about Engels' depiction of

39 Cf. Schüttpelz 2010.
40 Cf. Doty and Hynes 1993, p. 14, and Benjamin Disraeli 1998.
41 Cf. Julius 2010, starting at p. 264.
42 Orwell 1958, p. 17.
43 Hunt 2009, p. 18. At a good fifty printed pages, the chapter is also the longest in the whole book.
44 MECW 4, p. 329.

the 'great towns' is the claim to completeness, which contrasts confusingly with the exhibited partiality of the observer's position. This can already be seen in the opening of the chapter, where the reader is invited by an experienced 'I' to approach London by ship: 'I know nothing more imposing than the view which the Thames offers during the ascent from the sea to London Bridge'.[45] This marked perspective then quickly gives way to a brief generalised critique of civilisation, one outraged by the atomisation of people in the modern city, and then turns into a long, encyclopaedic survey, a veritable catalogue of the 'bad quarters' of London, and finally of all the major cities of the United Kingdom (Dublin, Edinburgh, Liverpool, Nottingham, Glasgow …), before culminating in the investigation of Manchester. But here too, Engels first presents the various suburbs in detail before finally focusing on the 'central city'. In the various city overviews, Engels explains the urban layout of the streets, the distribution of the factories and the various neighbourhoods, with particular attention to the hygienic conditions of the workers' quarters. In Manchester, Engels also examines in great detail the predominant forms of block development and, finally, the construction of the individual houses. To illustrate the courtyard system, Engels inserts floor plans and maps he made himself, and he also illustrates with small sketches the scandalous practice of no longer lying the bricks together as usual 'with their long sides touching' but with 'their narrow ends touching', which saves material but makes the walls thinner and more wind-permeable.[46] From the built substance of the cities to the clothing and food of the city dwellers, the urban form of life of the 'working class' is almost systematically recorded. Overall, the chapter has an enumerative and juxtaposing structure. How does Engels manage to make the 'facts of the narrative' meaningful?

First of all, it must be stated that no *stories* are told. There is no event that triggers the narration, no incidents to be told, no tension, no narrative timing. Even the somewhat episodic character of Boz'/Dickens' *Sketches* ('suddenly') is largely absent. At one point, we are told that the Chartist leader Feargus O'Connor wore a 'fustian velvet suit' – the 'proverbial costume of the working-men' – on his visit to Manchester during the 1842 insurrection, earning him the 'defeaning applause of the working-men'.[47] This micro-narrative comprises only one sentence, and only derives its narrative or at least anecdotal quality from the fact that it sums up the previously given detailed description of typical workers' clothing.

45 MECW 4, p. 328.

46 MECW 4, p. 359.

47 MECW 4, p. 367. Translation revised.

A central means of condensing meaning in Engels is through the depiction of prominent, clearly delineated tableaus. Thus, right at the beginning of the chapter, in the London section, three living situations are described that are meant to illustrate the worst possible degree of destitution. The reader is presented with the smallest flats and cellar holes without furniture or other furnishings, in which entire families vegetate and die on rotten straw without anyone noticing. More significant than the content for the mode of presentation is how the three descriptions are introduced. After a lengthy description of a 'bad quarter', it continues: 'The foregoing description furnishes an idea of the aspect of the interior of the dwellings. But let us follow the English officials, who occasionally stray thither, into one or two of these workingmen's homes'.[48] The joint walk composes the guiding and structuring fiction, linking the individual 'facts' in the movement of walking: the narrator/describer moves through the city and carefully notes what he sees. Turns of phrase that suggest ambulatory observation and narration can be found again and again throughout the chapter. Engels' pedestrian, however, differs in one essential respect from the flâneur, who will later become the privileged storyteller of urban modernity. In Engels' case, the ambulant narrator is an investigator, he does not allow himself to drift, but is rather motivated from the beginning by the urgent desire to look behind the façade. Again and again, he initially describes a sometimes even attractive exterior, behind which abysses of misery and violence open up. The very beginning of the chapter sets the tone for this *critical* movement of the gaze and thought. After the impressive view of London from the Thames, the second section begins with the all-important 'but':

> But the sacrifices which all this has cost become apparent later. After roaming the streets of the capital a day or two, making headway with difficulty through the human turmoil and the endless lines of vehicles, after visiting the slums of the metropolis, one realises for the first time that these Londoners have been forced to sacrifice the best qualities of their human nature, to bring to pass all the marvels of civilisation which crowd their city; that a hundred powers which slumbered within them have remained inactive, have been suppressed in order that a few might be developed more fully and multiply through union with those of others.[49]

48 MECW 4, p. 334.
49 MECW 4, pp. 328–9.

The whole city of Manchester, according to another example, was organised socio-spatially and urban-architecturally in such a way 'that a person may live in it for years, and go in and out daily without coming into contact with a working-people's quarter or even with workers, that is, so long as he confines himself to his business or to pleasure walks'.[50] But as soon as one strays from the familiar paths, one inevitably finds 'misery and grime'.[51] Engels wants to expose the one under the other, and at the same time he claims that the operation of concealment is part and parcel of the present social order: without 'so systematic a shutting out of the working class', without the 'shameful' and 'hypocritical plan' of the big cities, capitalism could not function.[52] Engels' distinction between façade and core is not merely superficial: it gets at the core of the matter itself. The consequences of this way of thinking and writing extend into the mature Marx's critique of ideology and fetishism.

The narrator's desire to uncover does not rely on the contingency of his own view, and this also marks a difference to the flâneur. He systematically consults other reports, he supplements and substantiates his own observations with the police reports, press reports and commission reports being prepared everywhere in light of the catastrophic living conditions of the 'working classes' in the 1830s and 1840s, which can hardly be concealed any more. Furthermore, Engels' narrator examines these reports in view of his own experience. This makes Engels' text polyphonic, and in addition to the drawings and maps already mentioned, he also draws extensively on tables containing, for instance, statistical material for parliamentary inquiry reports.[53] On closer inspection, the text appears as a montage of extremely heterogeneous materials whose coherence must first be produced and cannot be assumed anywhere.

It is the reporter-subject who establishes this coherence, and it is a coherence that is marked *as produced* throughout. The reporter lets the reader participate in how he himself tries to make sense of the conditions he observes, many of which are at first hardly imaginable in their misery. There is no presupposed sovereignty of the writing subject here, but a documented striving for sovereignty.[54] Small narratives, scenes and tableaus are aids that the reporter-

---

50 MECW 4, pp. 347–8.

51 MECW 4, p. 349.

52 MECW 4, p. 349.

53 Cf. for instance, MECW 4, p. 404.

54 Strikingly, Engels explicitly rejects universal assertions, which only increases the authority of what he says. See, for example, MECW 4, p. 335: 'I am far from asserting that *all* London working people live in such want as the foregoing three families. I know very well that ten are somewhat better off, where one is so totally trodden under foot by society; but I assert that thousands of industrious and worthy people – far worthier and more to be respec-

subject uses to create order and find his way around; they are parts of his montages. The superordinate, pre-ordered space of a narrative (in the strong singular), which would be structured solely by a narrator-subject (however unreliable and fractured) and his perspective, voice or surplus-knowledge, does not exist. The observing reporter-subject surrenders to the observed situation, and to a certain extent replaces the sovereignty of the narrator with a clear – and as such always recognisable – political and moral positioning.

Engels solves the problem of representation, which he had formulated as a narrative problem in view of miserabilist literature, by making the organisation of his text more flexible, integrating heterogeneous materials, revealing possible approaches to expansion and continuation and allowing descriptions as ends in themselves. The price of this procedure is a certain tiring redundancy, which even Engels' acclaimed book at times cannot avoid.

---

ted than all the rich of London – do find themselves in a condition unworthy of human beings; and that every proletarian, everyone, without exception, is exposed to a similar fate without any fault of his own and in spite of every possible effort.'

CHAPTER 7

Class in Struggle

> Begone! I will not hear you. There can be no community between you and me; we are enemies. Begone, or let us try our strength in a fight, in which one must fall.
>
> MARY SHELLEY[1]

• • •

> What remains of the traditional modes of expenditure has become atrophied, and living sumptuary tumult has been lost in the unprecedented explosion of class struggle … Class struggle, on the contrary, becomes the grandest form of social expenditure when it is taken up again and developed, this time on the part of the workers, and on such a scale that it threatens the very existence of the masters.
>
> GEORGES BATAILLE[2]

∵

Engels ends *The Condition of the Working Class in England* with a battle cry, one which today's reader cannot help but associate with Büchner's 'Peace to the peasants! War on the palaces!' from *The Hessian Messenger*:

> The war of the poor against the rich now carried on in detail and indirectly will become direct and universal. It is too late for a peaceful solution. The classes are divided more and more sharply, the spirit of resistance penetrates the workers, the bitterness intensifies, the guerrilla skirmishes become concentrated in more important battles, and soon a slight impulse will suffice to set the avalanche in motion. Then, indeed,

---

1 Shelley 2009, p. 103. The title of this chapter recalls a novel title by the Neukölln council communist and proletarian educator Karl Schröder, representative of the radical Essen current within the KAPD in the 1920s.

2 Bataille 1997, pp. 176, 178.

 | DOI:10.1163/9789004685536_009

> will the war-cry resound through the land: 'Peace to the peasants! War on the palaces!' – but then it will be too late for the rich to beware.[3]

The slogan, which Büchner himself had borrowed, makes historical reference to the social and military escalation of the French Revolution: *Guerre aux châteaux, paix aux chaumières* – a battle cry attributed to Nicolas Chamfort and sung by the French revolutionary armies in 1792 as they marched across the Rhine to spread the message of the revolution.

Engels takes the latest explosive rhetorical device hurled into Germany from France's now explicitly *social* revolution and affixes it to the beginning of his last paragraph, namely, the phrase: 'war of the poor against the rich'. The phrase was well-known in the Vormärz after Ludwig Börne used it in his sixtieth 'Letter from Paris' of 30 November 1831. Börne writes in a period of intensified class struggles following the July Revolution, and this letter in particular refers directly to the latest developments of the silk weavers' revolt in Lyon of November 1831.

By quoting Börne, Engels tunes the final blast of his book to the note of proletarian unrest and insurrection. In his concluding paragraph, he outlines the course of development to be followed by the radicalisation and self-clarification of class struggle. Engels' brief sketch provides an entire typology of possible forms of class struggle, which corresponds to the predicted development in the future tense: an initially diffuse 'spirit of resistance' and a still vague sense of 'bitterness' will flare up in 'guerrilla skirmishes', which will eventually be relinquished to make way for the 'more important battles'. It is here that the final battle is prepared, which Marx, in *his* finale to *The Poverty of Philosophy*, calls 'total revolution'.[4]

Engels' typology of class struggle reflects the hypothesis that classes do not enter into struggle as ready-made entities but rather are only constituted through the struggle itself. 'Class' is a thoroughly polemical concept: it is senseless to speak of a class without at the same time positing an opposing class, an antagonistic class. And it is equally meaningless to speak of a class that does not engage in struggle: 'The classes are divided more and more sharply', writes Engels, since it is only through struggle that they set themselves apart and become perceptible in the first place.

As will be discussed in the conclusion, this radicalisation has costs, and not only those accrued by the sacrifices that every revolution demands, but

3 MECW 4, pp. 582–3. Translation revised.

4 MECW 6, p. 212.

also in terms of the exclusions and restrictions that concern the composition of the revolutionary subject and the making of the revolutionary class itself.

1 Witches' Sabbath as Early Modern Class Struggle: Tieck

The first armed workers' uprising in German literary history takes place in the work of Ludwig Tieck. The plot of the 1832 novella *The Witches' Sabbath* [*Der Hexensabbat*] is set in the last years of Philip the Good's reign in Arras, Burgundy. In the enlightened, early capitalist atmosphere of a major city full of various 'trades' – Burgundy was the centre of a global textile industry in the mid-fifteenth century – a witch craze suddenly breaks out, completely unforeseen to most of those involved. Led by an old beggar-woman, who seems to be casting suspicions indiscriminately, and with the vigorous support of the new bishop, who everyone thought at first was a simpleton, pogrom-like scenes break out across the city; marauding 'mobs' and the 'rabble' play major roles.[5]

Failing to detect any logic behind the craze, the rich and educated 'burghers' initially assume it will be a temporary phenomenon.[6] 'The all-too-wise men', as Tieck smugly calls, cannot make any sense of the events.[7] As more and more burghers are themselves accused and thrown into prison, Peter Carrieux, 'one of the richest men in the country', has the bright idea 'to arm the many workers in his factories and send them to assist the burghers'. Appalled, representatives of the burghers reject the idea, fearing 'civil war' and the 'downfall of their city'.[8]

The workers, however – 'wallpaper weavers', as they are called, all of them 'good journeymen' – have already procured weapons and stand ready to strike at the behest of Guntram, an elder journeyman with plenty of experience in rebellion. Carrieux assuages them and orders them to 'get back to work'. To Guntram, Carrieux justifies the demobilisation by pointing to the social situation and the class alliances that would likely emerge in the city: 'The townspeople would not stand by us, the deputies are on the fence, fearing that the nobles might make moves against us'.[9] Guntram, on the other hand, is the

5 Tieck 1988a, pp. 41, 44, 85–86, 138, 143, 150, 158, 160, 182, 184, 189. I owe my friend Alexander Schmitz for the reference to Tieck's *Hexensabbat*.

6 Tieck 1988a, p. 189.

7 Tieck 1988a, pp. 189, 140.

8 Tieck 1988a, p. 153.

9 Tieck 1988a, p. 154.

'the real hero of the active resistance'.[10] He is certain that with the right amount of determination, this recalcitrance can be overcome:

> As you wish, said Guntram; but I have more experience in these things than you. I took part in the great uprising in Ghent, I used to be a soldier. Where clamour and skirmishes broke out, I followed my own heart. It is often a trivial thing that brings the whole city and the countryside to erupt in turmoil.[11]

The story goes on to reveal that both Carrieux and Guntram are right in different ways, and this does not end well for them. Carrieux gets arrested, while Guntram continues to mobilise the workers. The latter must now admit that his theory was correct, but that the other side has long since imposed its vision of order without compromise. The revolting workers believe they are fighting for the common good, as Guntram makes clear when says, 'We want to defend your city'.[12] In the end, however, they find themselves facing off against the very alliance predicted by Carrieux:

> They [the workers] stormed out shouting and made off for the bishop's palace. But no townspeople joined; where tumult was heard the shops closed their doors; the bishop's house and the Inquisition were barricaded shut. The journeymen raged and smashed what they could. But they all dispersed as soon as Count Etampes sent a group of horsemen led by a knight to the scene. Those brave enough to stay had to stand for an uneven fight with the armed horsemen. Only after several were killed and seriously wounded did the rest take off, at which point they were chased down the alleys.[13]

The indifferent, wait-and-see attitude of the burghers immediately turns into harsh rejection after the workers' defeat: when confronted by the prince's envoy, a representative of the burghers claims to have nothing to do with the rebels. It was, he claims, 'by no means the burghers that was up in arms, but rather a mob of workers'.[14]

---

10 Walter Münz, 'Nachwort', in: Tieck 1988a, pp. 301–35, here p. 320.

11 Tieck 1988a, pp. 154–5.

12 Tieck 1988a, p. 154.

13 Tieck 1988a, p. 188.

14 Tieck 1988a, p. 189.

Tieck's historical novella makes use of two distinct temporal levels and ties them together: the fifteenth century, and Tieck's present. Starting in a time of widespread social mobilisations erupting in unrest and revolutions, Tieck flashes back to a time which can be understood quite accurately as the birthplace of that new type of society which finally prevails in the Vormärz. In presenting a longer history of capitalism, French social historiography in the twentieth century has shown how capitalism dates much further back than the industrial era; according to Fernand Braudel (and the subsequent *world systems theory* propagated by Immanuel Wallerstein), the origins of capitalism can be traced back to the Northern Italian and Flemish-Burgundian trade and manufacturing centres from the fifteenth and sixteenth centuries.[15] Furthermore, the capitalisation of the urban societies of Northern Italy and Flanders shape the process of class formation.

Tieck provides an intricate snapshot of the social dynamics that arise once money and capital emerge as determining factors of social formation. It becomes clear that the tensions between the nobility, the burghers and the workers which openly erupt during the witch craze were already latent in the social fabric beforehand, and thus may have fomented the outbreak of the craze, though Tieck nowhere elaborates this. In any case, the end of the story suggests that the whole witch craze can *also* be interpreted as a symptom of existing class tensions.

From the very first pages of the novella, urban society appears deeply divided, with 'distrust' underlying all interaction.[16] The most important division is between nobility and burghers; the former have privileges, estates and castles, but no cash; the latter have learned to make their money work for them (and through their money, wage earners), and are therefore no longer willing out of patriotism or social conscience alone to let the nobles have their way. According to one burgher in the story, the 'crisis of our time' is conversely also rooted in the fact that the nobility does not want to seal its economic impotence with a resignation from political power: 'A struggle against the nobility will be just as necessary in the future as it was against the abuses of the Church until now'.[17]

In his characteristically terse manner, Tieck encapsulates the new social situation in a conversation that the old knight Beaufort, himself heavily in debt, must have with a count who accosts him for money:

15 Cf. Braudel 1984, pp. 89–174; Wallerstein 2004, pp. 66–129.

16 Tieck 1988a, p. 6.

17 Tieck 1988a, p. 39.

> Just this once, replied Beaufort, I will be unable to repay the sum you have requested: it is too high, it exceeds my credit. I have recently lost capital, my estates have brought little return, and everything I have had to build outside has already consumed many a year's income in advance. There's nothing I can do, even risk my own ruin, that would convince the bourgeois merchants or large factory owners to lend me an advance for you … They are certainly rich … but just think of all the cash expenses a carpet weaver has, what large sums he must pay out daily to his workers and subordinates. In this he must never fall behind, for a single week's delay would ruin him. The same goes for the timber merchant and cloth weaver. If they dared to withdraw such a large sum of capital from their business at once, they would lose all their credit instantly as soon as the other burghers found out. That is why their wealth only seems so great, since large sums of money are always pouring out, and they have to prepare in case external payments do not arrive, or merchants who owe them go bankrupt.[18]

In this situation, which can still roughly be grasped through the old estate system, but with cracks everywhere, the wage laborers become the decisive factor. The social order of the city consists of the three estates and underclass – 'rabble and burghers, nobility and clergy'.[19] But where do the workers fit?

On the one hand, they clearly qualify as burghers; they are the necessary counterpart to the 'bourgeois merchants' and 'large factory owners', for the townspeople rely on the workers in the 'struggle against the nobility'. On the other hand, however, the bourgeois capitalists are already beginning to fear the workers gaining power.

The workers too question their standing in the social order. On the one hand, they are ready to defend their city alongside their bourgeois employers; their armed struggle, at least according to its initial motivation, is not yet a class struggle *against* the bourgeoisie. On the other hand, they know that their social position alongside the burghers is totally dependent on them and their wage payments. When Carrieux is detained, the 'angry Guntram gathers all the journeymen, servants and unskilled workers' – an extraordinarily heterogeneous mixture in itself – 'and tells them that they would all be forced to become beggars now that their employer had been arrested'.[20] In other words, the (artisan) worker is always in danger of falling into the ranks of the rabble.

18 Tieck 1988a, p. 176.

19 Tieck 1988a, p. 182.

20 Tieck 1988a, p. 187.

The worker moves between the bourgeoisie and the rabble, but this is not a difference simply between different estates, but rather between status and non-status, between participating in the official order and being excluded from it. The fact that this exclusion is so easy – since all it requires is the ceasing of wages for any number of reasons – ultimately makes the whole order of estates untenable.

Guntram detects this untenability once he realises that he and his fellow class brothers are in danger of becoming rabble. But he also misjudges the situation entirely, perhaps due to his experience. When he mentions having taken part in the 'great uprising in Ghent', he means the great disputes between the proponents of urban-bourgeois self-government and those in favour of royal or ducal territorial rule.[21] After years of skirmishes, the Ghent militia had to admit defeat to Philip the Good in 1453. In these kinds of disputes, journeymen like Guntram were considered an integral part of the guild-organised burghers. *But now*, just a few years later – and Tieck's novella dramatises this socio-historical epochal threshold – this part of society has become uncanny to the rest, and must be cast off. The burghers would now rather enter negotiations with their old, noble adversaries than become dependent on the power of their former allies. To put it bluntly: the workers' struggle – for the freedom of the city, for Enlightenment, against the nobility and clergy – only becomes a struggle between classes, a struggle between workers and bourgeoisie, through the reaction of the bourgeoisie. In that very moment, however, the struggling workers are excluded from the society to which they originally sought to belong. If the modern proletariat emerges from the lower classes of the urban 'rabble' on the one hand and the craftsmen, above all the journeymen, on the other, then Tieck shows how these two wellsprings have always flowed into one another since the beginnings of capitalism. In the proletariat, both will have become indistinguishable.

2 The Witches' Sabbath of the Class Struggles in France: Börne

Tieck's analysis of society in *The Witches' Sabbath*, which clearly builds upon themes developed in *The Young Master Carpenter* concerning the disintegration of the old bourgeoisie and decline of journeymen craftsmen, acquires its striking relevance only against the background of the actual class situation at the time the novella was written, especially that of France after the July Revolu-

21 Tieck 1988a, p. 154.

tion. To truly grasp the power of Tieck's novella to make sense of its epoch, it is worth comparing his analysis with texts by Börne and Heine written at the same time.[22]

In his already mentioned sixtieth letter from Paris, Börne presents the situation of the bourgeoisie as the self-inflicted dilemma of a middle class that has lost its political bearings. In the relatively 'free' countries like France and England, according to Börne, no official inequality of privileges veils the inequality of living conditions, and this makes them particularly susceptible to social unrest: 'But where the middle classes have won equality, the lower classes see inequality. They become aware of their miserable condition, and sooner or later the war of the poor against the rich must break out'.[23] This war, however, is the fault of the bourgeoisie, and it ultimately comes at their expense as well. Instead of fighting for social equality and adequate political representation of the poor – the July Revolution merely extended census suffrage, rather than abolishing it – the bourgeoisie resorted to further depriving the poor of rights and property. In doing so, however, they only played into the hands of their old enemy, the recently vanquished nobility:

> The hopeless delusion of the bourgeoisie hastens ruin ever more terribly. Ever since winning their freedom, they cast their gaze on those beneath them, half out of fear, half out of arrogance, all the while failing to notice those above them, a defeated but still living enemy only waiting for them to look away. The aristocrats in France and England know very well how to make use of this fear and arrogance. They discretely incite the rabble against the citizens and proclaim to the latter: join us or meet your demise. The naive citizen believes this and does not understand that his own liberty, his own prosperity will falter so long as the poor do not join him in equal freedom, in equal prosperity; he does not understand that as long as there is a rabble, there is a nobility, and that as long as there is a nobility, his peace and happiness are in danger.[24]

Instead of preventing the poor from becoming an easily manipulated 'rabble' in the first place, the nouveau riche bourgeois mimic the old nobility. Just as the 'rich shopkeepers of Paris, bankers and factory owners', were recently insul-

22 Cf. Hörmann 2011, '"Der Krieg der Armen gegen die Reichen": Börne's Shifting Perspective on Proletarian Social Revolution', pp. 233–52.

23 Börne 1986, p. 329.

24 Börne 1986, pp. 329–30.

ted by the nobility as '*scoundrels*' [*Canaille*], they themselves now talk, 'as is fitting, all day about scoundrels, by which they mean everyone who does not wear a fine coat and has no income aside from the work his hands bring him each day'.[25] In the eyes of the bourgeoisie, the worker has long since become rabble.

3 Social War on Lake Zurich: Weitling

Both Tieck's historical novella and Börne's Paris correspondence focus on narrating and reporting revolutionary paroxysms. The 'social war', however, which Engels sees 'openly declared' as a 'war of all against all' in the 'great towns', smoulders rather than erupts in major battles.[26] In the typology of class struggle, this corresponds to the stage in which the workers' 'bitterness' first flares up in 'individual guerrilla skirmishes'. In two issues of *Junge Generation* dating from March and May 1843, Wilhelm Weitling collects 'Scenes from the Theatre of War', almost seismographically recording the social revolutionary upheavals in Switzerland, in France, England, in Germany, Ireland, Norway and Spain.[27]

The 'war of the poor against the rich', depicted by Weitling in his European revue, is clearly a reaction to rampant pauperism. While poverty is often portrayed as insidious and corrosive, especially in miserabilist literature, Weitling's approach is to dramatise and exacerbate the issue; his portrayal follows a more 'loaded' logic and rhetoric.[28] For example, in the first section of the first episode, set in 'Arau', Switzerland, we read: 'Misery is starting to take over here'.[29] Weitling counters this dynamic of immiseration which opens up both episodes in the 'Scenes' with an escalating counter-dynamic of 'impoverished delinquency'.[30] In Lyon, 'neither life nor property are safe anymore', and in Paris 'disorder is beginning to take a turn for the worse'.[31] Finally, of Berlin it is said: 'Poverty and crime are so rampant here one can only think of the future with horror'.[32]

---

25 Börne 1986, p. 330.
26 MECW 4, p. 329.
27 *Die junge Generation*, No. 3 (March 1843), pp. 40–43, and No. 5 (May 1843), pp. 71–3.
28 Cf. Suter 2016, p. 170.
29 *Die junge Generation*, p. 40.
30 Bescherer 2013, p. 76.
31 *Die junge Generation*, pp. 40–1.
32 *Die junge Generation*, p. 43.

Whereas the crimes reported in the first episode are indeed downright horrifying and destructive, with repeated stories of cruel violence against women, in the second episode the war correspondent does something different: he tries to find starting points of a rising social protest movement in the delinquency, since the 'crimes' depicted are now directed exclusively against property. The first 'scene' reads *in total*: 'Zurich. Here in the villages by the lake, misery bares its teeth. Here and there people are saying: it won't last another two years like this. If people learned about communism, things might change in only a few months'.[33] The following 'scene' from Paris states: 'Here people are beginning to have more respect for poverty than for property … The children take to thieving in droves'.[34]

Weitling presents property crimes as a form of social self-defence, which can at best pave the way for the desired revolutionary change. Once the prisons are 'overcrowded' and 'full to the brim', then even the representatives of the current order will realise that society can no longer be maintained in its current form.[35] Although still inspired by the beautiful dream of a self-abolition of the ruling order – in which 'those who mock and doubt communism would then have to resort to communism themselves if they wanted to live in peace and enjoy life' – Weitling is nevertheless aware that the decisive step has yet to be taken.[36] In Ireland, he reports, the 'people' have begun to transform the slow-burning conflict into an open war:

> The people hold assemblies to which they go armed, and decide on plans for insurrection. On 11 March, the whole peasantry marched into Waterford armed with bludgeons ready to storm the poorhouse. Many farmers from Werford and Kilkeney counties joined in as well. The military was called in to restore calm as usual.[37]

From now on, however, the development of class struggles in the Vormärz followed a path of escalation and militarisation, which ultimately led to an outright 'guerrilla war' against property.[38]

33 *Die junge Generation*, p. 71.
34 *Die junge Generation*, p. 71.
35 *Die junge Generation*, pp. 40–1. and p. 71.
36 *Die junge Generation*, p. 72.
37 *Die junge Generation*, p. 72.
38 Weitling 1974, p. 249 and pp. 253–4. See the investigative report by the Zurich government secretary Johann Caspar Bluntschli 1843, starting at p. 109. The complex is reviewed in Seidel-Höppner and Höppner 2005; and pointedly in Meyer 1999, pp. 257–71.

4 *Primitive Rebels* in Lower Lusatia: Willkomm

Ernst Willkomm's novel *White Slaves* not only chronicles the genesis of the 'free' working class as a story of the transformation of serfs into wage slaves, it also recounts the development of forms of class struggle connected to each social form. More precisely, it describes how modern class struggle emerged from pre-modern forms of social conflict. The class conscious, striking wage worker appears in Willkomm as heir and successor to the 'archaic' primitive rebels. As with his history of the transformation of social labour, Willkomm succeeds in capturing transitional social-historical phenomena through the internal historical construction of his novel.

The 'white slaves' of the title, as previously mentioned, inhabit both historical levels of the novel: they appear as both the serfs of Count Boberstein in the long flashback which recounts the prehistory of the novel's events, and as the 'free' wage labourers in the factory run by the Count's sons.

To each timeline also corresponds a distinct form of struggle by the unfree or dependent workers. In the second timeline, it is the textile workers' strike led by Martell, the outcast half-brother of the factory owning von Stein brothers. In the first timeline, during the end of the eighteenth century, it is a group of *primitive rebels*, as Eric Hobsbawm might say, a band of 'social rebels' led by a mythical robber captain whom the peasants of the area reverently call the 'Prince of the Heath'.[39]

Johannes Lips, as he is really called, gathers around himself 'a band of at least a hundred of the most daring, rash, and ravenous men, thirsting for fire and plunder – the dreaded wild horde of the Heath, which, unsuspected and unseen, climbed the walls of the noble estates on a cloudy night, invaded the castles and stole the most precious jewellery'.[40] The band lives in a remote corner of the Lower Lusatian Heath, a forested region in Southern Brandenburg, which is 'almost inaccessible' even to those familiar with the place, and completely off-limits to strangers.[41] They make a living from robbery, but are on good terms with the neighbouring peasants, since they have nothing to fear from the band.[42]

Now, however, these robbers have turned into *avengers* who atone for the 'despotism of the masters' and greed of the rich and powerful.[43] In carrying

39 Hobsbawm 1959.
40 Willkomm 2013, p. 339.
41 Willkomm 2013, p. 224.
42 Willkomm 2013, p. 339.
43 Willkomm 2013, p. 243.

out revenge, the 'forest brothers' adhere to fixes rules.[44] They do not murder – except in self-defence – but rather aim to humiliate 'the robbed, if [they were] notorious as brutal lords' through corporeal punishment and stealing their property, in order to bring them to reason; the ultimate goal is 'repentance'.[45] The band's strict code of honour fits with the reputation of their 'prince', a 'man of distinguished decency and fine manners' always at pains to keep his men from unnecessary cruelty.[46] Before punishing Count Boberstein, he makes a speech:

> 'Brothers of the forest', he addresses them. 'Today at sundown you heard from me what crimes Count Magnus von Boberstein committed against defenceless innocents. You know whom I have gathered you to avenge, and why this band of oppressed and disenfranchised men has joined us! Tonight, a first step will be made towards punishing the reigning evil, and if the father of the night and the spirit of just retribution, whose voice came to me, protect us, then our revenge will be a blessed one. But no wicked deeds! No murder! Not a drop of human blood shall stain our hands. We are the henchmen of Nemesis, who rules invisibly over us. Wherever we appear in her name, it is to improve our earthly lot. Swear that none will commit wicked deeds, that no one will do anything unless I command!' The robbers swore without hesitation.[47]

The portrayal of the robber prince and his band corresponds in most respects with the phenomenon Hobsbawm calls 'social banditry'.[48] Social banditry is an 'endemic peasant protest against oppression and poverty: a cry for vengeance on the rich and the oppressors, a vague dream of some curb upon them, a righting of individual wrongs'.[49] The life path of Johannes Lips also largely matches Hobsbawm's archetype: initially hired more than twenty years ago as a private tutor for the still young but already wild son of Count Magnus, the middle-class Johannes comes into conflict with the estates order. It all begins when he falls in love with the count's sister and begins a secret tryst with her. The count catches wind of this and – as Johannes recounts some two decades later – unleashes 'his tyranny, his unkindness, his deranged view of humanity and its division into

44 Willkomm 2013, p. 343.
45 Willkomm 2013, pp. 339, 375.
46 Willkomm 2013, p. 236.
47 Willkomm 2013, pp. 343–4.
48 Hobsbawm 1959, p. 13.
49 Hobsbawm 1959, p. 5.

different estates' on Johannes.[50] As a result, the latter is pilloried and flogged – a punishment which Johannes finds particularly humiliating since it is normally reserved for serfs, not for freemen.[51] Johannes did something that, in Hobsbawm's words, 'is not regarded as criminal by his local conventions, but is so regarded by the State or the local rulers'.[52] In doing so, he places himself outside the official order, but does not leave the framework of what is commonly considered 'honourable'; indeed, the conflict with the official order even earns him the reputation of being a delinquent and grants him the venerable status of a social rebel.[53]

The social bandit is considered a 'just man' precisely because he is an '*outlaw*'.[54] This paradox leads to an inevitable mythicisation of this figure. Real banditry is doubled by a myth inherent to banditry itself – without this myth there is no social rebel. The myth suggests that the rebel's transgressions can be sorted neatly, like some 'Robin Hoodism': the social rebel takes from the rich (and only from the rich!) and gives to the poor (keeping nothing for himself); he is thus never simply a 'professional criminal'.[55]

The mythical doubling corresponds to a construction of two distinct worlds: an 'official' world that has fallen into disarray and a 'parallel or subsidiary system' represented by the rebel who puts the official world back in order.[56] Willkomm illustrates this point particularly well: he describes an almost standardised procedure by which the peasants call upon the figure of the social rebel to punish the rich and powerful for violating social norms. To do so, emissaries deploy a series of watchwords in order to hail Johannes.[57] Once summoned, Johannes helps self-appointed 'judges draw up the decrees' that the parallel system will put into effect.[58] That such an abundance of power and influence, which can no longer be effectively controlled by any other entity, can also lead to hypertrophic self-mythification is demonstrated by a message that Johannes sends to the peasants seeking help:

> 'Go', he continued more briskly, 'go back to the derelict huts of the enslaved people and tell them that Johannes of Heath, their prince and lord,

50 Willkomm 2013, p. 240.
51 Willkomm 2013, pp. 319–20.
52 Hobsbawm 1959, p. 15.
53 Willkomm 2013, p. 321.
54 Willkomm 2013, p. 262; Hobsbawm 1959, p. 4.
55 Hobsbawm 1959, p. 20.
56 Hobsbawm 1959, p. 6.
57 Willkomm 2013, p. 248.
58 Willkomm 2013, p. 271.

> has returned from the wasteland to preach a new religion. It will bring peace to the poor and downtrodden, and war and relentless judgment to the lawless oppressors! I will destroy serfdom or die fighting for the cause!'[59]

The messianic self-fashioning remains strangely disjoined, since it neither fits with other depictions of Johannes' character nor does it have any ramifications for the plot; even the play on words with Johannes' nom de guerre, *Haide*, and the German word *Heide*, which means heathen, feels unconnected. Perhaps Willkomm himself falls for the myth of the social rebel, and pursues it beyond the point at which it matters for his novel. Or, and more likely, he wants to show how his character succumbs to his own myth. As the plot advances, the hubris accompanying Johannes' self-messianisation becomes more disgraced than supported. None of the interventions by the judge of the parallel world have the intended effect in the long run; indeed, they often end up bolstering the tendencies they set out to thwart.

The robber prince's first act of intervention occurs early on in the story, when Magnus receives an anonymous 'threatening letter'. The letter, which is 'written in a disguised handwriting', reads as follows:

> Four weeks after receiving this, Röschen Sloboda, known as Haideröschen, will marry the farmer Clemens Ehrhold. You, Count, will immediately grant permission to the said Clemens Ehrhold and accept Röschen Sloboda as your subject. Furthermore, you will not hesitate to hand over a dowry of three hundred Reichsthalers to the aforementioned Röschen and, on the day of the wedding, to which you are hereby invited, to present the newlyweds with a letter of freedom as an extraordinary wedding gift. You will graciously give an answer within twice four and twenty hours by firing your rifle from the same window through which the little Wend girl eluded your pursuit. If you should agree upon the aforementioned conditions but fail to give the required signal, then an hour later all the windows of your castle will be shattered by a hundred shots at once and divine retribution will strike you in the triumph of your unworthy crimes![60]

The 'haughty demand' formulated in the letter is intended to dissuade Magnus from pursuing Röschen any further. After the first assaults, Johannes was called

59 Willkomm 2013, p. 250.
60 Willkomm 2013, pp. 185–6.

in to prevent anything worse from happening. But the threatening letter, which Magnus pretends to accept, only gives him the 'diabolical' idea of kidnapping and raping Röschen Sloboda on her wedding night; the letter of freedom he actually offers the couple for their wedding is only issued for the following day – the night before, the young Count still executes his *jus primae noctis*.[61]

The mole-catcher Heinrich, who later serves as the peasant's emissary with a new request for Johannes' aid, reproaches him for the fatal mistake of the threatening letter, but at the same time legitimises it through God's greater wisdom. Faith in the power of the rebel, it seems, does not shake so easily:

> Despite your omniscience, it seems you are not well informed about the circumstances. For example, you know nothing of the tremendous progress made by your former pupil with his efforts. – Forgive me, Mr Johannes, if I cannot hide my astonishment! When, several months ago, you so willingly accepted the offer I presented to you and by it compelled the craven Count Magnus to do justice to a poor, oppressed girl, I thought you saw through the secret plans of this unscrupulous man. Who could have guessed that this threat would have such terrible consequences! – Well, what happened had to happen according to God's will, and not in vain. Röschen Sloboda's dreadful wedding night has sown dragon's teeth, which will soon arise to wreak bloody retribution.[62]

Johannes' second act of intervention in the story has even graver consequences. After the death of the old Count, the serfs are determined to rise up; they do not want to pass easily into the possession of the wicked young Count Magnus. Johannes agrees to make 'common cause' with the peasants.[63] In a spooky scene embellished with all fixtures of gothic romance, the serfs meet with Johannes' band one night in a remote misty clearing on the heath:

> From all sides of the encircling heath, black figures and grey-white shadows staggered toward the middle of the clearing, growing enormous in the indistinct distance. Here crowded a black knot of confused people, surrounded by a semicircle of white statues, sitting motionless on blocks, rotten rootstocks and half-split tree trunks, illumined only by the red glow of a crackling fire swirling pitch-black clouds of smoke towards the sky. These were the Wendish wives and daughters of the serfs in their

61 Willkomm 2013, starting at p. 217.
62 Willkomm 2013, pp. 241–2.
63 Willkomm 2013, p. 250.

> shimmering raincoats. A gentle breeze carried a monotonous murmur of voices towards our wanderers. Countless dark flames flickered far across the clearing, as if subterranean earth spirits were holding up huge lamps from their caves. Here and there a giant snake slithered across the ground in the same gloomy burnt colour, its head crowned in luminescent thorns. This spook was caused by the many rotten tree stumps and dead trees with their roots, whose damp wood now phosphoresced in the darkness.
>
> Little by little, the crowd of Wends grew to several thousand, including the women accompanying them. In the middle of this crowd sat the prince of the forest.[64]

The peasants and robbers then solemnly swear to punish the wicked. After careful preparations, the conspirators set fire to the heath; the fire reaches Boberstein Castle on the day of the old Count's funeral, and the noble mourners manage to escape at the last minute. From the fiery inferno, the fleeing Magnus hears, at first indistinctly, then more and more clearly, 'a roaring cry as if from a thousand voices at once'. It was the 'jubilation' of peasants who finally confronted the count. Johannes at first harangues Magnus: 'This poor, maltreated and despised people is mild even in its judgement. They do not want to destroy you, they do not want to torture you slowly to death, but merely knock on your dormant conscience and shine the burning torch of retribution into the dark folds of your soul!'[65] The Count is allowed to leave amid a hail of curses from the peasants. The work of revenge is done: 'Magnus was punished, expelled, the castle of his fathers reduced to ashes and dust'.[66]

As Willkomm's novel progresses, the maximal short-term efficacy of this punitive action – the success of a peasant rebellion can hardly resound more – is decisively put into perspective through recounting its long-term impact. Although Magnus does not return to Lusatia for several years, he handles the 'administration of his prized possessions' from afar. He marries 'abroad to a rich heiress', who bears him the three sons we already know, who finally 'inherit everything that was left of the great Boberstein estate in equal parts'.[67] Adrian, Aurel and Adalbert, however, rebuild Boberstein not as a castle, but as a factory. The rebellious peasants achieve their goal and are indeed freed from serfdom – but their newfound freedom only drives them into the arms of their old

64 Willkomm 2013, pp. 337–8.
65 Willkomm 2013, p. 373.
66 Willkomm 2013, p. 377.
67 Willkomm 2013, p. 382.

oppressor's sons, and beats them there with a new form of slavery: the 'slavery of freedom', wage slavery. As the title already announces, this is the story of *White Slaves*.

A bitter lesson of the story is that the transformation of the old slavery into the new one is in some respects driven by the slaves themselves and even made possible in the first place by their rebellion. By burning down the castle, they establish a *tabula rasa*, which prepares the ground for the innovation of the political-economic regime led by Count Magnus's three sons. The rebellious peasants themselves become agents of that 'creative destruction' which, according to Joseph Schumpeter, accompanies every capitalist innovation.[68] Karl Marx names the process of establishing the capitalist mode of production the 'so-called primitive accumulation of capital' – so-called because where Adam Smith and other bourgeois theorists of capitalism see a 'diligent, intelligent and above all frugal elite' at work, Marx finds something quite different, namely, 'conquest, subjugation, robbery, murder, in short, violence'.[69] Marx's succinct résumé is well known: 'Thus were the peasantry violently expropriated from the land, driven from their homes, turned into vagabonds, and then whipped, branded and tortured by grotesquely terroristic laws into accepting the discipline necessary for the system of wage labour'.[70] In Willkomm, 'violence' in its raw form *also* emerges from the subjugated themselves, and this violence prepares the ground for that more subtle kind of violence that will be carried out by the 'mute compulsion of economic relations'.[71]

Willkomm's telling of the long-term failure of the peasants' revolt can serve as an illustration of the 'tragedy of the social bandit', to which Hobsbawm's interpretation of the phenomenon also alludes. According to Hobsbawm, the social bandits' 'revolutionary traditionalism' is at best an antidote to the shocks that traditional social systems are subject to once they are seized by the 'jaws of the dynamic modern world'.[72] To understand the modern world and take advantage of its dynamics, however, exceeds the social bandit's horizon: '[T]he bandit is helpless before the forces of the new society which he cannot understand. At most he can fight it and seek to destroy it'.[73] Yet this attempt is doomed to fail from the outset, the social bandit is always fighting a losing battle. That is why, according to Hobsbawm, he makes such an excellent subject for the

68 Cf. Schumpeter 1994, 'The Process of Creative Destruction', pp. 81–6.
69 Marx 1976, pp. 873–74. Translation revised.
70 Marx 1976, p. 899. Translation revised.
71 Marx 1976, p. 899. Translation revised.
72 Hobsbawm 1959, p. 24.
73 Hobsbawm 1959, p. 25.

'romantic poets', who are more interested in the 'ideals' of social bandits than in the material conditions of their existence; these poets are fascinated by those 'songs' made up about the social bandits sung 'round the fireside' and which 'maintain the vision of the just society, whose champions are brave and noble as eagles, fleet as stags, the sons of the mountains and the deep forests'.[74]

5 Rescuing the Rebels

With his book, Hobsbawm wanted to rescue the primitive rebels from oblivion and from the 'rationalist and "modernist" bias' of a historiography that could see them as little more than 'marginal' phenomena of progress.[75] In the end, Hobsbawm honours the social rebels as bearers of a myth that points beyond them; ultimately, however, he sees their real historical role as very similar to the historiography he opposes. This is evident not least in the fact that he sets up a sharp opposition between archaic social rebels and modern social movements, which is primarily intended to demonstrate the extent to which the former (necessarily) lag behind the latter.

Perhaps fulfilling Hobsbawm's mission of rescuing the rebels requires a more careful elaboration of the myth's epistemic content. Willkomm takes the (uniform and stereotypical) myth of the social bandit and repeats all its essential features. But he also transforms the myth and pushes it beyond itself by integrating it into a work of literature.

In terms of their internal organisational structures, Willkomm attributes an almost early communist programme to his social bandits:

> For this reason, after each successful robbery of a rich person, one tenth of the stolen goods was deposited into a fund where the poor could at least benefit. The rest was divided equally amongst the robbers. Johannes himself would not even receive a larger share of the booty. He did, however, allow the band to present him with an honorary gift at the beginning of each quarter. This society thus had its own kind of constitution, admittedly in very crude form and perhaps without any of them having thought about it, but nonetheless one which sought to realise the idea of a possible equal distribution of wealth and labour.[76]

74 Hobsbawm 1959, p. 28.
75 Hobsbawm 1959, p. 2.
76 Willkomm 2013, p. 340.

As if to counter any suspicion that this was merely a senseless anachronistic projection, in the last sentence of the quotation, the narrator makes a brief aside to make explicit the latent ideological tendencies of the time. The narrator constructs a political unconscious – 'perhaps without any of them having thought about it' – that he sees at work in the story and through which he relates the story back to his own narrating present. The programme of a 'possible equal distribution of wealth and labour' was first formulated in the German-speaking world in the 1840s, in Willkomm's own time. As the narrator himself suggests in his short aside quoted above, it is historically quite plausible that this programme already circulated as an 'idea' in 'very crude form' in the two time periods narrated in the novel: around 1832, the time in which the main plot takes place, the early communist programme was first coherently formulated in neo-Babouvist circles in France in the context of the Lyon uprising; but it had been introduced already as early as the 1790s, the time in which the earlier narrative takes place, for example in Gracchus Babeuf's 'Conspiracy of Equals', to whom the neo-Babouvists around Filippo Buonarroti refer in the 1830s. With his early communist fable about the social bandit Johannes Lips, Willkomm does more than merely tell a political 'myth' – in the sense of an illusion, as Hobsbawm sometimes suggests – he constructs the history of the origins of a theory, communism, through which his own present time becomes decipherable.

By presenting the ideology of the social rebels as the germ form of a highly contemporary political theory, Willkomm encourages the reader to bring the seemingly archaic practices of the insurgents to bear on the present. At first, they are depicted as primitive characters: the peasants and robbers are staged as vestiges of a bygone era who must inevitably be steamrolled by a new age that is already everywhere underway. The rituals and 'old values' of the peasant and rebel community are, one could say, romantically exaggerated and nostalgically idealised in Willkomm – and thus should be criticised for being ideologically distorted and historically inaccurate. But perhaps Willkomm is not so concerned with how Lower Lusatian peasants actually acted, thought or felt at the end of the eighteenth century; rather, his aim is to tell a 'myth' whose essential function is contrastive. What exactly is reprehensible about the modern world becomes apparent through the contrast between, on the one side, the values and conceptions of honour upheld by the common peasantry and, on the other, the depravity of the aristocratic and bourgeois world. When Willkomm describes the unruly culture of peasant solidarity, then, following E.P. Thompson, one could say this refers not only and perhaps not even primarily to a 'solidarity *with*', but also a 'solidarity *against*'.[77] The culture of

77 Thompson 1966, p. 487.

solidarity should not be read mainly as a positive expression of certain values, but as an expression of opposition to others. The gothic romantic portrayal of nightly meetings and solemn oaths, the secret loves tended over decades, the enmities cherished for just as long, the intensely pursued plans for revenge, the widespread clinging to individual experiences of suffering and humiliation, and the defiant refusal to move beyond them, just because a higher logic of history commands it, all this points to a world beyond the *cash nexus*, to a world held together by more than money, competition and profitability.[78] The myth of the conspiring peasants makes it clear that there is more lacking in the modern world than just bread for the poor. By fighting for sufficient means of survival, the poor demonstrate in their practical forms of struggle that mere survival is not enough. The communism shown here begins with the 'idea of a possible equal distribution of wealth and labour', but goes way beyond it. A society in which this idea could be realised in practice – as Willkomm's account of the peasant uprising suggests – would have to be held together by more than the sheer conviction that this form of the social organisation of production, distribution and consumption is the most reasonable one overall. Rather, very strong political and communitarian affects would have to be brought into play, like those expressed in the rituals of the Lower Lusatian peasants and social bandits.

6 Revenge and Class

> The subject of historical knowledge is the struggling, oppressed class itself. Marx presents it as the last enslaved class – the avenger that completes the task of liberation in the name of generations of the downtrodden. This conviction, which had a brief resurgence in the Spartacus League, has always been objectionable to Social Demo-

78 Surprisingly, Willkomm's accounts largely coincide with the stories of the 'Black Lamp' conspiracies in West Riding of Yorkshire discussed by Thompson 1966, pp. 472–84. With Peter Linebaugh, one could also read Emily Brontë's *Wuthering Heights* as further evidence of the recurrent theme of nocturnal, proletarian, insurrectionist gatherings on the moor: 'The empty landscape and ominous turbulent weather which open *Wuthering Heights* indicate the terror and fear of the Other (Irish, Gypsy, proletarian). It is a shadowy representation of the actuality when the people of the north prepared for civil war by practicing military evolutions upon the moors by the light of the moon' (Linebaugh 2014, p. 85). Secret nocturnal meetings in open fields by torchlight as a specifically English practice of the early workers movement are also reported by Engels 1844, '*The Times* on German Communism', MECW 3, pp. 410–13, especially p. 412.

> crats. Within three decades they managed to almost entirely erase the name of Blanqui, at the thunder of whose name the preceding century had quaked. The Social Democrats preferred to cast the working class in the role of a redeemer of *future* generations, in this way cutting the sinews of its greatest strength. This indoctrination made the working class forget both its hatred and its spirit of sacrifice, for both are nourished by the image of enslaved ancestors rather than by the ideal of liberated grandchildren.
>
> WALTER BENJAMIN[79]

∴

In 'revolutionary periods', Hobsbawm writes in his book *Primitive Rebels*, 'vengeance' ceases to be 'a private matter and becomes a class matter'.[80] Willkomm's *White Slaves* is a prime example of this turning point. Here, 'class' as a politically acting collective subject first constitutes itself out of the affect of revenge. 'Class' coheres around a feeling of having to avenge a crime or disgrace, an injury perpetrated on individuals, but which could have affected everyone: collective subjectivation under the sign of revenge.

The narrative of *White Slaves* revolves around the rapes perpetrated by Count Magnus on the women in the village and castle. The Count's direct and violent access to the physical and mental integrity of his female subjects, which is partly even protected by the old 'rights of lordship', are restricted to the first timeline in the novel, the background to the present.[81] In the second timeline, such abuses no longer take place. In the past storyline, the peasants – mostly men – want to avenge their tormented and dishonoured wives and daughters. They in turn make the following social and political demands: the call for 'liberation of the people from the grip of domination, whatever name it may bear'; the common oath not to rest 'so long as there are still masters abusing their power to the detriment of their subjects; as long as a people on earth still lives who wail in poverty, misery and oppression, and must wander about without rights'.[82] Such revolutionary surpluses result only secondarily from solidarity with Röschen; they are side-effects of still very personal feeling of revenge.

79 Benjamin 2006, Thesis XII, p. 394. Translation revised.
80 Hobsbawm 1959, p. 25.
81 Willkomm 2013, p. 218.
82 Willkomm 2013, pp. 218–19.

Yet though these demands point far into the future, they are, however unconsciously, already at hand. The peasants' humbled desire for justice detaches from its immediate cause and undergoes a universalisation that thrusts it beyond the peasant's local horizon. In this universalisation, however – which concerns all 'people on earth' – the new social and political demands of the peasants can be linked to the still unconscious, latent early communist sentiments of the social rebel band. The initial affect of revenge is collectivised, paving the way for class action.

In the second timeline, too, the path leads through the family: now it is the young children who become victims of an injury, which in turn leads to the class subject constituting itself as a collective of revenge. Young children are made to work in the factories, whose machines seize and mutilate them. This is what happens to little Hans for example, the ten-year-old son of the spinner Martell. While gathering wool flocks under the spinning machine in the factory, his left foot is 'torn half off' and 'squashed flat', his father reports. Adrian's reaction redoubles the scandal. Martell's account once again makes use of all the topoi of miserabilist literature:

> 'The foot is gone, my poor boy a cripple! Well, that can happen, it is a misfortune, as any job brings! The boy should not have become a wool spinner and crawled under the machine if he wanted to keep all his limbs intact! – Am I not reasoning quite soundly and without taking sides? … I am not complaining at all, I just take my crushed boy in these arms of mine, close his screaming mouth with his trembling lips and carry him home to lay him here, here in this wretched, gloomy hut, into the lap of his sobbing mother and exchange a look of misery with her. – I did that, as I believe was my duty, and I did it with a broken heart. A few hours passed – hours I missed from work – before the doctor arrived with the medicine, ointments and herbs that I could afford with my few pennies. Finally, dead tired, I went back to the factory, where in the meantime my neighbours, kind humans that they are, had arranged my post in such a way that no harm could come to the machine or the weave. Nevertheless, can you believe it, Mr von Stein penalised me for the whole affair by deducting half a day's pay from my wages, withheld the poor boy's small earnings altogether and threatened to fire me! – But sir, my child, I say, my boy, my dearest has been crushed to a cripple – God knows whether he will ever recover, and whether I can afford to pay the costs of his recovery! Be cheap and merciful, sir!'
>
> 'Cheap!' he snapped at me. 'Who do you call cheap? Me letting myself fall to ruin for the sake of a crippled child? You should have asked God to

> let that mouth to feed die the sooner, the better, so you would not have to worry about him any longer! Machines sometimes improve what men do badly in their ignorance! It was a sign from heaven, why did you not heed it? And enough, I cannot pay for incomplete work'.
>
> 'That's what Mr von Stein said, and he's still alive?' Eduard said, while Paul clasped his hands in horror.[83]

In *White Slaves*, the 'horror' at the inhumanity of the system is finally channelled against the human representative of that system; the organised workers' desire for revenge is directed against Adrian as the owner of the factory. With Walter Benjamin one could say, the cut sinews of their own children only give the workers more strength, allowing them to rise up against those who have treated them like underage children themselves. At the height of the labour struggle, the 'vengeful' labour leader Martell demands 'restitution' from his half-brother.[84] In a melodramatic showdown, he puts Adrian in a 'school' – the hard school of the factory – and forces him to work on one of his own spinning machines.[85] In doing so, Martell wishes Adrian to 'feel the same agony' that he inflicted on his workers and especially their children.[86] Martell commands:

> 'You will do a whole day's work with me alone on the factory floor!'
>
> 'Ten hours?' cried Adrian in fright. 'I beg you –'
>
> 'You are mistaken, Mr von Stein', Martell interrupted him. 'Not ten, but twelve hours, according to your latest decrees. That is how long fine spinners must work. You will stay here with me for twelve hours and you shall work with me so that you may experience first-hand how your factory workers must live, so that you may feel how sweet, how exhilarating, how nourishing for mind and body this existence, this earthly calling, is!'
>
> 'For God's sake, Martell!'[87]

In addition to the physical strain, it is the horror at the lengthening of time – or as Rancière puts it: the 'pain of stolen time' – that now afflicts Adrian.[88] Martell had previously described Adrian's order to extend the normal working day

83 Willkomm 2013, starting at p. 246.
84 Willkomm 2013, p. 192.
85 Willkomm 2013, p. 204 and pp. 193–4.
86 Willkomm 2013, p. 196.
87 Willkomm 2013, pp. 272–3.
88 Rancière 1989, p. vii. Translation revised.

as a 'kind of torture'.[89] Now, Adrian suffers this fate in his own body: '"Another eleven hours!" Martell said to Adrian. "For someone who spins just to enrich his knowledge, a real child's play!" "Eleven hours!" repeated Adrian and, despairingly, lets the cart roll again'.[90]

Yet the real torment of the workers in the 'torture caves' (Weitling) of the factory lies in the fact that they are entirely at the mercy of the infernal machines who want to be served and to whose rhythm the workers are forced to adopt: 'Adrian would have faced a battery of loaded guns with less fear than the demonic power of the machines that thrust their gleaming steel hands towards him!'[91] Adrian (and the reader) finally learns how to keep these demons happy through a lesson Martell gives his brother in machine operation:

> 'I don't ... understand ... what's happening', stuttered the frightened man.
> 'What's happening to you is easy to understand, and presents no threat at all', Martell replied. 'All that matters is that you devote all of your attention to your work. – You may follow me if you wish, Mr von Stein, and memorise what I tell you! As soon as you lift this bracket here and turn this screw to the left, the machine connects with the big steam shaft and the work begins. The spindle carriage runs forward towards you for about a cubit and a half, then it stops for one second. Use this second to lift the hook here above the staples, causing the spun yarn to be rolled up ... You see, this work is so simple that even a child can do it, which is why you have employed so many children, whom you pay only half as much as us adults! – Are you ready?'[92]

While training him on the machines, Martell once again reminds his brother of the mutilated and killed children, the original impetus for Martell's desire for revenge. The whole scene exudes the grimly ironic touch of a cruel game, especially when the machines fully transform for Adrian – as for a child – into wild monsters that chase after him: 'He heard the creaking and gnashing of their steel teeth, the rolling and rattling of the elongated carriages! His plea turned into a shout that faded away amidst the roar of the machine'.[93]

While Aurel, the other brother, who has long sided with the workers, still sees Adrian's 'punishment' as a 'peculiar, original and in a certain sense magnificent

89 Willkomm 2013, p. 269.
90 Willkomm 2013, p. 281.
91 Willkomm 2013, p. 274.
92 Willkomm 2013, pp. 274–5.
93 Willkomm 2013, pp. 280–1.

kind of revenge', the course of action eventually gets out of hand.[94] Adrian gives up, throwing himself into the machine, which finally tears its owner and long-time profiteer to shreds:

> 'I don't want to live!' cried Adrian in a fit of excitement, his face twisting in convulsive spasms … Adrian pushed himself upright behind the backward-rolling spindle carriage, stretched out his arms, brushed the metal blades of the iron shaft with the hair on his head, which was immediately set in motion by the steam engine, and in the next instant he was – scalped! A horrible scream of pain pierced through all the walls – his hands seized the flashing, swinging shaft, and ripped apart, a bloody garland, hanging from the steaming iron shank!
>
> The machine stopped – along with the machines in the other halls where the scream had been heard. The spectators at the door rushed in breathlessly – then a second scream, similar to the first, was heard from below, and all was silent.
>
> Martell bowed his head and said sombrely: 'God has judged him!'[95]

7 The Machine Breakers

Louise Otto-Peters's novel *Schloss und Fabrik* [*Castle and Factory*] presents another example of how the desire for revenge and retribution can lead to collective class action.[96] Here it is an unborn child who, together with its mother, falls victim to the tyranny of the factory owner Felchner. A factory worker named Berthold talks about his pregnant wife in the pub:

> 'That's it', said Berthold, crying out in painful rage: 'She had to work at the factory again today, lifting heavy things, she said she couldn't do it – but a supervisor thought she was just pretending – but she really couldn't do it – she drags herself around until the end of the day – then she comes home and lies down – and never got up again – the child is dead because it came too soon and also had a gruesome end –' he gulped down the schnapps

94 Willkomm 2013, p. 277.

95 Willkomm 2013, pp. 284–5.

96 Otto-Peters' novel, in which the author not only describes revolutionary events but also incorporates revolutionary discourses of the time in a variety of ways – for instance, including long passages from the *Rheinische Jahrbücher* – was censored immediately upon publication. Cf. Ludwig 2004.

> and with it, the bitter tears that fell into the glass.
> 'That's horrible!'
> 'A disgrace!'
> 'Double murder'.[97]

The workers decide to take the law into their own hands and 'show the murderers how we can punish them, we want to judge them ourselves for once'. But instead of going after the factory owner's life, they only want to 'curse him' and 'threaten to destroy all the machines and the entire factory'.[98]

When the uprising breaks out, the destruction of machines is repeatedly coupled with revenge.[99] At this point, we hear the screams of 'long Lise', who, it is suggested, has lost children herself and perhaps for this reason was 'the most adamant' in destroying 'the machines with axes, sticks and logs':

> A machine for every child! ... The machines don't stop there, each one has more than one child murder on its conscience. Our retribution is still far too merciful! A child is worth more than a machine, it has a soul and life, but the machines are dead and only feign living, and are even vile enough to be capable of murder![100]

Revenge remains a decisive motive for struggle in Otto-Peters's novel: 'They had *something to avenge* from the factory owner: hunger, frostbite, vulnerability, illness, mutilated limbs, the death or affliction of their children, rough treatment and all the hardship and worry they face day after miserable day'.[101] Nevertheless, the narrator, who now speaks in a pointedly detached manner, leaves no doubt that revenge, although understandable, may not be the best guide for collective political action:

97 Otto-Peters 1996, p. 291.

98 Otto-Peters 1996, p. 291.

99 The historical template for Otto-Peters' narrative of rebellion is the uprising of the weavers in the Silesian villages of Peterswaldau and Langenbielau from 3 to 6 June 1844, which was put down by the Prussian military. In the course of the revolt, the Silesian weavers destroyed machinery, looted and ravaged the villa of the notorious factory owner Zwanziger. The weavers' uprising was a real media event. News of the uprising and its literary treatment – not least through Heine's poem 'Die armen Weber' [The Poor Weavers] – spread throughout Germany and Europe within weeks. Heine's poem, for example, appeared as early as 10 July in the exile newspaper *Vorwärts!* in Paris, edited by Karl Marx. For a collection of social, historical and literary sources, see Kroneberg and Schloesser 1979.

100 Otto-Peters 1996, p. 299.

101 Otto-Peters 1996, p. 313.

> But a vague *instinct* urged them in the same way towards revenge, an instinct which called on them to avenge themselves for everything good and noble and capable of educating their souls and those of their children that had been smothered and beaten to death by all their external misery, and all they had to do was let their immorality and savagery run rampant in its worst and most unbridled form.[102]

The word 'instinct' is stressed to indicate how the rebellious workers are further characterised in the novel, since their 'immorality and savagery' ultimately coincides with their animalisation. Their 'hundred-voiced howls', their 'raw, hideous sounds', their 'animalistic wails' lack one thing above all: an articulate *human* voice.[103] As a 'wild' and 'raging mob', the insurgents show at least some closeness to the pack; the 'pack of rabble' [*rottierende Pöbel*] had already been a common expression since Kant.[104]

Furthermore, it seems that the proximity to the instinctual animal also accounts for the (negative) affinity the insurgent workers have for the machines: both are considered not human; they are without consciousness and morality; therein lies a disturbing symmetry between animals and machines. If, according to 'long Lise', children have 'a soul and life', unlike machines, then her next sentence should grant the stark opposition that logically follows: namely, that the machines are without soul and dead. Instead, Lise states that although these machines are 'dead', they can 'feign living' – and thus have enough uncanny half-life to be able to 'murder'. If the beaten proletarians in the Vormärz are repeatedly portrayed as seemingly dead or living dead, then machines reflect their uncanny mirror image back to them.[105] This mirror image likeness of worker and machine was already noticed by ancient economics, in which the slave is defined as an 'animate instrument' that has no *logos* and is thus incapable of rational human speech.[106] In Otto-Peters, the

102 Otto-Peters 1996, p. 313.

103 Otto-Peters 1996, pp. 298, 314.

104 Otto-Peters 1996, pp. 298–9. and p. 316. Kant's *Anthropology* states: '[T]he part [of the people] that exempts itself from these laws (the unruly crowd within this people) is called a *rabble* [*pöbel*] (*vulgus*); whose illegal association is *the pack* [*Rottieren*] (*agere per turbas*); this conduct that excludes them from the quality of a citizen', Kant 2007, p. 407 (7: 311). Translation revised.

105 In Hess 1845, pp. 40–1, it is said that wage labour only serves the proletarian 'to eke out his miserable existence, to conserve it, as one conserves a corpse'.

106 On the nature of the slave as a being between animal and machine, cf. Aristotle's *Politics*, first book, chapters three to five, 1253b–1255a (Aristotle 2007, pp. 5–8).

topos of resemblance returns in modern form as a basic justification for breaking machines, as can be seen here in a discussion amongst rebellious workers:

> Another said: 'And you know how the cursed machines are to blame for the fact that we earn so little now, they make our hands unnecessary. Well, let's turn the thing around and destroy the machines, they are our worst enemies!'
>
> 'Away with the machines, let's smash them all!' shouted the crowd.[107]

Workers and machines are afflicted by the same likeness that plagues all 'worst enemies': enmity breeds similarity. The machines can make the 'hands' of the workers 'unnecessary', since neither have a head to guide their 'hands'; workers and machines are merely executing organs. The workers suspect this, which is why they try to *reverse* these conditions – but *only* reverse them, as the novel makes clear, not completely redesign them. In the end, the whole destruction of machines remains at the level of 'vandalism'.[108]

In her novel, Louise Otto-Peters ultimately condemns the machine breakers. This condemnation is reinforced by the fact that the philanthropic factory owner's daughter Pauline – a popular, albeit naïve character – appears to be quite sympathetic, but in this respect only confirms the alleged animal-like nature of the workers: in the workers' revolt, she hears merely an 'outcry of insulted human nature, which had been degraded and reduced to an animal stupor'.[109] For Pauline, as for Otto-Peters, the revolt is nothing more than an unconscious, spasmodic knee-jerk reaction without rational control or reasonable goal.

8 Is It O.K. to Be a Luddite?

The collectively organised destruction of (proto)industrial and agricultural machinery took place throughout Europe and on the American plantations in the late eighteenth and early nineteenth centuries.[110] Machine wrecking reached its historical peak in England 1811–12 with the Luddite movement. *Luddism* has since become synonymous with the sabotage of machinery in

107 Otto-Peters 1996, p. 297.
108 Otto-Peters 1996, p. 316.
109 Otto-Peters 1996, p. 314.
110 See Hobsbawm 1967a, 'The Machine Breakers'.

general. Ever since the early nineteenth century, the Luddites have been steadily condemned, and Otto-Peters' assessment can be taken as representative in this regard. According to Hobsbawm, twentieth-century historians adopted the view from 'nineteenth-century middle-class economic apologists' that 'the early labour movement did not know what it was doing, but merely reacted blindly and gropingly, to the pressure of misery, as animals in the laboratory react to electric currents'.[111] Ironically, the main 'conveyor belt' of this condemnation was the historiography of the workers' movement itself: a productivist, self-proclaimed progressive, parliamentary-reformist, restrained workers' movement of the late nineteenth and early twentieth that precisely did *not* want to see its own forerunners in the wild insurgents of the early nineteenth century.[112] In contrast, the historiography of the New Left since the 1950s has sought to rehabilitate and re-evaluate the machine breakers. This dialectic of condemnation and rescue renews itself right up to our present day: each new phase of technological development has its attendant opposition movements that see themselves as neo-Luddite or are decried as such. 'Is it O.K. to be a Luddite?' asked Thomas Pynchon in 1984, a question repeatedly posed and answered anew with the ongoing development of computer technology, brain research and bionics.[113] We shall return to this.

Hobsbawm and Thompson's historiographical rescue of the Luddites follows two strands of argument. First, they point out that the machine breakers were by no means acting blindly and irrationally, but rather according to implicit and partly explicit theories and strategies, which suggests their actions were more sensible than their critics were willing to acknowledge. Second, Luddism created cutting-edge forms of organisation and solidarity that were quite forward-looking. Thompson adds a third strand here, one that has cropped up several times in debates since then, from Pynchon to Peter Linebaugh, and perhaps

111 Hobsbawm 1967a, p. 7.

112 On the role of those historians who were close to Fabianism and the Labour Party, see Hobsbawm 1967a, pp. 7–8; Thompson 1966, p. 592. Wilhelm Liebknecht, one of the founders of the organised labour movement in Germany, codified the condemnation of the machine breakers for the subsequent movement in his great speech of 1872, 'Knowledge is Power': 'Do not misunderstand me, I am no opponent of machines. The machine-breakers, who were so active among the workers of England at the dawn of large-scale industry in that country, were entirely reactionary, and were acting in accordance with a false view of things, and were therefore bound to fail – for the benefit of mankind, but *not* for the individual working man. It is precisely the curse of our present-day civilization, that every general progress is useful only to a privileged minority, but makes the situation of the disinherited masses relatively and absolutely worse' (Liebknecht 1928, pp. 45–6, translation revised).

113 Pynchon 1984.

has even become more relevant now: the Luddites, Thompson shows, were one of the first modern political movements to use *myth*, or more precisely, their own *self-mythicisation*, as a weapon in political struggle. The fact that – apart from the concrete destruction and mysterious threats and letters of confession – only myths, rumours and suspicions about the Luddites have survived, but hardly any reliable source material, has proved to be an extremely effective means of propaganda and agitation. This is especially true during a media and communication revolution, which *also* took place in the first half of the nineteenth century. With these three strands, it is now possible to break down more precisely how Louise Otto-Peters and Ernst Willkomm treat – and mistreat – machine breaking.

First of all, the machine wreckers portrayed in Willkomm and Otto-Peters are not as irrational as they are made out to be; and second, both texts by and large propagate common prejudices about their acts of sabotage. For example, contrary to what a certain sensible worker named Franz claims in Otto-Peters' novel, the fact that the angry workers first indiscriminately destroy all the machines and then proceed to loot the factory owner's villa is no proof that these actions are inherently executed in a blind rage. Rather than 'hostility to machines as such', this form of action suggests that the workers seek to 'pressure' the factory owner Felchner in general by indiscriminately destroying his property.[114] Such actions, according to Hobsbawm, were a 'traditional and established part of industrial conflict' when it came to preventing wage cuts or layoffs; Hobsbawm thus ironically labels these and similar forms of action 'collective bargaining by riot'.[115] Whether such actions end in success or in disaster, as happens in *Castle and Factory*, depends on the power relations and intelligence of those involved. A conversation between the factory owner Felchner and his daughter Pauline shows that even in the scenario Otto-Peters narrates, failure was not inevitable; Felchner could have pursued a different path than calling on soldiers from the nearby garrison to help, in turn causing a bloodbath among the insurgents. Pauline instead proposes settling the dispute though a social partnership model, a quite realistic suggestion at the time:

> Come, father, let's go out there together, let us dare – and then I will ask them: what do you want? Go back to your homes and your work, we will give you better wages for it and your children shall have school and will

114 Hobsbawm 1967a, p. 9.
115 Hobsbawm 1967a, p. 9.

> work only four hours a day. However, anyone who does not go home will justly be punished. Come, father, let's try once more, only this time listen to your daughter![116]

But Felchner does not listen, and Pauline's 'reasonable' attempt at mediation fails. When the military suppresses the uprising, Felchner pays dearly for his intransigence: a stray bullet kills Pauline, leaving 'twenty corpses' on the battlefield of the social war. Felchner himself dies bitterly shortly thereafter.[117]

The sensible worker Franz had several reservations during the course of the uprising and refused to take part in the 'blind destruction' of 'defenceless things'.[118] This argument has been and continues to be used against machine breakers: according to this view, it is not the 'defenceless', innocent and politically neutral machines that are to blame for social misery, but rather the owners and beneficiaries of the machines who use them to exploit their workers. As Thompson shows, the cheap accusation that the machine wreckers are fighting against 'things' rather than social conditions amounts to little. As the few testimonies demonstrate, especially the more detailed threats and confessions, the Luddites certainly had a systemic critique that saw in machines the centrepiece of a strategy for the transformation of society as a whole. When machines are used on a large scale, sufficient workers must be provided to operate them *under conditions determined by the machines themselves*. Workers must be prepared to carry out monotonous, stultifying, unhealthy and often life-threatening work without pause, especially at the early stages of technical development. Machines deskill the former craftsmen, depress wages, create unemployment, destroy an 'entire way of life'.[119] In short, machines are not simply 'things', but integral parts of a *system*, the 'factory system', and that is why the Luddites destroy them.[120]

The Luddites are not so foolish as to fight against 'things', they are rather so wise as to fight against their own *reification*: 'As if your living cloth-dressers were all machines like your frames and shears' exclaims Caroline to the enraged textile manufacturer Robert Moore in Charlotte Brontë's novel *Shirley*, after his new machines have been destroyed by Luddites.[121] Moore, of course, sees nothing problematic about the machines as such.

116 Otto-Peters 1996, pp. 136–7.
117 Otto-Peters 1996, p. 319.
118 Otto-Peters 1996, p. 311.
119 Thompson 1966, p. 291.
120 The surviving writings of the Luddites are collected in Binfield 2004.
121 Brontë 2007, p. 62.

Willkomm's *White Slaves* also makes the argument that the machine wreckers fall short and hit the wrong target. After Adrian's death, Martell is put in charge of managing the factory. As the baton is handed over, Aurel, the philanthropic owner, gives a speech expounding his programme for social reform, with machines playing a crucial role:

> There exists a very large number of people who are convinced that the invention of machines and their use in various factories is an unprecedented disaster for the entire human race. Ever since they have been employed, poverty, misery, hunger, sorrow and crime among the lower classes have risen to a truly appalling and dangerous degree! It is therefore the duty of every true philanthropist to advocate with all his might for the abolition of the machines, to provide the poor with new work and sufficient earnings, and thus to restore to them the sole possession which has become theirs, the capital of their industrious hands! – These people, these well-meaning but short-sighted zealots are wrong!
>
> No, dear brethren and friends, machines are a blessing from God, a boon to humanity! Their maintenance, their spread and improvement must be the wish of every honest man; but they must only be used for the liberation, not subjugation, of the working classes! … The machine-owner must – God grant that we live to soon see this time – be required by law to use these levers of power to make work easier and grant those who produce more with the machines to share in the benefits of this increase! The machine-owners and manufacturers must be prevented from hoarding all the profits; there must be a proportionate, reasonable redistribution between him and his workers! If this happens, then want, poverty, discontent and vice will diminish among the people! Then the worker will bless the invention of the machines, love and revere his employer, remain loyal and devoted to him with heartfelt commitment, endure with him and for him without complaint![122]

The first thing to notice is that Willkomm's Aurel proposes a social model against the machine breakers which historically could only be achieved through the pressure of the machine breakers themselves. As early as 1802, machine wreckers in the West Riding of Yorkshire advocated for a set of fiscal welfare policies to moderate the implementation of machines: 'proposals were in the air for the gradual introduction of the machinery, with alternative em-

122 Willkomm 2013, pp. 314–15.

ployment found for displaced men, or by a tax of *6d.* per yard upon cloth dressed by machinery, to be used as a fund for the unemployed seeking work'.[123]

Willkomm also has a financing model for the socially responsible modernisation of production:

> 'I propose', continued the captain [Aurel], 'that my brother Martell be required to double the wages of his workers, and guarantee them a share in the total profit. This sum, however should not be paid in cash, but in interest, so that the amount of capital in circulation not only remains undiminished for greater benefit, but even increases from year to year! In this way the factory owner is not deprived of his large funds, which he cannot do without, nor is the worker deprived of the modest profit to which he is entitled. Upon request, the workers will be given a report on how things stand at the end of the year, and depending on whether the business has improved or deteriorated, the workers' share in the profit will be determined. But under no circumstance may the workers' wages be diminished, so that they may always lead a dignified life and never be degraded to the status of helpless slaves! – Are you prepared, Martell, to step in and manage the factory under these conditions?'
>
> 'Absolutely!' said Martell. 'I want to be a man among men, not a despot among slaves. I'd rather starve than that!'[124]

The model sounds economically plausible, and evens promotes a noble social and ethical cause, a classic win-win situation for both capital and labour. However, one factor remains unconsidered, even though it is mentioned in the pathos of social partnership rhetoric – albeit only in the mode of the analysed imagery. For while the factory flourishes under Martell's leadership, Aurel sets out to sea again to inspect the 'overseas connections and assets'.[125] As can be seen here, slavery on the company-owned plantations at the periphery remains the commercial basis even for the newly achieved class reconciliation in the centre. The (literal) *labour aristocrat* Martell anticipates Lenin's theory of imperialism in a very eerie way by managing production for his brother using a system of proto-corporatist co-management. The merchant capitalist Aurel remains in charge of the cotton plantation, and together they solidify their cherished class alliance on the backs of transatlantic slaves. Ultimately,

123 Thompson 1966, p. 526.
124 Willkomm 2013, pp. 317–18.
125 Willkomm 2013, p. 319.

the proto-welfare 'achievements' of the workers in the centre receive additional financing from the extra profits of the (post)colonial slave economy.[126]

Large machinery, which can now be further expanded through Martell's moderating influence without much opposition at the main factory, remains a prerequisite for plantation slavery, even in terms of the logic of production. For only an industrially operated production of textiles oriented towards a world market requires those huge quantities of raw cotton that only a plantation economy can produce; as long as 'free' workers are allowed to opt out, such plantations can only be worked by slaves. Drawing on the resistance of plantation slaves in the USA, who also destroyed tools and machinery on a large scale, Peter Linebaugh points out:

> They grew the cotton that was spun and woven in Lancashire. The story of the plantation slaves has been separated from the story of the Luddites. Whether separation was owing to misleading distinctions between wage and slave labour or to artificial or racial differences is unclear.[127]

Perhaps it is Willkomm's historical blindness that the 'white slaves' can celebrate their class compromise as a form of 'reconciliation' with the factory system only by forgetting the plight of the 'Black slaves'. Beyond that, it perhaps also articulates the unconscious insight that the one depends on the other, and that reconciliation can perhaps only be enjoyed and propagated when one forgets and is *willing to forget* that which remains unreconciled.

9 Towards a Pure Strike: Georg Weerth's Fragment of a Novel

Social rebels and machine wreckers are transitional figures, actors in a '*transitional* conflict', and Willkomm and Otto-Peters deploy them precisely as such.[128] When Thompson ironically writes that Luddism is best described as a '"peasant's revolt" of industrial workers', who, 'instead of sacking the *chateaux*', now attack machines, this also applies for the historical construction of the novels examined here.[129] For Otto-Peters, 'castle' and 'factory' are symbols of different systems of oppression, which nevertheless intertwine and stand

126 Cf. Lenin 1933, especially the eighth chapter, 'Parasitism and the Decay of Capitalism', pp. 90–8.
127 Linebaugh 2014, pp. 89–90.
128 Thompson 1966, p. 551.
129 Thompson 1966, p. 600.

in continuity, as seen in Willkomm. In England, and perhaps in Germany as well, as Otto-Peters suggests, the Luddite's offensive also led to a class alliance between the old landowning nobility and the new industrial bourgeoisie, a coalition of castle and factory. As Willkomm (and Linebaugh) make clear, one may confidently add the (post)colonial plantation owners to this new alliance of the propertied classes.

As transitional figures, social rebels and machine wreckers are always Janus-faced and thus particularly well suited as figures of a society in transition. They hark back to the time of the old, often still paternalist trade and guild orders: the Luddites were 'the last Guildsmen'.[130] Their forms of political action still emanated from a 'world of the benefit society, the secret ceremony and oath … the craftsmen's meeting at the house of call'.[131] Willkomm casts this look back in a surprisingly unsentimental manner. It is true that the factory workers of 1832 discuss how Count Magnus's direct oppression was more overt and thus more bearable than his son Adrian's wage slavery, and it is also true that the rebellious peasants of the 1790s loathe young Count Magnus, while upholding the honour of old Count Erasmus. But Johannes Lips, the leader of the 'Forest Brothers', had already been humiliated and tormented by this allegedly 'good' Erasmus, which is why the old bandit cannot understand the reverence that his peasant supporters have for the old tyrant. And so, when the castle burns, the old Count's body, laid out for burial, is simply left to the flames – uninterred and without a blessing. The struggles of the past remain unreconciled, carried into the present.

At the same time, the social rebels and machine wreckers also point ahead to a world of unionised agitation and parliamentary representation of the working class. They look ahead to a world in which capital and labour confront each other without reserves, without relying on old values. In this world, the working class struggles for higher wages, adequate labour laws and work day regulations. This world will be characterised by a higher form of struggle: the strike.

The strike is the pure form of struggle of an industrial working class, the form struggle takes in a world that comes *after* that transformation staged by the primitive rebels and machine wreckers in the social novels. In the class struggles portrayed in these novels, the strike is already everywhere, but still impure, still mixed with old, wild and unbridled values and notions of honour. In Georg Weerth's untitled novel fragment of 1846, one can see the purification

130 Thompson 1966, p. 552.
131 Thompson 1966, p. 601.

of the 'strike' as a form of struggle, and with it the purification of the class figuration of the workers constituted through struggle.[132]

In this text, Weerth places the three dominant social groups of the time in confrontation with each other, as if in an experiment, in order to illuminate their underlying relationships. First there is the Baron d'Eyncourt, who owns a small castle in a tributary valley of the Rhine; he is heavily in debt due to his lavish lifestyle and had to sell his land holdings to the successful textile manufacturer Preiss, who is already marked by his name as the embodiment of the *cash nexus*. Preiss takes advantage of poor working conditions to produce low-quality cheap textiles, and floods the market with them. Finally, there is the Martin family, all of whom work in Preiss's factory: the widow, prematurely aged after the death of her husband, her eighteen-year-old daughter Marie and the ten-year-old Gretchen. They are then joined by the son Eduard, after spending two years in Manchester learning to be a 'mechanic', and now returning home to the Rhine to join the others in the Preiss factory.[133] In doing so, he hopes to revolutionise conditions there: 'It is my firm intention to stir up all the workers far and wide against that old scoundrel'.[134]

According to Wilhelm Heinrich Riehl's slightly later terminology, the Baron can be regarded as a typical representative of the 'aristocratic proletariat'.[135] The storyline that centres around his debt and the 'help' that Preiss lends him also serves the narrative function of introducing the age-old 'paternalist code' that regulated the relationship between rulers and ruled in pre-industrial times.[136] Weerth presents this code as vanishing, only fully recognisable from the vantage point of its disappearance. When the Baron talks to his daughter about giving up everything and going abroad 'where nobody knows us' – he in fact simply wants to flee his creditors – Bertha is quick to reject the plan, and reminds him of the emotional bonds that have developed with the subordinates:

> And [where] do you find people who love you more than those who surround us here, whom you all know by name since youth, in whose cottages

132 The fragment of about 120 printed pages was only published in its entirety for the first time in 1965. On the history of its emergence and publication, see Unseld 1965 as well as Goette and Schlosser 1976.

133 Weerth 1976, p. 307.

134 Weerth 1976, p. 311.

135 Cf. Riehl 1866, pp. 298–311.

136 Cf. Thompson 1966, pp. 544, 550.

> you have sat, who you support in times of need, whom you always help with words and deeds, and who all revere you as their lord and father?[137]

One piece of advice the Baron offers his 'many poor friends' is to not let themselves be proletarianised.[138] When some fishermen from the village have the idea to 'send their two splendid boys, one barely twelve, the other only fourteen years old, to work in the city because the children have been promised a good wage', the Baron intervenes and advises the parents against it, claiming that the children would be 'ruined by all the work'.[139] And later, Preiss's devoted accountant Weber complains that the Baron repeatedly 'tells the villagers that their children are being spoiled in the factories', which 'sometimes turns away the best workers' from Preiss.[140] The Baron does not realise that *active* proletarianisation – being placed in 'free' wage labour relations – only becomes possible once *passive* proletarianisation has already taken place, i.e. once the previous means of securing subsistence have been destroyed; he does not understand that he himself is quite involved in this destruction, since he can only clear his debts by selling those lands on which the farmers and fishermen have made their subsistence until now.

The 'paternalist code', which the Baron d'Eyncourt upholds purely for moral reasons rather than any economic grounds, lives on even among his subordinates, who have long since become Preiss' wage labourers. This becomes clear when Eduard, who has matured into a class-conscious worker in England, begins to rail against the evil factory owner Preiss only a few minutes after returning to his mother's cottage. Preiss is a 'true devil' who slurps 'the sweat and blood of countless unfortunates' and sucks 'the marrow out of their bones'. Marie and her mother protest against this characterisation. Preiss is no angel, says Marie, but at the very least everyone can be 'glad that Mr Preiss keeps his factory going, that he gives us work, that we earn a living that way'.[141] And Preiss's son August, the acting manager (who has secretly converted to socialism), is said to have 'a warm interest in the welfare of his subordinates, a concern as firm and sincere as everything that moves this otherwise awkward man'.[142]

As the plot progresses, the 'paternalist code' is increasingly delegitimised by Eduard's appearance in the factory; the class relationship is purged of all

137 Weerth 1976, p. 277.
138 Weerth 1976, p. 277.
139 Weerth 1976, p. 278.
140 Weerth 1976, p. 299.
141 Weerth 1976, pp. 310–11.
142 Weerth 1976, p. 316.

obsolete moral and emotional remnants. This purification process takes place mainly in a long speech that Eduard gives to some workers during a lunch break, shortly after he re-enters Preiss's factory. It begins with a greeting: 'I come bearing greetings from the English workers! They are not much better off than you, and so are naturally your friends'.[143] First of all, the internationalist reference to the class brothers and sisters 'across the sea' takes the wind out of the sails of the chauvinist propaganda espoused by the factory owners.[144] These owners justify every wage cut with competition on the world market.[145] And second, it reveals the global frame of reference in which Eduard's class-conscious learning process took place:

> Before his trip to England, it would have been impossible for him to say even three or four sentences in the correct order. – Now his tongue was loosened, and the experience of two years gave him the courage to resolutely address the workers of his homeland. He had diligently attended the meetings of the workers in England – Manchester was the right place for him, and before long he could understand the speeches of his comrades, express his opinions in a foreign language, and take part in all the movements of that mighty people.[146]

The apologists of the old guild order already (or still) knew that travelling educates, and at the meetings of the English workers, Eduard receives a truly revolutionary lesson. He learns from them that the only way 'to change something' is 'to unite with others to confront the masters'. When asked the obvious question about whether that means starting 'a small war' – a 'guerrilla war', as Engels and Weitling put it – Eduard plays his trump card: 'Indeed, a war without rifles or sabres, a resistance that consists solely in not working anymore'.[147]

'But that's not so clear yet', objects a critical worker. This indeed requires some explanation, and gives Eduard the chance to use the knowledge he acquired from the meetings of the English workers:

> Effortlessly, he learned about the forces that shape our time – industry, commerce, politics. Everything was present in his mind, he knew more

143 Weerth 1976, p. 338.
144 Weerth 1976, p. 343.
145 Cf. Weerth 1976, p. 339.
146 Weerth 1976, p. 342.
147 Weerth 1976, p. 338.

> than many professors in his hometown about things like free trade, free competition, overproduction, the proletariat, for he had been educated by life itself, by direct observation. A natural interest made his free senses more receptive to every correct impression than was perhaps possible for those who had done the most rigorous study of all the world's most important writers.[148]

Eduard then gives the attentive workers as well as the reader a crash course in political economy. How can refraining from an action – work – be a more effective 'resistance' than war with 'rifles and sabres'? We learn that the English 'wool combers' – the core troops of the Luddites, perhaps not coincidentally – had initially profited from the boom in trade and industry. We learn how they became 'family men' during this period of prosperity, since they were now able to 'honestly provide for their wives and children'. But we also learn how these workers *had* to work, which made them vulnerable to blackmail by the factory bosses, who for their part 'sought to reduce production costs in every way possible', above all by cutting wages. The workers were 'beguiled' by the mention of economic crises, and refrained from resisting. Once on that slippery slope, they accepted more and more cuts until finally wages 'sunk so low that a poor comber could not possibly survive'. While some wool combers decide to 'give up the thankless occupation altogether and take up another line of work' – the decision to make use of that freedom of choice which belongs to the foundation of 'free' labour – others are opposed to the idea, since the situation is no better in other branches of industry: 'Everywhere an initially tolerable wage had tempted people to marry and increase the population. There were more than enough people to fill all the jobs'.[149]

Marx will later describe this same dynamic in the well-known 25th chapter of *Capital* as the 'general law of capitalist accumulation':

> But if a surplus population of workers is a necessary product of accumulation or of the development of wealth on a capitalist basis, this surplus population also becomes, conversely, the lever of capitalist accumulation, indeed it becomes a condition for the existence of the capitalist mode of production. It forms a disposable industrial reserve army, which belongs to capital just as absolutely as if the latter had bred it at its own cost.

148 Weerth 1976, p. 342.

149 Weerth 1976, p. 339.

> Independently of the limits of the actual increase of population, it creates always ready exploitable human material for capital's own changing valorization needs.[150]

Under these conditions, as Weerth's Eduard already knew in 1846, 'all friendly negotiations with the factory owners are useless'. If a 'surplus population of workers' wants to stop being merely 'exploitable human material', then the workers must stop letting themselves be played against each other; solidarity must replace competition. And so, the wool combers re-enact the classic scene of the *Secessio Plebis*: they take leave of the city and meet 'one Sunday morning on a nearby hill beneath the open sky'. In contrast to the Luddites and primitive rebels who gather at night in secret locations, these workers meet out in the open, in a non-conspiratorial manner, which suggests that they have nothing to hide. And so, 'after a brief discussion', they all agree that no change in the situation can be expected from 'decisively violence steps'.[151] The solution to the problem is then staged in Eduard's speech as a collective epiphany:

> 'What if', they said all at once, 'instead of rising up wildly, all 30,000 of us [the total number of wool combers at that location] put our arms in our laps, and instead of doing a lot, did absolutely nothing at all for a while? What if we neither sharpened weapons nor spun wool, but in a word, suddenly started acting like nobles and took a stroll that lasted several weeks on end? Wouldn't that knock some sense into our masters just as well as the bloodiest attack?'[152]

The idea that emerges 'all at once' is compelling precisely because it builds upon counterintuitive assumptions: not 'rising up wildly', but letting their arms sink down, not 'doing a lot', but 'absolutely nothing', not handling things, but letting them be. That promises success. Not acting like the 'masters' – such as the factory owners who always pretend to be busy – but like the 'noblemen' who have to pass the time but not turn it into money.

The imagery of a *dolce far niente* evoked here, however, remains unfulfilled – regrettably, one is tempted to say. Instead, Weerth describes even more precisely the material and economic consequences of doing nothing as a form of

---

150 Marx 1976, p. 784. Translation revised.
151 Weerth 1976, p. 340.
152 Weerth 1976, p. 340.

struggle. In a particularly bold train of thought, Eduard outlines how the non-action of the wool combers spreads widely and leads to mass solidarity, without relying on the idealistic goodwill of the participants. Rather, it lies in the nature of the action itself:

> If we stop work now, then suddenly the whole business comes to a standstill for them – we wool combers will have no more wool to comb, the spinner will have no more wool to spin, the weaver will have no more yarn to weave, the dyer will have no more garments to dye, the printer will have nothing more to print, the grocer will have nothing more to sell, and so on ad infinitum – the whole wool industry will come to a standstill. By stopping our work, we force all the other workers in wool manufacture to lower their arms as well, and since they are mostly just as unhappy as we are and can only wish that their relationship with the factory owners would change in some way, they will also make no fuss and half voluntarily, half out of necessity, join our side and expand the ranks of our party.[153]

There are also consequences on the other side, which Eduard relishes in describing: without workers, the factory owners 'can no longer run their factories, everything is at a standstill for them. Their capital no longer turns a profit'. Finally, the customers are driven away since this puts their business also at risk of shortages: the strike not only stops production, it also brings sales and distribution to a standstill.

Machinery plays an important, yet *ambivalent* role in the work stoppage: on the one hand, the use of large machinery in a strike can be turned against the factory owners themselves, since they 'have invested their fortunes in large, mighty facilities' – in extensive machine aggregates – 'which must always be kept running if their owners are not to suffer enormous losses'.[154] The 'constant capital' of machinery must be constantly put into motion and animated by 'variable capital', by paid living labour power, otherwise the enormous investments could not be amortised. On the other hand, new machines can also replace human labour power, and they do so precisely where human labour power threatens to withdraw through strikes. Worst of all is when, during a strike, 'some new invention in machinery' appears which 'replaces physical labour, so that the workers, if they really wanted to work for the former wages, or even at lower wages than before' – that is, in the case of defeat – 'are com-

153 Weerth 1976, p. 340.
154 Weerth 1976, p. 340.

pletely cast aside and must perish in the deepest misery'.[155] Marx will later reformulate Eduard's insight in a theoretically more polished form. In *The Poverty of Philosophy*, he even starts from the same context, the labour struggles of the English textile workers:

> In England, strikes have regularly given rise to the invention and application of new machines. Machines were, it may be said, the weapon employed by the capitalists to quell the revolt of specialised labour. The *self-acting mule*, the greatest invention of modern industry, outcompete the rebellious spinners.[156]

In *Capital*, Marx succinctly declares machinery to be 'the most powerful weapon for suppressing strikes, those periodic revolts of the working class against the autocracy of capital'.[157]

Weerth's Eduard already knows that the miracle remedy of the strike usually leads the workers into bitter defeats. For although the factory owner needs the workers to keep his factory running, the workers also need the wages in order to survive, and so it is 'obvious that the factory owners are always more capable of enduring such a dispute than their workers'.[158] But workers' defeats are never total, for every struggle is already a victory simply by launching in the first place and thus interrupting 'peaceful' and 'free' business as usual. Labour struggles build on each other until 'little by little all the working classes', Eduard envisions, 'get accustomed to this kind of warfare', until finally, in an acute crisis of 'overproduction', 'a generalized uprising breaks out, leaving no stone of the current institutions unturned, and a whole population takes its first step towards happiness under new laws and institutions'.[159]

The road map to revolution outlined here will remain valid for at least the next hundred years in the radical workers' movement; every *revolutionary* uprising therefore had to begin with the strike as the central form of struggle. Conversely, the strike was also the central component of every great plan to *reform* society by integrating the working class: only by striking could workers demonstrate that society does not function without them, that they are integral to society and should therefore be recognised and treated as such. In spite of

---

155 Weerth 1976, p. 341.
156 MECW 6, p. 207. Translation revised.
157 Marx 1976, p. 562.
158 Weerth 1976, p. 341.
159 Weerth 1976, p. 342.

the great division of the workers' movement into revolutionaries and reformists, the strike comes to be the preferred form of struggle by 'free' wage labour in general. And both strategic variants, reform and revolution, work according to the same utopia of de-differentiation, which Eduard alludes to in his speech: the initially separated 'working classes' will unite through the generalized form of struggle of the strike, and finally appear as the 'whole population'. This is not a presupposed factor (as, for example, with contemporary social statisticians), but a goal to be achieved, first to be realized. The 'whole population', as something integral, undivided, and singular, is novel, produced by those 'new laws and institutions' yet to be won.

In the course of the nineteenth century, the linking of 'free' wage labour, contractually guaranteed employment, and the 'strike' as form of struggle becomes an unquestionable matter of course. This coincides with a stabilisation of linguistic usage. The English term *strike* was 'imported' as early as the Vormärz alongside knowledge about the phenomenon itself. That an unbound, highly mobile commercial assistant like Weerth plays a significant role in this import business might be more than an aperçu. Finally, in the 1870s – after previous 'malapropisms such as "strick", "stricke" and the like' in the 1850s and 1860s – 'the Germanised word *Streik* becomes common both in scientific literature and in the speech of workers and businessmen. Shortly thereafter, derivates begin to appear in compound words such as *Streikkämpfe* (strike wave), *Streikreglement* (strike rules), *Streikposten* (picketing)'.[160]

Peter Linebaugh and Marcus Rediker add a global-historical touch to the conceptual history of the strike when they remark that the very word 'strike' originates from a context that was by no means characterised by 'free' wage labour, but rather by diverse, mixed forms of 'free' and 'coerced labour', namely Atlantic maritime shipping in the seventeenth and eighteenth centuries: 'The sailors of London, the world's largest port … in 1768 struck (i.e. took down) the sails of their vessels, crippling the commerce of the empire's leading city and adding the strike to the armory of resistance'.[161] In fact, 'free' wage labour is by no means exclusively bound to the strike as a form of struggle, since the tactic was developed in different labour conditions from the beginning. Even in the regime of free wage labour, the strike is only one weapon among others in the 'armory of resistance'. This was often still known during the Vormärz (and since then increasingly forgotten), and will have to be borne in mind again in the future – in this book and in social reality.

160 Tenfelde and Volkmann 1981, p. 12.

161 Linebaugh and Rediker 2000, p. 219.

10 The Struggle for the Family Wage, the Feminisation of Factory Work and the Masculinisation of the Workers' Movement

If the strike became the preferred form of struggle for 'free' wage labourers in the Vormärz, as the previous section argued, then this explicitly excludes working class women. In his study *Vom Scheitern der deutschen Arbeiterbewegung* [*The Failure of the German Workers' Movement*], Erhard Lucas characterises the 'workers' movement as a men's movement', and argues that making the strike the central form of struggle played a decisive role in the masculinisation of that movement.[162] When workers organise to stop working, they put their very lives at stake: without wages, survival becomes precarious. Edward's co-workers already see this when he introduces the strike to them as the form of struggle of the English workers: 'But how do they survive if they are out of work and earn nothing?'[163] The strikers also put the lives of their entire family at risk. Children start to go hungry very shortly after wages are withheld, and it is above all women also in proletarian families who have to handle this, regardless of whether they also have work. Lucas shows how women, as advocates and representatives of the family as a whole, were cast in the role of domestic strike-breakers in the eyes of many class-conscious male heads of household. As an exemplary proletarian woman says to her earnest, striking husband during the great labour struggles in the Ruhr region of the 1920s: 'What do I care about your proletarian class consciousness, I want bread for the children, what don't you understand!'[164]

The workers' movement was by no means purely a men's movement at its outset, nor did it ever end up becoming so later on. While Lucas writes that 'women's factory work was the exception' as 'the workers' movement first formed in Germany around 1860', this exceptional character is already based on the struggles of the 1840s, when the workers' movement in Germany was first constituted – and left incomplete.[165] The early struggles of the movement were often struggles for a family wage, which made it possible for proletarian women to take leave of the factories in the first place, very shortly after they had been driven there just like their male class brothers. It was not until after the family wage had been enforced that women were finally confined within the private sphere of increasingly petty bourgeois proletarian families.[166] The

162 Lucas 1983, pp. 45–69.
163 Weerth 1976, p. 341.
164 Lucas 1983, p. 61.
165 Lucas 1983, p. 62.
166 For Peter Linebaugh, the establishment of modern gender relations and the enforcement

process of *liberation and exclusion* from the factory and eventually from wage labour in general can be seen in all its ambiguity particularly well in Weerth's character Eduard.

When Eduard returns from England and enters the cottage with the three girls and women who, after the death of his father, form the last remaining members of his family, he promises them first of all that now 'a new life begins': 'You can relax now', he promises the mother, 'and Marie shall no longer work in the factory, and Gretchen should go to school. I will work for all of you, and I will earn enough!'[167] Eduard is particularly incensed that ten-year-old Gretchen had to work 'for two years in the cotton mill'. The conditions and consequences of women's and children's work are described later in the novel. Right at the end of pay day, at the lowest level of the internal hierarchy of the factory, 'the inhabitants of the spinning mill' line up behind the adult male workers to pick up their wages from the counter:

> Women, nine months pregnant, thirty-years old with grey, even white hair if the poor girl's hand had not previously brushed the dust of cotton from her head out of a remnant of vanity. Mothers whose breasts threaten to burst because at home a small child in nappies eagerly awaiting since noon stretches out his little hands in vain trying to find them. Old hags turned to skeletons by the magic wand of industry before they even died. Girls, pale and degenerate, with jaundiced shoulders, sagging breasts hardly veiled by threadbare garments, hair in dirty pig tails sweeping down their backs, crooked fingers hid beneath their tattered aprons, eyes vacant and glassy, dimmed by lashes full of dust, a catchy tune on the lips, venery in the bones. And now the children: humpbacked little boys with twisted legs and horrifying scrofula, and little girls, trained to work like weasels or poodles, fixed to the purring spindle, to the rattling machine, before the first buds of youth ever blossomed, before the first red flashed across their cheeks in dawning splendour, before they knew that they were children, that they were human beings, before they forgot the first curse and learned the first prayer, before they had rejoiced three times, before they had kissed three times, before they had a chance to live their life. Drained and depleted from the torture of work, no meat on

---

of a sexual division of labour are nothing but a strategy in the system of *enclosures*, cf. Linebaugh 2014, p. 80. The classic contribution from a socio-historical perspective is Hausen 1981.

167 Weerth 1976, p. 309.

> the bones, no blood in the veins, no brain in the heads – like ghosts freshly risen from the grave or withered flowers condemned to die the morrow.[168]

The cruelty of the industrial 'exploitation of little children, on this scale and with this intensity' – which E.P. Thompson considers to be 'one of the most shameful events in our history' – requires no further explanation by Eduard in the novel.[169] Nor is it necessary to discuss the fact that young mothers and old women should not be involved in industrial production in the way described. That Gretchen and the mother accept Eduard's insistence on acting as the family breadwinner seems to be a foregone conclusion. But what is not self-evident is why Marie – a twenty-year-old young woman who, after all, provided most for the family's subsistence during the last two years while Eduard was in England – should 'no longer work in the factory', as Eduard decrees, and hence Marie confronts him with a series of brash rejoinders. Although Marie does not directly resist his command to take leave of the factory, she does challenge Eduard's irate tirades against that 'scoundrel' and 'devil' Preiss; instead of class hatred, Marie still follows the old paternalist code.[170] Eduard, in turn, can only sense 'foolishness, nothing but foolishness' and 'nonsense' in Marie's rebuttal, whereas Marie aptly states that the two siblings 'cannot communicate'.[171] Why not?

Eduard's and the narrator's rejection of young women's wage labour and factory work stems from two grounds. First, young female adult workers – called 'girls', in contrast to the 'mothers' and 'hags' on the one side, and 'children' on the other – also undoubtedly suffer from the poor working conditions in the factory: they are 'pale', with eyes 'vacant and glassy'.[172] Poor working conditions affect both male and female workers alike, but in different ways. Thus, secondly, a gender-specific factor must be brought into play which speaks out particularly against young women working in factories. This factor is moral in nature: factory work seems to present an ethical quandary for young women, at least that is how the descriptions of female wage earners can be read. For they are not only 'pale', but 'pale and degenerate', 'their sagging breasts hardly veiled' and, to make matters worse, have 'a catchy tune on the lips' and 'venery in the bones'. Anyone who sings a 'catchy tune' – in contrast to 'the songs of children' in the factory, which, as described later, 'sounds like a prisoners' song' – obvi-

168 Weerth 1976, pp. 327–8. See also Engels' description, MECW 4, pp. 452–3.
169 Thompson 1966, p. 349.
170 Weerth 1976, p. 310.
171 Weerth 1976, p. 312.
172 Weerth 1976, p. 327.

ously cannot take the injustice and suffering inflicted on them seriously, they must be frivolous and catch all kinds of sexual diseases like 'venery' quite easily.[173]

It is thus fitting that Eduard confronts his sister with a vague suspicion of prostitution already in their first conversation after his return, which Marie immediately recognises and denies. When Marie defends the manufacturer's son, August, because he is 'always so good to her', we read: 'Eduard cast a sharp glance at his sister; – she blushed and batted her eyes. – "I will never do anything that I cannot answer before my brother," Marie replied at last'.[174]

Shortly after Eduard stakes out his claim as the main breadwinner, he begins to act as the family tyrant. As soon as Marie disagrees with him, 'he slammed the table with a clenched fist and shot an angry glare towards his sister. Marie didn't dare look up'.[175] Latent violence is the other side of the protective function that Eduard claims to assume; in return, Marie's opinion is systematically debased and ridiculed ('nonsense', 'You don't know any better').[176] Her ability to think in general is ultimately subordinated to Eduard's: 'come and forgive me', he begs her, 'but also promise me that you will think like me in the future'.[177]

Whether Marie will submit to this dictate remains unclear for the time being. What does become clear is the kind of social constellation that results when everyone else submits to Eduard's insolence. This becomes apparent at the large collective assembly in the factory courtyard during lunchtime, as Eduard explains the meaning of the strike. The formula of the 'workers' movement as a men's movement' finds its anticipated, if unintentionally comic, culmination here. The separation of spheres – which will only become a reality in society as a whole once the demand for a subsistence family wage succeeds – is already prefigured in the factory yard; 'the women and girls' stand together on one side and whisper back and forth about Eduard's appearance:

> 'Look how nice he's dressed!'
> 'And how handsome and strong he has become!'
> 'What a tremendous beard!'
> 'And such intrepid eyes!'[178]

173 Weerth 1976, p. 343.
174 Weerth 1976, p. 313.
175 Weerth 1976, p. 310.
176 Weerth 1976, p. 311.
177 Weerth 1976, p. 313.
178 Weerth 1976, p. 338.

Meanwhile, on the other side of the court, the men pay close attention to what Eduard has learned in England and partake in his lesson on the basics of political economy and the possibilities of proletarian intervention. The women hear nothing of this. However, both men and women agree that Eduard's appearance alone makes him an almost superhuman being:

> Eduard's eyes shone with enthusiasm as he spoke. It seemed as if he grew taller and more beautiful as he spoke, his giant limbs towering over all his surroundings, and the audience stunned and hanging on his eloquent lips.[179]

After concluding that one becomes 'more beautiful' and 'clever' in a foreign country, the women almost outdo each other in their obsequiousness: '"I'll do anything Eduard wants!" "I'll do more than that!"' The men then repeat the same gesture of submission, albeit on a different basis, for after all they had already discussed the matter with him at length: they mutually reaffirm their willingness to participate in the labour struggle, 'and since Eduard knows best, I will do what he commands', one worker clarifies on behalf of all the others.[180]

Weerth's Eduard can surely be read as a premature caricature of the class-conscious worker who, as a figure, will populate the proletarian and socialist-realist literatures of all countries and languages from the late nineteenth century onwards. However, the shrewd irony that usually characterises Weerth's writing is strikingly absent when it comes to portraying Eduard: the caricature is clearly unintentional. The questions remains as to the socio-historical background of this so un-Weerthly act of literary violence.

The history of the implementation of wage labour, or more precisely, the history of the dominance of industrial labour, can and must always also be told as a gender history of labour. The complicated and ambiguous history of the gender-political aspects of the labour movement can be seen especially in that very movement's rejection of wage labour: in many cases, the struggle against poor working conditions cannot be separated from the ousting of women from gainful employment.

Using official statistical material, Engels was already able to show in the *Condition of the Working Class in England* that the standardisation of factory work was not only linked to a de-skilling and devaluation of individual jobs, for example in textile production, but also to a comprehensive feminisation of

179 Weerth 1976, p. 342.
180 Weerth 1976, p. 343.

labour. Both processes, in turn, are inextricably linked to the increased use of large machinery; in the section on the 'factory hands', the 'fact that machinery more and more supersedes the work of men' is substantiated by impressive figures:

> Of 419,590 factory operatives of the British Empire in 1839, 192,887, or nearly half, were under eighteen years of age, and 242,296 of the female sex, of whom 112,192 were less than eighteen years old. There remain, therefore, 80,695 male operatives under eighteen years, and 96,599 adult male operatives, *or not one full quarter* of the whole number.[181]

The struggle of the early workers' movement was first and foremost a struggle against the deterioration of working conditions in the factories. The use of machines had not made work any easier, but rather more dangerous and harmful to health. That this knowledge was already widespread at the time can be seen not least in the countless sick, stunted, mutilated, and dying children that appear in the social literature of the Vormärz. The only sense in which work can be said to have become easier is insofar as specialised training was no longer necessary, which is why women and children were tasked with carrying it out, since it was obvious that they would be paid less.

At the same time, the workers' movement also fought to increase the proportion of adult men that were gainfully employed, especially in industrial work. First to be mentioned are the defensive struggles of male workers, many of whom still considered themselves craftsmen and defended this status with all their might. This brings us back to the core of the textile workers' struggles and thus to the core of Luddism. Recent research has been able to demonstrate a gender bias in Luddite actions, since 'very rarely – indeed, if at all – did the machine breakers fight against machines that took over the work previously done by women, e.g. spinning and all the preliminary work, scraping, carding, stretching etc. So if a specific activity already had a feminine connotation, then the machine was also spared'.[182] In short, the Luddites had nothing against women's work being replaced by machines. If, on the other hand, a machine replaced work that had to be done by more highly-qualified men, then the factory owners started assigning women to work on these machines, since a machine and a low-paid woman was less costly for capital than a highly-paid, status-conscious and headstrong craftsman-worker. The Luddites them direc-

181 MECW 4, pp. 434, 436.
182 Schlottau 2006, p. 112.

ted their resistance against precisely *those* machines which replaced previously 'male' jobs with either machines or women. When 'demands for the abolition of women's work' arose in the early workers' movement and especially in the later nineteenth century, this can be interpreted as machine breaking by other means: in both cases, the aim is the restitution of a high-wage sector for skilled male workers.[183]

Now, the phenomena of 'well-paid [male] workers whose income was usually sufficient to support a family' had certainly existed at times before industrialisation.[184] However, especially in view of the gendered social and political upheavals associated with industrialisation – upheavals that often threaten to distort the view of the 'before' – the family form must not be taken for granted historically. The demands pertaining to family and gender in the early workers' movement – such as the demand for a family wage in Weerth's novel fragment – are structurally nostalgic; they invent traditions of the good old days when men were still paid well enough for good work that they could support their children and wives, who meanwhile stayed at home and took care of the household. Yet this construction is anachronistic in a strict sense; it can be called an 'invented tradition' insofar as it represents less a look back at the actual (gender) relations in the working classes *before* industrialisation than a projection, a preview of the kinds of relations that the workers' movement will begin to fight for later in the nineteenth century. To condense by way of aphorism, one could say that the struggle for the family wage was not so much a struggle for a higher wage, but first and foremost a struggle for the right to family, a struggle to impose the nuclear family form throughout society, across classes.[185]

Joan Wallach Scott understood the outlined 'invention of tradition' as a 'story' (in scare quotes!) that was already told in the early nineteenth century about the development of industrialisation and the 'transfer of production from the household to the factory' – with the aim of dividing the new social constellation in general and the labour market in particular into gendered and hierarchical spheres. The 'story' claims that 'in the pre-industrial period women were thought to have successfully combined productive activity and childcare, work and domesticity'. The introduction of a specially delimited sphere of wage labour and finally the separation of domestic and productive spheres in the 'factory system' supposedly did away with this harmony; women's employment as now done exclusively outside the home was thus considered highly problem-

183 Schlottau 2006, p. 131.

184 Schlottau 2006, p. 115.

185 On the social history of the bourgeois-proletarian nuclear family, Tilly 1995, pp. 127–44.

atic and ultimately an 'anomaly'.[186] According to Scott, however, this 'story' is simply not true in its most important points, or is at best 'oversimplified':

> In the period before industrialization women already worked regularly outside their homes. Married and single women sold goods at markets; earned cash as petty traders and itinerant peddlers; hired themselves out as casual laborers, nurses or laundresses; made pottery, silk, lace, clothing, metal goods, and hardware; wove cloth and printed calico in workshops.[187]

The form of the list is central to Scott's argument: before industrialisation, women did many different kinds of work, and people switched jobs constantly according to the demands of the market. The movement was not generally 'from work at home to work away from home, but from one kind of workplace to another'.[188]

The heterogeneity of work also reflects back on the central category of 'woman' itself. It is actually anachronistic to speak of 'woman's' work, according to Scott, since the differences between women, even within the working classes, were greater than those between men and women. For Scott, the only meaning 'woman' has *as a category of the labour market* is in designating cheap and unskilled labour, which renders invisible the 'long tradition of skilled female crafts (in dressmaking or millinery, for example), or because they were recruited to new kinds of jobs'.[189] And conversely, with the strict gendered segregation of the labour force, the 'exemplary "worker"' is increasingly identified with the 'skilled male craftsman'.[190] The 'myth of the artisan', which, according to Rancière, both determined the self-perception of the early workers' movement and bewitched its later historiography, also dominates the history of the gender division of labour.

The traditional, heterogenous practice of women's work is now suddenly declared a problem for society as a whole with the onset of industrialisation and the attendant mass hiring of female workers in the factories – and initially by the early workers' movement. The scandalous conditions in the factories draw attention to the women working there. The social and humanitarian problem, however, is primarily identified in their lack of families or distance

186 Scott 1998, p. 400.
187 Scott 1998, p. 403.
188 Scott 1998, pp. 404–5.
189 Scott 1998, p. 422.
190 Scott 1998, p. 401.

from them. Weerth's image of the young woman who has become unattractive through work and will therefore never find a man can serve as an illustration here, as well as his 'miserable picture' of the mother whose breasts ache from factory work while her infant cries for its mother's milk at home. There is no question that these problems also existed in reality. But it is ideological to make this a problem of the 'working woman' per se and thus foreclose alternative lifestyles for women. Both before and during industrialisation, most women workers were 'young and single'.[191] For them, wage labour was only a short phase of life, one which required no qualifications and was therefore paid poorly from the outset. In addition, before and during industrialisation, many married women, including mothers, remained employed without having the same problems as the female factory workers. The old model of changing jobs at regular intervals proved to be quite amenable to the problem of reconciling family and work, without confining women to the home. The British historian Bridget Hill has used the figure of the 'spinster', the unmarried (usually elderly) woman, to discover a wealth of possible non-familial feminine forms of life that existed in the period between 1660 and 1850, which though culturally often considered more or less problematic or even ostracized, were quite viable economically.[192] Moreover, Hill suggests, the presumed connection between marriage and family must also be reexamined: between 1551 and 1851, the percentage of families with a single parent – and here we must assume a predominant number of them to be single mothers – was 19 percent on average, as compared to 16 percent today.[193] Being unmarried was disreputable, but not impossible.[194]

Against this background of diverse economic and (non)familial forms of life – which should not be nostalgically glorified merely because they were diverse, since the diversity mostly arose from the necessity of having to somehow make ends meet – the process of female proletarianisation in the Vormärz had the following characteristics: before industrialisation, women from the poor and working classes were by no means fully integrated into economic circuits centered on the family and the household, but rather engaged in many differ-

191 Scott 1998, p. 404.

192 Hill 2001. The number of the spinsters should not be underestimated: in 1851 there were 1.8 million or 8.9 percent of the total population in England; at the end of the seventeenth century the proportion was probably still 16–18 percent; similar figures can be assumed for the whole of Europe, cf. Hill 2001, p. 11.

193 Hill 2001, p. 9.

194 There were opportunities for 'Single Women in Agriculture' and for 'Single Women in Manufacturing', especially in the textile industry, cf. Hill 2001, pp. 16–27 and pp. 28–42.

ent kinds of paid work that varied primarily by one's stage of life.[195] Though these can all certainly be classified as wage labour, they do not yet correspond to the ideal type of 'free' wage labour, which finds its most adequate realisation in industrial factory work. In the course of industrialisation, the possibilities of a 'mixed' reproduction not based purely on 'free' wage labour are limited; this applies to both men and women – we have called this process 'passive proletarianisation' – but it affects the living conditions of each differently. And so, the economic and cultural possibilities for single women as well as their conditions of acceptance become increasingly restricted, like all options for life without a husband and family. The ideal of the married woman who stays at home to do housework and care for children instead of working in the factory becomes dominant amongst the proletariat as well. As already indicated, the workers' movement plays a decisive role in this process; the ideal of the nuclear family, economically sustained by the father with a family wage, emerges as a goal within the struggle of the working class. Literary figures such as Georg Weerth played no small part in formulating and popularising this agenda.

The demands of the workers' movement present themselves as a chain of rhetorical substitutions in which one scandal is always explicitly named and assailed in order to point to another unnamed and larger context. Starting from the inhumane working conditions of women and children – but also men – in the early industrial factories, child factory labour in particular becomes a target and its prohibition a popular demand. Along with child labour, however, women's factory work is also to be forbidden, since this contravenes woman's nature and impairs the ability of female factory workers to reproduce.

Through women's factory work, however, the question of women's work as such arises: proletarian women, like bourgeois women, should no longer have to work, in part to show that proletarian men are every bit as capable of providing for their families as are bourgeois men. In a certain sense, this claim shows the continuation of the old patriarchal idea of the head of the household, which is inscribed in the cultural source code of the workers' movement as a continuation (albeit thoroughly transformed) of the crafts movement. Precisely with this claim to inherit the 'true bourgeoisie', the workers' movement transformed the patriarchal ideal of the head of the household into that of the breadwinner of the bourgeois nuclear family. The ideal of the proletarian family, which economically depends entirely on the work of the family head, may have been imaginatively derived from the master craftsman's house, but

195 On the biographical 'flexibility of female labour power' at the beginning of industrialisation, see Schrupp 1999, pp. 25–6.

in reality more closely resembles the Prussian civil servant household, as Karin Hausen has shown. Much of what the workers' movement fought for in terms of family and social policy was first tested by the Prussian state on its civil servants, including the 'the payment of regular salaries, paid increasingly solely in money' (without which it is impossible to budget sensibly and with foresight) 'and the growing demand for pensions' (without which there would be no future security for women leaving paid work).[196]

The phase of early industrialization in which more women than men actually worked in the technically most advanced areas of social production, in large factories, can be seen as the 'bottleneck' through which the history of women's proletarianisation had to pass: from the mixed reproduction of the pre-industrial phase, which also revolved around principles of marriage and family, but still knew non-familial as well as economically and socio-culturally 'autonomous' forms of life, to the proletarian housewife, who depends on her husband's family wage and has thus become completely dependent, economically and socio-culturally.[197] Paradoxically, women's exclusion from wage labour altogether and their confinement to the domestic sphere was sparked by women's work in a public place outside the home on a mass scale, that is, in the factory.[198] This process, which has dragged on for at least a hundred years and is naturally marked by counter-movements, obstacles and divergences, can be analysed as the homogenising and disciplining of life options for proletarian women; its mirror image is the homogenising and (self)disciplining of the proletariat as a class.

The production of a closed and self-justifying system of a gender division of labour – distilled into the 'conceptual pair "sole breadwinner" and "housewife"' – offers a particularly clear illustration of how the tactics and strategies used by different agents can complement each other and work towards a common goal, even though those involved confront each other as irreconcilable enemies.[199] Scott has shown this in regards to the '"problem"' of the woman worker via the interaction of economic science, work organisation, trade unions and workplace safety legislation.[200] It is not necessary to see a conspiracy of men, a fated outcome of the logic of capital or a liberal-paternalist salvation narrative at work here; it is probably enough to note *post festum* (and only *post festum*) that the strategy of the gender division of labour proved particularly

196 Hausen 1981, p. 68.
197 On the metaphor of the bottleneck for modernisation, see Schlottau 2006, p. 112.
198 For a summary of the historical course described, see Schrupp 1999, p. 24.
199 Schlottau 2006, p. 112.
200 Scott 1998, pp. 461–75.

functional for capitalist accumulation for a few decades, and therefore prevailed. Later, this system was loosened again and has since largely fragmented, as many aspects of our present moment reveal: a widespread dissolution of the single breadwinner model; increasing rates of women's employment in occupational fields that were either previously predominantly occupied by women before or are now devalued as 'feminine', especially in terms of pay; the creation of an extensive low-wage sector in which women are disproportionately represented. What is remarkable is that the decomposition of the system of the gender division of labour produces phenomena similar in kind to what transpired before, during its formative phase, and thus must be contextualised in the historical process. Nonetheless, one should be wary of any premature euphoria concerning this transformation of the capitalist regime of accumulation. The conclusion that the gender division of labour becomes more fragile – or conversely, that the flexibilisation of the gender regime challenges capitalism as such – should be avoided.[201]

201 See Freundinnen und Freunde der klassenlosen Gesellschaft 2015a.

CONCLUSION

The Return of Romantic Anti-capitalism

In Georg Weerth's unfinished novel, the strike is presented as the mature form of struggle of a self-conscious industrial working class. The strike is the 'pure' form of class struggle that best corresponds to 'pure', 'free' wage labour. Just as the regime of wage labour ideally functions without coercion and violence, relying on the pure legal form of the sale of labour power – of course with the mute compulsion of sheer survival in the background – so the strike is a non-violent form of struggle based solely on withdrawal, on not exerting one's own labour power. The strike succeeds without any passionate, violent excess – affective excess, on the other hand, is precisely what marks the social rebellion in Willkomm's *White Slaves* as well as the machine breaking in Otto-Peters' *Castle and Factory*. Of course, for Weerth, this does not rule out a cool, calculated use of violence in strike situations. In England, for example, Weerth's Eduard reports, when the 'peaceful struggle' does not continue, then sometimes at night transpires 'riotous assemblies in front of the palaces of the most wanton', where the strikers demands are backed by 'wild shouting', and even 'stones occasionally fly … into the rooms'. Strike-breakers were brought to (class) reason by the threat that, if necessary, they would be 'beaten up, their houses demolished or otherwise harmed'.[1] For Weerth, it is precisely the instrumental and strategic – not moral or passionate – relationship to violence that constitutes the superior, because disciplined, character of the strike as a form of struggle for the working class. The striking workers thus rise to the level of rationality of their opponent.

The typology of forms of struggle that can be gleaned from the social novels of the Vormärz also implies, through the values represented in the novels, a history of progress from the still pre-modern (undisciplined-archaic) social rebels to the Luddites, whose modernity is not yet entirely transparent to themselves, up to the modern, self-conscious striking working class.[2] However, this (presumed) progress in forms of struggle also entails a change in the class composition of those who struggle: a uniforming and standardising of the pro-

1 Weerth 1976, p. 341.

2 The story of maturation is also told by Marx in *Capital*: 'It took both time and experience before the workers learnt to distinguish between machinery and its employment by capital, and therefore to transfer their attacks from the material instruments of production to the form of society which utilizes those instruments' (Marx 1976, pp. 554–5).

 | DOI:10.1163/9789004685536_010

letariat, which from the middle of the nineteenth century onwards presents itself more and more exclusively in the figure of the adult, male, white industrial worker.

There have always been, of course, counter-tendencies to this idealised history of progress, and these can be observed right at the beginning of the constructed sequence. Hobsbawm notes that even in the early days of industrialisation, workers in England often used the destruction of machines as a weapon when the 'simple withdrawal of work' was not effective: for instance, when a constant influx of freshly proletarianised individuals prevented solidarity and united action, or when production was so 'scattered' that a synchronous work stoppage could hardly be organised, as in the 'domestic system' of textile industry. Here, only the nocturnal troops of Luddites could 'guarantee an effective stoppage'.[3] Machine wrecking allowed an inclusive heterogeneous proletariat to collectively spring into action, a motley Vormärz proletariat, and not just an exclusively industrial proletariat. Wrecking machines 'might be used', Hobsbawm writes nonchalantly, 'by all sorts of people, from independent small producers, through the intermediate forms so typical of the domestic system of production, to more or less fully-fledged wage-workers'.[4]

It was not only in the transitional period of the Vormärz, when the 'factory system' of industrial capitalism was just getting off the ground, that the 'strike' as a form of struggle could still come up against limits – limits at which *other* forms of struggle of a *different*, broader and more inclusive proletariat had to be brought into play. Throughout its existence – and especially in the present phase of a progressive deindustrialisation of capitalism – other forms of direct action remain virulent, even if only marginally noticeable, under the surface during the long period of dominance of the industrial system and the industrial labour force. Suppressed since the Vormärz, 'immature' forms of class struggle like social rebellion and machine breaking are constantly reappearing. This is because the progression 'from the rabble to the proletariat' (Conze) and further 'from the proletarian to the industrial worker' (Florian Tennstedt), an idea invented in the Vormärz and orchestrated by authors like Weerth, did not and still does not exist as a one-way, exclusive street. The industrial worker too remains a 'virtual pauper' (Marx), and thus at least virtually tied to the pauper's forms of struggle.[5]

To enter the virtual, the hidden, the secret or counter-history of the social bandits and Luddites is to leave behind 'hard' social history and switch to the

3 Hobsbawm 1967a, pp. 11–12.
4 Hobsbawm 1967a, p. 11.
5 Marx 1993, p. 604; Conze 1954; Tennstedt 983.

register of the imaginary. At the same time, however, this step reveals a fundamental element of the imaginary, irreducible to ideology, already inherent in the underlying social-historical phenomena themselves, and even gives them their full historical coherence.

In his essay on the relation between Luddism and Romanticism, on 'Ned Ludd and Queen Mab', Peter Linebaugh notes the political dimension of the imaginary: 'The imaginative faculty can be political. There was a poiesis of the Luddites'.[6] Luddism, machine breaking and social rebellion in any case were deeply romantic movements; their protagonists were moved by the belief in a better yesterday to be reclaimed and realised, now more than ever. This better yesterday – the paternalist code, the fair wage, meaningful work – is a construction through and through; the tradition that invokes it is an invented one, like all romantic traditions. But machine breaking as a political movement is romantic in an even more specific sense. The Luddites are romantic because, like the authors and political propagandists of Romanticism, they willingly surrender from the beginning to the power of self-made myths and use them as weapons in political struggle.[7] The nightly meetings outside, the secret rituals and oaths whose protocol and wording are still unknown today, the circulated rumours about hidden weapons and far-reaching underground connections – all of this stages an archaicism both romantic and eminently modern at the same time. In a certain sense, the mythical practices represent an inversion of the ideal of publicity and transparency that became widespread in the course of the bourgeois revolutions of the late eighteenth and early nineteenth centuries. The Luddites practise an exodus from the public sphere, but at the same time depend on modern means of communication since they use them to spread their secret message. The Luddite myth is modern – and not archaic or backward-looking – in two respects: firstly, the machine breakers and their followers practise conspiratorial forms of solidarity, which become more necessary in the face of police and spy networks expanding with the characteristically modern centralisation and bureaucratisation of political rule. In *Castle and Factory*, the spy who corrupts the social body become a central plot device; the figure of Schumacher, the police superintendent, is inspired by the real figure of Stieber, the police superintendent and agent, who himself became an almost mythical figure in the Vormärz (and beyond).[8] It is also from the prac-

6 Linebaugh 2014, p. 106.

7 On the connection between Romanticism and myth, see Graevenitz 1987. On the deconstruction of Romantic mythopoiesis, see chapter two of Nancy 1991, 'Myth Interrupted', pp. 43–70.

8 For more on Stieber and his anonymously published first book *Die Prostitution in Berlin und ihre Opfer* [*Prostitution in Berlin and its Victims*] of 1846, see the subsection 'Fiction and Correction: Statistics of Prostitution' in the third chapter of this study.

tices and myths of the Luddites that the outlines of an 'opaque' 'working-class culture' emerge, without which even the legal, official trade union movement could not have established itself.[9]

The second genuinely modern aspect of Luddite mythopoesis arises from their secrecy: because no one knows anything about it, but everyone wants to talk about it, stories are circulated about the Luddites, whose protagonists exceed every common human measure from the outset. First and foremost is the eponymous *Ned* (or *General* or *Captain*) *Ludd* himself. Indeed, the Luddites themselves referred to this 'mythological name', and circulated stories about the origin.[10] Allegedly, in 1799, as Pynchon quotes the *Oxford English Dictionary*, Ned Ludd was a boy who smashed a stocking frame 'in a fit of insane rage'. A little later, his name became proverbial: wherever a machine was sabotaged, it was said 'Ludd must have been here'. By 1812, when the Luddite movement became a mass movement, the historical Ned Ludd was 'well absorbed into the more or less sarcastic nickname "King (or Captain) Ludd"'. He had become, as Pynchon notes, something essentially different: 'all mystery, resonance and dark fun'.[11]

Fighting against the superhuman power of machines and against the even greater and more opaque power of the 'factory system', Ned Ludd himself became a figure of superhuman power. The struggle of the Luddites is also about 'limits of humanity': machine breaking is a militant form of struggle against the reduction of the worker to the status of a machine. In this way, the Luddites also upset the man-machine boundary, which has remained contested since the rationalist fantasies of the Enlightenment. Whoever fights against *L'homme machine* has to become a kind of fighting machine himself, or at any rate be more than a 'mere human being' whose 'bare life' – as Tieck had already noted – is exhausted precisely in its mechanical functioning.

Ned Ludd belongs to the long line of mythical figures in which modernity – partly with recourse to archaic arsenals – symbolises itself in its own counter-images and counter-figures. From the Golem through Frankenstein to Superman, capitalism creates its own monsters.[12] Ned Ludd's mythical fame stems from the fact that he takes on superhuman actors; that is why he cannot be a normal mortal. Of course, it was clear to everyone that 'ordinary people' were behind the actions; the vehement repression aimed to show as clearly as

9 Thompson 1966, p. 494.
10 Linebaugh 2014, p. 79.
11 Pynchon 1984.
12 Cf. Barzilai 2016; Breyer et al. 2017.

possible that Luddites were mere mortals who could therefore also be killed in public. However, the 1812 *Frame Breaking Bill*, which declared the destruction of machinery a capital offence punishable by death, only confirmed the superhuman character of the Luddites. From that point on, they were treated as enemies of the state and set *hors-la-loi*. Even the army had to move in and occupy the whole of northern England to handle them. General Ludd's fame as a *true* general thus became all the more immortal.[13]

As an allegory of popular counter-power, General Ludd continues a historical series that goes back at least as far as Robin Hood.[14] Above all, however, Luddism exhibits a close proximity to literature from the very beginning: central protagonists of English Romanticism referred quite sympathetically to Luddism, from Mary and Percy Shelley to Lord Byron and Thomas Carlyle.[15] And even in Charlotte Brontë's *Shirley*, the current class struggles of the 1840s, such as the last flare-up of Chartism in 1848, are backdated to 1812: through the Luddite uprisings, a safe bridge could be built to an even more distant, mythically transfigured past, in which the relation between the classes was (supposedly) not yet as disastrously fractured as it was at the end of the 1840s, when Disraeli had to diagnose the complete break-up of the *one* English nation into *two nations*.[16] *Shirley* thus takes seriously the romantic anti-capitalism of the Luddites, even though the novel opposes the Luddites in its central political statements.

If there has been a uniformisation and standardisation of the proletariat since the Vormärz, then this class configuration is haunted from its origins by the spectre of the 'virtual pauper', who cannot be banished by any welfare state protection or by any bourgeoisification of the social imaginary. Parallel to the containment of class struggle in developed capitalist societies and the integration of the 'official' labour movement into society, there is another history, the history of an 'other' workers' movement, the history of all those social figures who embody the spectre of the 'virtual pauper' and haunt the cherished social order throughout the nineteenth and twentieth centuries.[17] It is the history of groups and individuals whose membership in the (waged) working class has always remained questionable, but whose complete prolet-

13 In his maiden speech in the House of Lords, to which he belonged by birth, Lord Byron defended the Luddites, cf. Dallas 1824, p. 213.

14 On the self-perception of the Luddites as 'Sherwood Lads', cf. Thompson 1966, pp. 552–75.

15 See Fox, 2002; McNally 2011, especially the section 'Jacobins, Irishmen and Luddites: rebel-monsters in the age of *Frankenstein*', pp. 77–111.

16 Cf. Eagleton 1975, starting at p. 45.

17 See Roth 1974; Negri 2005.

arianisation has never been in doubt. It is the history of the unqualified and the de-skilled, of migrants, of 'anti-socials', of the too young and the too old, of the unwilling, the subdued and the surplus, who, as figures of an obscure counter-history, always stand for more than their identification and cataloguing. In them, one could say, class society looks at its own ugly face which it openly showed at the beginning of its history and which it has been trying to conceal ever since.

The history of the other, dissident workers' movement is the history of a spook; for this reason alone, it is impossible to neatly separate 'real' from 'imaginary' aspects in this history. And yet it is a robust 'history of class struggle'. It tells of the continuing virulence of other, wilder forms of struggle, not confined to the cherished form of the 'pure' strike, in which the old social rebelliousness and machine wrecking persist to the present day. Parallel to the development of social democracy as a state-bearing force since the beginning of the twentieth century, and parallel to the rise and fall of really existing state socialism, there exists a history of shirkers and vagabonds who evaded the prevailing deification of labour shared across all other ideological divides. These figures, who politically and theoretically found a home more in anarchism and later in the aesthetic-political avant-garde movements than in the classical workers' parties, remain available to us today in almost no other way except their poetic manifestations. In German literature, for example, there is Erich Mühsam or Ernst Toller, whose drama *Die Maschinenstürmer* (*The Machine Breakers*) was published in 1922 at the final end of the German Revolution.[18] Another literary monument to this tradition comes from the scrounging artist Hugo Ball with his novel *Flametti oder Vom Dandysmus der Armen* (*Flametti or On the Dandyism of the Poor*).[19]

In the social struggles of the 1960s, 'deadbeats' and slackers again appeared on the scene. *Ne travaillez jamais!* demanded the Situationists in the middle of the wildcat general strike of May 1968.[20] In the movement of Italian *Autonomia Operaia*, the 'workers' autonomy' of the 1960s and 1970s, whose best-known theorist to date is Antonio Negri, intellectual dissidents of the old workers' parties and a young generation of freshly proletarianised, mostly unskilled ('mass') workers came together under the motto of a 'refusal of work' to declare war on 'factory society'.[21] A notorious class definition of *Autonomia* reads: 'The

18 Toller 2019.

19 Ball 2014.

20 On the history of the Situationist International, see Jappe 1999.

21 Cf. Tronti 2019, 'Factory and Society', pp. 12–35.

working class is the class that refuses to work'.[22] In this environment, elements of social rebellion and machine breaking resurface and form new alliances, perhaps pointing more towards the future than the past. One of the basic positions of *Autonomia*, for example, is the rejection of the neutrality of machinery and technology. Machinery, Raniero Panzieri argues, cannot take on just any social meanings, even when used for other purposes and by other people. Rather, it is materially congealed domination, the materialised form of the command of dead labour over living labour. Therefore, a revolutionary working class must abandon the idea that one can simply take over the social aggregate of machinery in a revolution. *There can be no free use of the assembly line, there can be no use of the assembly line in a free society* – the operaists claim.[23] Any inquiry into the material and organisational processes of labour in the present must therefore also be an inquiry into the ever more precise possibilities of sabotage against them.[24]

Against the active proletarianisation in the factories, the workers' districts of Turin, Bologna and Venice experimented with alternative forms of material reproduction, which were supposed to cushion the effects of passive proletarianisation. These align completely with Weitling's ideas of a 'guerrilla war against property': collectively organised shoplifting carried out as 'proletarian shopping'; paying only a previously discussed 'moral price' for public goods such as local transport, electricity and water, called *autoriduzione*.[25]

In addition to practical engagement in the social struggles in the factories and districts, Italian *Autonomia Operaia* also practised a strong politics of expression, especially in its second wave in the 1970s. *Autonomia* produced intense imagery and catchy slogans linked to contemporaneous phenomena of pop culture, from hippie to punk: from the films of Elio Petri (such as *La classe operaia va in Paradiso*), which were also recognised in high culture, and the novels and poems of the neo-avant-gardist Nanni Balestrini, from simple slogans such as the *rifiuto del lavoro* to complex theoretical neologisms such as 'autonomous self-valorisation' (*autovalorizzazione*) by which the proletariat was said to have suspended capital's law of value.[26] The militant theorist Toni

22 Thus according to the Bolognese autonomist Franco Berardi, 'Bifo', in conversation with a well-known French comrade with whom he found asylum after the defeat of the Italian movement, cf. Guattari 1978, p. 57.

23 Cf. Panzieri 1980.

24 Cf. Alquati 1974; 2013. A good introduction is the obituary by Armano and Sciortino 2010.

25 On the history of the Italian movements, see Balestrini and Moroni 2023.

26 Elio Petri, *La classe operaia va in Paradiso*, Italy 1971. The film was awarded the Palme d'Or at the 1972 Cannes Festival.

Negri continues to draw on the conceptual and pictorial poetic legacy of *Operaismo* today: the buzzwords *empire* and *multitude* have indeed managed to introduce previously marginal debates into a broader public discourse.

In the present, after the third industrial revolution and computerisation have completely transformed life and work, the last offshoots of a hidden tradition of social rebels and machine breakers can be called the *neo-Luddites*, who see a new struggle of *human beings* against *technology* raging at the given level of the productive forces.[27] Among the neo-Luddites, there are not only those who despise technology as such, but a number of ambiguous figures who question technological-scientific development from its spearhead. One might think of the historian of technology David Noble, who, 'in the heart of the beast', at MIT, finally comes around to a 'Defence of Luddism' – and is fired for it.[28] Or one may recall the 'Unabomber' Ted Kaczynski, who, after graduating from Harvard, taught as a mathematician at Berkeley before retiring to a cabin in Montana, from where he letter-bombed the world of academic scientists and international airline managers. Kaczynski's invisibility and elusiveness is emblematic of a scene that wants to evade mass media image production and yet can only become politically effective through its counter-images, which are also disseminated by mass media. The Unabomber is thus the most faithful revenant of the night conspirators from the northern English moorlands of the 1810s. There are no images and no news of him between his exodus into the woods and his arrest; he finally only becomes perceptible on the *net* (in all its meanings, up to and including Lutz Dammbeck's film of the same name about Kaszynski). Just as Thompson proved the political and theoretical validity of the threatening letters of the Luddites, Kaszynski's manifesto *Industrial Society and its Future* can also be read as an adequate political and theoretical expression of the current situation (if only as *one* adequate expression).[29] It would be worthwhile to place the Unabomber manifesto next to Bruno Latour's pronouncements on the need for a new 'war of the worlds', a *Gaia-War*: a proximity between Kaszynski's cabin in Montana and Sciences Po in Paris would not be easily dismissed.

Even if the continuous counter-history of an 'other' proletarian movement can be constructed from the early modern rabble via the Luddites to the Situationists and *Autonomia Operaia*, even if a coherent (neo)Luddite imaginary can be traced from Mary Shelley and Lord Byron to Ernst Toller and Thomas Pynchon, these movements and their imaginaries remain marginal. They are

---

27 On the current debate, see Jones 2006; Jarrige 2014; Biagini 2012.

28 Cf. Noble, 1995. On Noble's life and thought, see the obituary by Rancourt 2010.

29 Dammbeck 2005.

fringe figures on the banks of the great stream of history, who at most derive a broader appeal and significance from the fact that they succeed in asserting themselves as *avant-garde*. In the present day, these figures seem to be multiplying – the margins become the new centre – and it is again the history of technical development that plays an essential role in this. Where the Luddites opposed the replacement of human labour by machines, today this process has progressed to an unimaginable extent. Automation, the development of the productive forces in general, has progressed so far that, at least in the old centres of the capitalist mode of production, living labour is being pushed further and further out of social production (and in the new centres, for example in China and India, the situation will probably not be any different in the medium term; *jobless growth* has been observed in India for years). In Marxist terms: constant capital eats up variable capital. This has consequences for both sides of the labour-capital relation. On the side of capital, all the phenomena that Marx described under the heading of a 'tendential fall in the rate of profit' are increasingly asserting themselves; to go into this here in detail would lead us too far astray.[30] On the side of labour, more and more labour power remains unused, the sellers of labour power become superfluous. In the present moment, what Hegel already logically anticipated in his *Elements of the Philosophy of Right*, and what Marx pointed out in *Capital* as the 'general law of capitalist accumulation' in terms of surplus populations, is finally catching up with us historically: 'The abstraction of production makes work increasingly *mechanical*, so that the human being is eventually able to step aside and let a *machine* take his place'.[31]

There is currently little evidence to suggest that the other side of Marx's prediction will be realised in the foreseeable future, namely, that the release of human labour power from the production process will lead to an increase in 'disposable time'. And so, instead, mass precarity becomes the signature of our epoch: surplus human beings, partly exploited without restraint, partly immobilised in obviously pointless jobs, become the dominant figure of contemporary socialisation. Whatever this form of social (dis)integration may look like in detail, *nobody has free time here*. Instead, the precarious are under an intens-

30 The 'law of the tendential fall of the rate of profit' is developed in the third section of the third volume of *Capital*, Marx 1991, pp. 315–75. According to this law, the increased use of ever more expensive machinery leads, in order to recoup these investments, to the simultaneous squeezing out of the production process of the only source of surplus value and thus the actual anchor of all profit-making: living labour power. For a concise and contemporary exposition, see Mattick 2011.

31 Hegel 1991, § 198, p. 233.

ified 'time stress', as Guy Standing has put it.[32] The economic exposure of a remerging 'passive proletarianisation' drives those affected into an ever more restless and chaotic hyperactivity.

What large sections of the metropolitan precariat and, on a global scale, the 'informal proletariat' of the southern periphery have in common with those proletarian figures described here is that *the strike* no longer serves them as an adequate form of struggle.[33] For all those who depend on selling their labour power to secure their livelihood, but can no longer find any serious demand for it, the 'work stoppage' is no longer an option to make one's social opponent break out in a nervous sweat; what once was called the 'power of production' has been completely lost to them.

Instead, the precariat and the global surplus proletariat are left with what could be described as *nuisance value*, which somehow must be exercised in ways other than through cherished forms of struggle like the strike.[34] In political and social scientific debates of recent years, outwardly extremely diverse social articulations such as the riots and looting in the French banlieues and in London, uprisings in North Africa, occupations of squares in the crisis-hit states of southern Europe and the seemingly inexhaustible stream of migrants have been interpreted as expressions or symptoms of one and the same basic phenomenon: the rendering superfluous of labour power (to which the rendering superfluous of life and the cutting off of life opportunities is always attached).[35]

To synthesise these extremely diverse forms, the intellectual advocates of the precariat have in recent years repeatedly brought a profoundly bourgeois myth from the Vormärz into play, a myth that also allows the new social formation – 'a new group in the world, a class-in-the-making' – to be linked to an old source of horror.[36] For Standing, the precariat is 'the new dangerous class', while Negri, along with Michael Hardt, also writes of a return of the 'dangerous classes'.[37] The concept of the 'dangerous classes' was popularised in the Vormärz by Honoré Antoine Frégier in his 1840 work *Des classes dangereuses de la population dans les grandes villes, et des moyens de les rendre meilleures*. Fré-

32 Standing 2011, p. 130.

33 Still indispensable is Davis 2006; see also Freundinnen und Freunde der klassenlosen Gesellschaft 2015b.

34 I owe the term 'nuisance value' to Claus Offe, from a conversation at the height of the EU-Greece crisis in Florence during early February 2015.

35 Breman 2010. On the global 'surplus proletariat' as a background to the new migration movements, see Nail 2015.

36 Standing 2011, p. vii.

37 Hardt and Negri 2004, ch. 2.1 'The Dangerous Classes', pp. 103–157.

gier was 'Bureau Chief at the Seine Prefectur', as the title page of the German translation published in the same year announces, and thus a police functionary like our well-known Stieber.[38] Whether Frégier's concept is actually useful and capable of grasping the current phenomenon as a whole is certainly questionable. But the fact that it is being circulated again at all must be seen as a symptom all the more. For what actually returns is the *need for myth*, in this case the myth of the dangerous classes. It is the need for a myth that threatens to become dangerous to the ruling conditions. Beyond concepts and programmes, which Standing and others offer in abundance, what is most obviously lacking in the present is a poetic language, an *imagery* in which the present could communicate with itself about itself. That is to say, what is missing is a repertoire of images, figures and conceptual patterns to which the same coherence and binding force could accrue in the present as can be reconstructed – with all its colourfulness and multiversality – for the Vormärz proletariat.

Whenever there is talk of a 'return of the dangerous classes', it is hard *not* to think of gangster rap from a present cultural point of view: the threat to the official property order through the obscene display of an excessive desire for wealth with the simultaneous conspiratorial gesture of a mafia gang for those who have been left behind, the 'archaic' value systems and role models which, precisely in their deviant exaggeration, only reflect capitalist *business as usual*. And this association is reinforced by the fact that the 'dangerous classes' of the Vormärz were already recruited essentially from migrant and post-migrant sections of the population. But perhaps the parallel is too obvious; maybe it would be more interesting to look for the neo-proletarian imaginary of the present in those social and cultural experiences and inventions that initially still cling to the aspired or threatened status of their own (cultured) bourgeoisie, but are already imbued with the knowledge of the impending (or long since occurred) social decline: for instance, in the novels of Iain Levison or Thomas Melle.[39] Or in large parts of 'pop literature' since the 1990s, where the cynically or melancholically experienced 'transcendental homelessness' (Lukács) of the protagonists is repeatedly contrasted with the boring but supposedly still intact (welfare state) world of the parents' generation. That the ostentatious disorientation is not only generational or metaphysical, but possibly also due to all the 'made-up jobs' (according to the Hamburg punk band *Schneller Autos Organisation*) with which the protagonists struggle – and whether it is the job-

38 Frégier 1840a; 1840b.

39 Levison 2002; Levison 2003; Melle 2014; Melle 2016.

like nature of the jobs that is problematic, or rather their obviously made-up and superfluous status: this was and is rarely put up for discussion. Finally, one could think of a novel such as Jenny Erpenbeck's *Go, Went, Gone*, which envisions a world (*our* world) where meaning and social participation are only made available through gainful employment, but precisely this is withheld from ever larger parts of the population: the young and the old, the poor and the marginalised, and not least, the refugees of this world, who are at best sucked into the invisible realms of informal work and spat out again when demand dwindles.[40] Finally, it is worth recalling the radical manifesto *The Coming Insurrection*, which caused a furore in feuilletons and backrooms at the end of the noughties. The authors from the 'Invisible Committee' lament the fact that in the 'vague aggregate of social milieus, institutions, and individualized bubbles that is called, with a touch of *antiphrasis*, "society", … [t]here's no longer any language for common experience'. Without such a language, however, revolution is meaningless: 'we cannot share wealth if we do not share a language'.[41] The authors trust that 'struggles' will create this new language, but at the same time, and this is the really unique quality of the text, the 'Invisible Committee' creates such a language itself. If *The Coming Insurrection* has repeatedly (and rightly) been ascribed a special 'poetic' quality, this does not simply mean that the manifesto is 'nicely written'. Above all it signifies the creative work involved in producing imagery with which experiences can be articulated and around which militant collectives can come together. Along these tracks, one could look for lines of coherence for a contemporary poetry of class, one which could also encompass widely divergent cultural inventions and thus foreshadow the contours of a new, a different proletariat of the present.

The class – the 'class for itself' – 'constitutes itself' in struggle, Marx wrote, in the 'struggle of class against class'. The paradox that the goal of the process must already be presupposed can be solved by understanding the struggle of classes as a production process for *myths* of class. The dialectical transformation from 'class in itself' to 'class for itself' is one that takes place in struggle. Now, at the end of our investigation, it becomes clear once again and with new lucidity that this conversion can only be made if the class represents itself in a myth of itself – and also always threatens to lose itself in the various myths. The struggle of classes, especially in its mythopoetic dimension, is thus a solution *in practice* for problems that cannot be solved theoretically and logically in terms of representation.

---

40 Erpenbeck 2017.

41 Invisible Committee 2009, pp. 25–6.

The mythical creation and doubling of classes and their struggle affects not only the 'romantic' early forms, not only the marginal figures and deviants summarised above in the auxiliary term of an 'other', multiversal heterogeneous proletariat, but also the 'official', hegemonic working class and its movement. Weerth's Eduard, for instance, can be read as a veritable allegory of a purified, uniformed and homogenously steeled working class, perhaps even as a prefiguration of the 'socialist superman'. The heterodox 'other' tradition may have the advantage that its myths – the machine breakers and social bandits, for example – are less self-evident to us today. They seem more appealing, stranger, *more poetic* (in the sense of Eduard Gans). But even the class-conscious striking worker, who will at some point join the closed ranks of social democracy and communist parties – and whose annihilation in these ranks can already be sensed in his early Vormärz forms – has a poetry of his own. The labour struggle, the strike, is poetic because it is productive: the class is the production of its struggle, the struggle is the *poiesis* of the class, and the more contained the struggle, the purer the class formation that emerges.

Yet the labour struggle, *every* labour struggle, also bears traces of poetry because it causes an interruption of the ruling 'prose of circumstances'. The labour struggle is and remains poetic because, as an interruption, it harbours an element of unpredictability – no matter how rigidly the bureaucrats of the revolution in the established workers' parties and unions try to banish this element. In the final analysis, the strike, at least for the worker, is a struggle for life and death, for *he who does not work, shall not eat*.[42] Even if this struggle is increasingly regulated in history by 'social partnerships', there remains a virtually excessive moment in every strike which can always be released. Violence can break out on both sides. On the side of the strikers, divisions can emerge between those who play by the rules and those who suddenly see the rules as part of the problem; the strike can eventually expand and universalise, right up to the *unconditional proletarian general strike*, which ultimately leads to the death of the opponent, to the death of capital, since capital is nothing but accumulated dead labour, always dependent on living labour to reanimate it.[43] The unpredictability, the essentially incalculable element of the strike is also already reflected in Weerth, when Eduard has to admit that every strike can also end in the 'bitterest' defeat of the workers.[44] But the moment

42 Cf. Paul's 2nd epistle to the Thessalonians 3:10–11.

43 Cf. Roller 1905. On the poetry of the proletarian general strike, see Benjamin 2004. The poetological consequences of Benjamin's conception are drawn by Hamacher 1991.

44 Weerth 1976, p. 341.

is immediately recaptured in the unshakeable optimism of long foresight: *the struggles will accumulate, each new struggle builds on the experiences of the previous ones, in the end we must win.* For Weerth's Eduard, this confidence goes hand in hand with states of open 'enthusiasm'.[45] While the optimism of the workers' movement – its view of a liberated future, its expectation of a coming classless society – expresses an ideology of progress that mistakes itself as 'science', it also, however secretly, rides on the 'enthusiasm' of romantic anti-capitalism.[46]

45 Weerth 1976, p. 342.
46 Marx 1844, 'Contribution to the Critique of Hegel's Philosophy of Law', MECW 3, p. 184.

EPILOGUE

Romantic 'Anti-capitalism' from Above

Ludwig Tieck was not the only romantic to be suddenly and shockingly confronted with the social dislocations of capitalist modernity on a trip to England. The glimpse of 'factory towns', where the great 'mass of poor, stunted and lazy riff-raff' literally vegetate 'in the most tormenting dependence on their employer' threw not only Tieck's Leonhard off course. On 19 July 1826, Karl Friedrich Schinkel wrote to his wife Susanne from Liverpool about a well-known metropolis:

> England has been enlarged and embellished twofold and in many places three and fourfold in the last 50 years, as long as the machines have been running. This is an extraordinary phenomenon which must strike every attentive traveller. But the peak has also come and the speculation has become exaggerated. In Manchester, where we were yesterday, 400 new cotton mills have been built since the war, among them several buildings the size of the Royal Palace in Berlin, thousands of smoking obelisks of steam engines all around, whose height of 80 to 180 feet destroys all impression of the church towers. All these plants have produced such enormous masses of goods that the world is overflowing with them, 12,000 workers now rotting in the streets because they have no work, after the city has already sent 6,000 Irishmen back to their fatherland at its own expense. Other workers can only earn 2 shillings, about 15 groschen a week, for 16 hours' work a day. – One is very much in doubt as to what will become of this terrible state of affairs. – More of this in person. You see there are many interesting things to observe in this country.[1]

In the journal, he adds that the 12,000 unemployed workers thrown out onto the street were 'now coming together to revolutionise', whereas 'a lot of English military are being assembled for security': 'beautiful people, privates and officers, magnificent horses they ride'.[2]

Schinkel visited England together with his 'perhaps closest friend', Peter Beuth.[3] The two were travelling on state business; Beuth's office and function

1 Schinkel 1990, 'Brief an seine Frau Susanne, 19. 7. 1826', p. 187.
2 Schinkel 1990, *Tagebuch*, p. 160.
3 Trempler 2012, p. 177. See also Wolzogen 2016, Vol. 1, pp. 334–35 an pp. 337–8.

 | DOI:10.1163/9789004685536_011

shed light on the function of the trip. Initially a member of the State Council, Beuth was from 1819 director of the Technical Deputation for Trade and, from 1821, director of the Royal Technical Institute established according to his plans, which was renamed the Royal Trade Institute in 1827; this was later to become one of the nuclei of the Technical University of Berlin. Even as a young man, Beuth belonged to the 'Young Prussian network' that organised the implementation of the Prussian reforms behind the great figures of Barons Stein and Hardenberg. In 1809–10, he was particularly involved in drafting the freedom of trade as part of the 'closest circle of advisors around Hardenberg'.[4] In this circle he worked intensively with his friend, the jurist and historian Friedrich ('Fritz') von Raumer, who in turn was a close confidant of Ludwig Tieck. Beuth was also friends with the philosopher Karl Wilhelm Ferdinand Solger from his Berlin school and Halle student days, another Tieck intimate. Beuth got to know Schinkel at Solger's 'Friday Society' in Berlin, introducing him to Hardenberg in 1809.

Like many of the young Prussian elite, Beuth invoked the 'divine Smith' already as a student.[5] With Adam Smith in the hand, Prussia's economy and society was to be reformed, but under state control. Like many of his generation, Beuth was convinced that Smithian economic liberalism did not necessarily have to be linked to democracy – as the functionaries of the Chinese economic miracle still know or at least practise today (as shown by Giovanni Arrighi in his *Adam Smith in Beijing*).[6] Like Smith, however, Beuth and his colleagues also know that 'long-protected conditions should not be suddenly exposed to the open air': even the organisers and propagandists of free trade – and not just its critics – were aware of the need to first protect 'free trade' to then be able to slowly expand it. *Freedom of trade demands promotion of trade* – this sums up Beuth's credo, and just as he became the 'instructor of a working nation', Schinkel became its architect.[7]

For Beuth, promoting trade and commerce means first and foremost *education* [*Bildung*]: industrial training, the collection, organisation and improvement of design and production knowledge, the development of machines, the import and synthesis of scattered knowledge. Beuth's institute provides its

4 Wolzogen 2016, pp. 336–7.

5 Thus wrote Beuth's patron Ludwig von Vincke, quoted in Wolzogen 2016, p. 339 Even later in 1823, he will make a pilgrimage to the grave of the revered economist in Glasgow during a trip to Scotland, cf. Wolzogen 2016, p. 352.

6 Arrighi 2007.

7 Wolzogen 2016, p. 241 and p. 338. I was unable to find a source for the honorary title 'Vater der preussischen Gewerbeförderung' [Father of the Prussian Promotion of Trade], which is cited in many places but not verified anywhere.

few students, who are selected strictly on the basis of their qualifications and not their origins, with 'laboratories, workshops and, above all, contact with domestic and foreign masters of the profession'.[8] The functional elite of the soon to be expanding Prussian economy are recruited from the students. In 1844, the later 'railway king' August Borsig, graduate of the Trade Institute and pioneer of Prussian mechanical engineering, christened the first locomotive to be completely designed and built in Prussia under the name 'Beuth'.[9]

The training at the Institute was flanked by social organisational work. Out of loose, informal meetings, Beuth suggests the institutionalisation of an 'Association for the Promotion of Trade and Industry', in which 'factory owners, master craftsmen, pharmacists … men of means, landowners, bankers, art dealers, artists, ministers, privy and state councillors' come together; the heterogeneous composition of the association underscores that what matters here are only the aims, not any presupposed socio-cultural identities.[10] The trade association only seeks to promote trade and in this circular definition of itself can take no account of political prejudices or class conceits. Of all things, it takes seriously the romantic ideals of free association and turns them upside down on their economic feet.[11] In the association, Schinkel was 'head of department III for architecture and the fine arts'.[12]

Where contacts with foreign specialists do not come about of their own accord, Beuth or his students have to actively gather information, to 'acquire know-how'. On regular 'technological trips' to France and above all Great Britain, which are firmly institutionalised in the curriculum as a kind of internship abroad, they learn about the state of the development of the productive forces. They are shown workshops, factories and machines, department stores and market halls, as well as infrastructure projects like bridges and canals; they eagerly take notes and make drawings – if not directly on site, then in their rooms that evening. The whole thing goes back to Berlin in diplomatic mail or baggage. In addition, Beuth directly acquires machines and production equipment, which he disassembles and sends to Prussia in order to circumvent export bans and customs duties. Bribes were most certainly paid.[13] While it is

8 Wolzogen 2016, p. 346.

9 On Beuth's activity as a trade promoter, see Geheimes Staatsarchiv/Preussischer Kulturbesitz 2014.

10 Wolzogen 2016, p. 347.

11 The fact that Beuth and Schinkel were also members of Achim von Arnim's and Adam Müller's *Deutscher Tischgesellschafti* [*German Table Society*] shows once again how progressive liberal attitudes and antisemitic exclusion could go together in Prussia at the time.

12 Rottau 2012, p. 227.

13 Cf. Wahren 2016, pp. 34–5. and pp. 39–40.

too simple to place the Institute's entire travel activities 'under the general suspicion of industrial espionage', Schinkel and Beuth's trip to France and Great Britain in 1826 was not completely innocent of this.[14]

Schinkel accompanied his friend as more than just an experienced draughtsman, a skill not entirely unimportant.[15] Beuth had already written to Schinkel from Manchester during his trip to England in 1823 that it was possible to gain important and necessary experience in England, especially as a contemporary architect and designer concerned with keeping up with the times. He reported on the 'wonders of the new age':

> The machines and their buildings, called factories. Such a box is eight or nine storeys high, sometimes forty windows long and usually four windows deep. Each floor is twelve feet high; all are vaulted, with nine feet span the whole length. The columns are iron. The beam that lies on it too, with side walls and surrounding walls like map sheets, not two and a half feet thick on the second floor.[16]

During his trip to England, Schinkel was driven by the question of how to build the new 'factories' – soon to be erected *en masse* in Prussia on Beuth's initiative – in such a way that they were not merely 'boxes'. More precisely, how to build these 'boxes', once they had become historically necessary, so that they could develop their own, contemporary poetry? For Schinkel, the ultimate task of all architecture, including modern functional buildings, is to convey 'the historical and the poetic'.[17] The buildings which manifest Schinkel's English experience most clearly, this much can be anticipated, are the *Bauakademie* on *Werderscher Markt* – itself a 'box', albeit with a carefully designed rhythmic façade – and the annex to Beuth's Trade Institute in *Klosterstrasse*: the first building in Berlin to have a 'skeleton construction with cast-iron supports made from Prussian manufacture' and a curtain façade.[18]

In addition to these inspirations, Schninkel also brings back with him an artistic revulsion towards the English factory towns, whose descriptions clearly

14 Wolzogen 2016, p. 349.

15 'Baron von Stein brough a "landscape painter" with him on his trip to England in 1787, but he spent a conspicuously long time at factories' (Wolzogen 2016, p. 349).

16 Beuth to Schinkel, quoted in Schulz 2012, pp. 105–6.

17 Thus said Schinkel in 1835 on the occasion of the designs for a prince's residence, quoted in Philipp 2012, p. 23.

18 Schulz 2012, p. 110. The building was destroyed in the Second World War and can only be seen in Eduard Gärtner's painting *Die Klosterstrasse* from 1830 in the Alte Nationalgalerie. On the Bauakademie, cf. Wahren 2016, p. 28.

resonate with the social aesthetic laments of Tieck's Leonhard: 'It makes a terribly uncanny impression: enormous masses of buildings by only master workmen, without architecture and for the barest needs alone, made of red brick', he noted in his diary in Manchester.[19] A poetry of building that would meet the purposes and needs of the new age without stripping it of all artistic aspirations – if only such a poetry could be found, one could add with Leonhard, the lives of the people who have to live and work in the new buildings and with the new products would not be reduced to 'bare life'.[20]

The search for a poetry of industrial modernity culminates in a watercolour that Schinkel gave to his friend Beuth in 1837 and which, as a result of a perhaps false, or at least hasty, description of the picture by the recipient himself, has survived under the title *Beuth, Riding on Pegasus* – hasty, because the naked figure in rear view, which Beuth claims to be a representation of himself ('I float on the Pegasus above a factory town I built'), turns out on closer inspection to be at least ambiguous in gender. The upswept blond hair, the earrings and the bosom at any rate suggest a disjunction between the allegory and its personal model.[21]

Be that as it may, it is not only the figure's gender that remains ambiguous in the picture. For the figure, which must be read as an allegory of poetic imagination and poetic inspiration through the Pegasus on which it rides, also blows soap bubbles.[22] Here is an attribute of a fantasy run riot, producing merely colourful appearances which spawn soap bubbles that must always burst – this is one way of reading the enigmatic inscription intended for intimate communication between friends. On 'Ischia', according to the second soap bubble from the left, Beuth planned to build a villa, but nothing ever came of it.[23] Moreover, the allegory hovers not only over a 'factory town' and an 'industrial landscape', but also and above all over Beuth's own study, which is shown as a 'fictitious insertion' at the bottom of the picture, wrapped in a wreath of smoke.[24] In this study, which appears even greyer than the smoky factory town itself, files are stacked on top of each other and labelled as such: *Acta Gewerbeverein* [*Proceedings of the Trade Institute*]. The dream of a planned industrialisation portrayed in Schinkel's allegory, in which economic growth

19 Schinkel 1990, p. 160.
20 Cf. Tieck 1988b, p. 62.
21 Cf. Schulze Altcappenberg 2012, p. 205.
22 On the motif of the Pegasus in Schinkel's work, see Trempler 2007, starting at p. 84. On the connection between Pegasus and fame, cf. Brink 2011, pp. 287–8.
23 The other bubbles are labelled '7000000 Eink.', 'Araber' and 'Min. Gloria', cf. Schulze Altcappenberg 2012, pp. 205, 210.
24 Schulze Altcappenberg 2012, p. 205.

(every chimney smoking, a canal thick with traffic) can be combined with generous spatial design (the entire city densely greened under the clouds of smoke, the factory complex in the right foreground resembling a villa or a palace with a rectangular courtyard), the great dream of a planned, socially ordered and aesthetically designed modernisation springs first and foremost from hard bureaucratic work; but the dream could always turn out to be hot air, a mere soap bubble.

On the one hand, the allegorical enigma of the iconography – which becomes even more pronounced when one adds the other paintings Schinkel gave to Beuth – is certainly due to a friendly irony that reassures the other's self-esteem precisely by not taking him and his plans too seriously. On the other hand, however, Schinkel also acknowledges that the joint political-aesthetic project moves historically in a still open, perhaps even groundless space, where success and failure remain still up in the air. England (the dreamt-up scenery resembles the landscape of northern England) serves not merely as a guide in this context. For Schinkel, the revolting English workers loom as a threat behind all lofty plans, even if they are only rarely mentioned as openly as in the quoted letter to his wife.

With their English experience, the Beuth/Schinkel duo seeks and finds solutions to all the problems that the romantic Leonhard/Tieck associated with the freedom of trade. The interplay between the Trade Institute and the Trade Association largely covers the tasks that realistic nostalgists like Tieck or Rau assigned to the guilds, especially in training the young craftsmen and tradesmen: old knowledge is collected, tested and transferred, new knowledge is acquired and innovations promoted. Projects that go beyond the horizon of individual companies are socially anchored in the association, in the interaction of the various political, economic and cultural actors. And all of this is to be done without the smell of corruption or the securing of a sinecure – 'quality and transparency' were Beuth's key demands.[25] Thus, one of the central projects of the new association is the publication of a journal in which lectures and discussions are documented and continued: *Negotiations of the Association for the Promotion of Trade and Industry in Prussia*. The first issue of the journal reproduces Beuth's inaugural address to the association on 15 January 1821. Here Beuth emphasises the demand for transparency by offensively invoking the old prejudices against the guild system and thus shooing his new association brothers out of their comfort zone, as one would say today: '*The time of comfort*, where prices and quality could be made to one's liking, is over; the time of

25 Wolzogen 2016, p. 346.

hardship has come, and forces one to replace those lost advantages in a natural and modern way. *One lives no longer so easily, but equally as safe*; it is the time of *effort*'.[26]

The new era is still a 'time of hardship' – Beuth and Leonhard agree on that. Yet Beuth would emphasise that hardship is *necessary* to finally be able to live 'safely' in a 'natural and modern' way, and that means, *always* modern, moving forward with the times.

Schinkel's contribution to overcoming the hardship that even Beuth sees approaching, at least temporarily, with the freedom of trade lies largely in the politics of taste and affect that Leonhard so meticulously illuminates. Leonhard saw, particularly in the design of functional and consumer products, a 'tastelessness' at work, spreading 'from England', 'a kind of Puritanism that regards all ornament, everything not strictly necessary, as heresy' (JTM, p. 60). Leonhard, in contrast, put forward his theory of the 'necessary ornament' that must be given to 'bare life' as 'decorative dressing' in order to make life truly human and worth living.[27] Schinkel would agree with the critical diagnosis of the problem just as much as he would support the general orientation of the solution: in both views, 'poetry' stands for that 'necessary ornament', which, precisely because of its necessity, must always be something more, something different than mere ornamentation. Whereas Tieck's Leonhard as a master carpenter must insist on the individuality of the craftsmen's solution which, in the end, always relies on his deeply individual idiosyncrasies, Schinkel, both as an architect and a planner responsible for cultural policy, takes a different path. Even with individual signature buildings such as the *Friedrichswerder Church* or the *Bauakademie*, he opts for the use of prefabricated elements; ultimately, Schinkel's solutions are based on seriality.[28]

The contrast becomes even more clear when Schinkel, together with Beuth, moves into Leonhard's very own domain: the design of furniture. Leonhard feels particularly incensed about the 'square, jagged' furniture that he as a cabinetmaker now has to produce for the English taste of the time, and which seems to him like 'complete barbarism': the 'sadly monotonous and dark mahogany wood', everything 'hard, austere and artless'. Especially enraging to Leonhard are the 'extremely uncomfortable daybeds that I now have to make,

26 Quoted in Wolzogen 2016, p. 347.

27 Cf. the section 'Political Passions, Aesthetic Taste' in the first chapter of the present study.

28 For example, the designs for the unrealised department store, 'Unter den Linden', cf. Schulz 2012, pp. 111–12. The continuity between Schinkel and Neues Bauen [New Building], especially in Mies van der Rohe, was highlighted early on by Posener 1972.

which always look unfinished, and even more so by the secretaire, as they are called, or writing bureaus' (JTM, p. 60).[29] Schinkel would also agree that all the everyday things we use – from architecture to furniture – always seem 'dull' when design is dispensed with altogether. Yet, for all the closeness of the criticism, Leonhard's description of the detested English 'movables' (JTM, p. 59) remains not so distant from Schinkel's own concrete furniture designs. The graphic table, for instance, which he designed for Beuth's official flat in *Klosterstrasse*, and which can be seen in a portrait Schinkel made of Beuth in his flat in 1838, looks exactly like that – stark, 'hard, austere', even 'artless'.[30]

More important for the comparison of Tieck's Leonhard and Schinkel, however, is that for the latter, although furniture (like all everyday products) should be designed, this design should no longer be in the hands of individual artist-craftsmen, but rather can be taken over and finished by specialists. In other words: the poetry of an object shall indeed be developed individually out of its function, but no longer by individual artists, rather from the combination of design specialists and executive workers. This new, extremely modern conception of the design and manufacturing process appears most clearly in a book project that Schinkel published together with Beuth on behalf of the Royal Technical Deputation for Trades in two instalments in 1830 and 1837: *Models for Manufacturers and Craftsmen*. In these books, Schinkel and Beuth briefly introduce the basic concepts of design, and then provide concrete templates for designing buildings, furniture, textiles, durables and even machines, with detailed descriptions and numerous extremely high-quality copper plates. Beuth does not leave his readers in the dark about the aim of the enterprise, and he meets them where they are qua profession and function – at commercial interest:

> Just as the higher quality of goods in general at the same price secures sales, so does that part of them arising from the form and giving the goods their higher allure affects them to a higher degree. Whoever produces the most efficient and at the same time the most beautiful goods can count on a secure and lasting sale, no matter how much the buyer's ignorance, fashion and crudeness may influence the choice of purchase.[31]

---

29 The reference to office furniture in particular is certainly not coincidental, because the fashion for furniture spreading from England accompanied an economy in which paperwork at the desk played an increasingly important role.

30 See the illustration in Schulze Altcappenberg 2012, p. 204, description on p. 207; Kupferstichkabinett SMB, SM 54.11. On Schinkel's furniture designs, see Kropmanns 2012.

31 Königlich-technischen Deputation für Gewerbe 1830, 'Vorwort', signed by Beuth, p. iv.

The programme of a general improvement of taste in the spirit of promoting commerce suggested by the models was by no means one of those soap bubbles with which Schinkel gently teased Beuth in the Pegasus allegory. The volumes of *Models*, which repeatedly makes reference to English designs, were a complete success; they 'shaped the products of Prussian manufacturers and factories for decades, exactly in line with Beuth's claim to combine practicality and beauty'.[32] But with the serial production of beauty – and not with the complete artlessness of functional objects, for which design plays no part – Leonhard's individual craftsmanship is finally put to an end. For if mass-produced items are just as good and just as beautiful as what Leonhard and his peers can offer, only cheaper, then the market and the consumer will have always already decided. And when the editors stress that the models are to be used only for 'faithful imitation and copying', and by no means should be independently 'developed', they express an enormous distrust of the taste of craftsmen like Leonhard:[33]

> The appropriate application to our needs, as well as that of all ornaments, can only be the result of study, criticism and one's own talent; it belongs to the realm of art, just as does the creation of those models that have emerged freely from the inner life of the artist. The manufacturer, the craftsman as such, should make no claims to this, but merely limit himself to acquiring that education and skill necessary to grasp the spirit of the models given him and to imitate and execute them in this spirit to the best of his ability. If the craftsmen have often left this path, if those who have acquired some knowledge and skills in the schools of craftsmanship believed themselves called upon to apply them to their own compositions: this has produced nothing pleasant, but rather something more vulgar and abhorrent than if that knowledge had remained foreign to them.[34]

Tieck's and Schinkel/Beuth's similar sounding critique of the 'tastelessness' of the time as well as their shared idea about the necessary poetic dressing of everyday objects lead, however, to completely opposite conclusions in social political terms – with regard to the position of craftsmen, for example. Where Tieck's Leonhard upholds the ideal of a unified form of life for craftsmen, Beuth's and Schinkel's project suspends this ideal almost programmatic-

32 Wahren 2106, p. 29.
33 Trempler 2007, p. 177.
34 Königlich-technischen Deputation für Gewerbe 1830, p. v.

ally: craftsmen become 'hands', executive organs. For Beuth and Schinkel the emphasis on the craftsman's universal education by Weitling and his ilk, as well as the claim to an all-round development of individuality, means nothing. The two Prussian civil servant-artists even radically oppose the radical *poetry of class*, as it develops alongside the emerging journeyman-worker movement at the same time (accompanied and prepared by Tieck), by denying the craftsmen any further claim to education and self-development from the outset. Poetry and class are to remain separate things from now on, and the more the demands of the class are met in other areas, the more vehemently the Prussian state advocates this separation.

The 'time of hardship' which Beuth mentions in his inaugural address of the trade association was naturally very different for master craftsmen and manufacturers on the one hand, and journeymen and workers on the other. Since the introduction of the freedom of trade, pauperism afflicted large sections of the old crafts as well as those employed in the hitherto state-protected manufacturing sector in Prussia, and yet it only appears in passing, if at all, in Beuth's and Schinkel's work. Nevertheless, the state, the king and his officials did not remain idle here. In the 1820s, King Frederick William III ordered the construction of two huge churches for the poor in order to counteract the spiritual and moral neglect rampant in the newly emerging slums in the north of Berlin, by *Hamburger Tor*, *Oranienburger Tor* and *Rosenthaler Tor*. The contract was awarded to Schinkel, who convinced the king that four smaller churches would serve the purpose better. Finally, in the 1830s, interrupted by the great cholera epidemic of 1832, which hit these slums particularly hard, the 'suburban churches' of St. Elisabeth (*Invalidenstrasse*), Nazareth (*Wedding*), St. Johannis (*Moabit*) and St. Paul (*Gesundbrunnen*) were built.

In the 1830s and 1840s, numerous philanthropic initiatives were devoted to the slums of *Neu-Vogtland* (so called because of the numerous poor migrants from the central German *Vogtland*) and *Feuerland* (named after the blast furnaces of the new Borsig works, which never went out, even at night). Bettina von Arnim's *Armenbuch* [*Book of the Poor*], for example, which planned on combining statistical surveys and poetic narratives, bears literary historical significance here.[35] Von Arnim's first socially critical book of 1843, *Dies Buch gehört dem König* [*This Book Belongs to the King*], already confesses in the dedicatory formula of the title (though not in its complicated literary facture) the

35 Bettina von Arnim never completed the *Armenbuch*, probably because, after the Silesian weavers' revolt, publication would have been censored. A reliable edition is offered in Arnim 1995, pp. 369–555 and pp. 1047–1150.

actual addressee of her social commitment; the last part of the *Königsbuch*, entitled 'Experiences of a Young Swiss in the *Vogtland*', gathers reports by the Swiss teacher Heinrich Grunholzer from this very Berlin slum.[36] Von Arnim's romantic concern for the poor, which cares not only for the material but above all the spiritual and moral needs of the poor, seems not so distant from the initiatives of Wilhelm Weitling. In contrast to Weitling and his comrades, however, who rely purely on the self-activity of the working classes, the romantic von Arnim addressed the state directly, or more precisely, romantically: to the king as the shepherd and father of his people. Similarly, Lorenz von Stein, after his experiences with *Geschichte der sozialen Bewegung in Frankreich von 1789 bis auf unsere Tage* [*Socialism and Communism in Modern-Day France*], recommends in his widely read writings of the 1840s and 1850s a 'kingship of social reform' to prevent the spread of socialism and communism in Germany.[37] Franz von Baader too, whose 1835 memorandum *Über das dermalige Missverhältnis der Vermögenslosen oder Proletairs zu den Vermögen besitzenden Klassen der Sozietät* [*On the Present Disproportion of the Propertyless or Proletairs to the Property-owning Classes*] recommends above all the establishment of a social 'diaconate' that gives the 'proletairs' a voice and representation through priests for the poor.[38] The quintessence of romantic social welfare lies in the politics of affect: it is about restoring and deepening an emotional attachment of the 'people' to 'their' king and thus to 'their' state.

Schinkel participated in this romantic-affective social policy in many ways: as a city planner able to observe the disastrous consequences of the absence of any planning in England in times of wild urbanisation; as an architect of pastoral architecture, represented by the suburban churches; but also as an architect of prestigious royal buildings such as *Stolzenfels* Castle near Koblenz; or with his expert opinions on the completion of Cologne Cathedral, which was to create and strengthen a 'bond between the people and the monarchy', especially among the predominantly Catholic population of the recently annexed Rhineland.[39]

The social reformist project of a romantic politics of affect was often ridiculed even in the Vormärz: in Moses Hess's review of Lorenz von Stein in Herwegh's *Twenty-One Sheets from Switzerland*, in Otto Lüning's ironic Arnim contrafactum *This Book Belongs to the People*, in Engels' jibes against Franz von Baader's 'somnambulistic mysticism and unphilosophy' or in Ferdinand

36 Arnim 1995, pp. 329–368 and the commentary pp. 1039–46.

37 Stein 1921, Vol. 3, p. 41.

38 Baader 1957, p. 241.

39 Werquet 2012.

Freiligrath's poem 'From Below Up!', where a 'proletarian machinist' curses the king and queen from the engine room of a Rhine steamship, which he himself sails towards *Stolzenfels*.[40] Perhaps this mockery was too easy. For the romantic politics of affect in particular has proved to be astonishingly long-lasting and strong; without this affective side, the successful model of the Prussian welfare state, whose foundations were laid in the Vormärz and the Revolution, might never have existed.

The inclusive universalism of *subversive* romantic anti-capitalism always addressed itself 'to everyone'. From the outset, the *official* romantic double of promoting commerce and social welfare was addressed to the king, to the authorities, to the state. The welfare state as it developed in the course of the century would have been unthinkable without this Prussian, authoritarian foundation. By addressing the state, however, the promised material and cultural security of the 'people' was limited to its *subjects*: the 'social policy' programmes that emerged in the 1840s all aimed at a national domestication of the proletariat – in the figurative as well as literal sense of housing policy. From now on, there are to be no more 'journeymen without a homeland', no more 'homeless class', but only 'German workers'; the 'journeymen without a homeland', who, of course, continue to exist, are marginalised and excluded ideologically as well as materially as they fall out of state care.[41] The process of national enclosure is prepared and accompanied by the metropolitan class compromise, as drafted at the end of Ernst Willkomm's novel *White Slaves*: the erosion of solidarity with those now excluded – the plantation slaves of the Global South, as well as women, wanderers and vagrants – is rewarded to the now cherished (national, 'free', male) working class with a bigger piece of the growing economic pie. The economic nationalism of the working class is the nail in the coffin of the motley proletariat whose story this book has told. And in the 'cleansing' of this class, all the reactionary and regressive varieties of romantic anti-capitalism come into play, which I deliberately put aside in my study, precisely because this is all too often ideologically equated with the former. Where the working class is already addressed as 'the people', it soon no longer sees itself as a 'lower folk' – as a 'people in blouses, jackets, smocks and caps' (Weitling) – but above all as a 'national people' and soon all too often as a 'national race'. Moses Hess, one of the heroes of our story, learned the consequences of the rampant antisemitism in the workers'

40 Hess 2004; Lüning 1845–7; Engels 1842, 'Alexander Jung', MECW 2, p. 296; Freiligrath 1980, pp. 88–90; Freiligrath 1846; the poem 'From Below Up! [*Von Unten Auf!*]' is part of the 1846 cycle Ça *ira!*

41 Cf. Riehl 1861.

movement of the 1850s and 1860s, and even left the movement (temporarily) to write *Rome and Jerusalem*, one of the founding documents of Zionism.[42]

With the exclusion of its heterogeneous, insubordinate elements, and the uniformisation of the working class, the now national workers' movement gains political clout and, in the course of the nineteenth and twentieth centuries, fights for a hitherto unimaginable improvement in real living conditions. As Étienne Balibar points out, 'for roughly a hundred years, the labour movement, on the one hand, and the bourgeois state, on the other, had, relatively speaking, unified a national bourgeoisie and proletariat', and these two internally homogeneous blocks have in turn entered into a long-lasting strategic partnership, a national class compromise.[43]

Even this class compromise has never been a bed of roses for the incorporated national working class. The society arched over by the national welfare state remains a class society. Compulsion – the generalised (though still class-specific) compulsion to sell one's labour power as well as the always preceding '*coercive* implementation of the fiction that labour power *is* a commodity' – remains at the core of all social policy (and all promotion of commerce as well).[44] To cushion this, to make it tolerable in the first place – that is the purpose of the affective *surplus* which all romantic social policy aims to provide.

Based on this, we should finally ask about the *poetry of the welfare state* that inherits and continues our *poetry of class*: what is the political imaginary of a social formation that must presuppose a comprehensive integration of all classes and a harmonious, 'social partnership' containment of class struggle, but which can never and must never completely achieve this integration, because otherwise it would deprive itself of its own commercial basis? And with regard to the poetry of the working class whose integration in the national welfare state is claimed everywhere: what self-narrative does it use to 'manage' the 'cognitive dissonance' of the fact that it is both *inside* and *outside* the social whole?[45] It is so far inside that it presupposes an identification of its own interests with the national interest and defends this interest against any (supposed) onslaught from outside. But it is so far outside that its own (individual

42 Hess 1918; Weiss, 2015, pp. 170–184; see also the first three contributions in Heid and Paucker 1992 by Herzig (pp. 1–18) Grab (pp. 19–34) and Brumlik (pp. 35–42).

43 Balibar 1991, p. 180.

44 Offe 1985, p. 55. On the history of the welfare state as a history of compulsory work and the sorting out of those unable or unwilling to work, see Lapinski 1928; Karlsruher Stadtzeitung 1985; Gruppe Blauer Montag 2008.

45 On the narrative 'management of cognitive dissonance', Koschorke 2018, pp. 155–9.

as well as collective) experience of persistent 'wage slavery' can hardly ever be addressed: namely, the experience of a stolen lifetime, given up for a job that may sometimes be physically easier than in Weitling's time (and even that is not always true), but has by no means become less dull and humiliating.[46]

But that would be another story. Or, in any case, a different conclusion and a different continuation of our story – linked and intertwined with this one just as the *other*, dissident workers' movement, whose twists, turns and return I have recounted in the concluding chapter of this study, is linked and intertwined with the *official* workers' movement of national class compromise. This latter story, which has been told to us for so long as one final, irreversible triumph, has completely unravelled and come to an end before our eyes. What matters is to reweave the threads – or bravely cut them once and for all.

46 The empathetic description of the everyday work of one's own mother is one of the most authentic but least discussed passages in Eribon 2013, pp. 86–87: 'A worker's body, as it ages, reveals to anyone who looks it the truth about the existence of classes'.

Bibliography

Sources and Primary Literature

Aristotle 2017 [335 BCE], *Politics*, translated by C.D.C. Reeve, Indianapolis: Hackett.

Arnim, Bettine von 1995, *Werke und Briefe*, Volume 3, *Politische Schriften*, edited by Wolfgang Bunzel et al., Frankfurt: Deutscher Klassiker.

Auerbach, Berthold 2014 [1846], *Schrift und Volk. Grundzüge der volksthümlichen Literatur, angeschlossen an eine Charakteristik J.P. Hebel's*, in *Schriften zur Literatur*, edited by Marcus Twellmann, Göttingen: Wallstein, 7–173.

Aveling, Edward and Eleanor Aveling-Marx 1888, 'Shelley and Socialism', *To-Day*, April 1888, 103–16.

Baader, Franz von 1957 [1835], 'Über das dermalige Missverhältnis der Vermögenslosen oder Proletairs zu den Vermögen besitzenden Klassen der Sozietät in betreff ihres Auskommens, sowohl in materieller Hinsicht, aus dem Standpunkte des Rechts betrachtet', in *Gesellschaftslehre*, Munich: Kösel, 235–50.

Ball, Hugo 2014 [1918], *Flametti or On the Dandysm of the Poor*, Cambridge: Wakefield Press.

Beck, Karl 1846, *Lieder vom armen Mann with a preface to the House of Rothschild*, Leipzig: Bernhard Hermann.

Bensen, Heinrich Wilhelm 1847, *Die Proletarier. Eine historische Denkschrift*, Stuttgart: Franckh'schen Buchhandlung.

Binfield, Kevin (ed.) 2004, *Writings of the Luddites*, Baltimore: Johns Hopkins University Press.

Blake, William 1988, *Milton: a Poem in 2 Books*, in *The Complete Poetry and Prose of William Blake*, edited by Davis V. Erdman, New York: Anchor, 95–144.

Bluntschli, Johann Caspar 1843, *Die Kommunisten in der Schweiz nach den bei Weitling vorgefundenen Papieren*, Zürich: Orell, Füssli und Co.

Börne, Ludwig 1986 [1832–1834], *Briefe aus Paris*, Wiesbaden: Fourier.

Brontë, Charlotte 2007 [1849], *Shirley*, Oxford: Oxford World Classics.

Büchner, Georg 2000–2013, *Sämtliche Werke und Schriften. Historisch-kritische Ausgabe mit Quellendokumentation und Kommentar*, edited by Burghard Dedner and Thomas Michael Mayer, Darmstadt: Wissenschaftliche Buchgesellschaft [MBA].

Büchner, Georg 1993, *Complete Plays*, London: Penguin.

Buonarroti, Philippe 1836 [1828], *Buonarroti's history of Babeuf's conspiracy for equality*, London: H. Hetherington.

Carlyle, Thomas 1840, *Chartism*, London: James Fraser.

Carlyle, Thomas 2005 [1843], *Past and Present*, Berkeley: University of California Press.

Dallas, Alexander Robert Charles 1824, *Recollections of the life of Lord Byron, from the year 1808 to the end of 1814, exhibiting his early character and opinions, detailing *the progress of his literary career, and including various unpublished passages of his works. Taken from authentic documents, in the possession of the author*, London: Charles Knight.

Defoe, Daniel 2007 [1719], *Robinson Crusoe*, Oxford: Oxford University Press.

[Dickens, Charles] 1995 [1836], *Sketches by Boz*, London: Penguin.

Disraeli, Benjamin 1998 [1845], *Sybil or The Two Nations*, Oxford: Oxford University Press.

Dronke, Ernst 1981 [1846], *Aus dem Volk & Polizeigeschichten. Frühsozialistische Novellen 1846*, edited by Bodo Rollka, Cologne: C.W. Leske.

Dronke, Ernst 1987 [1846], *Berlin*, edited by Rainer Nitsche, Berlin: Rütten und Loening.

Eribon, Didier 2013 [2009], *Returning to Reims*, Los Angeles: Semiotext(e).

Erpenbeck, Jenny 2017 [2015], *Go, Went, Gone*, Cambridge: New Directions.

Frégier, Honoré Antoine 1840a, *Des classes dangereuses de la population dans les grandes villes, et des moyens de les rendre meilleures*, Paris: Baillière.

Frégier, Honoré-Antoine 1840b, *Über die gefährlichen Classen der Bevölkerung in den grossen Städten und die Mittel, sie zu bessern*, 2 Volumes, Coblenz: Hergt.

Freiligrath, Ferdinand 1980, *Ferdinand Freiligraths Werke in einem Band*, edited by Werner Ilberg, 4th edition, Berlin/Weimar: Aufbau.

Freiligrath, Ferdinand 1846, 'From Below Up!', available at: https://allpoetry.com/Von-Unten-Auf!

Gans, Eduard 1995 [1836], *Rückblicke auf Personen und Zustände*, edited by Norbert Waszek, Stuttgart-Bad Cannstadt: frommann-holzboog.

Grimm, Jacob 1819, *Deutsche Grammatik*, Volume 1, Göttingen: Dieterichsche Buchhandlung.

Gutzkow, Karl 1986 [1850], 'Der Roman des Nebeneinander', in Gerhard Plumpe (ed.), *Theorie des bürgerlichen Realismus*, Stuttgart: Reclam, 211–12.

Harrington, James 1992 [1656], *The Commonwealth of Oceana and A System of Politics*, edited by John G.A. Pocock, Cambridge: Cambridge University Press.

Hegel, Georg Wilhelm Friedrich 2005 [1821/1822], *Die Philosophie des Rechts. Vorlesung von 1821/22*, edited by Hansgeorg Hoppe, Frankfurt: Suhrkamp.

Hegel, Georg Wilhelm Friedrich 1991 [1820], *Elements of the Philosophy of Right*, Cambridge: Cambridge University Press.

Hegel, Georg Wilhelm Friedrich 1975 [1835], *Lectures on Aesthetics*, Volume II, Oxford: Clarendon Press.

Heine, Heinrich 1976 [1831–7], *Sämtliche Schriften in zwölf Bänden*, edited by Klaus Briegleb, München/Wien: Hanser.

Herwegh, Georg 1886, 'Bundeslied für den Allgemeinen deutschen Arbeiterverein', in: [Rudolf Lavant], *Vorwärts. Eine Sammlung von Gedichten für das arbeitende Volk*, Zürich: Verlag der Volksbuchhandlung in Hottingen, 472–473.

Hess, Moses 1845, 'Ueber die Noth in unserer Gesellschaft und deren Abhülfe', in: Hermann Püttmann (ed.), *Deutsches Bürgerbuch für 1845*, Darmstadt: C.W. Leske, 22–48.

Hess, Moses (ed.) 1845/1846, *Gesellschaftsspiegel. Organ zur Vertretung der besitzlosen Volksklassen und zur Beleuchtung der gesellschaftlichen Zustände der Gegenwart*, Elberfeld: Bädeker.

Hess, Moses 1918 [1862], *Rome and Jerusalem: A Study of Jewish Nationalism*, New York: Bloch Publishing Company.

Hess, Moses 1959, *Briefwechsel*, edited by Edmund Silberer, s'Gravenhage: Mouton and Co.

Hess, Moses 1961, *Philosophische und sozialistische Schriften 1837–1850. Eine Auswahl*, edited by Auguste Cornu and Wolfgang Mönke, Berlin: Akademie.

Hess, Moses 1845, 'On the Essence of Money', *Rheinische Jarhrbücher zur gesellschaftlichen Reform*, Darmstadt: C.W. Leske (available at https://www.marxists.org/archive/hess/1845/essence-money.htm)

Hess, Moses 2004 [1843] 'Socialism and Communism' in: Hess, Moses, *The Holy History of Mankind and Other Writings*, edited by Shlomo Avineri, Cambridge: Cambridge University Press, 97–115.

Der Hülferuf der deutschen Jugend. Herausgegeben und redigirt von einigen deutschen Arbeitern 1841, Bern, September–November 1841.

Hundt, Martin (ed.) 2010, *Der Redaktionsbriefwechsel der Hallischen, Deutschen und Deutsch-Französischen Jahrbücher (1837–1844)*, 3 Volumes, Berlin: Akademie.

Instituten für Marxismus-Leninismus beim ZK der SED und beim ZK der KPdSU (eds.) 1970, *Der Bund der Kommunisten*, Dokumente und Materialien, Volume 1: 1836–1849, Berlin: Dietz Verlag.

Institute of Marxism-Leninism of the C.C., C.P.S.U. 1958, *Reminiscences of Marx and Engels*, Moscow: Foreign Languages Publishing House.

Jantke, Carl and Dietrich Hilger (eds.) 1965, *Die Eigentumslosen. Der deutsche Pauperismus und die Emanzipationskrise in Darstellungen und Deutungen der zeitgenössischen Literatur*, Freiburg/Munich: Karl Alber.

Die junge Generation 1842/1843, [Geneva] January 1842–May 1843.

Kant, Immanuel 2007 [1798], *Anthropology from a pragmatic point of view* in *Anthropology, History, and Education*, edited by Günter Zöller and Robert B. Louden, Cambridge: Cambridge University Press, 227–429.

Königlich-technischen Deputation für Gewerbe (eds.) 1830, *Vorbilder für Fabrikanten und Handwerker*, Berlin: August Persch.

Köpke, Rudolf 1855, *Ludwig Tieck. Erinnerungen aus dem Leben des Dichters nach dessen mündlichen und schriftlichen Mitteilungen*, 2 Volumes, Leipzig: Brockhaus.

Lafargue, Paul 1907 [1883], *The Right to be Lazy and Other Studies*, Chicago: Charles Kerr.

Lenin, V.I. 1933 [1916], *Imperialism: The Highest Stage of Capitalism*, London: Lawrence & Wishart.

Liebknecht, Wilhelm 1928, *Voices of Revolt Volume VII: Speeches of Wilhelm Liebknecht*, New York: International Publishers.

Livy 1919 [27–9 BCE], *History of Rome, Volume I: Books 1–2*. Translated by B.O. Foster. Loeb Classical Library 114, Cambridge: Harvard University Press.

Lüning, Otto (ed.) 1845–7, *Diess Buch gehört dem Volke*, 3 Volumes, Bielefeld: A. Helmich.

Marx, Karl and Friedrich Engels 1975–2004, Marx and Engels Collected Works [MECW], 50 Volumes, London: Lawrence & Wishart.

Marx, Karl 1976 [1867] *Capital Volume 1*, New York: Penguin.

Marx, Karl 1991 [1894] *Capital Volume 3*, New York: Penguin.

Marx, Karl 1993 [1857–8], *Grundrisse*, New York: Penguin.

Mead, Edward 1989 [1843], 'The Steam King' in Peter Scheckner (ed.), *An Anthology of Chartist Poetry. Poetry of the British Working Class, 1830s–1850s*, Cranbury: Fairleigh Dickinson University Press, 287–288.

Melle, Thomas 2014, *3000 Euro*, Berlin: Rowohlt.

Melle, Thomas 2016, *Die Welt im Rücken*, Berlin: Rowohlt.

Milton, John, *Paradise Lost* 1832 [1667], in *Milton's Poetical Works in Two Volumes*, Volume 1, New York: J.H. Turney, 15–274.

Möser, Justus 1775, 'Von dem Verfall des Handwerks in kleinen Städten', in *Patriotische Phantasien*, edited by his daughter J.W.J. von Voigt, born Möser, Berlin: Nicolai, 181–209.

Mundt, Theodor 1837, *Die Kunst der deutschen Prosa. Aesthetisch, literargeschichtlich, gesell- schaftlich*, Berlin: Veit.

Niebuhr, Barthold Georg 1811, *Römische Geschichte*, Volume 1, Berlin: Realschulbuchhandlung.

Otto-Peters, Louise 1996 [1846], *Schloss und Fabrik. Erste vollständige Ausgabe des 1846 zensierten Romans*, edited and with an epilogue by Johanna Ludwig, Leipzig: LKG.

Parent-Duchâtelet, Alexandre Jean Baptiste 1836, *De la prostitution dans la ville de Paris, considérée sous le rapport de l 'hygiène publique, de la morale et de l 'administration: ouvrage appuyé de documens statistiques puésés dans les archives de la Préfecture de police*, Paris: Libraire de L'Académie Royale de Médecine.

Proudhon, Pierre-Joseph 1888 [1846], *System of Economic Contradictions, or, The Philosophy of Misery*, Boston: Benjamin R. Tucker.

Proudhon, Pierre-Joseph 1994 [1840], *What is Property?* edited by Donald R. Kelley and Bonnie G. Smith, Cambridge: Cambridge University Press. Püttmann, Hermann (ed.) 1845, *Deutsches Bürgerbuch für 1845*, Darmstadt: C.W. Leske

Püttmann, Hermann (ed.) 1845/1846, *Rheinische Jahrbücher zur gesellschaftlichen Reform*, 2 Volumes, Darmstadt: Leske, 1845 and Belle-Vue bei Constanz: Verlagsbuchhandlung zu Belle-Vue, 1846.

Püttmann, Hermann (ed.) 1846a, *Deutsches Bürgerbuch für 1846*, Mannheim: Heinrich Hoff.

Püttmann, Hermann (ed.) 1846b, *Prometheus. Organ zur sozialen Reform*, Herisau: Literarischen Instituts.

Püttmann, Hermann (ed.) 1847, *Album. Originalpoesien*, Borna: Reiche.

Rau, Karl David Heinrich 1816, *Ueber das Zunftwesen und die Folgen seiner Aufhebung*, 2nd edition, Leipzig: Georg Joachim Göschen.

Riehl, Wilhelm Heinrich 1861, *Die deutsche Arbeit*, Stuttgart: Cotta.

Riehl, Wilhelm Heinrich 1866 [1851], *Die bürgerliche Gesellschaft. Die Naturgeschichte des Volkes als Grundlage einer deutschen Sozialpolitik*, Volume 2, 6th edition, Stuttgart: Cotta.

Riehl, Wilhelm Heinrich 1873 [1854], *Die Familie. Die Naturgeschichte des Volkes als Grundlage einer deutschen Sozialpolitik*, Volume 3, 7th edition, Stuttgart: Cotta.

Roller, Arnold 1905, *The Social General Strike*, Chicago: Debating Club No. 1.

Ruge, Arnold (ed.) 1843, *Anekdota zur neuesten deutschen Philosophie und Publicistik*, 2 Volumes, Zürich/Winterthur: Verlag des Literarischen Comptoirs.

Schade, Oskar (ed.) 1865, *Deutsche Handwerkslieder*, Leipzig: Vogel.

Schinkel, Karl Friedrich 1990 [1826], *Die Reise nach Frankreich und England im Jahre 1826*, edited by Reinhard Wegner, Munich/Berlin: Deutscher Kunstverlag.

Schulz, Wilhelm 1985 [1851], 'Georg Büchners nachgelassene Schriften', in Walter Grab, *Georg Büchner und die Revolution von 1848. Der Büchner-Essay von Wilhelm Schulz aus dem Jahr 1851. Text und Kommentar*, Königstein/Taunus: Athenäum, 51–82.

Shelley, Mary (with Percy Shelley) 2009 [1818/1831], *The Original Frankenstein. Two New Versions, Mary Shelley's Earliest Drafts and Percy Shelley's Revised Text*, edited by Charles E. Robinson, New York: Vintage.

Shelley, Percy Bysshe 1987, *The Selected Poetry and Prose*, London: Wordsworth.

Sieyès, Emmanuel 2003, *Political Writings: Including the Debate Between Sieyes and Tom Paine in 1791*, Indianapolis: Hackett Publishing.

Smith, Adam 1976 [1776], *An Inquiry into the Nature and Causes of the Wealth of Nations*, edited by R.H. Campbell and A.S. Skinner, 2 Volumes, Indianapolis: Liberty Classics.

Stein, Heinrich Friedrich Karl vom und zum 1833, *Die Briefe des Freiherrn von Stein an den Freiherrn von Gagern von 1813–1831*, Stuttgart/Tübingen: Cotta.

Stein, Lorenz von 1921 [1850], *Geschichte der sozialen Bewegung in Frankreich von 1789 bis auf unsere Tage*, edited by Gottfried Salomon, 3 Volumes, Munich: Drei Masken Verlag.

[Stieber, Wilhelm] 1846, *Die Prostitution in Berlin und ihre Opfer. Nach amtlichen Quellen und Erfahrungen. In historischer, sittlicher, medizinischer und polizeilicher Beziehung beleuchtet*, Berlin: A. Hofmann und Comp.

Stirner, Max 2018 [1845], *The Unique and its Property*, Berkeley: Ardent Press.

Sue, Eugène 2015 [1843], *The Mysteries of Paris*, New York: Penguin.

Tieck, Ludwig 1985 [1845], *Phantasus, Schriften in zwölf Bänden*, Volume 6, edited by Manfred Frank, Frankfurt: Deutscher Klassiker.

Tieck, Ludwig 1986 [1839], *Des Lebens Überfluss*, in *Schriften in zwölf Bänden*, Volume 12, *Schriften 1836–1852*, edited by Uwe Schweikert, Frankfurt: Deutscher Klassiker, 193–249.

Tieck, Ludwig1988a [1832], *Der Hexensabbat*, Stuttgart: Reclam.

Tieck, Ludwig 1988b [1836], *Der junge Tischlermeister. Novelle in sieben Abschnitten*, in *Schriften in zwölf Bänden*, Volume 11, *Eigensinn und Laune. Schriften 1834–1836*, edited by Uwe Schweikert, Frankfurt: Deutscher Klassiker, 9–418 [JTM].

Tieck, Ludwig 1988c [1835], *Die Vogelscheuche. Märchen-Novelle in fünf Aufzügen*, in *Schriften in zwölf Bänden*, Volume 11, *Eigensinn und Laune. Schriften 1834–1836*, edited by Uwe Schweikert: Deutscher Klassiker, 419–731.

Tocqueville, Alexis de 2012 [1835], *Democracy in America Volume 1*, Indianapolis: Liberty Fund.

Tocqueville, Alexis de 2021 [1835/1837], *Memoirs on Pauperism and Other Writings: Poverty, Public Welfare, and Inequality*, Notre Dame: University of Notre Dame Press.

Toller, Ernst 2019 [1922], 'The Machine Breakers' in *Ernst Toller: Plays Two*, London: Oberon Books, 27–126.

Tristan, Flora 1982 [1842], *The London journal of Flora Tristan, 1842, or, The aristocracy and the working class of England*, London: Virago.

Tristan, Flora 1983 [1843], *The Workers' Union*, Urbana: University of Illinois Press.

Der Urwähler. Eine Wochenschrift, redigiert von Wilhelm Weitling. Organ des Befreiungs-Bundes 1848, Berlin: Rudolph Liebmann (four issues, October–November 1848).

Venedey, Jacob (ed.) 1834/35, *Der Geächtete. Zeitschrift in Verbindung mit mehreren deutschen Volksfreunden*, Paris.

Vischer, Friedrich Theodor 1857, *Die Dichtkunst*, Stuttgart: Carl Mäcken.

Vischer, Friedrich Theodor 1986 [1857], 'Theorie des Romans', in Gerhard Plumpe (ed.), *Theorie des bürgerlichen Realismus*, Stuttgart: Reclam, 240–7.

Wachenhusen, Hans 1855, *Die Grisette. Ein Pariser Sittenbild*, Berlin: Verlags Comptoir.

Wagner, Georg Wilhelm Justin 1831, *Statistisch-topographisch-historische Beschreibung des Grossherzogthums Hessen*, Bd. 4: *Statistik des Ganzen*, Darmstadt: Leske. Weerth, Georg 1975/1976, *Vergessene Texte. Werkauswahl*, edited by Jürgen-W. Goette, Jost Hermand and Rolf Schloesser, 2 Volumes, Cologne: Leske.

Weerth, Georg 1976 [1846] 'Romanfragment', in *Vergessene Texte. Werkauswahl*, Volume 2, Cologne: Leske, 271–394.

Weitling, Wilhelm 1844, *Kerkerpoesien*, Hamburg: Hoffmann und Campe.

Weitling, Wilhelm 1907, 'Ein Stück Selbstbiographie', in Hermann Schlüter, *Die Anfänge der deutschen Arbeiterbewegung in Amerika*, Stuttgart: Dietz, 56–66.

Weitling, Wilhelm 1971 [1845 and 1838/1839], *Das Evangelium des armen Sünders/Die Menschheit, wie sie ist und wie sie sein sollte*, Reinbek: Rowohlt.

Weitling, Wilhelm 1974 [1842], *Garantien der Harmonie und Freiheit*, edited by Ahlrich Meyer, Stuttgart: Reclam,

Weitling, Wilhelm 1931a [1859], *Theorie des Weltsystems*, edited by Ernst Barnikol, Kiel: Walter G. Mühlau.

Weitling, Wilhelm 1931b [1848–9], *Klassifikation des Universums*, edited by Ernst Barnikol, Kiel: Walter G. Mühlau.

Weitling, Wilhelm 1931c [1856], *Der bewegende Urstoff. In seinen kosmo-elektro-magnetischen Wirkungen*, edited by Ernst Barnikol, Kiel: Walter G. Mühlau.

Weitling, Wilhelm 1991, *Grundzüge einer allgemeinen Denk- und Sprachlehre*, edited by Lothar Knatz, Frankfurt:

Willkomm, Ernst Adolf 2013 [1845], *Weisse Sclaven oder die Leiden des Volkes*, Leipzig: Kollmann (Reprint Berlin: Holzinger).

Zetkin, Clara 1971 [1928], *Zur Geschichte der proletarischen Frauenbewegung Deutschlands*, Frankfurt: Roter Stern Verlag.

Secondary Literature

Adler, Hans 1998, 'Der soziale Roman', in Gerd Sautermeister and Ulrich Schmid (eds.), *Hanser Sozialgeschichte der deutschen Literatur vom 16. Jahrhundert bis zur Gegenwart*, Volume. 5: *Zwischen Revolution und Restauration 1815–1848*, Munich: Deutscher Taschenbuch Verlag, 195–209.

Alquati, Romano 1974, *Klassenanalyse als Klassenkampf. Arbeiteruntersuchungen bei FIAT und OLIVETTI*, edited by Wolfgang Rieland, Frankfurt: Fischer.

Alquati, Romano 2013 [1964], 'Struggle at FIAT', translated by Evan Calder Williams (available at https://viewpointmag.com/2013/09/26/struggle-at-fiat-1964/)

Anderson, Kevin 1999, 'Marx on Suicide in the Context of His Other Writings on Alienation and Gender', in Karl Marx, *Marx on Suicide*, edited by Eric A. Plaut and Kevin Anderson, Evanston: Northwestern University Press, 3–28.

Armano, Emiliana and Raffaele Sciortino, 2010, 'Ciao Romano. Erinnerung an Romano Alquati', in *Sozial.Geschichte Online* 3, 192–197 (available at https://duepublico2.uni-due.de/receive/duepublico_mods_00022662)

Arrighi, Giovanni 2007, *Adam Smith in Beijing: Lineages of the Twenty-First Century*, London, Verso.

Bachleitner, Norbert 1993, *Der englische und französische Sozialroman des 19. Jahrhunderts und seine Rezeption in Deutschland*, Amsterdam/Atlanta: Rodopi.

Balestrini, Nanni and Primo Moroni (eds.) 2023 [1988], *The Golden Horde Revolutionary Italy: 1960–1977*, London: Seagull Books.

Balibar, Étienne 1991 [1988], 'From Class Struggle to Classless Struggle?' in Étienne Balibar and Immanuel Wallerstein, *Race, Nation, Class*, London: Verso, 153–184.

Badiou, Alain 2003 [1997], *Saint Paul: The Foundation of Universalism*, Stanford: Stanford University Press.

Barzilai, Maya 2016, *Golem. Modern Wars and Their Monsters*, New York: NYU Press.

Bataille, George 1997 [1933], 'The Notion of Expenditure' in *The Bataille Reader*, edited by Fred Botting and Scott Wilson, Oxford: Blackwell, 167–181.

Bataille, George 1988 [1949], *The Accursed Share*, New York: Zone.

Bauman, Zygmunt 1982, *Memories of Class. The Pre-History and After-Life of Class*, London: Routledge and Kegan Paul.

Benjamin, Walter 2004 [1921], 'Critique of Violence', translated by Edmund Jephcott, in *Walter Benjamin: Selected Writings, Volume 1, 1913–1926*, edited by Marcus Bullock and Michael W. Cambridge: Belknap, 236–252.

Benjamin, Walter 2005 [1933], 'Experience and Poverty', translated by Rodney Livingstone, in *Walter Benjamin: Selected Writings, Volume 2, Part 2, 1931–19434*, edited by Howard Eiland, Michael W. Jennings and Gary Smith, Cambridge: Belknap, 731–6.

Benjamin, Walter 2006 [1940], 'On the Concept of History', translated by Harry Zohn, in *Walter Benjamin: Selected Writings, Volume 4, 1938–1940*, edited by Howard Eiland and Michael W. Jennings, Cambridge: Belknap, 389–400.

Bescherer, Peter 2013, *Vom Lumpenproletariat zur Unterschicht. Produktivistische Theorie und politische Praxis*, Frankfurt/New York: Campus.

Biagini, Cédric 2012, *L'emprise numérique. Comment internet et les nouvelles technologies ont colonisé nos vies*, Montreuil: Editions L'Échappée.

Bloch, Ernst 1995 [1959], *The Principle of Hope, Vol. 2*, Cambridge: MIT Press.

Bosse, Heinrich 1999, 'Zur Sozialgeschichte des Wanderlieds', in Wolfgang Albrecht and Hans-Joachim Kertscher (eds.), *Wanderzwang – Wanderlust. Formen der Raum- und Sozialerfahrung zwischen Aufklärung und Frühindustrialisierung*, Tübingen: Niemeyer, 135–57.

Bosse, Heinrich, *Bildungsrevolution 1770–1830* 2012, edited by Nacim Ghanbari, Heidelberg: Winter.

Brass, Tom and Marcel van der Linden and Jan Lucassen, 'Conference on the history of free and unfree labor', in *Free and Unfree Labor: The Debate Continues*, edited by Tom Brass and Marcel van der Linden, Bern: Peter Lang, 1997, 5.

Braudel, Fernand 1984 [1979], *Civilization and Capitalism, 15th–18th Century. Volume 3: The Perspective of the World*, London: Collins.

Breman, Jan 2010, *Outcast Labour in Asia. Circulation and Informalization of the Workforce at the Bottom of the Economy*, Oxford: Oxford University Press.

Breyer, Till and Rasmus Overthun and Philippe Roepstorff-Robiano and Alexandra Vasa (eds.) 2017, *Zeitschrift für Kulturwissenschaft: Monster und Kapitalismus*, Issue 2.

Brink, Claudia 2011, 'Fama', in Uwe Fleckner, Martin Warnke and Hendrik Ziegler (eds.), *Handbuch der politischen Ikonographie*, Volume 1, Munich: C.H. Beck, 285–92.

Brown, Heather A. 2012, *Marx on Gender and the Family. A Critical Study*, Leiden: Brill.

Buck-Morss, Susan 2009, *Hegel, Haiti and Universal History*, Pittsburgh: University of Pittsburgh Press.

Bunzel, Wolfgang 2011, 'Das Junge Deutschland', in Claudia Stockinger and Stefan Scherer (eds.), *Ludwig Tieck. Leben–Werk–Wirkung*, Berlin/Boston: de Gruyter, 120–30.

Bürger, Christa (ed.) 1974, *Ludwig Tieck: Der blonde Eckbert / Die Elfen. Materialien zur romantischen Gesellschaftskritik*, Frankfurt: Diesterweg.

Cannadine, David 1999, *The Rise and Fall of Class in Britain*, New York: Columbia University Press.

Christolova, Lena 2014, 'Vom Bund der Geächteten (1834–1836) zum Bund der Gerechten (1836–1840). Anomie und Ausnahmezustand im Vormärz', in Jutta Nickel (ed.), *Geld und Ökonomie im Vormärz, Jahrbuch des Forums Vormärz Forschung 2013*, Bielefeld: Aisthesis, 215–36.

Clark, Gregor and Anthony Clark 2001, 'Common Rights to Land in England, 1475–1839', *The Journal of Economic History* 61.4, 1009–1036.

Clark, T.J. 1982, *The Image of the People. Gustave Courbet and the 1848 Revolution*, London: Thames and Hudson.

Conze, Werner 1954, 'Vom "Pöbel" zum "Proletariat". Sozialgeschichtliche Voraussetzungen für den Sozialismus in Deutschland', *Vierteljahrschrift für Sozial- und Wirtschaftsgeschichte* 41.2, 333–64.

Conze, Werner 1984, 'Proletariat. Pöbel, Pauperismus', in *Geschichtliche Grundbegriffe. Historisches Lexikon zur politisch-sozialen Sprache in Deutschland*, Volume 5, edited by Otto Brunner, Werner Conze and Reinhart Koselleck, Stuttgart: Klett-Cotta, 27–68.

Dammbeck, Lutz 2005, *Das Netz – die Konstruktion des Unabombers. Im Anhang: Die industrielle Gesellschaft und ihre Zukunft (Unabomber-Manifest) von FC*, Hamburg: Edition Nautilus.

Davis, David Brion 1999, *The Problem of Slavery in the Age of Revolution 1770–1823*, New York/Oxford: Oxford University Press.

Davis, David Brion 2014, *The Problem of Slavery in the Age of Emancipation*, New York: Alfred A. Knopf.

Davis, Mike 2006, *Planet of Slums*, London: Verso.

Debord, Guy 1995 [1968], *Society of the Spectacle*, New York: Zone.

Derrida, Jacques 1992 [1991], *Given Time: 1. Counterfeit Money*, Chicago: University of Chicago Press.

Doty, William G. and William J. Hynes 1993, 'Historical Overview of Theoretical Issues: The Problem of the Tricksters', in: *Mythical Trickster Figures. Contours, Contexts, and Criticism*, edited by Doty and Hynes, Tuscaloosa: University of Alabama Press, 13–32.

Eagleton, Terry 1975, *Myths of Power. A Marxist Study of the Brontës*, London: MacMilllan.

Epstein, S.R. 2004, 'Property Rights to Technological Knowledge in Premodern Europe 1300–1800', *The American Economic Review* 94, 382–7.

Epstein, S.R. and Maarten Prak (eds.) 2008, *Guilds, Innovation, and the European Economy, 1400–1800*, Cambridge: Cambridge University Press.

Essbach, Wolfgang 1988, *Die Junghegelianer. Soziologie einer Intellektuellengruppe*. Munich: Fink.

Essbach, Wolfgang 2005, 'Elemente ideologischer Mengenlehren: Rasse, Klasse, Masse', in Justin Stagl and Wolfgang Reinhard (eds.), *Grenzen des Menschseins. Problem einer Definition des Menschlichen*, Wien: Böhlau, 727–55.

Fox, Nicolas 2002, *Against the Machine. The Hidden Luddite Tradition in Literature, Art, and Individual Lives*, Washington: Shearwater Books.

Freud, Sigmund, 1990 [1921] *Group Psychology and the Ego*. New York: Norton.

Freundinnen und Freunde der klassenlosen Gesellschaft 2007, '28 Thesen zur Klassengesellschaft', *kosmoprolet* 1, 10–51. (Available in translation online https://www.kosmoprolet.org/en/28-theses-class-society).

Freundinnen und Freunde der klassenlosen Gesellschaft 2015a, 'Abseits des Spülbeckens. Fragmentarisches über Geschlechter und Kapital', *kosmoprolet* 4, 10–31.

Freundinnen und Freunde der klassenlosen Gesellschaft 2015b, 'Reflexionen über das Surplus-Proletariat. Phänomene, Theorie, Folgen', in: *kosmoprolet* 4, 34–59.

Frost, Alphonso A., Jr. 1989, *Ernst Dronke. His Life and His Work*, New York: Peter Lang.

Füllner, Bernd 2006, *Georg-Weerth-Chronik (1822–1856)*, Bielefeld: Aisthesis.

Füllner, Bernd 2012, 'Zur Entstehungs- und Zensurgeschichte der sozialistischen Lyrikanthologie "Album. Originalpoesien von Georg Weerth … und dem Herausgeber H. Püttmann"', in Bernd Kortländer and Enno Stahl (eds.), *Zensur im 19. Jahrhundert. Das literarische Leben aus Sicht seiner Überwacher*, Bielefeld, 111–26.

Geheimes Staatsarchiv/Preussischer Kulturbesitz 2014, *Klosterstrasse 36. Sammeln, Ausstellen, Patentieren. Zu den Anfängen Preussens als Industriestaat* [Katalog], Berlin: Geheimes Staatsarchiv Preussischer Kulturbesitz.

Ghanbari, Nacim and Saskia Haag and Marcus Twellmann 2011, 'Einleitung: Das Haus nach seinem Ende', *DVjs* 85.2, 155–60.

Giesselmann, Werner 1993, *'Die Manie der Revolte'. Protest unter der Französischen Julimonarchie (1830–1848)*, 2 Volumes, Munich: Oldenburg.

Goette, Jürgen-Wolfgang and Rolf Schlosser 1976, 'Vorbemerkung', in Georg Weerth, *Vergessene Texte. Werkauswahl*, edited by Jürgen-W. Goette, Jost Hermand and Rolf Schlosser, Volume 2, Cologne, 265–70.

Gorz, André 1982 [1980], *Farewell to the Working-Class*, London: Pluto Press.

Grab, Walter 1987, *Dr. Wilhelm Schulz aus Darmstadt. Weggefährte von Georg Büchner und Inspirator von Karl Marx*, Frankfurt: Büchergilde Gutenberg.

Graeber, David 2011, *Debt: The First 5,000 Years*, Brooklyn: Melville House.

Graevenitz, Gerhart von 1987, *Mythos. Zur Geschichte einer Denkgewohnheit*, Stuttgart: Metzler.

Griffin, Emma 2010, *A Short History of the British Industrial Revolution*, New York: Palgrave Macmillan.

Gruppe Blauer Montag 2008, *Risse im Putz. Autonomie, Prekarisierung und autoritärer Sozialstaat*, Berlin/Hamburg: Assoziation A.

Guattari, Félix 1978, *Wunsch und Revolution. Ein Gespräch mit Franco Beradi (Bifo) und Paolo Bertetto*, Heidelberg: Wunderhorn.

Hamacher, Werner 1991, 'Afformativ, Streik', *Cardozo Law Rev*, vol. 13, no. 4, 1133–57.

Hardt, Michael and Antonio Negri 2004, *Multitude: War and Democracy in the Age of Empire*, New York: Penguin.

Harvey, David 2006, *Paris, Capital of Modernity*, New York/London: Routledge.

Haupt, Gerhard 2002, 'Neue Wege zur Geschichte der Zünfte in Europa', in *Das Ende der Zünfte. Ein europäischer Vergleich*, Göttingen: Vandenhoeck und Ruprecht, 9–37.

Hauschild, Jan-Christoph 2013, *Georg Büchner. Verschwörung für die Gleichheit*, Hamburg: Hoffmann und Campe.

Hausen, Karin 1981 [1976], 'Family and Role-division: The Polarisation of Sexual Stereotypes in the Nineteenth Century – an Aspect of the Dissociation of Work and Family Life' in *The German Family: Essays on the Social History of the Family in Nineteenth- and Twentieth-Century Germany*, edited by Richard J. Evans and W.R. Lee, London: Routledge, 51–83.

Heid, Ludger, and Arnold Paucker (eds.) 1992, *Juden und deutsche Arbeiterbewegung bis 1933. Soziale Utopien und religiös-kulturelle Traditionen*, Tübingen: Mohr Siebeck.

Hill, Bridget 2001, *Women Alone. Spinsters in England 1660–1850*, New Haven: Yale University Press.

Hirschman, Albert O. 1997 [1977], *The Passions and the Interests: Political Arguments for Capitalism before Its Triumph*, Princeton: Princeton University Press.

Hobsbawm, Eric J. 1959, *Primitive Rebels. Studies in Archaic Forms of Social Movement in the 19th and 20th Century*, Manchester: Manchester University Press.

Hobsbawm, Eric 1967a [1964], 'The Machine Breakers', in *Labouring Men. Studies in the History of Labour*, Garden City: Anchor Books, 7–26.

Hobsbawm, Eric 1967b [1957/1964], 'The British Standard of Living, 1790–1850', in *Labouring Men. Studies in the History of Labour*, Garden City: Anchor Books, pp. 75–121.

Hobsbawm, Eric 1967c [1964], 'The Standard of Living Debate: a Postscript', in: Eric Hobsbawm, *Labouring Men. Studies in the History of Labour*, Garden City: Anchor Books, pp. 141–147.

Hobsbawm, Eric and Terence Ranger (eds.) 2012 [1983], *The Invention of Tradition*, Cambridge: Cambridge University Press.

Hörmann, Raphael 2011, *Writing the Revolution. German and English Radical Literature, 1819–1848/49*, Zürich/Berlin/Münster: LIT.

Hörmann, Raphael 2012, '"Zum sogenannten, so gescholtenen Pöbel". Die radikale Aufwertung der Sozialen Unterschichten bei Börne und Büchner', *Georg Büchner Jahrbuch* 12, 2009–2012, Berlin/New York: de Gruyter, 143–63.

Hughes, Linda K. 2010, *The Cambridge Introduction to Victorian Poetry*, Cambridge: Cambridge University Press.

Hundt, Irina 2004, '"Sich mit warmen Herzen an der Zeit und ihren Interessen betheiligen". Bettina von Arnim, der Fall Schlöffel und der Roman *Schloss und Fabrik* von Louise Otto', *Louise-Otto-Peters-Jahrbuch*, 163–170.

Hunt, Tristram 2009, 'Introduction', in Friedrich Engels, *The Condition of the Working Class in England*, London: Penguin, 1–31.

Invisible Committee 2009 [2007], *The Coming Insurrection*, Cambridge, MIT Press.

Jappe, Anselm 1999, *Guy Debord*, with a Foreword by T.J. Clark, Berkeley: University of California Press.

Jarrige, François 2014, *Techno-Critiques. Du refus des machines à la contestation des technosciences*, Paris: La Découverte.

Johnson, Christopher H. 1983, 'Response to Jacques Rancière', *International Labour and Working Class History* 24, 21–6.

Jones, Steven E. 2006, *Against Technology. From the Luddites to Neo-Luddism*, New York/London: Routledge.

Jordan, Don and Michael Walsh 2008, *White Cargo. The Forgotten History of Britain's White Slaves in America*, New York: NYU Press.

Joyce, Patrick 1991, *Visions of the People. Industrial England and the Question of Class 1848–1914*, Cambridge: Cambridge University Press.

Joyce, Patrick 2010, 'What is the social in social history?', *Past and Present* 206, February, 213–48.

Julius, Anthony 2010, *Trials of the Diaspora. A History of Anti-Semitism in England*, Oxford: Oxford University Press.

Karlsruher Stadtzeitung 1985, 'Mit dem Dreirad durch den Sozialstaat', *Wildcat* 35, 45–55.

Kemmann, Ansgar 1996, 'Evidentia, Evidenz', in *Historisches Wörterbuch der Rhetorik*, edited by Gert Ueding, Volume 3, Tübingen: Niemeyer, 33–47.

Kluge, Arnd 2007, *Die Zünfte*, Stuttgart: Franz Steiner.

Kocka, Jürgen 1986, 'Traditionsbindung und Klassenbildung. Zum sozialhistorischen Ort der frühen deutschen Arbeiterbewegung', *Historische Zeitschrift* 243, 333–76.

Kocka, Jürgen 1990, *Weder Stand noch Klasse. Unterschichten um 1800. Geschichte der Arbeiter und der Arbeiterbewegung in Deutschland seit dem Ende des 18. Jahrhunderts*, Volume 1, Bonn: Dietz.

Kocka, Jürgen 1995, 'Das europäische Muster und der deutsche Fall' in *Bürgertum im 19. Jahrhundert*, Volume. 1, *Einheit und Vielfalt Europas*, Göttingen: Vandenhoeck und Ruprecht, 9–75.

Koschorke, Albrecht 2015, *Hegel und wir*, Berlin: Suhrkamp.

Koschorke, Albrecht 2018 [2012], *Fact and Fiction*, Berlin: De Gruyter.

Koschorke, Albrecht and Nacim Ghanbari and Eva Esslinger and Sebastian Susteck and Michael Taylor 2010, *Vor der Familie. Grenzbedingungen einer modernen Institution*, Konstanz: Konstanz University Press.

Koselleck, Reinhart 1987 [1967] *Preussen zwischen Reform und Revolution. Allgemeines Landrecht, Verwaltung und soziale Bewegung von 1791 bis 1848*, Stuttgart: Klett-Cotta.

Koselleck, Reinhart 2000, 'Gibt es eine Beschleunigung der Geschichte?', in *Zeitschichten. Studien zur Historik*, Frankfurt: Suhrkamp, 150–77.

Koselleck, Reinhart 2010, 'Die Auflösung des Hauses als ständischer Herrschaftseinheit. Anmerkungen zum Rechtswandel von Haus, Familie und Gesinde in Preussen zwischen der Französischen Revolution und 1848', in *Begriffsgeschichten. Studien zur Semantik und Pragmatik der politischen und sozialen Sprache*, Berlin: Suhrkamp, 465–485.

Krantz, Mark 2011, *Rise Like Lions. The History and Lessons of the Peterloo Massacre of 1819*, Manchester: Bookmarks.

Kroneberg, Lutz and Rolf Schloesser 1979, *Weber-Revolte 1844*, Cologne: Leske.

Kropmanns, Birgit 2012, 'Die Möbelzeichnungen Karl Friedrich Schinkels. Versuch einer Kategorisierung', in Schulze Altcappenberg and Johannsen (eds.), *Karl Friedrich Schinkel. Geschichte und Poesie. Das Studienbuch*, Berlin: Deutscher Kunstverlag, 235–242.

Lapinski, P. 1928, 'Der "Sozialstaat": Etappen und Tendenzen seiner Entwicklung', *Unter dem Banner des Marxismus* 4.7, 377–418.

Lehning, Arthur (ed.) 1987, *Unterhaltungen mit Bakunin*, Nördlingen: Greno.

Levison, Iain 2002, *A Working Stiff's Manifesto: A Memoir of Thirty Jobs I Quit, Nine That Fired Me, and Three I Can't Remember*, New York: Soho Press.

Levison, Iain 2003, *Since the Layoffs*, New York: Soho Press.

Linden, Marcel van der 2008, *Workers of the World. Essays toward a Global Labor History*, Leiden: Brill

Linden, Marcel van der, and Karl Heinz Roth 2014a [2009], 'Introduction', in Marcel van der Linden and Karl Heinz Roth (eds.), *Beyond Marx: Theorising the Global Labour Relations of the Twenty-First Century*, Leiden: Brill, 1–20.

Linden, Marcel van der, and Karl Heinz Roth 2014b [2009], 'Results and Prospects', in: Marcel van der Linden and Karl Heinz Roth (eds.), *Beyond Marx: Theorising the Global Labour Relations of the Twenty-First Century*, Leiden: Brill, 445–85.

Linebaugh, Peter 2006, *The London Hanged. Crime and Civil Society in the Eighteenth Century*, London/New York: Verso.

Linebaugh, Peter 2008, *The Magna Carta Manifesto. Liberty and Commons for All*, Berkeley: University of California Press.

Linebaugh, Peter 2014, 'Ned Ludd and Queen Mab. Machine-Breaking, Romanticism, and the Several Commons of 1811–12', in *Stop, Thief! The Commons, Enclosures, and Resistance*, Oakland, PM Press, 77–107.

Linebaugh, Peter and Rediker, Marcus 2000, *The Many-Headed Hydra, Sailors, Slaves, Commoners, and the Hidden History of the Revolutionary Atlantic*, Boston: Beacon.

Loose, Margaret 2014, *The Chartist Imaginary. Literary Form in Working-Class Political Theory and Practice*, Columbus: Ohio State University Press.

Löwy, Michael 1979, *Georg Lukács – From Romanticism to Bolshevism*, London/New York: New Left Books.

Löwy, Michael 2005 [2001], *Fire Alarm. Reading Walter Benjamin's 'On the Concept of History'*, London: Verso.

Löwy, Michael and Robert Sayre 2001, *Romanticism Against the Tide of Modernity*, Durham: Duke University Press.

Lucas, Erhard 1983, *Vom Scheitern der deutschen Arbeiterbewegung*, Frankfurt: Roter Stern.

Lucassen, Jan (ed.) 2008, *Global Labour History. A State of the Art*, Bern: Peter Lang.

Lucassen, Jan, Tine De Moor and Jan Luiten van Zanden (eds.) 2009, *The Return of the Guilds*, Cambridge: Cambridge University Press.

Ludwig, Johanna 2004, '"Ich martere mich selbst mit diesen Problemen …": Die Zensurgeschichte und zeitgenössische Bewertung des Romans *Schloss und Fabrik*', in Eva Schöck-Quinteros and Hans Kloft and Franklin Kopitzsch and Hans-Josef Steinberg (eds.), *Bürgerliche Gesellschaft – Idee und Wirklichkeit. Festschrift für Manfred Hahn*, Berlin: Trafo, 179–200.

Lukács, Georg, 1971 [1923], *History and Class Consciousness: Studies in Marxist Dialectics*, Cambridge: MIT Press.

Lukács, Georg, 'Eichendorff' 1993 [1940], in *German Realists in the Nineteenth Century*, Cambridge: MIT Press, 50–68.

Manning, Patrick 1990, *Slavery and African Life. Occidental, Oriental, and African Slave Trades*, Cambridge: Cambridge University Press.

Mattick, Paul 2011, *Business as usual: The Economic Crisis and the Failure of Capitalism*, London: Reaktion Books.

McNally, David 2011, *Monsters of the Market. Zombies, Vampires and Global Capitalism*, Leiden: Brill.

Mehring, Franz 1963 [1902], 'Gesellschaftsspiegel' in *Gesammelte Schriften*, Volume 4: *Aufsätze zur Geschichte der Arbeiterbewegung*, Berlin: Dietz, 170–5.

Meillassoux, Claude 1981 [1975], *Maidens, Meal and Money: Capitalism and the Domestic Community*, Cambridge: Cambridge University Press.

Meyer, Ahlrich 1999, *Die Logik der Revolten. Studien zur Sozialgeschichte 1789–1848*, Berlin/Hamburg: Schwarze Risse – Rote Strasse.

Meyer, Ahlrich 2014 [2009], 'A Theory of Defeat. Marx and the Evidence of the Nineteenth Century', in Marcel van der Linden and Karl Heinz Roth (eds.), *Beyond Marx:*

Theorising the Global Labour Relations of the Twenty-First Century, Leiden: Brill, 259–79.

Mohl, Ernst Theodor 1971, *Marginalien zum Nachdruck der von Moses Hess redigierten Zeitschrift 'Gesellschaftsspiegel', nebst Fussnoten zur neueren Marx- und Hess-Forschung*, Glashütten: Auvermann.

Moretti, Franco 2013, *The Bourgeois. Between History and Literature*, London/New York: Verso.

Müller, Margrit, Heinrich R. Schmidt, and Laurent Tissot 2011, 'Introduction' in *Regulierte Märkte. Zünfte und Kartelle/Marchés régulés. Corporations et cartels*, Zürich: Chronos, 9–22.

Na'aman, Shlomo 1978, *Zur Entstehung der deutschen Arbeiterbewegung. Lernprozesse und Vergesellschaftung 1830–1868*, Hannover: SOAK.

Nail, Thomas 2015, *The Figure of the Migrant*, Stanford: Stanford University Press.

Nancy, Jean-Luc 1991 [1986], *The Inoperative Community*, Minneapolis: University of Minnesota Press.

Negri, Antonio 2005, *Books for Burning: Between Civil War and Democracy in 1970s Italy*, London: Verso.

Noble, David F. 1995, *Progress Without People. New Technologies, Unemployment, and the Message of Resistance*, Toronto: Between The Lines.

Offe, Claus 1984, *Contradictions of the Welfare State*, London: Hutchinson.

Offe, Claus 1985, *Disorganized Capitalism*, Cambridge: MIT Press.

Orwell, George 1958 [1937] *The Road to Wigan Pier*, New York: Harcourt, Brace and Company.

Österreichisches Biographisches Lexikon: 1815–1950, Volume 1, 1957, Wien: Verlag der Österreichischen Akademie der Wissenschaften.

Panzieri, Raniero 1980 [1961], 'The Capitalist Use of Machinery', in *Outlines of a critique of technology*, edited by Phil Slater, London: Humanities Press, 44–68.

Pelger, Hans 1975, 'Dokument einer literarischen Opposition in Deutschland', in *Deutsches Bürgerbuch für 1845*, edited by Rolf Schloesser, Cologne: Leske and Europäischen Verlagsanstalt, XIII–XXXVI.

Philipp, Klaus Jan 2012, 'Poesie und Architektur um 1800', in Schulze Altcappenberg and Johannsen (eds.), *Karl Friedrich Schinkel. Geschichte und Poesie. Das Studienbuch*, Berlin: Deutscher Kunstverlag, 23–30.

Poovey, Mary 1994, 'The Social Constitution of "Class"', in Wai Chee Dimock and Michael T. Gilmore (eds.), *Rethinking Class. Literary Studies and Social Formations*, New York: Columbia University Press, 15–56.

Posener, Julius 1972, *From Schinkel to the Bauhaus. Five Lectures on the Growth of Modern German Architecture*, London: Lund Humphries for the Architectural Association.

Priddat, Birger P. 2005, '"Reiche Individualität" – Karl Marx' Kommunismus als Konzeption der "freien Zeit für freie Entwicklung"', in: Ingo Pies and Martin Leschke (eds.), *Karl Marx' kommunistischer Individualismus*, Tübingen: Mohr Siebeck, 124–46.

Pynchon, Thomas 1984, 'Is It O.K. To Be A Luddite?', *New York Times*, 28. 10. 1984 (available at https://www.nytimes.com/books/97/05/18/reviews/pynchon-luddite.html).

Rancière, Jacques 1978, 'Utopisten, Bürger und Proletarier', in *Kursbuch 52: Utopien, 1: Zweifel an der Zukunft*, edited by Karl Markus Michel and Harald Wieser, Berlin: Rotbuch, 146–58.

Rancière, Jacques 1983, 'The Myth of the Artisan: Critical Reflections on a Category of Social History', *International Labour and Working Class History* 24, 1–16.

Rancière, Jacques 1989 [1981], *The Nights of Labor: The Workers Dream in Nineteenth Century France*, Philadelphia: Temple University Press.

Rancière, Jacques 1994 [1992], *The Names of History*. Minneapolis: University of Minnesota Press

Rancière, Jacques 1999 [1995], *Disagreement*, Minneapolis: University of Minnesota Press.

Rancière, Jacques 2003 [1990] *Short Voyages to the Land of the People*, Stanford: Stanford University Press.

Rancière, Jacques 2012 [1981], *Proletarian Nights*, London: Verso.

Rancourt, Denis C. 2010, 'David F. Noble: In Memoriam', *Counterpunch*, 3. 12. 2010, (available at http://www.counterpunch.org/2010/12/30/david-f-noble-in-memoriam/).

Reid, Robert 1986, *Land of Lost Content. The Luddite Revolt, 1812*, London: Heinemann.

Roth, Karl Heinz 1974, *Die 'andere' Arbeiterbewegung und die Entwicklung der kapitalistischen Repression von 1880 bis zur Gegenwart*, Munich: Trikont.

Rottau, Nadine 2012, 'Schinkel der Moderne – Gewerbeförderung und Design', in: Hein-Th. Schulze Altcappenberg, Rolf Johannsen and Christiane Lange (eds.), *Karl Friedrich Schinkel. Geschichte und Poesie* [Katalog], Munich: Deutscher Kunstverlag, 227–29.

Ruckhäberle, Hans-Joachim 1975, *Flugschriftenliteratur im historischen Umkreis Georg Büchners*, Kronberg/Taunus: Scriptor.

Ruckhäberle, Hans-Joachim (ed.) 1977, *Frühproletarische Literatur. Die Flugschriften der deutschen Handwerksgesellenvereine in Paris 1832–1839*, Kronberg/Taunus: Scriptor.

Sanders, Mike 2009, *The Poetry of Chartism*, Cambridge: Cambridge University Press.

Sayre, Robert and Michael Löwy 2016, 'Die (antikapitalistische) Romantik in der *Theorie des Romans*', in Rüdiger Dannemann (eds.), *Lukács 2016. Jahrbuch der Internationalen Georg-Lukács-Gesellschaft*, Bielefeld: Aisthesis, 145–62.

Schaub, Gerhard 1977, 'Statistik und Agitation. Eine neue Quelle zu Büchners *Hessischem Landboten*', in Herbert Anton and Arthur Henkel (eds.), *Geist und Zeichen. Festschrift für Arthur Henkel zu seinem 60. Geburtstag*, Heidelberg: Winter, 351–75.

Schlottau, Klaus 2006, 'Maschinenstürmer gegen Frauenerwerbsarbeit: Dea ex machina', in Thorsten Meyer and Marcus Popplow (eds.), *Technik, Arbeit und Umwelt in der Geschichte. Günter Bayerl zum 60. Geburtstag*, Münster: Waxmann, 111–32.

Schmitt, Carl 2007 [1932] *The Concept of the Political: Expanded Edition*, Chicago. University of Chicago Press.

Schmitt, Carl 2011 [1919], *Political Romanticism*, Routledge: London.

Schoeps, Julius H. 1977, 'Agenten, Spitzel, Flüchtlinge. Wilhelm Stieber und die demokratische Emigration in London', in Horst Schallenberger and Helmut Schrey (eds.), *Im Gegenstrom. Festschrift zum 70. Geburtstag von Helmut Hirsch*, Wuppertal: Hammer, 71–104.

Schrupp, Antje 1999, *Nicht Marxistin und auch nicht Anarchistin. Frauen in der Ersten Internationale*, Königstein/Taunus: Ulrike Helmer.

Schulz, Bernhard 2012, 'Schinkels englische Reise – Wendepunkt oder Intermezzo? Die Industrie und die Poesie des Bauens', in Schulze Altcappenberg and Johannsen (eds.), *Karl Friedrich Schinkel. Geschichte und Poesie. Das Studienbuch*, Berlin: Deutscher Kunstverlag, 105–115.

Schulze Altcappenberg, Hein-Th. 2012, '"Letzte Lebensphilosophie". Die Allegorien auf Peter Beuth', in: Schulze Altcappenberg and Johannsen (eds.), *Karl Friedrich Schinkel. Geschichte und Poesie. Das Studienbuch*, Berlin: Deutscher Kunstverlag, 199–210.

Schumpeter, Joseph A. 1994 [1942], *Capitalism, Socialism and Democracy*, London: Routledge.

Schüttpelz, Erhard 2010, 'Der Trickster', in Eva Esslinger and Tobias Schlechtriemen and Doris Schweitzer and Alexander Zons (eds.), *Die Figur des Dritten. Ein kulturwissenschaftliches Paradigma*, Berlin: Suhrkamp, 208–24.

Scott, Joan 1998 [1991], 'Woman Worker', in *History of Women in the West, Volume IV: Emerging Feminism from Revolution to World War*, edited by Geneviève Fraisse and Michelle Perrot, Cambridge: Harvard University Press, 399–426.

Seidel-Höppner, Waltraud and Joachim Höppner 2005, 'Wilhelm Weitlings "Guerillakrieg des stehlenden Proletariats". Dokumentation einer Legende', in Helmut Bleiber and Wolfgang Küttler (eds.), *Revolution und Reform in Deutschland im 19. und 20. Jahrhundert*, 2nd Half-Volume: *Ideen und Reflexionen. Zum 75. Geburtstag von Walter Schmidt*, Berlin: Trafo, 79–93.

Sewell, William H. 1980, *Work and Revolution in France. The Language of Labor from the Old Regime to 1848*, Cambridge: Cambridge University Press.

Sewell, William H. 1983, 'Response to Jacques Rancière', *International Labour and Working Class History* 24, 17–20.

Simmel, Georg 1910 [1908], 'How Is Society Possible?' *American Journal of Sociology*, vol. 16, no. 3, 372–91.

Skinner, Quentin 2002, 'John Milton and the Politics of Slavery', in *Visions of Politics*, Cambridge: Cambridge University Press, pp. 286–397.

Speck, W.A. 2001, 'Robert Southey, Lord Macaulay, and the Standard of Living Controversy', *History. The Journal of the Historical Association*, Volume 86, Issue 284, 467–77.

Stadelmann, Rudolf and Wolfram Fischer 1955, *Die Bildungswelt des deutschen Handwerkers um 1800. Studien zur Soziologie des Kleinbürgers im Zeitalter Goethes*, Berlin: Duncker und Humblot.

Stagl, Justin 2014, 'Die Entstehung der Völker- und Volkskunde aus der Krise der Statistik, 1750–1850', in Gunhild Berg and Borbále Zsuzsanna Török and Marcus Twellmann (eds.), *Berechnen/Beschreiben. Praktiken statistischen (Nicht-)Wissens 1750–1850*, Berlin: Duncker und Humblot, 213–229.

Stagl, Justin/Reinhard, Wolfgang (eds.) 2005, *Grenzen des Menschseins. Problem einer Definition des Menschlichen*, Wien: Böhlau.

Standing, Guy 2011, *The Precariat. The New Dangerous Class*, London: Bloomsbury.

Stanziani, Alessandro 2008, 'Free Labor – Forced Labor: An Uncertain Boundary? The Circulation of Economic Ideas between Russia and Europe from the 18th to the Mid-19th Century', *Kritika: Explorations in Russian and Eurasian History* 9.1 (Winter), 27–52.

Strauss, Leo 1988 [1952], *Persecution and the Art of Writing*, Chicago: University of Chicago Press.

Stürmer, Michael 1979, *Der Herbst des Alten Handwerks. Zur Sozialgeschichte des 18. Jahrhunderts*, Munich: Deutscher Taschenbuch Verlag.

Suter, Mischa 2011, 'Ein Stachel in der Seite der Sozialgeschichte: Jacques Rancière und die Zeitschrift *Les Révoltes logiques*', *Sozial-Geschichte Online*, Issue 5, 8–37.

Suter, Mischa 2016, *Rechtstrieb. Schulden und Vollstreckung im liberalen Kapitalismus 1800–1900*, Konstanz: Konstanz University Press.

Tenfelde, Klaus and Heinrich Volkmann 1981, 'Einführung: Zur Geschichte des Streiks in Deutschland', in *Streik. Zur Geschichte des Arbeitskampfes in Deutschland während der Industrialisierung*, Munich: Beck, 9–30.

Tennstedt, Florin 1983, *Vom Proleten zum Industriearbeiter. Arbeiterbewegung und Sozialpolitik in Deutschland 1800–1914*, Cologne: Bund-Verlag.

Thompson, E.P. 1966 [1963], *The Making of the English Working Class*, New York, Vintage.

Thompson, E.P. 1967, 'Time, Work-Discipline, and Industrial Capitalism', *Past & Present*, No. 38, 56–97.

Thompson, E.P. 1976, 'Romanticism, Moralism and Utopianism: the Case of William Morris', *New Left Review*, 1/99.

Thompson, E.P. 1997, *The Romantics. England in a Revolutionary Age*, Woodbridge: Merlin.

Thompson, E.P. 2011 [1955], *William Morris: Romantic to Revolutionary*, Oakland: P.M. Press.

Tilly, Louise A. 1995, 'Paths of proletarianization. Organization of production, sexual division of labor, and women's collective action', in Johanna Brenner and Barbara Laslett and Yasmin Arat (eds.), *Rethinking the Political. Gender, Resistance, and the State*, Chicago: University of Chicago Press, 127–44.

Trempler, Jörg 2007, *Schinkels Motive*, Berlin: Matthes & Seitz.

Trempler, Jörg 2012, *Karl Friedrich Schinkel. Baumeister Preussens. Eine Biographie*, Munich: C.H. Beck.

Tronti, Mario 2019 [1966], *Workers and Capital*, London: Verso.

Ungern-Sternberg, Jürgen 2003, 'Proletarii', in *Der Neue Pauly*, edited by Hubert Cancik, Helmuth Schneider and Manfred Landfester, Volume 10, Stuttgart, 397–398 (available online in English at https://referenceworks.brillonline.com/entries/brill-s-new-pauly/proletarii-e1010020).

Unseld, Siegfried 1965, 'Georg Weerth – Lebenslauf eines Unbekannten', in Georg Weerth, *Fragment eines Romans*, Frankfurt: Insel, 5–18.

Vogel, Barbara 1983, *Allgemeine Gewerbefreiheit. Die Reformpolitik des preussischen Staatskanzlers Hardenberg (1810–1820)*, Göttingen: Vandenhoeck und Ruprecht.

Wadauer, Sigrid 2003, 'Paris im Unterwegs-Sein und Schreiben von Handwerksgesellen', in Mareike König (ed.), *Deutsche Handwerker, Arbeiter und Dienstmädchen in Paris. Eine vergessene Migration im 19. Jahrhundert*, Munich: Oldenbourg, 49–67.

Wahren, Reinhard 2016, *Baukünstler und Ingenieur. Eine Berliner Freundschaft: Karl-Friedrich Schinkel und Christian Peter Wilhelm Beuth*, Berlin: Hendrik Bässler.

Wallerstein, Immanuel 1974, *The Modern World-System: Capitalist Agriculture and the Origins of the European World-Economy in the Sixteenth Century*, New York: Academic Press.

Weerth, Marie, *Georg Weerth (1822–1856). Ein Lebensbild*, Bielefeld: Aisthesis, 2009.

Wehler, Hans-Ulrich 1987, *Deutsche Gesellschaftsgeschichte*, Volume 2: *Von der Reformära bis zur industriellen und politischen 'Deutschen Doppelrevolution' 1815–1845/49*, Munich: C.H. Beck.

Weiss, Volker 2015, *Moses Hess. Rheinischer Jude, Revolutionär, früher Zionist*, Cologne: Greven.

Wergin, Ulrich 1979, '"Einer der letzten Gäste auf dem Maskenball der Poesie". Ludwig Tieck, die Romantik und die Folgen. Nachwort', in Ludwig Tieck, *Die Vogelscheuche. Das alte Buch und Die Reise ins Blaue hinein*, 2nd Edition, Frankfurt: Zweitausendeins, 627–92.

Werquet, Jan 2012, 'Künstlerisches Ideal und historischer Aussagewert. Schinkel und die rheinischen Bauprojekte Kronprinz Friedrich Wilhelm (IV.)', in *Karl Friedrich Schinkel. Geschichte und Poesie. Das Studienbuch*, Berlin: Deutscher Kunstverlag, 261–72.

Williams, Raymond 1960 [1958], *Culture and Society: 1780–1950*, Garden City: Anchor Books.

Williams, Raymond 1972, *Gesellschaftstheorie als Begriffsgeschichte. Studien zur historischen Semantik von 'Kultur'*, Munich: Rogner & Bernhard.
Williams, Raymond 2015 [1976], *Keywords. A Vocabulary of Culture and Society. New Edition*, Oxford: Oxford University Press.
Wissell, Rudolf 1981 [1929], *Des alten Handwerks Recht und Gewohnheit*, Volume 3, edited by Ernst Schraepler, Berlin: Colloquium.
Wolf, Siegmund A. 1985, *Wörterbuch des Rotwelschen. Deutsche Gaunersprache*, 2nd edition, Hamburg: Hemut Buske.
Wolzogen, Christoph von 2016, *Karl Friedrich Schinkel. Unter dem bestirnten Himmel*, 2 Volumes, Frankfurt: H.W. Fichter Kunsthandel.
Zeuske, Michael 2002, 'Die Massensklaverei auf Kuba – extreme Bedingungen und quantitative Dimensionen', in *Sklavereien, Emanzipationen und atlantische Weltgeschichte. Essays über Mikrogeschichten, Sklaven, Globalisierungen und Rassismus*. Arbeitsberichte des Instituts für Kultur- und Universalgeschichte Leipzig 6, Leipzig: Leipziger Universitäts-Verlag, 82–9.
Zeuske, Michael 2004, *Schwarze Karibik. Sklaven, Sklavereikultur und Emanzipation*, Zürich: Rotpunkt.
Zlocisti, Theodor 1921, *Moses Hess. Der Vorkämpfer des Sozialismus und Zionismus 1812–1875. Eine Biographie*, Berlin: Welt-Verlag.

Film

Dammbeck, Lutz: *Das Netz*, 121 Min., Deutschland 2003.
Petri, Elio: *La classe oparaia va in Paradiso* [dt. *Der Weg der Arbeiterklasse ins Paradies*], 120 Min., Italien 1971.

Name Index

Alquati, Romano 258*n*
Aristotle 223*n*
Arnim, Bettina von 275–6
Arrighi, Giovanni 267
Auerbach, Berthold 3–4, 187
Aveling, Edward 16*n*
Aveling-Marx, Eleanor 16*n*

Baader, Franz von 8, 276
Babeuf, François Noël (Gracchus) 77, 273, 357, 371
Badiou, Alain 97
Bakunin, Mikhael 53*n*
Balestrini, Nanni 258
Balibar, Étienne 278
Ball, Hugo 257
Bataille, Georges 5, 197
Bauer, Bruno 78–9, 81, 142*n*
Bauman, Zygmunt 24*n*
Beck, Karl 124–9, 133, 141
Benjamin, Walter 18*n*, 32, 156, 186, 217, 219, 264*n*
Bensen, Heinrich Wilhelm 9–10
Berardi, Franco 258*n*
Beuth, Christian Wilhelm Peter Friedrich 266–275
Blake, William 5*n*, 74, 161, 162*n*
Blanqui, Louis-Auguste 95*n*, 101, 145, 217
Bloch, Ernst 155*n*
Bluntschli, Johann Caspar 206*n*
Börne, Ludwig 1*n*, 8, 52*n*, 198, 203–5
Borsig, August 268, 275
Bosse, Heinrich 61, 97
Braudel, Fernand 157, 201
Brontë, Charlotte 227, 256
Brontë, Emily 216*n*
Büchner, Georg 101–3, 106–110, 141*n*, 197–8
Buck-Morss, Susan 170–1*n*
Buonarroti, Filippo 52, 215
Buret, Eugène 88, 110
Bürger, Christa 33*n*, 46*n*
Byron, George Gordon (Lord Byron) 256, 259

Cannadine, David 24
Carlyle, Thomas 23, 157, 158*n*, 163, 256
Chamfort, Nicolas 198
Clark, T.J. 11*n*
Cooper, James Fenimore 189–90

Dammbeck, Lutz 259
Davis, Mike 261
Debord, Guy 174
Derrida, Jacques 156
Dickens, Charles 4, 187–8, 193
Disraeli, Benjamin 192, 256
Dronke, Ernst 17, 84, 120–1, 128–131, 135–142

Eagleton, Terry 256*n*
Engels, Friedrich 4–5*n*, 9, 17, 31*n*, 46*n*, 54, 65–8, 69*n*, 70*n*, 77, 81*n*, 84–6, 89–91, 112, 122*n*, 124–9, 131–3, 136–42, 144*n*, 146, 158–9, 163–70, 185–198, 205, 216*n*, 234, 242*n*, 244, 276, 277*n*
Eribon, Didier 279*n*
Erpenbeck, Jenny 263
Essbach, Wolfgang 90–2, 100, 104*n*, 106*n*, 107*n*

Fourier, Charles 144
Frégier, Honoré Antoine 261–2
Freiligrath, Ferdinand 5, 66, 77, 84, 128, 277
Freud, Sigmund 9, 81
Freytag, Gustav 138
Friedrich Wilhelm IV 79, 82

Gans, Eduard 1–3, 178, 264
Gorz, André 22*n*
Grimm, Jacob 3–4
Graeber, David 181, 182*n*
Guattari, Félix 258*n*
Gutzkow, Karl 109, 187

Hardenberg, Karl August von 26, 267
Harrington, James 7*n*
Harvey, David 1*n*
Hausen, Karin 241*n*, 250
Hegel, Georg Wilhelm Friedrich 1–3, 9–10, 31, 36, 53, 58, 78–81, 84, 103, 112*n*, 124*n*, 142, 144–5, 147, 189, 260
Heine, Heinrich 1, 3, 5, 8, 25, 52*n*, 66, 100, 159*n*, 204, 222*n*

Heinzen, Karl 84–5
Herwegh, Georg 20, 125*n*, 173, 276
Hess, Moses 16*n*, 17, 23, 54*n*, 69*n*, 84–91, 111*n*, 112–3, 115*n*, 118, 119–20*n*, 121, 175–7, 223*n*, 276–8
Hill, Bridget 248
Hirschman, Albert O. 40–1
Hobsbawm, Eric 11*n*, 15, 47, 123, 124*n*, 151, 152*n*, 207–9, 213–5, 217, 224*n*, 225–6, 253

Joyce, Patrick 18*n*, 23

Kaczynski, Ted 259
Kant, Immanuel 39, 223
Keller, Gottfried 79*n*
Kriege, Hermann 75
Kocka, Jürgen 30*n*, 32, 47–51, 152*n*
Köpke, Rudolf 33, 34*n*, 123, 124*n*
Koschorke, Albrecht 24*n*, 141*n*, 183, 186*n*, 278*n*
Koselleck, Reinhart 26, 173*n*

Lafargue, Paul 10*n*, 14, 155
Latour, Bruno 259
Lenhardt, Gero 10
Lenin, Vladimir 92, 229, 230*n*
Levison, Iain 262
Liebknecht, Wilhelm 225*n*
Linebaugh, Peter 8, 16, 124*n*, 169*n*, 178*n*, 182–3*n*, 216*n*, 225, 230–1, 239, 241*n*, 254, 255*n*
Linden, Marcel van der 149, 172*n*, 173*n*, 179*n*
Livy 70*n*
Löwy, Michael 15–17
Lucas, Erhard 240
Lukács, Georg 14–16, 18, 155, 185, 262
Lüning, Otto 113–14, 128, 276, 277*n*

Marx, Karl 8, 9*n*, 10*n*, 13, 16*n*, 17, 18, 20, 22–3, 46, 50, 53*n*, 54, 75, 78*n*, 79, 81, 82*n*, 83*n*, 84–5, 88*n*, 90–1, 103, 115–8, 119*n*, 124*n*, 125, 128, 132, 136*n*, 142–151, 154–5, 157*n*, 164, 167–9, 171–5, 177–8, 183–5, 189, 195, 198, 213, 216, 222*n*, 235–6, 238, 252*n*, 253, 260, 263, 265*n*
Mead, Edward P. 5*n*, 158–60, 184
Mehring, Franz 90*n*
Melle, Thomas 262
Meyer, Ahlrich 33*n*, 174, 206*n*
Milton, John 160*n*, 162*n*
Moretti, Franco 30*n*, 39
Möser, Justus 33*n*
Mundt, Theodor 3

Nancy, Jean-Luc 254
Negri, Antonio 256*n*, 257, 259, 261
Niebuhr, Barthold Georg 7, 8*n*
Noble, David F. 259

Offe, Claus 10, 12*n*, 176–7*n*, 261*n*, 278*n*
Orwell, George 192
Otto-Peters, Louise 99*n*, 131*n*, 133, 134*n*, 148*n*, 221–7, 230–1, 252

Panzieri, Raniero 258
Petri, Elio 258
Proudhon, Pierre-Joseph 142, 144–8, 150–1, 168, 185
Püttmann, Hermann 4–5, 16*n*, 52*n*, 66, 82–5, 86*n*, 92, 93*n*, 121, 128
Pynchon, Thomas 225, 255, 259

Rancière, Jacques 4, 12, 15, 19, 21, 31*n*, 54, 70*n*, 77*n*, 95–6*n*, 97, 101*n*, 219, 247
Rau, Karl David Heinrich 33–5, 271
Raumer, Friedrich von 267
Rediker, Marcus 8, 169*n*, 182*n*, 239
Ricardo, David 145–6
Riehl, Wilhelm Heinrich 28*n*, 35*n*, 80*n*, 232, 277*n*
Roller, Arnold 264
Roth, Karl Heinz 172*n*, 179*n*, 256*n*
Rousseau, Jean-Jacques 41, 105
Ruge, Arnold 78–83

Sayre, Robert 15–6, 17*n*
Schade, Oskar 58–9
Schinkel, Karl Friedrich 266–276
Schmidt, Julian 138
Schmitt, Carl 75, 106–7
Schnake, Friedrich 120–1
Schüler, Friedrich 103–4
Schulz, Wilhelm 109
Schumpeter, Joseph A. 13, 213
Scott, Joan Wallach 246–7, 248*n*, 250
Seeger, Ludwig 66
Sewell, William 51, 77*n*

Shelley, Mary 11, 197, 256, 259
Shelley, Percy Bysshe 5, 16, 66, 108, 256
Siebenpfeiffer, Philipp Jakob 103–4
Sieyès, Emmanuel 106
Simmel, Georg 9
Skinner, Quentin 162
Smith, Adam 40–2, 157*n*, 213, 267
Standing, Guy 261–2
Stein, Heinrich Friedrich Karl vom und zum 7, 8*n*, 26, 267, 269*n*
Stein, Lorenz von 276
Stieber, Wilhelm 119–20, 254, 262
Stirner, Max 81
Strauss, Leo 19
Sue, Eugène 114–5, 142–5, 189–90

Thompson, E.P. 11, 15, 17–8, 49–51, 152–5, 170*n*, 215, 216*n*, 225–7, 229*n*, 230, 231*n*, 232*n*, 242, 255*n*, 256*n*, 259
Tieck, Ludwig 5*n*, 11*n*, 16–7, 25–47, 49, 61, 72, 82, 122–4, 132, 139, 152–5, 199–205, 255, 266–7, 270–5
Tristan, Flora 98–9
Tronti, Mario 257*n*
Tocqueville, Alexis de 122*n*, 176
Toller, Ernst 257, 259

Venedey, Jacob 52–3, 85
Vischer, Friedrich Theodor 2–3

Wachenhusen, Hans 131*n*
Wagner, Georg Wilhelm Justin 102
Wallerstein, Immanuel 201
Weber, Max 81
Weerth, Georg 4, 17, 20, 51, 65–74, 77, 84–5, 230–244, 246, 248–9, 252–3, 264–5
Wehler, Hans-Ulrich 8*n*
Weidig, Ludwig 101, 102*n*, 108–9
Weitling, Wilhelm 4–5, 14, 17, 51–66, 72, 75–78, 89, 92–99, 100*n*, 104, 160–3, 170, 205, 220, 234, 258, 275–7, 279
Williams, Raymond 6, 15, 50, 64–5
Willkomm, Ernst Adolf 134–6, 149, 178–185, 207–221, 226, 228–231, 252, 277
Wissell, Rudolf 46*n*

Zetkin, Clara 99*n*